Gothic Images of Race in
Nineteenth-Century Britain

H. L. MALCHOW

Gothic Images of Race in Nineteenth-Century Britain

STANFORD UNIVERSITY PRESS

STANFORD, CALIFORNIA

1996

Stanford University Press
Stanford, California
© 1996 by the Board of Trustees of the
Leland Stanford Junior University
Printed in the United States of America

CIP data appear at the end of the book

Stanford University Press publications are distributed
exclusively by Stanford University Press within the
United States, Canada, Mexico, and Central America;
they are distributed exclusively by Cambridge
University Press throughout the rest of the world.

For Peter Cupchunas

Acknowledgments

An author who attempts to range through such extensive and often unfamiliar terrain, and to engage a subject that refuses to be captured by a single academic discipline, must owe a great debt to other scholars and specialists, and to friends and colleagues over many years. I am also deeply obliged to my students' lively discussion and intelligent criticism in a number of seminars and colloquia. Among my colleagues at Tufts University who have been generous with their time and comments, I must thank Sugata Bose, Carol Flynn, John Fyler, Gerald Gill, Martin Green, Jeanne Penvenne, and Laurence Senelick. I also owe debts of gratitude to Patricia Klaus, David M. Knight, David Cresap Moore, David Roberts, Kirsten Seaver, Nate Therien, and Alex Warwick. Special thanks are due to Norris Pope at Stanford University Press, and to the editors of *Past and Present* for their permission to publish a revised version of my article "Frankenstein's Monster and Images of Race in Nineteenth-Century Britain" here. Finally, whatever contribution this study has to make—indeed, the fact that it is seeing the light of day at all—is largely owing to the criticism and encouragement over many years of Howard Solomon, whose far-ranging and shrewd understanding of the now vast field of sexuality and gender studies and the construction of prejudice makes him a valuable resource, not only for academics such as myself, but for that larger community in which we live.

H.L.M.

Contents

"To Join in Holy Matrimony" 240. *"A Just Impediment"* 243. *"Being now come to Years of Discretion"* 248. *"Brute Beasts that have no Understanding"* 251. *"Ordained for the Procreation of Children"* 254. *"Envy, Hatred, and Malice"* 256.

Illustrations

15. "The Irish 'Vampire'" 128
16. Fred Leslie as the Creature in *The Vampire's Victim* 147
17. C. Léandre, "The House of Rothschild" 154
18. (a) A. S. Thomson, "New Zealand Girl with Her Half-Caste Nephew and Niece" 198
(b) H. A. Stark, Hostages to India" 199
19. Miss Jewell and Lobengula 240
20. Loben in War Dress 241
21. (a) "Loben and His Jewell" 244
(b) "I Suppose I Am Married" 245
22. "Imperialism" 246

Gothic Images of Race in Nineteenth-Century Britain

. . . no longer take things at second or third hand, nor look through the eyes of the dead, nor feed on the spectres in books

— *Walt Whitman, 'Song of Myself'*

Introduction

This book searches an area that lies somewhere in the borderlands between literature and history, between "representation" and reality. It is a shadowy place, both Platonic cave and Cimmerian den, in
which images of the ideal and the monstrous are intertwined. Shadowy,
but not unexplored: it has been nearly 50 years since Octave Mannoni's
Prospero and Caliban suggested that Europeans "project upon the colonial peoples the obscurities of their own unconscious—obscurities they
would rather not penetrate."[1] And it has been 30 years since Philip Curtin's magisterial *Image of Africa* drew scholarly attention back from the
"dark continent" itself to domestic European values, beliefs, and popular
myths—to the hobgoblin element that shaped Western "knowledge" of
the black. Since then, much has been written about how the West has
"constructed" non-European peoples, as projections of its own anxieties
and as rationalizations for and instruments in the extension of its economic and political power. The past two decades have seen important
explorations of the ways in which Europeans came to grips with the
"marvelous possessions," in Stephen Greenblatt's words, that their tech-
nology secured for them. This study is deeply indebted to the work of
many who have seen in the prolific European literature on other cultures
texts that reveal, between the lines and under the surface, more of the
observer than the observed.

In the first place, no one writing on European images of race can avoid
a debt to Edward Said and his provocative thesis that "Orientalism" was
an insistently hegemonic discourse, that European-constructed knowledge of the culture of the colonized principally and powerfully served
the purposes of domination and authority.[2] If Said's picture of the way

knowledge of the "Other" was produced and used now seems somewhat insensitive to the complex interaction of experience and mentality and to the ambiguities and conflicts within the texts he drew upon, nevertheless his study, and the deconstructionist assumptions upon which it rested, inaugurated a decade of reexamination of the texts by which Europeans have explained and manipulated the history and cultures of non-Europeans. The work, for instance, of Peter Hulme and Stephen Greenblatt on the Columbian Caribbean, or of Greg Dening on the South Pacific, draws us back into the European mind, to the limitations of understanding inherent in European culture—indeed, to the problem of language itself in revealing/concealing the reality of these alien worlds.[3]

Such domestication of foreign experience in the formation of a popular culture as well as a "science" of racial difference has also been explored by those who, in the wake of the structuralist revolution of the 1970's, have argued for a single field in which the images of race, sexuality, and class are interwoven systems that mutually confirm the hegemony of the European, heterosexual, bourgeois male. The efforts of Sander Gilman and G. L. Mosse have been important in drawing together these separate-seeming but intimately connected discourses of prejudice,[4] and an ever-widening range of feminist and gay scholarship has also been increasingly sensitive to the similarities in racist and sexist discourse, to, in the words of Joanna De Groot, "the theme of domination/subordination central both to nineteenth-century masculine identities and to the western sense of superiority."[5] This awareness of a nineteenth-century "reshaping and intensifying of a range of social boundaries and differences," of the parallel and homologous construction of "natural" inequalities of race and gender, importantly informs this study.

Nevertheless, the cultural historian apprehends a certain danger in too simple a duality of empowered male colonialist aggressor and subordinate female colonized victim. As with Said, one senses the need for more flexibility, for more dialogue between mentality and experience. "Race" was not simply a difference that, in the context of an expanding sphere of imperial power, could neatly and automatically be slotted into a system of prejudice prepared by domestic tradition. For one thing, those "traditions" themselves were neither unitary (among different social classes and regions) nor stable. For another, like all communication, the dialogue between European experience abroad and domestic culture required a language fit for the task. This study explores the creation of a popular vocabulary in the late eighteenth and nineteenth centuries by which racial and cultural difference could be represented as unnatural— a "racial gothic" discourse that employed certain striking metaphoric images to filter and give meaning to a flood of experience and information from abroad, but that also thereby recharged itself for an assault on domestic social and physical "pathology."[6]

Although an undertaking such as this must acknowledge the real contributions of critical theory, my chief interest does not lie in addressing that ever-growing, somewhat self-referential body of knowledge per se. Some may feel that, in consequence, this study is too empirical and opportunistic, employing concepts and approaches that might more cautiously, consistently, and exactly be used by those who have developed them for getting at a specifically interior logic of "the text." The need to explain change over time and to create a narrative, inevitably, however, draws the historian back to the larger world, to the surrounding environment, to biography, to the way texts serve both emotional and tangible interests. How texts are purposefully manipulated and employed—and how they are received—is of particular concern. That is, most historians are likely to assume the importance of "context" and have, of course, a natural affinity with what has been called "the new historicism" in literary studies.

This study tries to move back and forth between the imagined world of literature and the "real" world of historical experience, between fiction and romance on the one hand, and, on the other, what Sander Gilman has called the "parallel fictions" of the human sciences, of anthropology and biology,[7] between popular representations of the "unnatural" at home and abroad, between a domestic environment and that of empire. "Race," it has become a commonplace to observe, is an inherently fluid idea, whose meaning, like those of class or nationality, shifts over time, and seems at once concrete and intangible. Rac*ism* required a "demonization" (I do not use the word casually here) of difference. The gothic genre of the late eighteenth century, and its various permutations thereafter, offered a language that could be appropriated, consciously or not, by racists in a powerful and obsessively reiterated evocation of terror, disgust, and alienation. But the gothic literary sensibility itself also evoked in the context of an expanding experience of cultural conflict, of the brutal progress of European nationalism and imperialism, and was in part a construct of that phenomenon. There was, as Margaret Hunt has argued with respect to eighteenth-century travel literature, not so much a learning of racism from such texts, as a cross-fertilization and mutual reinforcement of beliefs.[8] This book explores both the gothicization of race and the racialization of the gothic as inseparable processes.

Important work continues to emerge on the social and cultural context of the idea of "race" in nineteenth-century science and social science. George Stocking's seminal studies of Victorian anthropological thought have been recently augmented by Christopher Herbert's rewarding exploration of the subjectivity of ethnological constructions of both domestic and foreign "savages" and Henrika Kuklick's presentation of what one may call the sociology of social science—that is, of the domestic social context of anthropologists as professionals and of their ideas.[9] Illuminating as this work has been, the present study does not concern itself, at least directly, with the production of a particular field of Victorian knowledge, with ethnology per se, with scholarly debate in the universities and professional societies, with the ways in which cultural factors shaped specific scientific and social scientific theories, systems, and proofs. This book is, in other words, not a formal excursion into intellectual history, but rather a tentative sampling of a vast field of popular culture, a field in which an ephemeral novel or play, sensational for a season and then forgotten, can hold as much meaning as the familiar artifacts of the Victorian intelligentsia.

The ground has been well broken for such an enterprise, at least with regard to late-nineteenth-century fiction and its context of a general fin de siècle malaise over cultural and sexual identity, empire, race, and nation. In particular, Patrick Brantlinger's *Rule of Darkness* and Elaine Showalter's *Sexual Anarchy*, from different perspectives, have fueled a general reexamination of a literature Brantlinger has christened "imperial gothic." These themes of anxiety over degeneracy and primitivism have found their way into explorations of the wider popular culture in this critical period as well—most notably in Judith Walkowitz's use of the gothicized Ripper sensation of the late 1880's to reveal an antifeminist politics of sexual danger.[10] My debt to this scholarship will be obvious, particularly in the later sections of this book. The themes and texts I search here range, however, well beyond and beneath the "imperial gothic" fiction of Haggard, Kipling, and Stevenson, and the chronological limits of the fin de siècle. In fact, it may be that the excellence of a decade or so of scholarship on this period has somewhat overburdened it as *the* critical era of crisis. Racial gothic, if not imperial gothic, has an older and deeper provenance.

Although this study closely reexamines the two defining classics of gothic literature that frame the nineteenth century, Mary Shelley's *Frankenstein* and Bram Stoker's *Dracula*, and has recourse to the themes and imagery of a number of lesser gothic pieces, it is not a study in literary criticism as such, and does not attempt an analysis of the gothic as a literary style. In establishing a "gothic" representation of racial difference as a powerful nineteenth-century phenomenon, I have followed a larger, no doubt looser and more popular, definition of gothic—as a *language* of panic, of unreasoning anxiety, blind revulsion, and distancing sensationalism, as well as a particular "*literature* of terror." Obviously, this language of terror was no monopoly of the novelist, but can be found throughout the discourse on racial difference at whatever level—in both the popular and establishment press, in scientific writing, in missionary and imperialist memoirs, and in travel books. It is not my argument that this spreading realm of representation, this regarding of the colonized and savage Other as weirdly unnatural, was simply a by-product of the gothic form of literature that preceded it, although indeed it often seems to have drawn directly on such a source. Gothic fiction and racial discourse were indeed closely intertwined, but they mutually influenced each other; moreover, both were shaped in large part by the audience they had in common, by the social and sexual, as well as racial, apprehensions of the literate middle and lower middle classes.

The gothic as a literary genre may be defined by characteristics[11] that resonate strongly with important aspects of the nineteenth-century literature of racial prejudice, imperial exploration, and sensational anthropology: themes and images meant to shock and terrify, and a style grounded in techniques of suspense and threat. If the archaic settings of many early gothic romances do not seem to have much significance for the kinds of connection this study explores (although archaism may, of course, evoke primitivism), other elements, such as highly stereotyped characters and an insistence on readable signs of depravity and the demonic concealed in physiognomy, dress, and mannerism are strikingly apt. Both the gothic novel and racist discourse manipulate deeply buried anxieties, both dwell on the chaos beyond natural and rational boundaries and massage a deep, often unconscious and sexual, fear of contamination, both present the threatened destruction of the simple and pure by the poisonously exotic, by anarchic forces of passion and appetite, carnal lust and blood lust.

David Punter has drawn attention to the gothic's "connections with the primitive, the barbaric, the tabooed": "where the classics offered a set of cultural models to be followed, Gothic represented excess and exaggeration, the product of the wild and the uncivilised."[12] This language is significant. To describe the gothic genre with such vocabulary (*primitive, barbaric, uncivilised*) and with jargon (*taboo*) derived from nineteenth-century tales of the cannibal South Pacific suggests just the kind of intimate connection between the gothic literary sensibility and a popular culture of racial fantasy and fear that this study attempts to explore.

The structure of this book reflects its enterprise; that is, its parts alternate from the realm of gothic fiction, which was itself at some level a response to expanding knowledge of cultural and racial difference, to that of an explicit nineteenth-century racial and imperial discourse covertly informed by fictional, mythic, and folkloric—that is, essentially domestic—traditions. Thus Chapter 1, which argues that Frankenstein's Monster must be read in the context of Caribbean slave rebellions, is followed in Chapter 2 by an extended analysis of cannibalism, an important—perhaps the most important—element of nineteenth-century racial discourse, which nevertheless drew deeply on popular domestic European culture—that is, from the "white cannibalism" of the madman, the criminal, the mob, the sailor, and the harpylike female. Here the purpose is not to offer a judgment on the reality or otherwise of customary cannibalism in the Pacific, Africa, or South America, but rather to demonstrate how the representation of the presumed cannibal nature of the primitive nonwhite—by missionaries, explorers, and ethnologists—was itself a gothic discourse, a fearful and sensational imagining of the unnatural and the unseen.

Chapter 3 returns to the gothic genre to explore the social context of the popular revival in the late nineteenth century of gothic fiction, and of the vampire story in particular. An attempt is made to join a close examination of Bram Stoker's own life with a reading of *Dracula* that draws out a subtext shaped by contemporary fears of identity, of sexual-cum-racial pollution, of "homosexual panic" and anti-Semitism. Bad blood, the unnatural crossing of sexual and racial boundaries and the threat of a new and secret vampiric race leads directly in Chapter 4 to the image of the half-breed and the way that image was progressively gothicized in the course of the nineteenth century. As with cannibalism, the object here is not to engage the reality of mixed-race culture beyond Europe, but to examine the representation of the half-breed, half-caste, or mulatto in popular science, the press, and literature. Like "race" itself, the idea of *the* "half-breed" was a largely arbitrary construction of the imagination, which took on a deeply gothic coloring as the concepts of race and nationality themselves became progressively reified in the course of a century of imperial conflict and expansion.

Obsession in fin de siècle Britain over the threat of collapsing racial identity resonated strongly with similar fears of the transgression of the boundaries of sexuality, with an exactly contemporary popular preoccupation with the social and imperial threat of masculine women and feminine men. Both were preceded by a fixing—that is, an overdetermining—of "natural" identity. In an epilogue that reexamines the press-driven moral panic over interracial intimacy at the "Savage South Africa" Exhibition of 1899, racial discourse is drawn back to a domestic locus of misogyny and ethnic prejudice. Of central interest in this concluding essay is not the "real" story, well narrated by Ben Shephard,[13] of the chief participants, Kitty Jewel and Peter Loben, but the way the popular press manipulated their histories.

It is my hope that this study will convincingly establish, not only the likelihood of an underlying racial element in gothic literature, but what is more important, the pervasiveness of the gothic in nineteenth-century racial discourse. Appreciation of the centrality of this sensational language of a hidden unnaturalness in racial and cultural difference is, in fact, fundamental to understanding, not only the ways in which racism drew a peculiar strength from powerful and emotive images, but the compelling, if covert, linkages that were thereby fused at both the conscious and unconscious levels with other areas of social discourse and prejudice: with misogyny, homophobia, class snobbery, and popular revulsion at poverty, madness, and disease.[14] Moreover, by insisting on an evolution of the gothic connection over time and on a particular rhythm of exchange between real and fictional, domestic and foreign, this study attempts to evade the reductionist and tautological problem of criticism that, having posited a "great surface network" unifying all such discourses, is fatally (for the historian's enterprise) static and can only substitute a kind of race-sex-class mantra for explanations of historical change.

Some may object that the themes and connections of this study are beyond the realm of formal "proof." This is, of course, strictly speaking true, but I believe that the density of gothic imagery and metaphor, over a wide range of texts, and the thick similarities and resonances that weave in and out of them, create a compelling case. Some may also feel that, given the vastness of nineteenth-century documentation, I have relied upon a relatively small number of texts, both within the genre of gothic fiction and within the much wider realm of nonfictional literature. This, too, is true, although my strategy was to look closely and reiteratively at a selection of sources that seemed to display a kind of "evidence" found throughout their respective genres. I have presented a variety of types of material and am confident that further and lengthier research would only strengthen the case.

There remains much to say about racial gothic, of course, which the requirements of space and time have not permitted here. More could certainly be done with gothic resonances in scientific, especially biological, discourse—on, for instance, the discovery of "cannibalism" in the animal world. An even wider field is offered by the complicated Victorian attitude toward "signs" of moral and physical depravity (at home and abroad) and how to detect and read them. This study has only scratched the surface of a gothic reading of signs—of secret languages and offensive odors, of the half-breed's earrings, the Maori's tattoos, and the incorrect clothing of the half-civilized "native." And then there are the most gothic signs of all, the disaggregated parts of bodies that fill nineteenth-century representations of domestic and racial outsiders—Queequeg's preserved heads and the phrenologist's skulls, the cannibal's filed teeth and the lips of the mulatto, the mutilated genitalia of the African woman and the Jewish man, the staring eyes of the cannibal, the criminal, the madman, the Jew, the homosexual, and the harlot.

CHAPTER I

Was Frankenstein's Monster
"a Man and a Brother"?

*The Black stripp'd, and appeared of a giant-like
   strength,
Large in bone, large in muscle and with arms a cruel
   length.*[1]

It is now commonly accepted that the gothic literary genre of the late eighteenth and early nineteenth centuries represented, if remotely and unconsciously, the central tensions of an age of social liberation and political revolution. The themes of unjust persecution and imprisonment that are central to works like Matthew Lewis's *The Monk*, Charles Maturin's *Melmoth*, and Eugène Sue's *The Wandering Jew*, together with the dilemmas of identity facing the liberated that permeate William Godwin's *Caleb Williams* and Mary Shelley's *Frankenstein*, obviously resonate with the events of an age that, as Chris Baldick has finely observed, witnessed humanity seizing responsibility "for recreating the world, for violently reshaping its natural environment and its inherited social and political forms, for remaking itself."[2] Criticism in this vein has, however, focused almost exclusively on domestic themes—the "demonizing" of the proletariat in an era of industrial and political revolution, or the self-exploration and "nascent feminism" of authors like Mary Shelley and Charlotte Brontë. In contrast, I shall offer a racial reading of Mary Shelley's *Frankenstein* as an important level of interpretation that meshes with Marxist and feminist efforts to locate the novel in its social and psychological context.

In the portrayal of her monster, it is at least as plausible that Mary Shelley drew upon contemporary attitudes toward nonwhites—in particular, on fears and hopes of the abolition of slavery in the West Indies—as upon middle-class apprehension of a Luddite proletariat or her own "post-birthing trauma."[3] Indeed, the peculiar horror of the monster owes much of its emotional power to this hidden, or "coded," aspect, and the subsequent popularity of the tale through several nineteenth-century editions and on the Victorian stage derived in large part from the convergence of its most emotive elements with the evolving contemporaneous representation of ethnic and racial difference. Of necessity, such an argument rests on evidence that is indirect, circumstantial, and speculative. There is no clear proof that Mary Shelley consciously set out to create a monster explicitly suggestive of the Jamaican escaped slave or maroon, or that she drew directly from any personal knowledge of either planter or abolitionist propaganda. That she did so is certainly not impossible. It is not, in any event, my purpose to prove explicit connections and direct sources. Nor is it my purpose to discover a hidden "key" that will unlock every level of meaning, intended or otherwise, in the novel. What does interest me is how closely Shelley's fictional creation in many respects parallels the racial stereotypes of the age, and how her exploration of the limits of the thinking of Rousseau and William Godwin on man and education, surely the most important subtheme in the novel, mirrors contemporary difficulties in maintaining universal humanistic ideals in the context of the slave economy of the West Indies and an expanding empire over nonwhite populations in Asia and Africa.

"Race" in the Napoleonic Era

The relationship of man to the rest of creation, and of European man to others, was a familiar problem posed afresh to the systematizing Enlightenment mind. This is not the place to describe again the development of the concept of race in the eighteenth century, except to note that these ideas already involved a good deal of projection, to use Mannoni's language, of Europeans' fears about their own savage practices and dark interiors, and that toward the end of the century they acquired a greater presence or centrality owing to informal travel, scientific or scholarly investigation, and imperial conquest.[4]

Educated Europeans of the early Enlightenment inherited a view of foreign peoples that was a mixture of fantasy and hearsay, often used to expose the venality of European life, as in Montaigne and Montesquieu, or, as in Hakluyt and Purchas, to administer a crude justification for economic penetration and religious conquest. Ironically, however, the hunger for systematic and verifiable knowledge that typified the mid-century *philosophe* served to reinforce, with a scientific gloss, this Eurocentric perspective. As the fantastic was exchanged for a natural science of plants, animals, and foreign peoples, there was an inevitable compulsion to rank, not only cultures, but types of people. This in turn encouraged the construction of "races" of men in parallel with the genera and species laid down by Linnaeus for the biological world as a whole. This search for an ordering of Nature by rank, by degrees of civilization, no doubt reflects a hierarchical mentality inherent in the aristocratic European tradition.

If Rousseau, in his famous assault on that tradition, offered the "natural man," the untutored savage, as an ideal, a model of precivilized innocence, this was, of course, no validation of other, specifically alternative, cultures. As Hayden White has argued, "the Noble Savage was a concept with which to belabor nobility, not to redeem the savage."[5] Moreover, the notion of natural man—read as humanity in general—yet subsumed the idea of the Wild Man of European tradition, from which it had evolved, a tradition that in fact forcefully resurfaced in both evangelical theology and Burkean conservatism in the era of social and political upheaval into which Mary Shelley was born. The Beast Within had to be displaced outward and downward, in the manner White has suggested,[6] in order to define the limits of a specifically bourgeois "humanity." An uncontrollable "inhuman" appetite, a rage to devour came to characterize both the foreign and pauper "native." James Gillray's well-known cartoon of sansculottes enjoying a meal of dismembered aristocrats precisely brings together the themes of bestial and threatening domestic poverty and a gothic cannibalism drawn from folktale grotesques, the Columbian Caribbean, and Captain Cook's South Pacific.

Mary Shelley grew to maturity in a highly charged intellectual and political atmosphere, in which revolutionary radicalism was on the defensive. Her parents' close association with radical politics, her husband's revolutionary idealism, and her own reading of Rousseau have been widely commented on, and the novel has been persuasively portrayed as, in part, an ambiguous rendering of her father's utopian and universal ideals.[7] If, however, we are to locate the novel in the context of the general assault on radical ideas, then it may be valuable to bear in mind that the black Jacobins in Haiti and the parliamentary struggle in England to abolish the slave trade guaranteed that issues of race played a significant contemporary role in the larger political debate surrounding the capacities and rights of mankind. Nor did a reciprocating awareness of the antislavery and the domestic radical movements fade after abolition of the British slave trade in 1807. In 1814 a proposal was made at the Congress of Vienna to renew the rights of French slave merchants. Within four weeks some 806 opposing petitions with 1,500,000 signatures from towns throughout Britain were sent to Parliament.[8] If nothing else, Negro slavery in the New World provided a common source of analogy and metaphor in the political polemic aimed at redressing or defending inequality in the Old. Like other radicals, Mary Shelley's parents, William Godwin and Mary Wollstonecraft, at least tangentially addressed questions raised by the West Indian slavery debate in their own writings.

Godwin, concerned to defend the universality of reason in humankind and its operation in the perfecting of governments and human society generally, attacked the familiar theory that climate had created types of men with different capacities, in his best-known work, *Political Justice*. Characteristically, however, he obscured his point by admitting some probable effect of climate on character in extreme cases, such as the tropics. Here his reliance on Hume led him to confuse racial and national character and further vitiated his object of demonstrating that it was, by and large, governments that shaped the characters of their peoples for good or bad.[9] Although he was, of course, an opponent of slavery, and scorned the argument that it was a tolerable institution because the slaves themselves seemed to tolerate it, Godwin nevertheless, in his rambling asides on Negro character, managed to affirm some of the common theories about Negro "differences" that one can find in the proslavery literature, as well as among the armchair theorists generally. Specifically, he accepted that Negroes came to sexual maturity earlier, had more passionate temperaments than Europeans, and possessed a natural indolence "consequent upon a spontaneous fertility" of the tropical environment. Moreover, while denying that racial differences posed any absolute barrier to the spread of political liberty, Godwin suggested, like many abolitionists, that instruction and guidance over a lengthy period of time would be necessary to prepare such people for freedom.[10]

If, even in the flush of optimism of the early years of the French Revolution, a radical like Godwin could offer only an ambiguous approach to racial equality—and some radicals, such as Cobbett, had no use for "nigger philanthropy" in any form—conservative polemic often encouraged racial or at least ethnic stereotyping in its emotional and intellectual response to utopian radicalism. The French wars, the abortive rebellion in Ireland, the spread of the ideals of the French Revolution to Haiti, and armed resistance to British suzerainty in India served to heighten xenophobia and validate ethnic prejudice as patriotic anti-Jacobinism. In this context, the assault on slavery, as well as its vigorous defense, established a discourse that served both to highlight inherent cultural, and increasingly racial, differences between the Englishman and the black, while at the same time offering allusive and metaphorical ammunition to the enemies of domestic radicalism. Those searching for answers to claims of "universal" humanitarian and egalitarian rights in Europe had only to wave a hand at the patent folly of enfranchising Jamaican slaves, Tipu's fanatical followers in India, or, for that matter, "the Hottentot Venus" lasciviously displayed in London in 1810.

The exhibition of this indentured black woman, Saartjie Baartman, to curious crowds in Regency London, the extraordinary interest taken in her physical form by the press, and the way her body, after death, was literally disassembled to prove spurious theories about Negro nature,[11] is a reminder of the way the cultural prejudices, fears, and deep-seated neuroses of the observer may impinge on "science" and literature, and wander from one arena to another. Here the physical "abnormalities" of the South African "Hottentot," hitherto unknown in England, served through popular caricature to reinforce ideas of polygenesis and racial hierarchy, but also more subtly in a reactionary political climate to encourage views of natural inequality generally. When studying even so bookishly inspired a text as *Frankenstein*, it may be well to bear in mind that a writer—and Mary Shelley led a far less closeted life than many young women in her milieu—exists within a popular as well as an intellectual culture. A journal recording the books she read indicates possible intellectual sources for Mary Shelley's ideas; other influences are necessarily obscure, but not therefore unimportant. Her first novel was the product of inner psychology and private domestic experience, but also of the wider enfolding, external environment of impinging and shifting values, attitudes and observations.

Free American and West African blacks were not unknown in the England in which Mary Wollstonecraft Godwin came to maturity, nor were they merely the objects of a distant Caribbean philanthropy. In his *Fables, Ancient and Modern*, published in 1805, William Godwin included a tale, "Washing the Blackamoor White," with the aside, "The other day I stopped involuntarily to look at a negro I passed on the street . . . there was nothing brutal or insulting or coarse in his manner."[12] Thousands of mostly destitute Negroes—freed slaves brought to England by their masters, ex-sailors who had manned ships and left them in English ports, and those who had fled America—were concentrated in London and the other major ports by the end of the eighteenth century.[13] If the fashion for little black boys in livery, or black footmen, as in Godwin's fable, had waned, blacks as beggars, prostitutes, and in the rougher occupations were relatively common. In 1810 and 1811, a black boxer from America, Thomas Molineaux, almost defeated the legendary English champion Tom Cribb in two widely publicized matches. These fights, attended by thousands, reported in *The Times*, and portrayed in the popular art of cheap prints and caricature,[14] drew the attention of polite society as well as the gaming world. Even the *Annual Register* for 1811 offered a report, with the justification that it "is so characteristic of the taste of the times, and its subject of so much contemporary importance, that we cannot but think it worth recording." An event such as this inevitably raised a sense in many of national and racial competition: "The Black's prowess was regarded by Cribb's friends with a jealousy which excited considerable national prejudice against him . . . the laurels of a British champion was in danger of being wrested from him by a Baltimore man of colour." The victorious Cribb was received by his friends "like a Nelson returning from a naval victory."[15]

It is not merely the case that blacks were from time to time in the public eye in Britain. At home as well, Mary Godwin had certainly been exposed, both through her father's writings and through house guests, to the hotly contested issue of the abolition of slavery. It is reasonable to assume that this provided one source of images and buried themes in the novel. William Godwin had covered the debates on the slave trade for the Whiggish *New Annual Register* in the 1780's and 1790's. In April 1791, he was actually present in the gallery of the Commons when William Wilberforce's motion to ban further import of slaves into the British West Indies went down to defeat.[16] If, as we have seen, he accepted in *Political Justice* that there were racial differences in character as well as body, his sentiments lay with the abolitionists, although not with Wilberforce's Tory evangelicalism. Godwin denied that differences of race or gender had any significant effect on an individual's ability to reason or to be educated. In his novel *St. Leon* (1799), a prison turnkey is represented as a Negro with "sound understanding and an excellent heart."[17] The political struggle for abolition and the potential of the freed Negro for improvement would have been subjects of common conversation in the home in which Mary was educated. For example, Dr. James Bell, an admirer of Godwin's, was introduced to him there in 1799. Bell was determined to go out to Jamaica "to lighten the woes and diminish the horrors of slavery." He died on the island shortly after arrival.[18]

The prominence of the antislavery issue in late-eighteenth-century European discourse had a direct impact on the characteristic depiction of the Negro in Western art. Rather than as an exotic, often in fancy dress, the black came to be visually represented as a naked or semi-clothed victim, an object of pity.[19] While the intention of the evangelical abolitionists may have been to portray the black slave as "a man and a brother," the actual effect of their propaganda—rendered vivid on canvas, medallions, and chinaware, in cheap prints and ballad sheets, on mementos of all kinds—was to reiterate an image of the Other as a special kind of childlike, suffering, and degraded being, rarely heroic, that became part of the common coinage of popular culture (ill. 1). Moreover, abolitionist propaganda inevitably drew counterblasts from the proslavery lobby. Apologists for Negro slavery manipulated scientific argument and injected into English popular culture, as well as into European po-

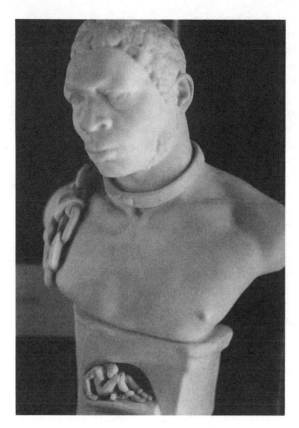

Ill. 1. Figurine (Wilberforce Museum, Hull).

litical and intellectual discourse, the paranoid fears, sexual fantasies, and indeed the whole range of racist stereotypes already current in Jamaican planter society. This served to create misgivings and ambiguities about race that were roughly parallel to the challenge to Paineite liberalism posed by émigré descriptions of Jacobin ferocity in Paris.

Finally, while admitting that Mary Shelley's world was suffused with both positive and negative representations of the black man in public discourse, that her father held strong opinions on the subject that, inveterate educator that he was, he would have communicated to his children, and that there was a real presence of the racial Other in the London of her childhood, one might still ask whether this offers sufficient probability that she absorbed these images in a way that would lead one to expect them to emerge in her first and most important work of fiction.

There is, in fact, proof that Mary Shelley did have recourse both before and during the writing of *Frankenstein* to a reservoir of information about blacks in Africa and in the West Indies. Turning to the journal she kept, and in which she meticulously recorded books she and Percy read, we find some interesting titles. In 1814 they both read the first two large volumes of Mungo Park's relation of the interior of Western Africa, an important milestone in European "discovery" of the continent. Later, the year Mary began *Frankenstein*, they read the third volume, containing the narrative of the death of Park.[20] In the winter of 1814–15, they also read a history of the British West Indies by the wealthy merchant-planter Bryan Edwards.[21] Edwards was a relatively liberal Jamaican, although proslavery. His work, narrating the history of the islands up to the late eighteenth century, dwelt upon differences of color and caste and the supposed racial characteristics of West Indian slaves from different parts of Africa, as well as the horrors of slave rebellions. Mary Shelley appears to have found the work engaging enough to spend "all evening" and "all day" engrossed in it.[22] Finally, although the journal indicates that the Shelleys finished reading John Davis's record of his travels through the American South after the *Frankenstein* manuscript had been dispatched to John Murray in London, the themes it treats—musing about the black as natural, Rousseauian man, the struggle of owners to retrieve fugitive slaves, the melancholy wilderness of the American "Alps" (the Blue Ridge mountains)—have a close affinity with those that Mary Shelley explores, just as his description of the pathetic condition of escaped blacks might suggest as well that of Frankenstein's fleeing Creature: "Exposed to such wanton cruelty the negroes frequently run away; they flee into the woods, where they are wet with the rains of heaven, and embrace the rock for want of shelter."[23]

It may also be significant that in the weeks just after Mary Shelley "conceived" the central idea for her story, but before she had given birth to the Creature in chapter 5, Matthew Lewis joined the little house party at Geneva.[24] While no record of his table talk survives, "Monk" Lewis was a famously voluble conversationalist, and he had just returned from his first visit to his own Jamaica plantation. The *Journal* of his experiences in the West Indies was not published in his lifetime, but its themes would certainly have been shared with his friends. Like those of Bryan Edwards, Lewis's opinions were liberal for the times ("the execrable slave-trade"), and his account contains flattering and sympathetic portraits of many of the blacks—slave and free—whom he met in Jamaica. But it also portrays a planter society that was "in the utmost alarm at rumours" of abolition, and indulges with some relish in a gothic representation of stories of Obeah poisonings and brutal acts of revenge perpetrated by escaped slaves.[25]

This dualism—the black's eagerness to please, combined with a propensity, when harmed or scorned, for exacting a bloody vengeance—had, as we shall see below, become a commonplace of racial discourse by the early nineteenth century. Suggestive of the emotional instability of the child, the woman, and the madman, it had already provided Lewis with material for a gothic drama, *The Castle Spectre*. Here, Earl Osmand's black servant, Hassan, consumed with a passion for revenge at his enslavement, vows sweet vengeance: "Am I not branded with scorn? . . . am I not now despised? What man . . . would accept the negro's friendship? What woman . . . would not turn from the negro in disgust? . . . Oh! how it joys me when the white man suffers!"[26] Lewis's vengeful black here speaks a language that closely parallels the despair and rage of Frankenstein's Creature.

It remains to examine the extent to which the language and themes in *Frankenstein* indicate a reflection at some level of the imagery and issues of contemporary race debate in the creation and fate of Mary Shelley's Monster.

Frankenstein

As is well known, *Frankenstein; or, The Modern Prometheus* had its origins at a house party near Geneva in June 1816 at which the eighteen-year-old Mary Wollstonecraft Godwin (she married Shelley the following December) was challenged to produce a ghost story. The resulting tale was published anonymously in March 1818, and was surprisingly successful. In the form of a gothic horror romance, it recounts, through the letters of Walton, an Arctic explorer, the tortured history of Victor Frankenstein, the young son of a Genevan magistrate, who, as a Faustian university student, aspired to create life, and whose creation—his monster, fiend, or demon—, rejected by his creator, flees to the wilderness, where he lives rough on nuts and berries. His appearance produces violent revulsion in all who meet him, however, in spite of the Creature's earnest attempts to make friends and do good. Educated vicariously and surreptitiously, he develops a sense of the injustices heaped upon him and turns to vengeance. He first murders Frankenstein's child brother, then causes the judicial murder of an innocent young woman, and finally, half-repentant, tracks down his creator to demand that he create a mate for him, vowing that they will live apart from mankind. This Frankenstein at first agrees to do, but he betrays his promise after reflecting on the dangers of a race of creatures arising from the union of two such monsters. The enraged Creature exacts a further terrible vengeance, first killing Frankenstein's friend Clerval, and then his bride

Elizabeth on their bridal bed. The novel concludes with a determined
Frankenstein pursuing his creation into the Arctic, only to die before
confronting the Monster, who mourns his maker and disappears into the
northern darkness with a vow of self-immolation.

A reading of this text that attempts to draw out an embedded racial
message must begin where racism itself begins, with physiognomy. The
Monster, it will be seen, is not merely a grotesque, a too-roughly cobbled-
together simulacrum of a man. He is, first, larger and more powerful
than his maker, and, second, dark and sinister in appearance. This suggests the standard description of the black man in both the literature of
the West Indies and that of unfolding West African exploration. Mungo
Park's *Travels*, which Mary Shelley had ready to hand, described the
Mandingoes as "commonly above the middle size, well-shaped, strong,
and capable of enduring great labour." A Negro guide who "mounted up
the rocks, where indeed no horse could follow him, leaving me to admire
his agility" indicates both great strength, and perhaps the simian dex-
terity with which the Monster eludes Frankenstein in the Alps.[27] The
Jamaican Bryan Edwards described the Mandingoes as "remarkably tall,"
while the Eboes were, he averred, a sickly yellow in complexion with
eyes that appeared to be "suffused with bile."[28]

By the early nineteenth century, popular racial discourse managed to
conflate such descriptions of particular ethnic characteristics into a general image of the Negro body in which repulsive features, brutelike
strength and size of limbs featured prominently. Frankenstein's creature,
when we first see him, is defined by a set of clichés that might be picked
out of such literature. His eyes are "dull yellow" and "watery," hair "a
lustrous black" and "ragged," and his black lips contrast with "teeth of
pearly whiteness." His skin was "in colour and apparent texture like
that of a mummy."[29] Mummies are, of course, ordinarily dark brown or
black in color, a fact that led to speculation about the racial origin of
the ancient Egyptians following the Napoleonic excavations. There was
already a tradition drawn from classical authors that the civilization of
ancient Thebes had originated in Ethiopia. The comte de Volney made
use of this in his *Ruins*, a book Mary Shelley knew and used as one of
the Monster's textbooks in the novel; Volney wrote of "the black complexion of the Sphinx."[30] This is not to say that Shelley intended to create a specifically Negro monster—elsewhere she writes of the Monster's
yellow skin[31]—but rather that, reaching into childhood fantasy and
imagination, she dredged up a bogeyman that had been prepared by a
cultural tradition of the threatening Other—whether troll or giant,
gypsy or Negro—from the dark inner recesses of xenophobic fear and
loathing.

This seems to me to be at least as reasonable a reading as the claim that the Monster is a feminine-masculine composite that transcends gender,[32] or that his alien hideousness reflects bourgeois fears of a threatening working class. The physical lineaments of the Creature suggest little that can be construed as feminine, nor do they explicitly raise the image of the wan and bowed pauper or proletarian laborer, often small in stature and poor in health. Frankenstein's Monster is robust and larger than life, ostentatiously rural rather than urban. Of course, the Monster as industrial worker does not have to be a literal image, but rather the enlarged fear of a collective threat. Nevertheless, at the level of physiognomy at least, a racial reading seems to me to be closer to the mark than a Marxist one.

Beyond size and repulsiveness, the most striking physical attributes of the Monster are his apelike ability to scamper up mountainsides and his endurance of temperatures that European man would find intolerable: "I was more agile," he says, "than they and could subsist upon coarser diet; I bore the extremes of heat and cold with less injury to my frame."[33] This description closely parallels the claims of the apologists for West Indian slavery. The Negro, it was said, had more brute strength than the white man and could stand the heat of the tropics, which would enervate, perhaps kill, a European.[34] One might, without stretching imagination very far, see in Frankenstein's futile chase after his creature in the Alps or the frozen waste of the Arctic a displaced image of the white planter's exhausting, and in Jamaica often futile, search for the runaway slave in the opposite extreme of the equatorial tropics.[35] Moreover, some apologists for slavery defended a subsistence slave diet of maize and water by claiming that the race did not require the white man's luxuries of meat and drink. This draws on a long European tradition that imagined wild men or natural men of the woods as, like Frankenstein's Monster, colossal vegetarians, images eighteenth-century naturalists helped to melt into that of more primitive races of men abroad, far down the ladder of racial hierarchy. Mungo Park commented on the largely vegetable diet of many Negroes.[36]

Shifting from the image to the story, however, we see that Shelley's Monster is no mere ape-man. He has an innate desire for knowledge, a capacity to learn, and feelings of right and wrong. He is, notwithstanding his hideous appearance, dreadfully wronged by a society that cannot see the inner man for the outer form. Here one might argue quite plausibly for an abolitionist rendering of the image of the Monster as "a man and a brother." However, Shelley's Creature is, if not a masculine and feminine composite, a compound of both sides of the slavery debate. He *is* wild and dangerous, unpredictable and childlike, but at the same time

has perhaps (as the Creature himself says) been made such by the circumstances of an unjust exclusion. And yet the depth of his rage and
destructiveness seems to stem from more than environment and frustration; it suggests an inherent bestiality lurking somewhere. How much
the Monster's excitable character is the result of his unique physiology,
and how much of his environment, is an ambiguity exactly paralleling
the central conundrum of the antislavery debate. Something of this ambiguity might even be said to be buried unconsciously in Godwin's own
good-natured telling of the fable about washing the blackamoor, which
he intended no doubt as an abolitionist homily that skin color mattered
only to the ignorant. But it would more commonly have been read with
another message, that the black could no more be educated into whiteness than a leopard could change his spots, that there were basic and
ineradicable racial differences, of which skin color was but an outward
sign.[37] The story was an old one. In 1776 the Reverend Henry Bate's
comic opera *The Blackamoor Wash'd White* was performed at Garrick's
Drury Lane Theatre. It contained a song with the lines:

> No, you're not an earthly creature,
>   But death's shadow in disguise!
> See him stamp'd on ev'ry feature!
>   What a pair of rolling eyes!
>   Don't come nigh me,
>   Let me fly thee,
>   Or I faint—I fall—I die!
>   See death yonder!—
>   Now I wonder
> Who outruns, the ghost,—or I?[38]

Violently contradictory and unbridled emotions were characteristics
commonly associated with the Negro. Mungo Park, who was killed by
natives in the upper Niger region, related numerous examples of violence—"The Jaloffs (or Yaloffs) are an active, powerful, and warlike
race"—and "savagery": "The Negro carried the body [of a deceased boy]
by a leg and an arm, and threw it into the pit with a savage indifference,
which I had never before seen." Edwards describes the blacks of Jamaica
who originated on the Gold Coast, "the genuine and original unmixed
Negro," as having a "firmness of body and mind; a ferociousness of disposition; but withall, activity, courage, and a stubbornness . . . of soul,
which prompts them to enterprises of difficulty and danger; and enables
them to meet death, in its most horrible shape, with fortitude or indifference."[39] Many writers, like John Leyden in 1799, made much, not only
of the violence of native Africans and slaves, in particular their thirst for

revenge, but also of their contrasting capacity for gratitude and affection: "The understanding is much less cultivated among the Negroes than among Europeans; but their passions, whether benevolent or malevolent, are proportionately more violent. . . . Though addicted to hatred and revenge, they are equally susceptible to love, affection, and gratitude."[40] It will be apparent how closely Leyden's choice of description—passionate revenge and loving gratitude—echoes Shelley's own characterization of her Monster. It was a common theme, which Mungo Park voiced in his observations, for example, of the "Feloops" near the Gambia River: "They are of a gloomy disposition, and are supposed never to forgive an injury. . . . This fierce and unrelenting disposition is, however, counterbalanced by many good qualities: they display the utmost gratitude and affection toward their benefactors." This combination of vengefulness and affection was, in fact, a stereotype commonly applied to any savage or primitive race, as when Edwards described the extinct "Caribbees" of the West Indies: "They will be considered rather as beasts of prey, than as human beings," were prone to brood over "past miscarriage" and possessed an "implacable thirst of revenge." "But among themselves they were peaceable, and towards each other faithful, friendly and affectionate."[41]

Mary Shelley's addition of *cruel* vindictiveness to the portrait of the natural savage accords with a contemporary shifting of attitude from that of Dr. Johnson's savage ("a man untaught, uncivilized") to the egregiously cruel as well as ignorant black, which was well established in mid-nineteenth-century opinion.[42] Writing in the 1790's, Edwards ascribed a particular cruelty to both the ancient Caribbees (an "unnatural cruelty") and the mulattoes and Negroes of his time: "It serves to some degree to lessen the indignation which a good mind necessarily feels at the abuses of power by the Whites, to observe that the Negroes themselves, when invested with command, give full play to their revengeful passions; and exercise all the wantonness of cruelty without restraint or remorse."[43]

It is possible to find in contemporary abolitionist representation positive images of the black as a powerful force for *justifiable* vengeance rather than a mere supplicating child, although this perspective remained somewhat exceptional. In 1811 the abolitionist artist George Dawe exhibited at the British Institution a larger-than-life painting, *A Negro Overpowering a Buffalo*, which depicted a massive black body tensed with brute strength. A few years earlier, Henri Fuseli, also an abolitionist, had given the public a towering, elemental, and heroic black in his *The Negro Revenged*. If Dawe's message was oblique, Fuseli's was direct, suggested perhaps by lines from Thomas Day's poem "The Dying

Ill. 2. Henry Fuseli, *The Negro Revenged* (Kunst-halle, Hamburg).

Negro": "For Afric triumphs!—his avenging rage / No tears can soften, and no blood assuage." A black male, larger than the white woman cling-ing to him, erect rather than kneeling, calls down the wrath of God on a foundering slave ship (ill. 2).[44] More commonly, however, the image of the black as a destructive force—with a suggestion of irrational besti-ality—drew from the propaganda of the Jamaica planter class, and was echoed by their parliamentary defenders. For example, in 1796 *The Par-liamentary Register, The Annual Register,* and presumably other Lon-don publications as well gave ample space to Henry Dundas's reply in the House of Commons to humanitarian concerns over the use of blood-hounds to hunt down Negro men, women, and children in Jamaica: "The Maroons were accustomed to descend from their fastnesses at midnight, and commit the most dreadful ravages and cruelties upon the wives, children, and property of the inhabitants, burning and destroying every place which they attacked, and murdering all who unfortunately became the objects of their fury."[45]

One might note here the coincidence that Shelley's implacably vengeful Monster murders both a woman and a child, and burns the De Lacey cottage to the ground. Such images were common to the literature on the West Indies with which Mary Shelley was recently familiar. She would, for instance, have read Edward's rather more explicit description of the horrors of a slave rebellion that saw widespread "death and desolation," he claimed: "They surrounded the overseer's house about four in the morning, in which eight or ten White people were in bed, every one of whom they butchered in the most savage manner, and literally drank their blood mixed with rum. . . . [They] then set fire to the buildings and canes. In one morning they murdered between thirty and forty Whites, not sparing even infants at the breast."[46] This nightmare Edwards put into verse, which, like Fuseli's canvas of 1807, may also echo, if in a more sinister tone, Thomas Day's poem:

> Now, Christian, now, in wild dismay,
> Of Afric's proud revenge the prey,
>   Go roam th' affrighted wood;—
> Transform'd to tigers, fierce and fell,
> Thy race shall prowl with savage yell,
>   And glut their rage for blood![47]

This essentially gothic image of frenzied blacks drinking the blood of their victims (Frankenstein accuses the Monster of being "his own vampire")[48] makes use of a common trope for a depraved and irrational lust for vengeance. It also brings together two characteristics of the racial primitive—a manic preoccupation with avenging grievances and cannibalism—that were gaining currency by the end of the eighteenth century. Conflicting European traditions of the vegetarian wild man and the cannibalistic savage parallel other contradictions—like that between affectionate gratitude and indifferent, casual cruelty—that were held to coexist in primitive natures. The notion of cannibalism as a characteristic of primitive peoples had been passed down from well-elaborated, if largely fanciful, sixteenth-century accounts of the Caribbean, and was lodged in popular culture by Defoe's *Robinson Crusoe* (recommended by Godwin for the education of children).[49] It was a tradition that, although often discounted in the early Enlightenment, was powerfully reinvested as a universal mark of primitivism in the late eighteenth and nineteenth

centuries and received apparent empirical corroboration in explorers' accounts of the South Pacific and Africa. Bryan Edwards, who believed that
cannibalism had once been widespread in the West Indies, drew attention to the debate on the extent of the practice in his *History*.[50]

While Mary Shelley's Monster cannot actually be charged with cannibalism, the subject is certainly raised, if obliquely, in the novel. William Frankenstein, the child whom the Monster strangles, his most horrific crime, charges him at first sight with this savage intention: "Ugly
wretch! You wish to eat me and tear me to pieces."[51] The charge is, of
course, unjust; it is part of the prejudice the Creature meets wherever
he turns. Although Victor Frankenstein metaphorically associates his
Monster with vampirism, it is Frankenstein himself who is the cannibal,
who tears "to pieces" both the corpses from which he assembles his
creature and the female mate he had begun to construct. Similarly, he
also takes on the savage's thirst for vengeance, and dedicates himself to
revenge the deaths of his brother and bride, to a relentless pursuit of
his own creation. As Anne Mellor and other critics have noted, Frankenstein and his Monster become indistinguishable: "The creator has become his creature."[52]

Ironically, like the scientific dismemberment of "the Hottentot Venus," dissection in Frankenstein's lab is a horror directly mirroring that
of savage myth. A racially prejudiced combination of vengeance and
cannibalism-via-dissection already existed, of course, in Shakespeare's
Shylock, and in the long European tradition of the blood libel generally,
just as a metaphorical cannibalism had been vividly and insistently associated with, first, the Parisian mob, and latterly the Parisian medical schools. In England, the Burke and Hare murders subsequently established more firmly in popular culture this association of a gothic
cannibalism/dismemberment with godless science, and one Victorian
edition of *Frankenstein* was published together with another work titled
London Medical Students. Ultimately, the clandestine and illegal search
for human flesh for medical school dissection was conflated with the
Frankenstein story itself on stage and in film.

There remains a further aspect of the Monster's physical appearance
and character that bears emphasizing in any search for a racialized image. A strong tradition, already familiar by the late eighteenth century,
and insisted upon by racist propagandists for slavery like Edward Long,
had it that Negroes were both particularly libidinous and possessed of
unusually large genitalia. William Godwin himself had written that:
"The heat of the climate obliges both sexes [of the Negro] to go half naked. The animal arrives sooner at maturity in hot countries. And both
these circumstances produce vigilance and jealousy, causes which inevi-

tably tend to inflame the passions."[53] Edwards related that Negroes were promiscuous, and possessed a strong sexual passion, which "is mere animal desire."[54] The threat that white women might be brutalized by oversexed black men of great strength and size became a cliché of racist writing, ready for appropriation in the creation of gothic horror and given an extra charge by the recently dramatized and exaggerated stories of the plight of white women in revolutionary Haiti.

Mary Shelley's Monster, because of his great strength and his unpredictable moods, his alternate plaintive persuasiveness and fiery rage, is suffused with a kind of dangerous male sexuality. In the film *Young Frankenstein*, Mel Brooks equips his Monster with a monstrous "Schlange." Beneath this juvenile satire is a valid, even perceptive, extrapolation from the original. Shelley describes her creation as not only eight feet tall but "proportionably large." Frankenstein's shocked reaction to his first sight of the living creature seems to invoke the image of a great, engorged, and threatening phallus: "Great God! His yellow skin scarcely covered the work of muscles and arteries beneath."[55] A similarly threatening masculinity may be suggested in his later awakening to find the Monster nakedly towering above him as he lies in his bed.

The murder of Elizabeth, Frankenstein's bride, would seem almost certainly to draw, either consciously or otherwise, upon the classic threat of the black male. The sharp contrast between the hazel-eyed, auburn-haired, high-browed, fragile white woman and the dark Monster was sharp in the 1818 version, but was made much starker in Mary Shelley's revision of 1831. Here we can see the construction of both race and a vulnerable femininity, the "angel in the house," progressing together toward the Victorian age. Elizabeth is described in this third edition as, not only of aristocratic, but of stereotypically northern, Teutonic beauty: "Her hair was the brightest living gold . . . her brow was clear and ample, her blue eyes cloudless . . . none could behold her without looking on her as of a distinct species, a being heaven-sent, and bearing a celestial stamp in all her features. . . . Her mother was a German."[56] It is this master-race maiden whom the Monster, her racial negative—dark-haired, low-browed, with watery and yellowed eyes, violently assaults in her bedroom and strangles as Othello smothers Desdemona.[57] The scene is emotionally and suggestively that of rape as well as of murder, or rather, as murder in lieu of rape.

Finally, the racial threat of an oversexed, rapidly propagating, monstrous Other is practically made explicit in Frankenstein's hesitation to create a mate for his Monster: "Even if they [the Monster and his bride-to-be] were to leave Europe [as the Monster had suggested] and inhabit the deserts of the new world, yet one of the first results of those sympathies for which the daemon thirsted would be children, and a race of devils would be propagated upon the earth who might make the very existence of man a condition precarious and full of terror. Had I a right, for my own benefit, to inflict this curse upon everlasting generations?"[58] Two interesting allusions are possible here. First, the idea of exile from Europe was already available in the Sierra Leone experiment in sending destitute blacks "back to Africa." By the time Mary Shelley was writing, this much-advertised experiment had come to be regarded largely as a failure. But, more pointedly, there was a strong parallel to the fear of "a race of devils" in conditions of autonomy in the recent history of Haiti and in highly exaggerated stories about the escaped or freed slave communities of mulattoes in the West Indies and the threat they posed to the white planter society, and in particular to its women. Once again, this was a fear the slaveowning class encouraged in their loud protests against humanitarian intervention. The year Shelley began her novel, there were reports that rebellious blacks in Barbados flew a flag portraying "a black chief, with a white woman, with clasped hands, imploring mercy."[59]

The image of blacks free from the discipline of a white master, in an environment where nature provided unlimited sustenance, breeding at a rate unrestrained by decency or prudence, was already available well before Carlyle's essay on the "Nigger Question." And in it lay much of the basis for the prediction of the inevitability of race war that is the preoccupation of much late-nineteenth-century racist literature. *Frankenstein* prefigures this racial Armageddon as much as it does the mad scientist of twentieth-century fiction and film.

Education and Moral Dilemma

The education of Frankenstein's monster occupies an important, indeed central, part of the story, involving a complicated and lengthy subplot at the De Lacey cottage. This has drawn the attention of literary critics, who see in it not just a digression that allows Mary Shelley to parade her grasp of Lockeian ideas on the acquisition of knowledge by sensory association (the Monster as tabula rasa), but also a sophisticated means of introducing the Rousseauian critique that true instruction must engage the emotions and requires loving contact. It is precisely this, of course, that the Monster is denied both by his creator and ultimately by the family from whom he secretly learns language and history. This is a reasonable view, which accords well with what we know of Mary Shelley's own reading of both Locke and Rousseau. It should not, however, preclude an examination of the novel as at some level also a comment on sharply focused and pragmatic contemporary issues, as well as on past educational theory.

It is apparent that the success of Victor Frankenstein's hubristic experiment immediately poses the central problem of the novel, the hinge upon which the moral of the tale turns. This is the dilemma of whether he is willing to acknowledge his responsibility to nurture and educate his creation in the ways of humankind, thus not only making his progeny safe for society but admitting the fact of his paternity and responsibility to both himself and the world at large. This he cannot force himself to do, and his flight from moral obligation has terrible consequences for all concerned. This ethical problem can be generalized. Can any parent, slave master, patron, or employer escape, without retribution, the moral obligation of providing for the welfare and education of those who are dependent upon him and who have been in some sense at least called into being, shaped, and perhaps deformed to serve his needs. This was a powerful and demanding issue, which not only hints at a common critique of Rousseau's own notorious avoidance of the obligations of paternity, but directly targets a central, perhaps the central, social question of the postrevolutionary, early-industrial age.

Frankenstein's refusal to admit responsibility for the creature he has made or to help it to achieve a full integration into the society of men, coupled with the potential threat of the brute strength of the Monster, has led some critics to the view that the story is a metaphor for domestic class relations in the era of early mechanization and Luddism. In such a reading, Frankenstein's refusal to ameliorate the condition of his Monster roughly anticipates the coming liberalism of the age of laissez faire and individualism. The Monster's later discovery of social injustice through his effort at self-education comfortably conforms to this interpretation. But these issues of accountability, paternalism, and the dangerous self-awareness of a subordinate class emerge with equal, if not greater and more immediate, force in nineteenth-century race relations.

Like Frankenstein, the white, gentlemanly abolitionist sought to give reality to an indeal, the potential humanity of the degraded slave. The slave, like the Monster, was in the eyes of some philanthropists indeed a tabula rasa, a cultureless creature ready to receive their moral teaching and their theology. In the optimism of the movement, others assumed that the abolition of the institution of slavery alone—in Frankenstein's story the mere act of creation—would be followed by inevitable improvement as the liberated black man found his place as a fully responsible, self-improving citizen. By the time Mary Shelley was writing, however, there were already deep misgivings. In Sierra Leone, the projectors of a free and self-respecting black colony had had to retrench their

expectations, impose discipline, and withhold self-governance. By the
second decade of the century, there must have been many even within
the abolitionist camp who also harbored doubts about at least the immediate result of wholesale abolition in the West Indies, and who were
anxious to deny their own responsibility for any horror that might
emerge. Denial is, of course, Frankenstein's first reaction to his own creation. Furthermore, the leaving of the Monster to his own devices in the
wilderness results in brooding grievance and childlike rage. Already mal-
formed by his creator, he does not rise to full humanity but reverts to the
beast, in part because of the prejudice of those he encounters, in part
because real self-improvement without an education involving discipline and a nurturing paternalist connection was as unlikely for him as
it seemed to many to prove unlikely for blacks in the West Indies.

Here it will be seen that *Frankenstein* strongly resonates with a great
and pressing social concern much in the mind of the upper- and middle-
class public. As with Frankenstein's Monster, there was a dual aspect to
the problem of education in the early nineteenth century: the advance-
ment, moral well-being, and happiness of those to be educated, but also
the safety of the society into which, in some degree, either the new urban citizen of the "dangerous classes" or the freed slave of the plantation
was to be admitted.

In Mary Shelley's world, these issues of responsibility and discipline
were sharply debated. The same evangelicals who advocated abolition
and missionary activity abroad pressed for Sunday schools and philanthropic instruction at home. The issue of the education of factory children, of women, and of slaves in the West Indies emerged in much the
same terms. Where did responsibility lie? What ought to be taught?
What was the (clearly anomalous) social role of an educated black or
worker or woman? Clearly, the problem facing the rejected Monster,
how to educate himself, and the disappointment he experiences on discovering that his efforts at self-tuition are of little use in winning acceptance, closely approximates the issues raised both by abolitionists and
domestic educational reformers of either a Benthamite, radical, or evangelical persuasion. Behind this were the frustrations inherent in the formal education of subordinate persons in a society that remained intensely patriarchal, class-bound, and color-prejudiced.

Like race prejudice and class snobbery, the racial and domestic educational issues were tightly intertwined. The two discourses drew from
and reinforced each other, and share the key questions of appropriate-
ness, responsibility, social control, and social danger. The historians of
education in this period have neglected the degree to which the "problem" of Negro education, a debate that raged at least in abolitionist and

proslavery quarters from the late eighteenth century until well after the American Civil War, influenced the tenor and substance of the domestic European debate over the educability of the poor and women. A further consideration of aspects of the novel in this light will be of some interest.

In the first place, it is appropriate to recall that the issue of whether black slaves ought to receive any education—enough, at least, to read the edifying homilies of religion—had long been a bone of contention between the Jamaican planters and the humanitarians. Knowledge is power, and the withholding of instruction was a highly symbolic entrenchment of the master-slave relationship. This suggests another debate: whether slaves ought to be baptized into a Christian church, which would bring them into the brotherhood of Christ and pose problems in their disposal as chattels. It is not a far-fetched reading of the novel to see some reflection of these issues in Frankenstein's refusal either to instruct or to name his creature. Mary Shelley's Monster is not only denied education; he is also denied a Christian name.[60] Frankenstein thus retreats from a commitment to a relationship, an attachment of sentiment and parentage, which is as repugnant to him as it would have been to the white slave master. The Monster's thirst for knowledge is, in fact, a thirst for deliverance from the condition of "a vagabond and a slave." What education he is able to glean from the conversation of the De Laceys (like that a "house-nigger" might have picked up from those he served) teaches him that one such as himself, lacking "unsullied descent" and even a name, is "doomed to waste his powers for the profits of the chosen few!"[61]

It might be thought that the Monster's articulateness, his precocious quickness of intellect in learning at second hand from overheard conversation, belies a close comparison with the slave stereotype. Certainly the most brutal stereotype, from, say, the pages of Edward Long, would deny the Negro sufficient intelligence to learn, but liberal opinion, that read by Mary Shelley, held otherwise. Edwards claimed that he had "been surprised by such figurative expressions [from his slaves], and (notwithstanding their ignorance of abstract terms) such pointed sentences, as would have reflected no disgrace on poets and philosophers. . . . Negroes have minds very capable of observation."[62]

"Observation" is the Monster's only means of self-education. Like the Negro slave, he is kept an outsider. In what is clearly a sense of self-recognition, he responds with weeping to Volney's tragic history of "the helpless fate" of the native inhabitants of America.[63] However, he not only identifies with the sufferers of this racial injustice, but, although protesting that "mine shall not be the submission of abject slavery," finally acknowledges to himself his own inferiority and despairs: "I became fully convinced that I was in reality the monster that I am. . . . I abhorred myself . . . I was the slave, not the master. . . . I, the miserable and the abandoned, am an abortion, to be spurned at, and kicked, and trampled on. . . . Your abhorrence cannot equal that with which I regard myself."[64] His response is at first rebellion, but this turns to despair and, ultimately, to suicide. The Monster's "education" has taught him self-contempt, just as the little education of the plantation black or freed slave served merely to reinforce his own awareness of inferiority. This mentality conforms to that observed by Edwards among the mulattoes in Jamaica, where an official system of racial identification "tends to degrade them [freed blacks and mulattoes] in their eyes, and in the eyes of the community to which they belong."[65]

It was a commonplace of the literature of slavery that the recently enslaved experienced deep depression and were, particularly those from some proud, warlike tribes, prone to either rebellion or suicide. Edwards remarks on the frequent suicides among the Eboes of West Africa and comments elsewhere that it was widely believed (although he disagreed) that "Negroes consider death not only as a welcome and happy release from the calamities of their condition, but also as a passport to the place of their nativity."[66] Matthew Lewis echoes this in his *Journal* of his visit to Jamaica in 1815–16.[67] The Monster's intended self-immolation brings together three clichés of this tradition: the low self-regard of the slave, slave suicide (a form of impotent rebellion), and destruction by fire (the common image of real rebellion).

From overheard conversations and readings, the Monster also learns the ethnic stereotyping of which he himself, as an alien, is ironically also a victim—of slothful Asiatics, degenerate Romans, and *ungrateful*, wicked Turks.[68] Indeed, the idea of gratitude, and its opposite, the corrosive sense of resentment, feature strongly throughout the novel. There is the story of the Christian Arab Safie and her Turkish father, who unnaturally rewards his Christian deliverer with treacherous ingratitude. When Justine, a poor relation living as a servant in the Frankenstein household, is unjustly accused of the murder of Frankenstein's brother, the charge of murder is made more horrible in the eyes of the public by its suggestion of "ingratitude" to the Frankenstein family, which has protected her. Then there is the repeated assertion of the Monster himself that if treated by someone with kindness, he "would bestow every benefit upon him with tears of gratitude" at his acceptance; "my virtues will necessarily arise when I live in communion with an equal," for his heart, the Creature says, "was fashioned to be susceptible of love and sympathy."[69] Again, this is a theme that features prominently in the literature on African and West Indian blacks with which Mary Shelley was familiar. Edwards, like others, was eager to affirm that, however violent and passionate the black or mulatto might be, there was a counterbalancing tendency to affection, and he speaks of "their disinterested gratitude and attachment where favours are shown them"; "if their confidence be once obtained, they manifest as great fidelity, affection, and gratitude as can reasonably be expected from men in a state of slavery."[70]

This projection of gratitude invokes the classic colonizer mentality, evident in the middle-class humanitarian as well as in the paternalist slaveholder. Those who are the receivers of liberation, protection, or education in the Christian virtues of patience and forbearance are expected to repay benevolent condescension with self-abasing thankfulness and loyalty. The cardinal sin in this system is "ingratitude," a failing Mary Shelley herself at one point calls "blackest ingratitude,"[71] and that the Victorians were later quick to ascribe to sepoy troops and Jamaican freed slaves. This discloses the paradox at the center of the humanitarian abolitionist enterprise: that while the *gift* of liberation transforms the slave into a freedman, it does so only through the good offices of white, middle- and upper-class patrons rather than by self-help. In this relationship, the idealized black, although a "man and a brother," is inevitably still on his knees as a grateful man and a younger brother.

The Victorian Frankenstein

Although Mary Shelley wrote five more novels before her death in 1851, none succeeded with the public nearly as well as *Frankenstein*. Only months after it appeared in the spring of 1818, Thomas Peacock could write to Percy Shelley, "*It seems to be universally known and read.*"[72] The three-volume edition of that year was followed in 1823 by a two-volume version, apparently to take advantage of the popularity of stage adaptations. A cheaper (one-volume) third edition, with revisions and illustrations, was aimed at a yet wider public in 1831, and this was often reprinted.[73] There was in fact either a new edition of the novel or an authorized reprinting in each decade of the century, and two in the 1830's, 1880's, and 1890's, as well as the versions included in collections of horror stories, in pirated (often American) editions, and in foreign translations. A shilling pocket edition appeared in 1888.

The successful stage adaptation of 1823, which helped to spread and sustain the novel's popularity, sparked a number of other dramatizations (at least fourteen in the following three years). Some of these were, in fact, burlesques, which suggests that the original work had already become part of the lumber of popular culture. The first and most successful of the stage adaptations, Richard Brinsley Peake's *Presumption; or, The*

Fate of Frankenstein, achieved an "enduring popularity" and "tremendous enthusiasm." Thomas Cooke, who made a specialty of weird and villainous roles, made the part of the Monster his own, and played it to packed houses for some 350 performances in London and Paris.[74]

On the Victorian stage, the Frankenstein story was inevitably altered to fit the melodramatic expectations of the audiences of the time. On the one hand, demonic and alchemical elements were emphasized; on the other, songs and dancing were interpolated in some versions, and a comic element was occasionally introduced to lighten the story. Catastrophic storms, the burning of the cottage, and avalanches provided spectacle, while the subtler tones of the novel were sacrificed to a simplified drama of innocence versus demonic terror. Mary Shelley's ambiguities disappeared. Cooke's Monster, effectively mimed, lost its articulateness and became the mute beast, tamable only by music. As Steven Forry has recently observed,[75] the Monster was Calibanized, although this was surely only an extension of the densely present, if buried, associations already linking Mary Shelley's Monster to the Calibanlike slave.[76] Certainly, the silencing of Frankenstein's creation closely parallels what Nicholas Ashton has seen as a general "silencing of the Other" in nineteenth-century Western discourse, a patriarchal insistence that African speech, like the words of women, was inherently different and less significant than that of European man.[77]

By turning the Creature into even more of a caricature, the Victorian stage enhanced its utility as stereotype, as image of the dark Other. It may be significant, for instance, that both the popularity of a variety of burlesques on the Frankenstein story (still being played as late as the 1880's), as well as the introduction of comic songs into even the more serious versions, coincides with the emergence of "nigger minstrels" as an enduring entertainment in London music halls and theaters.[78] In any event, the image of the Creature swaying to the charms of music at least suggests the caricature of the singin' and dancin' slaves of the Old South.

From the 1830's on, there was another type of association available to public view, one completing a triangular relationship between the images of animal, monster, and Negro, in the exhibition of the first large apelike creatures from Africa at the Regent's Park Zoo. Tommy the Chimpanzee captivated audiences in 1835 and displayed what seemed to be the learning ability at least of a child. He was followed two years later by a much-publicized orang-utan. Many Victorians, one assumes, responded like Queen Victoria herself, who commented, "He is frightful & painfully and disagreeably human."[79] About the same time, Edgar Allan Poe's story "The Murders in the Rue Morgue" (1843) brought to the public what Frankenstein's Monster might already have suggested, a homicidal simian.[80]

One would like to know more about the actual performances of the stage adaptations, and whether the available racial and simian associations of the Creature were introduced on the stage as they were in parliamentary debate and magazine caricatures. Cooke probably darkened his skin for his performance of the satanic Zamiel in an 1824 version of *Der Freischütz* to suggest the darkness of evil. Similarly, he, like others after him, used blue greasepaint in his portrayal of the Monster,[81] not with the direct intention of creating a racial villain, but to suggest both the lividity of a corpse and a sinister Otherness. A blue-skinned Monster would inevitably, however, have suggested, on the one hand, an Othello, and on the other, a nigger minstrel—Negro tragedy and Negro farce (ill. 3).

However this may be, the story clearly found its way quickly into popular metaphor and caricature, and such allusions seem to follow, not the publication of the three-volume novel in 1818, but the London stage plays of 1823. For example, in March 1824, in a parliamentary debate over Thomas Fowell Buxton's motion that the children of West Indian slaves be freed on achieving their majority, the foreign secretary, George Canning, explicitly connected the Frankenstein myth with the dangers of abolition:

> In dealing with the negro, Sir, we must remember that we are dealing with a being possessing the form and strength of a man, but the intellect only of a child. To turn the negro loose in the manhood of his physical strength, in the maturity of his physical passions, but in the infancy of his uninstructed reason, would be to raise up a creature resembling the splendid fiction of a recent romance; the hero of which constructs a human form, with all the thews and sinews of a giant; but being unable to impart to the work of his hands a perception of right and wrong, he finds too late that he has created a more than mortal power of doing mischief and himself recoils from the monster which he has made.[82]

Canning here seized upon three important racial parallels: first, the childishness of Monster and Negro slave; second, a supposed lack of moral judgment (this reading obviously derived from the stage plays rather than the novel, where the Monster has an acute sense of right and wrong); and finally, an implied sexual threat—the "maturity of his physical passions." Coincidentally, the play at this time was accompanied in a double bill at Covent Garden by another entitled *The West Indian*.[83]

This temptation to use the image of the Monster in the portrayal of

Ill. 3(a). T. P. Cooke as the Creature in *Le Monstre et le magicien*, Théâtre de la Porte-Saint-Martin, 1826 (Bibliothèque nationale, Paris).

"uncivilized" and unwhite peoples abroad inevitably wandered into domestic politics. As Chris Baldick has noted, Canning was "reclaiming the monster as a Burkean bogy figure," and in this enterprise the dumb, mimed figure of the stage fiend served better than the articulate reasoner of Mary Shelley's original creation.[84] The Monster in caricature was commonly used as a metaphor for radicalism during the Reform agitations of the early 1830's, the Chartist era, and the mid 1860's. If these were not Negro Monsters, they often suggested ethnic prejudice in associating the Creature with the Irish working man. "The Irish Frankenstein" in fact became something of a cliché in mid-Victorian humor magazines, and was used to comment on Daniel O'Connell in the 1840's

Ill. 3 (b). Paul Bedford as the Creature and Edward
Wright as Frankenstein in *The Model
Man* (*Illustrated London News*, Jan. 1850).

(*Punch*), the Fenians in the 1860's (Matt Morgan in *The Tomahawk*), and
the Phoenix Park murders in 1882 (John Tenniel in *Punch*) [ill. 4].[85]
  This is not to claim, of course, that there had always to be a racial or
ethnic component in Victorian appropriation of the Frankenstein metaphor. The story worked its way down into popular culture, to become a
kind of mythic or iconic element that was drawn up again into serious
literature, as in *Middlemarch*, where Lydgate's search for the life source
in primitive tissues clearly draws on Frankenstein's lab.[86] In *Mary Barton*, Elizabeth Gaskell compared the uneducated radical working man to
"a Frankenstein," in what had possibly become a commonplace allusion. That she received the idea from popular "knowledge" of the Frank-

Ill. 4. "The Irish Frankenstein" (*Punch*, 4 Nov. 1843).

enstein story rather than from a direct reading is indicated by her careless confusion of Frankenstein with his Monster, while the misreading
of the Monster on the popular stage as an inarticulate child served her
desire to represent the working class as childlike.[87] Pip's fear that Magwitch has become his own Frankenstein's Monster[88] seems free of racial
association as well, although his acute embarrassment over the possibility of public knowledge of the criminal's patronage suggests something
of the horror of the discovery of "bad blood," of a "white" having to recognize black relations.

   Frankenstein has endured in print, on the stage and screen, and as
metaphor in a way that belies the weaknesses of its literary construction. Indeed, the critical response then and later was slight and mixed,

with some praise from a minority of critics and much deprecation of the "immorality" of its apparent message. It is reasonable to assume that it survived partly because of the resonances it evoked and because of its usefulness in reinforcing racial and ethnic prejudice. Seen simply as a somewhat immature and certainly backward-looking exercise in gothic horror, with a message drawn from reflections on Enlightenment ideas of the perfectability of man—that is, from the preoccupations of the dated late-eighteenth-century radicalism of Godwin—the story's enduring success seems odd. As with any critical failure and popular success, one can attempt to explain it in terms of the appeal of mere sensationalism to an uncritical public. The rise of the vulgarly educated mass consumer of cheap literature in the nineteenth century offers this answer, but it is not, I think, a sufficient one. Some works that were "in tune" with changes in contemporary mentality achieved a larger-than-life stature and were "read" by the public in a way not perhaps intended. The nineteenth-century development of the Frankenstein story in drama and burlesque reflects this process.

The idea that the story is about science run amok, a critique of the mad, godless professional, in the sense that later became standard fare, was one such "reading," not exactly intended in the original but quite quickly developed on the stage.[89] Similarly, the change from the highly articulate Monster of Shelley's creation into the mute horror pursued by villagers, the manufactured zombie with a deformed and criminal brain, is also a later interpretation, reflecting perhaps the craniological and neurological ideas of mid-nineteenth-century science, as well as the requirements of stage and film sensationalism.

At a deeper and less obvious level, however, the conjunction of certain readily appropriable images with deep popular anxieties—about revealed religion versus science, or the place of women in the male world of empire and the professions, or the danger of proletarian revolution, or the threat of nonwhite races—is where the real explanation for the enduring appeal lies. Here it is that the subtext of racial image and character is important in explaining the appeal of a story that helped to formulate a popular emotional response to increasing contact with, and threats from, nonwhite cultures abroad. The Indian Mutiny, the Jamaican rebellions of 1831 and 1865, and the countless little wars fought by Victoria's armies against the Maori, Ashanti, Zulus, and Canadian Métis all contributed to the emotional appeal of a text that presented the Other as a rebellious, ungrateful child that owed its very existence to a white male patron. The story loops around, and what began as a series of ambiguous images inspired in part by the concept of the Noble Savage, as well as by the abolition versus slavery discourse of the late eighteenth century, played a role in reifying and entrenching racialist and colonialist values in the nineteenth and twentieth centuries.

Making Monsters

As developed here, the Frankenstein story has three levels of interest. First, it reveals a deeper kind of signification than is at first apparent. The Other, the outsider, the racially foreign, is probably buried in the whole genre of gothic horror. Second, while in the novel this message reflects contemporary ambiguity or confusion about "race," it entered popular culture at a time of shifting and hardening opinion, and in this context inevitably lent its weight to the construction of sensational (and more firmly pejorative) representations of race in the nineteenth century. Finally, the text and its subsequent development reveal inherent linkages between race and the other evolving concepts of class and gender.

A close reading of *Frankenstein* demonstrates how this well-known work of fiction depended at least in part for its inspiration, as for its effect, on the coded language of contemporary racial prejudice, as well as on a deeply embedded cultural tradition of xenophobia. It is necessary, consequently, substantially to amend Ann Mellor's judgment that "Mary Shelley created her myth single-handedly. All other myths of the western or eastern worlds, whether of Dracula, Tarzan, Superman or more traditional religious systems, derive from folklore or communal ritual practices." Nor can one entirely accept that the creature should be seen as "a sign detached from a visual or verbal grammar, without diachronic or synchronic context, without precursor or progeny."[90] *Frankenstein* did not, in fact, spring fully formed from Mary Shelley's imagination, but owed much of its language and power to Jamaican and Haitian slave rebellions and to uncertainties over the consequences of abolition. In this context, it displaced overtly xenophobic and racial fears to another, imaginary field. A mid-twentieth-century parallel can be found in the way American science fiction literature and film offered a strikingly similar displacement of contemporary fears of communist subversion and invasion. With the familiarity it achieved with the reading public, on stage, and in common discourse, *Frankenstein* attained the status of an icon of popular culture and thus itself became, albeit obliquely, a source for the reinforcement of ethnic and racial stereotypes, a reservoir of emotional ammunition that could be deployed against the Other both within and outside Victorian England.

In some sense, the story of *Frankenstein* itself, the construction of the Monster, is the fictional parallel of the "construction" of race and simul-

taneously of racial prejudice. It is not merely a case of the unknown portrayed as evil. Ironically, the Monster lives up to the expectations imposed upon him. "By reading his creation as evil," Anne Mellor has
observed, "Frankenstein constructs a monster."[91] She sees this as Mary
Shelley's own comment on the dangers of romantic imagination. Race
itself, however, is in its most emotive sense a construct of romanticism.
Imagination literally gave birth to reality. Prejudice, like the imperialism
that was its crudest manifestation, worked to produce the abject degradation and dependency it expected to find in the Other.

As the nineteenth century progressed, racism became ever more widely
diffused and achieved an acceptability, almost a consensus, in educated
society as well as at deeper levels of popular culture. As a result, what
was unconscious or only obliquely hinted at in a work like *Frankenstein*
could surface with explicitness in Victorian literature. For instance,
there was the fatal problem of "bad blood." In *Wuthering Heights*, the
savagery of Heathcliff, a "dark-skinned Gypsy" in appearance, "black as
Satan," is linked to his darkly suggested origin as a Lascar orphan on
the docks in Liverpool, while *Jane Eyre*'s madwoman is a passionate
West Indian, with "a goblin appearance . . . long dishevelled [black] hair"
and a "swelled black face."[92] Moreover, what was buried in the gothic
novel often became overt in the late-nineteenth-century adventure story.
William Harrison Ainsworth's popular *Rookwood* of 1824 produced Old
Barbara the Gypsy Queen, a repulsive old woman with blackened yellow
skin, "like an animated mummy," who ruled her "wild tribe" like an
"Obeah woman." Sixty years later, H. Rider Haggard achieved the same
sensational effect less allusively with the withered old Negro witch
Gagool in his *King Solomon's Mines*. Both recall elements of Godwin's
malignant old robber woman in *Caleb Williams*, whose "swarthy" complexion, "the consistency of parchment," "uncommonly vigorous and
muscular" arms, and "savage ferocity" lend a further racial coloring to
her avowed cannibal intention to "drink your blood!"[93]

As suggested in the Brontë novels, the problem of racial pollution, of
bad blood, was packed with associations revealing a peculiarly Victorian,
middle-class obsessiveness. It meshed, that is, with deep anxieties over
class and sexuality, with problematic issues of respectability and identity. In the course of the nineteenth century, apprehension over a *hidden*
racial identity became fear of "infection," via "miscegenation" and "the
half-breed," that took on a progressively gothicized form, as a terrible,
warping, secret aberration.[94] Heathcliff's masculine strength is perverted
into vindictiveness and sadism by his non-European otherness. He has
the inner contradictions of the half-breed, a childlike vengefulness and
cruelty, combined with a strong need for affection. In Bertha Mason, we

encounter a similar combination of gender and racial stereotype, the hysterical and uncontrollably passionate nature of her sex is amplified or liberated by her hidden blackness, by her nature as a drunken Jamaican "white" Creole. In her madness, she burns down Rochester's house, just as the monster destroys the De Lacey cottage, and commits suicide, just as the monster had intended to do.

Although I have emphasized the racial aspects of Frankenstein's Monster, other critics have pleaded for class-based and gender-based readings. In fact, these issues of class, gender, and race are all present in an intricately interwoven way. The Monster, unnaturally conceived without woman, oversized, oversexed, physically repulsive, and economically and socially marginal, encompasses three confused elements of middle-class nightmare: racial, sexual, and proletarian.

The 50 years that followed the French Revolution saw a hardening among the educated classes of social definition and categorization. This involved the "construction," albeit not out of entirely new materials, of an emerging (and threatening) urban working class, a segregated and subordinated second sex, and racially inferior colonized peoples. This triple evolution, and integration, of attitudes was an intimately interconnected response to changing social conditions—to industrialization, the separation of work from family, and the outward expansion of the state and economy. In each case, the formation of prejudice had, of course, a long linear and separable history, but it was in the early nineteenth century that they were welded together in a mutually reinforcing tripartite structure that could endure, because, like the triangular supports of a geodesic dome, each offered its own resistance to pressure on the others. This strength rested on a commonsensical invocation of science, nature, economic necessity, and tradition, and on a sharing around of metaphor appropriate to each area of social, sexual, and racial domination. In this, diffuse but heavily charged sources, such as popular romance and sensational theater, played a clandestine role in confirming the white English, upper-class male in the empire, the workplace, and the home.

CHAPTER 2

Cannibalism and Popular Culture

Cannibalism, the feeding on human flesh, is found in most barbarous tribes; a practice so revolting to our nature, that its existence anywhere was denied, until it was established by irrefragable evidence. . . . It prevailed in both the Americas, in the Oceanic Archipelago, and in many of the clusters of Polynesia. . . . It subsisted in the comparatively civilized empire of Mexico, and relics of it were discovered among the mild inhabitants of Peru. In New Zealand, the eating of human flesh is not merely an excess of occasional revenge, but is actually a luxurious gratification of appetite.[1]

Perhaps the single most emotive aspect of the monstrous non-European, the construction of the black savage that most closely relates to the gothic unnatural, is his presumed cannibal impulse. Either as customary practice or as ungovernable rage and vengeance, cannibalism has been associated with the wild barbarian beyond the pale from the dawn of European self-regard as a "higher" civilization. Since the Renaissance, however, the mythic and fabulous accounts of the ancient and medieval tradition have been displaced—perhaps *transformed* would be a better word—by mounting empirical "evidence." European expansion—the conquest of America, the exploration of the Pacific, and the partition of Africa—produced a dense, highly colored narrative of anthropophagy abroad.

By the late nineteenth century, there was hardly a "primitive" culture, from the Eskimo to the Tierra del Fuegans, that had not been accused of cannibal practice, cannibal inclination, or at least a cannibal past.[2] Finally, in the hands of the anthropologist and psychologist, the cannibalism of the savage ceased to be exceptional—the perverse custom of detached and degraded peoples at the ends of the earth—and became a buried universal. Ultimately, the black man's appetite became symbolic of the primitive origins of mankind and of the dark urges within us all.

Without accepting in its entirety William Arens's thesis—that there is no sufficient evidence of customary cannibalism anywhere—one can readily acknowledge that the testimony of missionaries appealing for subscriptions, converts looking for praise, explorers exaggerating their courage, or imperialists rationalizing their own methods of barbarism is highly prejudiced and must be treated with extraordinary skepticism. As

Christopher Herbert has argued, missionary ethnology's image of the Polynesian was "a wholly prefabricated one, a piling-on of monotonous rhetorical formulas which clearly exert a strong determining influence upon all their so-called empirical observation."[3] When Augustus Earle reported what he construed to be the evidence of cannibalism in New Zealand in 1827, he expressed just this tendency of the Western observer to anticipate the reality he "discovered": "I was more shocked than surprised, for I had been informed of the character of the New Zealanders long before my arrival amongst them."[4] Greg Dening has succinctly expressed the problem of evaluating "knowledge" constructed upon such a foundation: "It is impossible to distinguish fact from imagination in most accounts. . . . Some psychohistory of the nineteenth-century voyagers' preoccupation with cannibalism would be needed to unravel truth from revealing fiction."[5] Whether a "true" picture of indigenous life in the South Pacific can ever be reconstructed may be doubted, but appreciation of the depth of the cannibal obsession can be made to tell us much about the white observer. Clearly, cannibalism as a racial image conveniently served to invert reality by encoding as appetite those whom the European sought to incorporate.[6] But beyond this obvious reversal, or transference of guilt, there is more to be learned. Whether anthropophagy is pure fantasy or based on some version of actual practice, its rhetorical manipulation as an alien racial characteristic is a rich source of information about the social fears and cultural obsessions of Europeans.[7]

Rather than trace yet again the cannibal tradition through the literary record, from Montaigne's reflections on Brazil to Defoe's Caribs, and so to the "actual" accounts of explorers and missionaries in the eighteenth and nineteenth centuries, I shall begin, not with the cannibal located abroad in place and time, but with the man-eating traditions buried in British culture, in folklore and common metaphor, in crime and fiction. The thesis explored here is that the nineteenth-century image of the racial cannibal was built upon, interwoven with, and sustained by domestic discourse. Thus established, the "reality" of cannibalism abroad was itself redeployed in Europe in a process that Stephen Greenblatt has called "the reproduction and circulation of mimetic capital,"[8] becoming part of "a stockpile of representations" available for Europeans to draw upon in their own struggle—especially marked in the late nineteenth century—with problems of social, sexual, and spiritual identity.

Maggie Kilgour has persuasively hypothesized that cannibalism in *late*-Victorian literature is intimately related to the breakdown of certain notions of language and identity, both personal and national.[9] This section offers some further suggestions on that theme, focusing finally on the Victorian need for a *comic* presentation of cannibalism. Its chief interest, however, is in an early- and mid-nineteenth-century cannibal discourse, in a period that saw the transference abroad of domestic obsessions rather than their reimportation home amid fears of fin de siècle sexual and racial anarchy.

Like assertions of racial inferiority, accusations of cannibalism establish the community of the virtuous by projecting onto others evils feared within. Thus cannibalism juxtaposes in striking contrast victim and predator, innocent and depraved, sane and mad, white and black. The most graphic and emotive accounts of cannibalism are in fact those that involve, not like eating like, but the victimization of an opposite: of one sex devouring the other, of age feasting on youth, of the young feeding on the old, of the living violating the dead and buried, of one "tribe" or race consuming another.

In an important study of the European construction of the cannibal Carib, Peter Hulme has argued that the idea of "cannibals" generally, and of "cannibalism," was a product of the specific colonial discourse following from the Columbian encounter with Amerindians in the Caribbean. This discourse was determined, he maintains, by preexisting European conceptions, chiefly the dichotomy between the civilized and the barbarian, "two distinctive discursive networks" that were more important in determining ethnic identity in the Caribbean than "any observation of or interaction with native Caribbean cultures." The division of island natives into gentle Arawak and fierce Carib sprang largely from "the norms of white society." While Hulme does not deny the importance of historical interaction over time in shifting and refining the conceptual field within which the idea of cannibal was deployed, he contends that *cannibalism* as the image of ferocious consumption of human flesh is a term that can have "no application outside the discourse of European colonialism." Serving a hegemonizing purpose throughout the long period of European imperialism, the idea of the cannibal, Hulme suggests, nevertheless remained a mental construction that had less to do with the history of subsequent encounters with nonwhites—or even with the subsequent development of European self-identity and anxieties—than with that original moment of contact in the "special place" of America in 1492, an event constituting an "epistemological boundary."[10]

The virtue of Hulme's argument is that it draws us back to the importance of the mental baggage of the European observer himself in the formulation of the texts of colonial encounters, and cautions that the very language with which knowledge of the other is expressed carries "deeply colonialist," Europeanist values and significations. But it is his further insistence on the critical, determining, and fixing nature of the contact of 1492, and behind this the apparently eternal dichotomy of civilized and savage buried in the European mentality, that may be problematic for the historian. The difficulties that arise are not merely the doubts that those within the more "positivist" or "empirical" tradition may feel about his reading of subtexts.

In the first place, although the dichotomy between civilized and savage in the European tradition was important, it was not the only place where the domestic and the colonial met. Hulme himself observes that gender emerges in the Columbian account of the custom among the Caribs of wearing their hair long, "like women." This suggests more, it opens much larger areas for exploration, than his "Herodotean expectations" of Amazonian evidence suggest. There are vast areas of European prejudice and domestic construction—involving gender, sexuality, ethnicity, poverty, madness, and criminality—that may be relevant in shaping the image of the cannibal or of the racial "Other" generally. In fact, man-eating did have an application outside colonial discourse. Within European popular culture, at the level of folktale and metaphor, it had an existence quite separate from the literary discourse on the "anthropophagi" beyond Herodotus's civilized world. These traditions persisted after 1492, and Hulme offers little means of understanding their quite complex interaction with reports even of his own Caribbean "cannibals."

In the second place, Hulme's thesis allows for little subsequent interplay between a shifting European culture and the experience of a variety of non-European peoples. One might query whether the American experience, so admittedly vital in the early period, and doubtless casting a long shadow, really did define all subsequent discourse through time. For the historian of the nineteenth century, particularly, it would seem clear that important elements of Defoe's cannibal Carib, for instance, were displaced by the evolution of the idea of "race." The fluidity of this larger, overarching concept should be a warning that the social and ethnic significance of the cannibal, which was in some sense subsumed into racial typology, may be fluid as well.

Finally, the cannibal is neither merely the photographic negative of the civilized man nor simply the alter-image of the good—that is, passive—native. He serves to enforce social and sexual boundaries, not only by being the image of a savage opposite—for that, any savage, even the vegetarian wild man of European myth,[11] might serve—but by threatening literally to eradicate boundaries: by incorporating others within himself, he becomes the image of chaos beyond the structured world of personality, subordination, and hierarchy. That other racialized taboo of the nineteenth-century West—unnatural sexual congress of black and white and its dangerously half-bred child of miscegenation—has a similar meaning. Neither the miscegenist nor the cannibal is merely grotesquely different. The cannibal transforms his objects of desire by eradicating their separateness and then transmuting them into his own excrement. In the eyes of the racist, the miscegenist transforms the racial distinction of his partner into a similar, if living, pollution. In both, the transgression of taboo evokes an essentially gothic unnaturalness—a crossing of lines, a contamination, and an obscenity—not merely an "otherness."

Cannibal Gothic

> To be gnaw'd out of our graves, to have our sculs made drinking-bowls, and our bones turned into pipes, to delight and sport our enemies, are tragicall abominations, escaped in burning burials.
>
> — *Sir Thomas Browne, Urne-Buriall* (1658)

In European popular culture, deep revulsion at the idea of man-eating, although no doubt varying with time, class, and local custom, offers a double sensation—both *fear* of being eaten and *disgust* at eating, at sharing in that unmentionable feast. That cannibalism, both as event and as metaphor, should be a commonplace of gothic fiction, as well as of wider texts employing the rhetoric of the gothic for effect, comes as no surprise. Cannibalism evokes an even deeper response than Western sexual taboos, with which it has much resonance. It is such an obviously available trigger for sensational emotion that virtually all gothic literature employs some anthropophagic element, indicating the depth of the fear/disgust response it evokes—from Frankenstein's pulling apart of bodies to the soul- and blood-devouring demonism of Dracula. It is directly or indirectly suggested by the wide range of sadomasochistic gothic imagery: severing of body parts, drinking of blood, desecration of the dead, and handling, smelling, and ingesting the putrefied and the unclean. It evokes torture and murder, rape and incest—often in folklore involving the victimization of the most innocent, of children, boys, and young women.

In Britain, the bridge between the popular culture of cannibalistic folktales and gothic literature is most evident in two types of nineteenth-century sensationalism—the vampire story and that of the suspect pie-seller. The latter found its most popular form in the several versions of Sweeney Todd, the demon barber of Fleet Street, which T. P. Prest published in its most familiar version about 1840, to be followed two years later by a London stage version by George Dibdin Pitt.[12] Hack variations of the story continued to appear until at least the 1880's.

Ill. 5(a). Sweeney Todd, the Demon Barber of Fleet Street (London, ca. 1880): "I'll have him yet!"

In early modern Europe, the trade of the barber had been a low one, with associations, of bloodletting and sharp instruments suggestive of the abattoir, that perhaps entailed suspicions of the uses to which human blood and hair collected by the barber might be put. Human blood was, in fact, openly used for a variety of medicinal therapies. If there were also suspicions that it might find its way into blood puddings, or sausages, we are close to the popular foundations of the Sweeney Todd story. The nineteenth-century Sweeney, who turns his customers into meat for Mrs. Lovett's pies, may be based on the imported story of a fourteenth-century Parisian baker accused of using the flesh of infants, as well as on the more recent story of a revolutionary-era Parisian barber who murdered his customers,[13] but the theme of the serving up of human meat in pies to the unsuspecting is also a generic form of folk story.

Ill. 5(b). "Sweeney Todd clutched at the gold."

Like the story of the Scottish cannibal Sawney Beane, which received a wide publicity in eighteenth- and early-nineteenth-century English sensational literature, that of Sweeney Todd also involves an ethnic monster. The one suggests the anti-Scot prejudice of eighteenth-century English popular culture, the other the anti-Irish hatred that was a marked phenomenon of the industrial period. As Irish paupers poured into English cities, and Irish radicals preached revolution and dispossession, the crofter Scot was romanticized, and the rural Sawney yielded in popular imagination to the urban threat of the demonic Sweeney. In the last full version of the story, published anonymously about 1880 in serial form, illustrations exaggeratedly maintain the ethnicity of this particular cannibal—his low forehead, long upper lip, and pug nose—and contrast this Irish physiognomy with the idealized symmetry of the face and form of the upper-class English male (see ill. 5).[14]

If the late-nineteenth-century Sweeney is more sharply delineated as ethnic Other than earlier, this was by then an ethnicity that was not merely the result of custom and upbringing, but of inherent, "racial" difference. Sweeney's perversion, cannibalism, was itself progressively racialized in the course of the century, as an unnaturalness located by the missionary, the imperialist, and the scientific anthropologist in the primitive races of the South Seas or Africa. If earlier the supposed cannibalism of Amerindians was read as barbarism—that is, was placed in the context of the wild men of the European tradition—in the nineteenth century this was reversed. White cannibalism came to be read as racial primitivism, a blackness under the skin, until, at the end of the century, Kurtz's savagery is merely a form of "going native." The barrage of missionary, explorer, imperial, and anthropological narrative served to establish the cannibalism of the Fijian or the Congolese as a defining and racial phenomenon in the popular mind. Consequently, the Victorian deployment of the cannibal motif in literature could hardly be separated from racial allusion. But it was perhaps easier to gothicize the developing racial discourse than to racialize gothic literature, which often depended for its effect on fears of a *secret* depravity rather than overt difference. One solution, of course, was in the concept of bad blood, and the characteristic gothic horror of the late nineteenth century is the vampire—a half-breed cannibal who can "pass," caught between two worlds.

As with the cannibal Sawney and Sweeney, the vampires of the earlier gothic literature are domestic creatures. They are suggested by folk traditions common in Europe and receive at the hands of Byron and the anonymous creator of *Varney* a transformation from peasant into aristocrat, which further locates them in the context of postrevolutionary Europe. Varney is native to England. Significantly, Dracula, coming at the end of the century, is, overtly, a foreign and racial threat.[15] *Varney*, like *Sweeney Todd*, may occasionally invoke a racial, that is foreign, comparison: "She has received a severe wound in the arm, by some one . . . it would almost make one believe we are in the Cannibal Islands, to say the least of it."[16] But as the century progresses, such allusions shift their reference in the mind of the reader, away from Defoe's tamable savage and toward a growing colonial discourse, which ultimately objectified the idea of cannibalism as an inherent racial characteristic rather than merely a barbaric practice. Cannibalism as a primitive practice in the eighteenth century meant something quite different from cannibalism as a racial characteristic in the midnineteenth. In fact, the rigidifying of the concept of race is intimately connected, not only with the pseudoscientific discourse of phrenologists and comparative anatomists, but with the rediscovery/reinvention of cannibalism in the South Pacific via a language heavily indebted to domestic gothic idiom.

In 1884, Alfred St. Johnston commented that there was "a certain weird attractiveness about the subject of cannibalism, a grim fascination in its grisly horrors."[17] The audience he had in view were not penny serial readers but educated gentlemen, and his purpose was to place, with a characteristically late-nineteenth-century urbanity, recent anthropological evidence of South Pacific and African cannibalism in a larger field of knowledge, drawing together the primitive European past and the primitive non-Western present. That he begins with an invocation of the gothic, of the pleasures one might, like a novel reader, experience as voyeur of exotic horror, is of some interest, for it was precisely this approach that distinguished the representation of racial cannibalism in the nineteenth-century literature of the missionary, the explorer, and the scientist. In this sense, the cannibal text is not so much a dialogue between the European author and his native subject, whom he could engage, if at all, only at a distance, and often mediated by inadequate interpreters and second- or thirdhand accounts. Inevitably, the more important dialogue informing the cannibal text—and here the "facts" of observation may have less significance than the language used to describe them—is that between the author and his European audience. When the Methodist missionary Thomas Williams's account of his work among the cannibal Fijians was first published in London, one reviewer in a major literary journal expressed this relationship, this dialogue between author and readers' expectation, exactly: "It is not often that we have presented to us volumes so rich as those now before us are, in observation, in glimpses of wild life, and in descriptions of men, whose disposition and habits are all we can picture a savage's to be."[18]

The exotic landscape was central to the nineteenth-century tourist/explorer's discovery of the world beyond, places where, to quote the missionary hymn, "ev'ry prospect pleases and only man is vile."[19] A central irony in the romantic vision was that in the vastness of Nature, mere man seemed insignificant, even unnatural, and—as with Ruskin's goitered peasants in the valley of Chamonix—the more beautiful the view, the more jarring the human element was. When the missionary John Williams published his impressions of the South Pacific in 1837, he emphasized just this paradox—ethereal beauty ("grandeur, wildness, and sublimity") as a setting for "the most degraded and wretched state of barbarism . . . cannibals of the worst character . . . ferocious habits and cruel practices."[20] To this was added, particularly in the lushness of the

tropical landscape, a lurking moral danger to the white man himself—
something of the Garden of Eden, an eternally feminine seduction, offering ripe fruit but also pollution and corruption.

The mysterious, obscuring, and fecund jungle is the common locus for
nineteenth-century representations of cannibalism—not the blasted
wilderness and the rocky cave of the Cyclops's retreat, nor even Defoe's
malleable and utilitarian flora and fauna. When the medical officer Vincent Richards visited the Indian penal settlement at Port Blair, created
on the Andaman Islands in the Bay of Bengal in the wake of the Mutiny,
he was struck by the contrast between the most beautiful, dense, and
exotic scenery, on the one hand, and on the other, a convict settlement
where syphilis raged and the natives were as black as Africans, entirely
naked, and reputed to be cannibals. Women wore their dead husbands'
heads suspended from their necks. In this lush and sensual environment, the "revolting crime" of sodomy also flourished, not only in the
settlement but "amongst the native free population." The jungle also
concealed, he wrote—innocent of the symbolic significance of his observation—, a stronger, more vigorous, and more poisonous cobra than was
found on the mainland.[21]

Alfred St. Johnston drew the point that cannibalism "lingered longest
in the most beautiful regions,"[22] an assertion recalling Eugène Sue's
gothic invocation, in *The Wandering Jew*, of the steamy coast of Java:
"Magnificent and fatal country, where the most admirable flowers conceal hideous reptiles, where the brightest fruits contain subtle poi-
sons." Or Melville's Asia in *Moby Dick*: "Warmest climes but nurse the
cruelest fangs: the tiger of Bengal crouches in spiced groves of ceaseless
verdure. Skies the most effulgent but basket the deadliest thunders."
Such language enjoyed a very wide currency. At the end of the century,
for instance, the amateur naturalist James Rodway employed the same
mode in his descriptions of the tropical forests of Guiana—beautiful and
exotic, "a veritable paradise," which, however, concealed painful razor
grass and deadly snakes, "horrid" vampire bats, and mysterious birds,
whose midnight cries were like the shrieks "of some poor murdered victim" of cannibals.[23]

The *concealing* nature of the dense tropical world allowed the imagination of the white interloper and the distant novelist alike to color what
they could not themselves observe with an apprehension-driven gothic
sensationalism. In Africa, even General Wolseley, an earth-bound prag-
matist not given to flights of romantic fantasy, recoiled from the oppressive closeness and visually impenetrable surroundings: "What strikes
the stranger most in this weirdly-dark forest scenery, are the thousands
of twisted creepers and winders of all shapes and sizes which cross and

recross one another. . . . There is something indescribably ghostly in the midday twilight of these forests." Henry Morton Stanley, writing of the "sepulchral gloom" of the forests of Central Africa—inhabited, he claimed, by cannibals and pigmies—uses similar language, speaking of an entrapping "ravenous legion of snaky vines . . . serpent-like creepers." The associational route can become overtly a significant one—from darkness and obscurity to a coiling, deceitful entrapment, and so to the female: the masses of creepers were, Wolseley said, "like the tangled locks of some giant Meg Merrilies."[24]

Although Europeans suspected cannibalism wherever the "savage primitive" was to be found—in the windswept north among the Eskimo and in the forests of North America among the Iroquois, the steaming tropics were the favored narrative locus, where the cannibal of popular imagination best flourished. But the defining location of the moment was mobile. It shifted over time, reflecting the onward sweep of European exploration and domination, from the Caribbean world of the seventeenth and eighteenth centuries, thence to Asia and the South Pacific, and so to sub-Saharan Africa. By the second half of the nineteenth century, the journey into lush, fetid, tropical Africa became a progress into the cannibal realm. Canopied with trees and vines, the rivers up which the white intruder journeyed were labyrinthine cloaca, ever-narrowing, leading into the dark bowels of the cannibal's lair—journeys accompanied in theatrical retelling by cries from unseen throats for "niama, niama": "meat, meat."[25] A piece of popular sensationalism such as Herbert Ward's *Five Years with the Congo Cannibals* is itself a peripatetic progress through increasingly dense and more suspect territory, a progress that discovers ever-intensifying *degrees* of cannibal character as Ward journeys from the lower to the upper Congo. The people of the Bolobo district, "although not actually cannibals are, beyond doubt, one of the most cruel races met with in this part of Central Africa." Further on, the Monsole "are cannibals, but they confine themselves generally to eating enemies slain in battle." The Baui however "are great cannibals" who prey on weaker tribes, and the Bakundu "are voracious cannibals, a fact which they do not disguise." At his station far upriver, Ward imagined perpetual cannibal "orgies" just beyond his view. "I knew that I should never have far to seek to find my [Bangala] friends . . . indulging in a light repast off the limbs of some unfortunate slave." And on the "opposite side of the river," in the dense, impenetrable, and unseen out-there-somewhere, were yet more brutal and savage cannibals—an "inferior" type of cannibal of whom he had heard tales, with their filed teeth, surrounded by the skulls of their victims.[26]

In such an obstructed landscape, where the concealed closeness of the enemy obviated much of the advantage of modern weaponry, where decaying tropical vegetation limited the sweep of the domineering masculine gaze, just as it restricted the sweep of the Maxim gun, even a sympathetic observer found his dark fears of a ghoulish and sadistic perversity fermenting in the stench and oppressive closeness of his surroundings. And it is precisely this apprehension of the unseen that is fundamental to the nineteenth-century gothic discourse on cannibalism—an eternally unviewable act that has to be *imagined*, not witnessed. When the anthropologist Berthold Seemann visited Fiji in 1860, the mere sight of an iron pot hanging on a chief's wall, "large enough for two men," was enough to make "my imagination run riot."[27]

An important example of the gothicizing of geographical and anthropological discovery in the nineteenth century is the juxtaposition of scenic and floral beauty with the most disquieting form of the cannibal taboo—the eating of the dead and buried. "Mortuary cannibalism" served as nothing else to sensationalize and dehumanize the non-European, violating as it did taboos against both necrophilia and cannibalism. It also, at the very least, violated the principles of sanitary health, an area of domestic discourse already resonating with gothic fears of the contagion of decomposition. This provided an ideal field for the gothicization of racial difference: "While the Fijian turns with disgust from pork, or his favourite fish, if at all tainted, he will eat *bakolo* when fast approaching putrescence."[28]

Early-nineteenth-century exploration of the interior of Australia first furnished hints of the "horrid practice," as Sir Thomas Mitchell called it, of what he presented as probable grave-robbing for the purpose of devouring the corpses.[29] Although it now seems likely that the source of these ghoulish fantasies was merely the aboriginal practice of secondary burial, where bones of the deceased were exhumed and dutifully carried about, precisely because of its gothic sensationalism, Mitchell's secondhand "fact" that "dead men were sometimes dug up and eaten" was quickly embraced, repeated, and elaborated by others.

Subsequently, the Fiji Islands provided a more substantial cannibalism discourse in the colored accounts of missionaries urging Western intervention. Without directly challenging the actual practice of some form of cannibalism in Fiji, we may note the ease with which suspicions of man-eating slip into a predictable rhetoric of gothic excess. In 1836 the Methodist Missionary Society in London issued "An Appeal to the Sympathy of the Christian Public on Behalf of the Cannibal Feejeeans." In the eyes of their missionary correspondent, it was cannibalism, "this unnatural propensity," that perverted the morals of the islanders and led them into the most extreme "abominations" he could envisage, even to "absolutely rob the graves of their inhabitants," including those of "their own deceased children."[30] Two years later, the Reverend David Cargill made a similar sensational accusation, published in the Missionary Society's journal, affirming that "as if they were human hyenas, they disinter dead bodies, days beneath the ground."[31] His version highlighted Fijian preference for "the flesh of women" in an invocation of the gothic blend of the sexual and the morbid. We may note in both these narratives the construction of anthropophagy as an addictive vice that, like uncontrollable libidinousness or narcotic dependency, deformed all other areas of life.

A calmer observer, the naturalist Alfred Russel Wallace might describe a form of Amazonian mortuary cannibalism in 1853 without this kind of sensationalism, but even his account rests rhetorically on the effect of the juxtaposition of exotic flora and fauna with peculiar customs, and on the emphasized details of decomposition and odor: "The Tarianas and Tucanos, and some other tribes, about a month after the funeral, disinter the corpse, which is then much decomposed." Baked "with a most horrible odour" until reduced to a powder, this was then, he said, mixed with a liquor and drunk "till all is finished."[32]

In Africa, earlier reports of cannibalism had been discounted by Thomas Winterbottom, and at mid-century David Livingstone was, at first, careful not to spread the cannibal libel, stressing that the blacks he knew were much more likely to suspect the white man of cannibalism than to practice it themselves.[33] Such skepticism was, oddly enough, echoed by the racialist surgeon Robert Knox, who averred that he "had always doubted the fact of cannibalism having ever existed. . . . In Africa no such practise exists."[34]

Livingstone's distrust of what he called the "hobgoblin" element in the European relation of African customs was a shrewd recognition of the domestic folkloric locus of much of the cannibal tradition. But even Livingstone was not immune to the attraction of a gothicized rhetoric. His *Missionary Travels and Researches in South Africa* contains dark references to unexplained "depravities" and a detailed account of premature burial—that cliché of nineteenth-century gothic.[35] And in his last, terrible years of wandering in central Africa, Livingstone, too, came reluctantly to embrace a fully gothicized belief in a savage cannibalism of appetite (of "a depraved taste" for buried, putrefied human flesh).[36] Whatever the reality of human sacrifice among the "Manyuema" of the dark regions of the "Metamba country," it will be clear that Livingstone's darkening vision must reflect at some level his own failures in the tangled morasses that devoured both his health and his hopes of an African renaissance. This growing belief in a widespread cannibalism, which parallels Livingstone's tenacious credulity about the source of the Nile, must be seen in the context of the growing impenetrability of the forest swamp and the dangerous strangeness of the local peoples—a dark region where everything was corrupted, in Livingstone's mind, by the abomination, the hidden depravity, of the slave trade.

The imaging of Africa as locus of the gothic was, of course, already well under way before mid-century, grounded as it was in a sensational literary style characteristic of early nineteenth-century reportage. When the French missionaries Arbousset and Daumas visited the Cape in 1836, they told fanciful stories of "cannibal caves" to the north that would seem to resonate more with the criminal cannibalism of Sawney Beane's clan, or with Goya's drawings of bandit-cannibals,[37] than with Bechuana reality. They portrayed a "wild and ferocious" people who became "both robbers and cannibals," who attacked travelers "in open day" and dragged them into the dark places of their caves to be "devoured in secret." Like their Scottish counterparts, they had depopulated the surrounding countryside.[38]

By mid-century the rhetoric of African explorers, like that of the missionaries, had generally abandoned the calm and measured discourse of a Mungo Park or a Thomas Winterbottom for a gothicized narrative of adventure. Winwood Reade's notoriously racist relation of his experiences in *Savage Africa* commences with a progress through Madeira, off the West Coast, that parallels the ironies of Sue's Java: "It is but a lovely charnel-house this island of Madeira. It is a boudoir, and it is a hospital: a paradise, and a tomb . . . all changes suddenly like a horrible dream . . . the sun is darkness; the flowers are ashes; the warm, soft air is heavy with disease."[39] Mortuary cannibalism itself was dwelt upon by the German skull-collecting anthropologist Georg Schweinfurth, who, a few years later, published his own account of *"The Heart of Africa"*. Schweinfurth's narration slips easily from the pseudo-scientific discourse of the comparative anatomist into the rhetorical excesses of unrestrained gothic description. Native bearers who died from fatigue (that is, who were indirectly killed by Schweinfurth) were "dug from the graves in which they had been buried" to have their fat stripped away for consumption. Any guilt of his own complicity was here firmly displaced by "the horror that thrills through us at every repetition of the account of hideous and revolting custom."[40]

Returning to the urbane St. Johnston, who found a "weird attractiveness" in the subject of cannibalism in his erudite essay of 1884, we discover that his own interest had previously been focused by a tour through islands in the South Pacific. He published the diary of this excursion as a light and humorous monograph, which he called *Camping Among the Cannibals*. Here he regales his reader with anecdotes of cravings for "strange flesh," of Fijians who "frequently have enacted the part of ghouls, and digging the body up from the grave, have cooked it and feasted thereon."[41] But under St. Johnston's gothic horror, there stirs the essentially comic and trivializing purpose indicated in the title he chose. Just as gothic fiction slips so easily into parody—comic Frankenstein monsters and camp vampires—so the gothicized cannibal leads inevitably to the cannibal joke.

Cannibalism, White and Black

"Cannibals? who is not a cannibal?"
— *Melville, Moby-Dick*[42]

While white man-eaters did not disappear from popular view—there was, especially, the survival cannibalism of the Donner party in the American West and of the English crew of *Mignonette*[43]—as the century progressed, the practice became the more alien the more it was dwelt upon as a signifier of race. Exoticized and racialized, its unnaturalness became a boundary that defined biological identity, like the phenotypical measurements of the anthropologists' comparative anatomies. An earlier generation would not have refused, like Dickens, to believe that the men of the Franklin expedition could have resorted to cannibalism in the frozen north,[44] nor would they have arrested the survivors of the *Mignonette*.

And yet the language of racial cannibalism had its deepest origins in domestic discourse, traditions that both shaped the gothic and prepared Western perceptions of the racial Other. While some of the medieval and Renaissance elements of this discourse are obvious enough—the presumed cannibalism, for instance, of witches and Jews—it is a wider, more pervasive phenomenon than is commonly appreciated. Here we can but scratch the surface in a brief consideration of popular usage of the cannibal idea, in folk traditions, in the language used to describe both a dangerous underclass and the rapacious landlord and financier, the entrapping woman and the lecherous man, the madman and the criminal.

FOLK CANNIBALISM

In Britain, there were widely surviving local traditions—no doubt under assault in a nineteenth-century environment of rapid social change, education, and mobility—that suggest cannibal superstition and ritual. In Wales, for example, there was the ancient custom of the "sin-eater," someone paid to dine on bread, cheese, and beer placed on the breast of the recently deceased. In other parts of Britain (as in Bavaria), this took the form of the custom of the corpse cake, funeral food allowed to rise on or near the dead body.[45] The cannibalism suggested here, perhaps deriving from ancient, pre-Christian practice, no doubt came to relate in some way to the implied cannibalism of Holy Communion itself. Moreover, there were a variety of folk remedies that involved the actual ingestion of some part of the human body. In Denmark and northern Germany, blood was consumed well into the nineteenth century as a treatment for epilepsy—it being in fact the prerogative of executioners to sell the blood of decapitated criminals to those waiting, cup in hand. In some areas of France, peasants considered the fat of executed criminals a cure for scrofula and rheumatism. Executioners who sold strips of human fat for such medicinal purposes raised complaints among apothecaries that their trade was being infringed upon.[46] Mortuary cannibalism as medicinal therapy is also explicit in a custom found surviving at least as late as the mid eighteenth century in Sussex: the apparently popular superstition that an infusion made from the bones of a criminal would cure rheumatism. In 1743 the gibbetted corpse of the murderer John Breads, executed in Rye, disappeared piecemeal.[47]

This local superstition is clearly related to the much more widely held belief, popular in seventeenth-century apothecary lore, but surviving, it would appear, into the early twentieth century, that a bit of desiccated corpse, called "mummy," as an ingredient in a medicinal preparation, had wide curative power. The English College of Physicians included mummy and human blood in the official London pharmacopoeia as late as 1747. Stolen from gibbets or graveyards or imported from France, bodies were prepared by a customary process of drying and treatment with pitch and sold over the counter by apothecaries. Samuel Johnson's *Dictionary* indicates that mummy was still being sold in England, although as early as 1738, Chambers' *Cyclopoedia* dismissed the remedy as an invention of "the malice of a Jewish physician."[48] Dislodged from its place in official medicine by the same process that subordinated the apothecary to the polite and scientific profession of the university-educated doctor, it nevertheless survived at some level in popular culture. As late as 1908, the well-known German pharmaceutical company E. Merck offered in its catalogue "genuine Egyptian mummy, as long as the supply lasts, 17 marks 50 per kilogram."[49]

> And so it goes from rape and sodomy to incest and cannibalism.
> —Darnton, 'The Great Cat Massacre'[50]

In their seminal works on Africa, both Thomas Winterbottom, writing at the beginning of the nineteenth century, and David Livingstone, writing sixty years later, drew attention to the parallel between the exaggerated and sensationalized accounts of African depravity and European folktales of "hobgoblins and spectres," which were used, in Winterbottom's words, "to terrify children" and by frequent repetition "acquire[d] a degree of credit among the vulgar." Livingstone put it more succinctly: "The nursery hobgoblin of the one [the European] is black, of the other [the African] white."[51]

A deeper, if necessarily brief, consideration of the European folktale tradition might be of some interest in further explicating the construction of the racial cannibal in the nineteenth century. Of course, a full consideration of this theme would encompass the wider European tradition—the ogres and trolls of Germanic myth or the stories of *ancien régime* France with their world, as Robert Darnton has recreated it, "of raw and naked brutality."[52] But for present purposes, Katherine Briggs's monumental *Dictionary of British Folk-Tales* provides a convenient route into the gothic elements of at least British popular culture.[53] Here one finds roughly three types of cannibal tale, each of which has some obvious emotional and thematic relation to the representation of cannibalism abroad.

In the first, cannibalism is directly associated with peasant poverty— although, indeed, the whole genre of cannibal folktales probably refers at some level to this underlying theme, the cannibalism of duress, of survival, of eat or be eaten, in a premodern environment where famine was known and feared as a common occurrence. In these tales, the deed is nonetheless a transgression and requires some kind of punishment— usually a terrible confrontation with the spirit of the eaten. In one such story, "The Bone," of which there are many local variations, a member of a starving family robs a grave and brings back a bone from a corpse, which is then boiled in a pot for soup. Their meal is interrupted by a ghostly voice demanding the return of its bone.[54] The issue of interest here—beyond the image of the stew pot, which became a standard of the comic caricature of the African or Fijian cannibal—is the use of the desecration of the grave and the abuse of the corpse to add a deeper depravity to the offense. Such grave-robbing cannibalism resonates directly with the nineteenth-century descriptions of mortuary anthropophagy pervasive in racial narrative. Another tale, that of "The Liver," in a Scottish variation,[55] stands (like the story of Sawney Beane) between what may be called the cannibalism of starvation and that of perverse appetite. A man's wife dies, and he hungers for her liver, which he takes out of the corpse, roasts, and eats. She returns as a specter and charges him with the crime. Here hunger becomes desire—that is, preference. Although it is a tale of mortuary cannibalism, the corpse is female, and there may also be elements of sadism and sexual perversity. This type of story is a bridge to the second category.

The sexual content seems paramount in the next type, that of the male or female bluebeard who designs or at least wishes for the death of a mate in order to possess or consume a part of his or her partner. The tale of "The Golden Arm" is very similar to that of "The Liver," except that the desired body part, the golden arm, is not a postmortem after-thought of desire, but the very object of original obsession, for which the wife was pursued and wedded: the husband "was fonder of the golden arm than of all his wife's gifts," and when she died, "he got up in the middle of the night, dug up the body, and cut off the golden arm. He hurried home to hide his treasure."⁵⁶ Although not an outright tale of cannibalism, this story conforms to the type—the postmortem severing of a body part, which is secretly and shamefully possessed, hidden if not incorporated. The sexual overtones—the reduction and objectification of the woman to a desired part of the body—are clear.

An interesting inversion of the marital cannibal type is "Wanted a Husband," where it is the wife who is the grave-robbing cannibal, whose uncontrollable appetite (sexual or gastronomic) is suggested by her hav-ing had seven husbands. A gypsy lad learns of this widow and her wish to marry again. They wed, but he wakes on the wedding night to find her gone. On the third night of absence, he follows her to the graveyard, where he demands to know what she is eating: "'Corpse, you bugger, corpse!'"⁵⁷ Here we have a popular trope of gothic literature, woman as man-eater, who threatens to entrap and destroy innocent youth, a char-acteristic reversal of the "naturally" gendered roles of feminine victim and masculine villain.

The image of female depravity is the central element in a third type of tale—the popular theme of the murder of a small child by an evil mother or stepmother, who then serves parts of the body to an unwitting father for his supper. Briggs offers two such stories, variations on the familiar tale of "The Juniper Tree." Neither "The Little Bird" nor "The Milk-White Doo [Dove]"⁵⁸ presents the crime as an overt act of revenge (in the manner of *Titus Andronicus*) aimed at the father, but merely as the re-sult of rage and cupidity. In the one, a child breaks a favorite jug and is killed; in the second, the wife herself eats a hare intended for her hus-band's dinner and then substitutes his favorite child. These stories achieve their effect, of course, by perverting the maternal relationship, turning the nurturing female into witch (in both, her punishment is vio-lent death), and maintaining the benevolent distance of the father, who is drawn, Adamlike, into sin through his unwitting participation in the cannibal meal. In these no doubt ancient stories, there is also some re-flection of the Christian idea of the child as lamb of God.⁵⁹ As in Swift's Irish satire or Rubens's grotesque painting of Saturn devouring one of his infant children (ill. 6), the effect depends on the nightmare image of the

Ill. 6. Peter Paul Rubens, *Saturn Devouring One of His Children* (Museo del Prado, Madrid).

hideous destruction of the tenderly vulnerable. By the nineteenth century, of course, the progressive romanticization of the child as innocence rather than receptacle of Calvinist sin, freed even further the image of the abused and cannibalized child for sensational featuring in accounts of the racial Other,[60] as well as in the more oblique use of cannibalism in the imagery of the devouring mill and mine in domestic English social criticism.

Sensational nineteenth-century narrations of cannibal depravity (white or black) in the "contact zones" of racial conflict draw upon such sources so strongly that fact, fiction, and folklore become inextricably confused. That such confusion is often deliberately invoked to heighten narrative effect does not deny yet deeper, less conscious borrowings. For example, J. Ross Browne's "sketches of adventures" in California (1864), written in a style that deliberately merges fact and fiction, inevitably include the story of a woman "masculine" in size and strength who survived the ill-fated Donner party. He gives her a "wild and piercing expression of eye, and a smile singularly startling and unfeminine." She "had subsisted for some time on the dead body of a child . . . this horrible feast of human flesh." The woman is a simple innkeeper, but her past, that imagined gothic moment in the mountains, compels the narrator to construct her form and character out of his own sense of revulsion (he must imagine her hands to be "the same hands that had torn the flesh from a corpse and passed the reeking shreds to her mouth") and from his own memory of childhood fictions. Browne intends, of course, to sensationalize, but his self-conscious drawing on the folkloric to amplify a real, if terrible, event, reveals a strategy that is, in fact, often buried in "non-fictional" nineteenth-century texts of exploration and anthropology: "The picture of the terrible ogress that I had seen when a child, and the story of the little children which she had devoured, assumed a fearful reality, and became strangely mingled in my dreams with this woman's face."[61]

It is necessary to consider at somewhat greater length the domestic locus of cannibal representation, to follow the folkloric into the late-eighteenth- and early-nineteenth-century social world. If we exclude here the important category of the cannibal Jew, there remain three significant areas of domestic—that is, white—cannibal representation. That of the savage mob is clearly related to the folkloric theme of starvation cannibalism, but also to another category, that of the cannibal madman or madwoman, the frenzied desire of the (often pauper) insane to devour themselves and others. Both madness and poverty feature particularly in one extension of these middle-class fears, the criminal cannibal (especially the cannibal convict, an important example of white savagery, particularly powerful in the first half of the nineteenth century), while the cannibal sailor, a close relation, is, like the convict, associated with sexual and social deviancy, as well as poverty. A third category of domestic representation, also prefigured in the folkloric tradition, is that of woman as both cannibal and cannibal victim whose physiological and mental weaknesses make her both vulnerable to abuse and subject to hysteria. These three areas—poverty, femineity, and criminality—are, of course, far from mutually exclusive. The pauper, the woman, and the convict lack social and political power. That the rogues among them are demonized, invested with a deviancy that often has sexual overtones, served to justify and reinforce a more general coercion and exclusion.

CANNIBALISM AND THE WORKING CLASS

The most familiar use in domestic discourse of the cannibal theme was probably that of the threat of a savage underclass—especially powerful as metaphor during and following the French Revolution. Counterrevolutionary propaganda, from Burke's speeches to the fiendish representations of Gillray's cartoons (ill. 7), crudely joined the domestic Georgian image of the devouring mob with that of the alien and depraved foreigner, the starving French worker who was already invested in caricature and tradition with a strange and disgusting diet (ill. 8).[62]

Lee Sterrenburg has explored the use of cannibal imagery by the Victorians, especially Carlyle and Dickens, in their representation of the savageries of the French Revolution of 1789, and subsequently in the demonization of the revolutionary Left of 1830 and 1848.[63] The attempt to portray revolution in metaphors of incorporation, as a devouring, has, he claims, its roots in a repressed middle class's need to identify social classes, both above and, particularly, below themselves, as animalistic and appetite-ridden. The Victorians did not, of course, invent this particular metaphorical representation. However much it may have suited the vision of the nineteenth-century bourgeois, the savagery of the mob, its metaphorical cannibalism, was well developed in eighteenth-century polemic before Burke invoked the "cannibal appetites" of the sansculottes.[64]

It has been suggested that "an Enlightenment spirit" that separated the purposeful popular violence of the wars of religion from the sacred, and associated such ritualized excess with chaos rather than order, stands behind a shift in perception at least among the educated. In France, 1794 was a watershed: "After Thermidor the new sensibility began to take hold. In retrospect, people began to describe the violent mobs of years past as 'cannibals.'"[65] Of course, however catalytic the events of

Ill. 7. James Gillray, "Un Petit Souper, à la Parisienne" (1792) (British Museum).

the Terror and reaction may have been in both England and France, "a spreading humanitarianism"[66] was already well under way, marked by an essentially urban, middle-class aversion to blood sports, to slaughterhouse smells and filth, to cruelty to animals and children, to the public torture of criminals. This growing sensibility, reinforced in England by the Evangelical awakening, meant that popular acts of violence and rage, such as those witnessed during the Gordon Riots in London in 1780, were increasingly represented, not as inevitable and customary, nor even as merely dangerous to those with property to lose, but as deviant, savage and unchristian. As this revulsion from violence, pain, public disorder, and the sight of blood spread, it encouraged the gothicization, not only of the traditional, direct methods of organization and intimidation employed by the unfranchised at home, but also of the customs of non-Europeans abroad, whose cultures were seen still to express just that ritual violence, corpse desecration, and organized vengeance that Europeans were guiltily engaged in displacing from their own past.

Sensational press accounts of English urban and rural violence were, of course, common well before the counterrevolutionary writers took up this mode in denouncing the excesses of the Revolution. Newgate Calendar stories, with their violent and brutal details of lower-class crime, depended on the tender sensibilities of their readers for their effect. The style of Burke's denunciation of the savagery of mob violence as a form of depraved man-eating was not new. What may be of more interest is his employment of the term "cannibal*ism*" (although he may not have coined the word, the *Oxford English Dictionary* cites his usage as its first example) to denote both the actual and metaphoric cannibal practice of the mob: "By cannibalism, I mean their devouring, as a nutriment of their ferocity, some part of the bodies of those they have murdered."[67] His linkage of an actual cannibalizing of bodies with a metaphoric devouring of property in fact anticipated the political economy of the nineteenth century, the confusion of body and commodity within an ideology of possessive individualism. Burke demands "a warm opposition to the spirit of leveling, to the spirit of impiety, to the spirit of proscription, plunder, murder, and *cannibalism*."[68]

Twenty-five years earlier, the first edition of the *Encyclopedia Britannica* denied that man-eating had commonly been practiced anywhere—either in Europe in ancient times, in the Caribbean, or elsewhere: "It is greatly to be doubted if ever such a custom existed."[69] This was an enlightened skepticism that, *pace* Defoe, stretched back at least as far as the calm reasoning of the circumnavigator William Dampier's observations of 1688, that he "did never meet with any such People: All Nations or Families in the World, that I have seen or heard of . . . would scarce

FRANCE

Ill. 8(a). "France" (1772) (British Museum).

Ill. 8(b). James Gillray, "French Liberty" (1792) (British Museum).

kill a man purposely to eat him." Even the Indians of the Cannibal Islands "do trade very civilly with the *French* and *Spaniards*; and they have done so with us."⁷⁰

Although the second edition of the *Britannica* (1778), following stories of purported cannibal practices discovered in the South Pacific by Cook's first two expeditions, accepted the likelihood of the custom, it was also presented as probably common to most of mankind at certain stages of development.⁷¹ It is not until the third edition, published between 1788 and 1797, that we are presented with cannibalism as a socially dangerous, as opposed to merely bizarre, repugnant, and distant, practice, which would erode "the chief security of human life"—respect for the person—that "more frequently restrains the hand of the murderer, than the sense of duty or the dread of punishment."⁷² The middle-class, educated, and largely urban authors and readers of such encyclopedias in England as in France were increasingly, as polite society drew further apart from those below, sensitive to the dangers to person and property of the unrestrained "mob." Diderot's *Encyclopédie* asserted an antiprimitive perspective on "savages" as likely cannibals, "without laws, without *police* [order], without religion,"⁷³ which seems to have a domestic, as well as foreign, evil in view. The *Britannica* article in the third edition dwells on the evidence of contemporary cannibal practice among the Maori of New Zealand and the Battas of Sumatra. Its strategy, however, is to draw out a general principle that, more directly than Diderot's, responds to domestic rather than colonial anxieties—a message attuned to the fears raised by the devastating Gordon Riots of 1780, "the largest, deadliest and most protracted urban riots in British History,"⁷⁴ if not by the fall of the Bastille in 1789. After the Revolution,⁷⁵ this message took on a sharper urgency.

In England, urban and rural riots had been commonplace expressions of popular will—over the price of bread, religion, taxes, contested elections, and even the possession of the bodies of those who had been hanged. But they appear never to have been as ferocious as the eruptions of popular violence in France. The wars of religion had seen massacres in France that involved the symbolic consumption of parts of the bodies—ears, hearts, and livers—of Huguenots, while siege warfare during the civil wars inevitably led to a starvation cannibalism in Paris and elsewhere in which the "obvious victims" were probably the first to go.

In the Revolution, a "disruption of the order of the universe," public acts of collective, organized, ritualized violence—not a formless mass hysteria—may have been one terrible way the inarticulate had of responding to the general dissolution, of creating a kind of social—that is, public—bonding. The desecration of the bodies of the enemies of the

Republic—the dragging of them from place to place and the parading of body parts—no doubt drew on a long tradition. In the early stages of the Revolution, Brian Singer has argued, the circulation of body parts "through the major arteries of the city" was a ritual that engaged the entire society, the descriptions of which were "couched in the terms of a vocabulary of digestion: those participating in such acts are inevitably called 'cannibals,' 'anthropophagi,' or *buveurs du sang* (blood-drinkers)."[76] As Alain Corbin has observed, in these bizarre celebrations, "the Revolution simply repeated the Wars of Religion."[77] But it was a repetition that was focused and reinterpreted to serve their own ends by both revolutionary propagandists and their opponents.[78]

Lynn Hunt has shown that the radical representation of royalty as devourers, as *mangeurs de peuples*, justified an inverted cannibalism, that of the people, particularly the sansculottes, as *mangeurs de rois*. If, in revolutionary iconography, Hercules exacting vengeance on kings in general is emblematic of the nation-as-its-people emerging from thraldom, Louis's execution in particular could also be deployed as a ritual sacrifice, a metaphoric shared cannibalism like the mass, an eating of the king's body, not merely as vengeance, but as a means of symbolically transferring its sacredness to the people as a whole.[79] Others have explored a more overtly Freudian reading of the king's execution as a parricide, the consumption of the body of the father by the sons at a cannibal feast, which, Dorinda Outram has argued, became a preoccupation of bourgeois revolutionary mythology.[80]

Representations of the king's death and the Terror generally were dominated, not by radical apologists—there were very few engravings of the execution published in Paris—but by the propagandists of the counterrevolution, who saw in the stories of a populace that actually tasted Louis's blood quite another image—one that was gothic and demonic. Accusations of both metaphoric and actual cannibalism abound from the earliest days of the "unnatural" events in Paris. Lally Tollendal's characterization of the National Assembly as "cette caverne d'Anthropophage," quoted by Burke, is typical. In England, the Establishment and émigré press were only too willing to expand upon the theme of a sadistic revolutionary depravity: "The good people of France, if we may credit report, indulged some of their numerous prisoners, in the early periods of their blessed revolution, with soup, made out of the limbs of those human victims whom they sacrificed at the altar of liberty."[81] In fact, "Eusibius" subsequently explains, this particular report is "a groundless calumny," but its rhetorical "truth" is nevertheless established within this particular text by associating a bizarre French diet—French cooks can "toss up a dozen frogs into a delicious fricassee"—with that of African primitives—"To a Hottentot, cow's dung is a savoury garnish to a dish of guts and garbage"—and Asian cannibals.

Inevitably, as the embattled Revolution defended itself, as the nation became, via the *levée en masse*, the army, the image of the cannibal sansculotte was transferred. English propagandists sought to rehabilitate the image of the English military as emblematic of a king-and-God-fearing nation by emphasizing its alter-image in a French army that represented atheism, sansculottery, and cannibal depravity.

Anthony Aufrere's hysterical account of the atrocities committed by French troops during the campaign in Swabia in 1796 takes as its title *The Cannibal's Progress*, significantly invoking Hogarth in his portrayal of the ferocious sexual depredations, murders, and pollutions of the army of the Republic. Aufrere's pamphlet, widely reprinted at the time, is an important example of the deployment of metaphoric cannibalism, of an essentially gothic trope, in extending the reactionary assault on the plebeian revolutionary into a wider nationalistic and ethnic attack. The French are portrayed as men of enormous appetite ("two Frenchmen would devour at a meal as much as would serve three hard-working Germans three or four days"). They sexually violate pregnant women, those deformed by loathsome disease, and even the bodies of the dead, just as they violate Christ's dead body (in the churches they "trampled the host underfoot"). Their "barbarous excesses" are the product of the unrestrained animal lust but also the appetite—the greed—of the French pauper. They torture and burn to discover hidden property as well as hidden virgins. They even open new graves to pillage the corpses as well as to profane them, and they bring in their wake "the tribe of Jews . . . the refuse of Suabia."[82]

This gothicization of the army of the Republic resonates with the later "gothicization of poverty" that Gertrude Himmelfarb revealed in her examination of G. W. M. Reynolds's *Mysteries of London*, and its "pornography of violence" in the 1840's.[83] A generation after Burke, in the industrializing England of the early nineteenth century, representations of the degraded and demonized poor of the factory towns as cannibalistic savages—and as the victims of a cannibalistic economic system—give a somewhat different meaning to the familiar label "the hungry forties."

Contemporaneous with the age of revolutions and the early industrial period, gothic imagery of mob violence effectively substituted the urban collective savagery of the degraded and dispossessed for the original savage Carib of Defoe's desert island. When the surgeon Southwood Smith complained of the dangers of procuring bodies for dissection (itself a kind of cannibalism) in Scotland in the 1820's, he projected onto the "mob" a kind of cannibal savagery—one in particular "kindled a fire with [the empty coffin's] fragments, and surrounded it like the savages in Robinson Crusoe, till it was entirely consumed."[84] When Eugène Sue represented the vengeance of the mob in *The Wandering Jew* in a scene of "massacre and torture," he invoked the "butchery" of the "cannibal," and the scene was, he claimed, based on an actual occurrence of Parisian mob violence: "Each individual, yielding to a sanguinary frenzy, came in turn to strike his blow, or to tear off his morsel of flesh. Women—yes, women—mothers!—came to spend their rage on this mutilated form."[85] In England, *Varney, the Vampyre*, also published in the hungry forties, contains a similar evocation of the cannibalism of the proletarian mob. Here, as with Southwood Smith's complaint, there is also a characteristic inversion where the vampire, the true cannibal, is pursued by an enraged populace, who smash and burn his mansion: "They danced like maniacs round the fire; looking, in fact, like so many wild Indians, dancing round their roasting victims, or some demons at an infernal feast."[86]

Ironically, this image, distant from the original cannibal of Renaissance exploration myth, but close to the bourgeois fears of lower-class violence in urban Europe, was reexported to the non-Western world as part of the mental baggage of the missionary and explorer. If Defoe's Carib had served allusively to heighten the demonization of the European underclass in the eighteenth century, it was the Revolution and middle-class social apprehension of the early nineteenth century that shaped its specific monstrosity—an image that was then carried back to the racial Other. In the early nineteenth century, the severed head, that most powerful image of the Terror, became symbolic also of the South Pacific "cannibal." The fascinated horror with which early narratives of New Zealand invest the preparation of preserved heads clearly drew some of its inspiration and emotional force from recent European history.[87]

When Winwood Reade describes Africans in his *Savage Africa*, he does so with explicit reference to "the mob, which in all countries is tolerably brutal." The cannibal Fans, "whose physiognomy expressed good-natured stupidity," received him "with the enthusiasm of the mob. . . . Oh, if Hogarth could have seen my cannibals!"[88] Another account, contemporary with Reade's, Faulkner's *Elephant Haunts*, employs the same image. There is a frenzy among Faulkner's African bearers to disembowel, "like hungry wolves," and butcher the elephants he has shot: "Each elephant had a mob closely packed round it, yelling and fighting like demons."[89]

In the mature industrial period, Burke's cannibal proletariat, or at least the most degraded part of it, was increasingly represented by friend and foe alike as "a race apart" (Engels), "a nomad race" (Mayhew), a "residuum" of primitive savagery maintaining itself in the dark corners of an otherwise improving society.[90] The nineteenth-century middle-class search for domestic ethnographic detail, for "knowledge" of the hidden world of urban poverty, offers a close parallel to the contemporary search for the real nature of the primitive in the South Pacific or Africa. Christopher Herbert has christened Henry Mayhew's view of the slums of London a "Cockney Polynesia,"[91] while Catherine Gallagher has discovered another kind of cannibal association in the "biological economy" of a Malthusian middle-class social discourse that was obsessed with sewage, with the danger of an involuntary ingestion of the products of other bodies, with transcendable biological boundaries. Henry Mayhew's types of the sexually vigorous but essentially "parasitic" poor, the wandering nomads "preying" on the productive part of the population, are a threat to a social body that is vulnerable, not vigorous and resistant.[92]

By mid-century, sociocultural evolutionism was investing elements of the working classes in Britain with a mental primitivism whose characteristic impulsiveness, improvidence, and general childishness exactly paralleled the construction of the racial primitive in the expanding empire. As George Stocking has emphasized in his important study of the origins of the "science" of anthropology, this was the product of "a close articulation, both experiential and ideological, between the domestic and the colonial spheres of otherness."[93] One needs, however, to ground this articulation more firmly in a deeper popular culture that had long invested the outsider, particularly the Celtic outsider, with a demonic, primitive, and dangerous aspect.[94] Popular responsiveness to the racialization of cultural difference by the mid-Victorian intelligentsia had its roots, not only in the conjunction of social-evolutionist ideas, colonial expansion, and the creation of an urban industrial proletariat, but in folk myth and long-standing domestic prejudice directed at gypsies, Jews, and, especially in England, Celtic vagabonds.

Returning briefly to the story of Sawney Beane, we find there already a remarkable juxtaposition of precisely those elements that served to gothicize and racialize the nineteenth-century Celtic proletariat. The poverty of Sawney's origins (his parents were hedgers and ditchers), the association of criminal depravity (the murder and cannibalization of innocent travelers) with sexual depravity (the incestuous relationships that produced the "Blood-thirsty Clan" of "savages" living in Beane's cave), and the claustrophobic interior of the cave itself (a fetid place, a "Cimmerian Den" with its "intricate Turnings and Windings," a place of "perpetual Horror and Darkness"),[95] are themes reproduced time and again in the nineteenth-century middle-class literature of the (often Irish) urban slum, of Engels's Manchester, the Reverend Andrew Mearns's "Outcast London," or Jack the Ripper's Whitechapel.[96]

Stories of Celtic cannibalism had an ancient history, but the modern association of Celt and cannibal had a locus in—no doubt often fanciful—English stories of starvation cannibalism, reported in Ireland from the late sixteenth and early seventeenth centuries,[97] and resurfacing in the Great Famine of the 1840's. Echoing Chief Justice Lord Clonmell's late-eighteenth-century observation that in the rural parts of Ireland one felt "like a traveller in Africa, in a forest amongst Hottentots and wild beasts,"[98] Carlyle could refer to a place he visited in remote Kildare as "like a village in Dahomey," wild, exotic, and wretched, and to those who did well in the Famine as having prospered "by *eating* the slain."[99] Charles Kingsley makes the association more literal, seeing the poor rural Irish as a species of "white chimpanzees" who "were as perfect in the arts of forest warfare as those modern Maories whom they so much resembled."[100]

One supposed case of actual cannibalism near Ballinrobe was raised in Parliament in 1848, involving reports of a starving man tearing out the heart and liver of a corpse that had been washed ashore and eating them. The language of Lord John Russell's denial of the veracity of the report is itself of interest in its own representation of the primitive Irishman. The man, Russell said, was not starving or in actual distress, but rather was possessed of a "singularly voracious appetite." He did not appear to know that the corpse was a human trunk and in any event was stopped by his neighbors before actually eating any of it.[101] Here the ignorance and unmanageable appetite of the Irishman, and his willingness to consume what was decomposed into unrecognizability, as firmly establish his primitive character as any actual deed of cannibalism.

In England, the image of Irish savagery melts into a general representation of the gothicized poor. Here we have a double deployment roughly paralleling the duality of the cannibal taboo—one's fear of being eaten and the gorge-raising disgust at one's own, unwilling, participation in a cannibal feast. The underclass as imaged by the sensational press were alternatively represented either as criminal fiends or pauper victims— the former driven by a blood lust that produced both metaphoric and actual deeds of cannibalism, the latter fearing, we are told, a workhouse diet of the dissected bodies of deceased fellow paupers.

The cannibalistic savagery of the criminal insane formed a subgenre of the sensational Newgate Calendar story, from that of the Frenchwoman Mary Aubrey, hanged for killing and dissecting her English husband in the 1690's,[102] or of John Gregg of Clovelly in Devon, executed for having "emulated Sawney Beane" in 1740,[103] down to the sensational reports that Jack the Ripper removed and took away certain internal organs of the prostitutes he murdered.[104] Nor is the tradition, of course, an exclusively British one. In France, there is the infamous story of the cannibal brigand Blaise Ferrage in the mountains of the Aure, broken on the wheel in 1782 for robbing and then eating his victims. He preferred young women, on whose dead bodies he first satisfied his lust.[105]

While, as we shall see, such tales helped establish connections between, especially, sexual and criminal depravity and to associate both with poverty and deviant ethnicity, a subtler form of journalistic sensationalism employing the motif of criminal cannibalism was common in the English press from the 1850's on. Here the language used to describe the violent, brawling, often drunken behavior of usually working-class people brought before magistrates' courts often invokes the image of the cannibal to sensationalize class differences in England—an example of the fluid mobility of cannibal representation, which, having been exported, as it were, in order to gothicize the racial Other, flowed back again further to establish the depravity of the domestic subject.

In 1850 *The Times* reprinted an account from a provincial newspaper employing this mode of reportage. It was the story of a common beerhouse brawl involving, in fact, not overt cannibalism but all-in fighting and mutilation—the loss of an ear, a nose, the biting and tearing of the flesh of both defendant and complainant. But it was reported under the heading "Cannibalism" and represented as domestic brutality comparable to the objects of missionary activity abroad: "Wilder or more uncultured savages do not exist in any part of Africa than are to be found within a few miles of our homes."[106] This allusive manner of reporting violence in England became a commonplace in the second half of the century, apparently reflecting, not only journalistic irony, but the actual discourse of the courtroom itself. Another such story, involving bitten fingers, elicited a reprimand from the bench that the defendant "had been guilty of a disgraceful act of cannibalism unbecoming a man, much less an Englishman."[107] This metaphoric racialization of lower-class behavior can also be seen in philanthropic rhetoric as well, culminating, no doubt, in "General" William Booth's Salvation Army tract of 1890, *In Darkest England and the Way Out.*

Finally, there was the representation of the pauper class as cannibal victim. This took two forms. First, after the Anatomy Act of 1832, the corpses of the workhouse poor, along with those of criminals awaiting execution and hospital charity cases, were liable to become the subjects of medical school dissection. This was a fate greatly feared by the poor and attacked by their middle-class sympathizers as a kind of cannibalism. Ruth Richardson cites one such example in a cartoon attacking the Anatomy Bill of 1828, showing parts of human bodies hanging like butcher's meat outside a shop.[108] A darker evocation of cannibalism emerged after the New Poor Law Act and subsequent scandals over the provision of unsuitable or inadequate food in some unions, in a wide-spread fear among the poor themselves that workhouse food contained human remains, and that they were thus made unwitting cannibals. In *Sartor Resartus*, Carlyle develops this theme with Swiftian irony: the carcasses of the poor might be "salted and barrelled; could not you victual therewith, if not the Army and Navy, yet richly such infirm Paupers, in workhouses and elsewhere, as enlightened Charity, dreading no evil in them, might see good to keep alive?"[109] Even late in the century, a street ballad, "The Poor Workhouse Boy," still played on this idea.[110]

It is a short step from this suggestion of actual cannibalization of the working class—the cannibal cannibalized, as it were—to the larger motif of a cannibalizing political economy. This indeed became a familiar trope of the attack by both humanitarians and radicals on the emerging capitalist system, on an economic ideology that treated the human workforce as "hands," as dissected factors of production, on mill owners who "devoured" their labor, and on an urban environment portrayed as the excremental result of the "cannibal feast" of capitalist consumption. In 1795 Lambeth investigators were told of bodysnatchers who actually, rather than metaphorically, converted the material of the pauper workforce into commodities: "Human flesh has been converted into a substance like Spermacetti, and Candles made of it, and . . . Soap."[111]

Such representations of domestic exploitation both helped to shape and themselves received deeper confirmation from unfolding "knowledge" of savage peoples abroad. If the preservation and display of human heads in New Zealand suggested the barbarism of the Revolution, the growing *trade* in heads, encouraged by Europeans in the South Pacific, had its parallel in a contemporary gothic treatment of the sale of bodies and body parts for medical dissection in Paris and London (ill. 9).[112] A disturbing commodification of the human body—a metaphoric cannibalism—at home was thus readily complemented by representations of a yet more gruesome, but essentially homologous, trade among "real" cannibals abroad. Moreover, the two fields were drawn together by the common belief that the European merchant was instrumental in, if not initiating, at least extending and perpetuating the traffic ("it was not till Europeans proposed to buy [preserved heads], that the idea occurred to [the Maori] of preparing the heads of their enemies"). Like the upper-class surgeon who paid the resurrectionist or Burker, the European buying preserved heads in New Zealand was only a savage once removed: "How many of the savage sins of these savage islanders have been participated in by their European visitors!"[113]

In earlier centuries, it was the rural economy that provided a double cannibal metaphor, in the rude, antisocial, rustic existence of Sawney

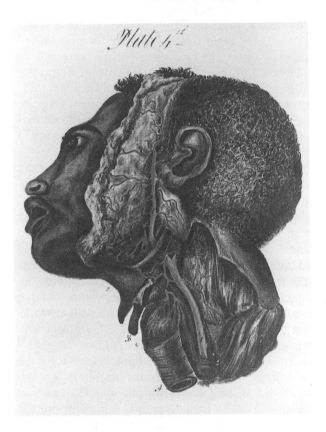

Ill. 9. Sir Charles Bell, *Manuscript of Drawings of the
Arteries:* "A Dissected Negro Head" (1797?) (National
Library of Medicine).

Beane, who had no notions of "Civil Society" and whose family belonged
to no "City, Town, or Village,"[114] or in the rapacious appetite of the en-
closing and engrossing landlord who, like Thomas Coke, could view the
depopulated scene round about his improved estate and say, "I am Giant,
of Giant's Castle, and have eat up all my neighbours." Although the landowner as vampire and cannibal lived on in the radical language of the
Anti–Corn Law League, for instance,[115] in the nineteenth century, it was
the urban bourgeois who metaphorically devoured the world, who imported beef from a starving Ireland, who turned the handle of Cruikshank's meatgrinder that processed seamstresses into cheap stuff for the
clothing trade (ill. 10), and who "partitioned" a cannibal Africa into mar-
kets that were represented as Christmas puddings or pies. The practice

TREMENDOUS SACRIFICE!

Ill. 10. George Cruikshank, "Tremendous Sacrifice" (1842) [British Museum].

of imperialism—which severed the colonized from his culture, dehumanized him, and reconstructed him as body parts, as working hands, broad back, large genitalia, and pearly teeth—was a form of dissection roughly analogous to the similar dismemberment and dehumanization of the domestic working class in the age of industrialization. In both cases, the cannibalism of the imperialist and the capitalist was projected upon a savage race.

The anthropologist Peggy Sanday has observed, "When projected onto enemies, cannibalism and torture become the means by which powerful threats to social life are dissipated. . . . In these cases cannibalism provides an idiom for deranged and antisocial behavior."[116] But in nineteenth-century domestic social discourse, the problem of just who was victim and who the cannibal often became confused. In *The French Revolution*, Thomas Carlyle suggested that the modern social system itself had become cannibalic, "based on the 'primitive' fact that 'I' can devour 'Thee'."[117] In such an omni-devouring culture, the working-class victim was also the working-class cannibal, an irony that Carlyle later, writing about the presumed killing of their own children by the poor to claim burial benefits, deployed with ambiguous effect:

> Our poor little Tom, who cries all day for victuals, who will see only evil and not good in this world: if he were out of misery at once; he well dead, and the rest of us perhaps kept alive? It is thought, and hinted; at last it is done. And now Tom being killed, and all spent and eaten, is it poor little starvling Jack that must go . . . ?[118]

WOMEN AND CANNIBALISM

Carlyle's powerful image of the cannibalized child also, of course, implies a cannibalizing mother, an emblem of the unnatural that grew in forcefulness as the Victorians refined the feminine ideal. Forty years after *Past and Present*, Carlyle's ironic association of domestic infant murder and cannibalism still found circulation in popular journalism: "If our mothers do not eat their dead children," as, *All the Year Round* assured its readers, was common practice among black cannibals abroad, "they do not scruple to kill them for a consideration."[119] But woman as child-eater was not an image confined to the allusive and metaphoric. The third edition of the *Encyclopedia Britannica* (1788–97) introduced (directly following an essay on the "depravity" of Sumatran cannibalism) a curious section on "Anthropophagia," a possibly "pretended" disease inducing some to hunger for human flesh. But the only example cited was that of a sixteenth-century Milanese woman whose "depraved" appetite led her to kill and salt children she had enticed into her house to eat. Of

Ill. 11. Antoine Wiertz, *Faim, folie, crime* (1853) (Wiertz Museum, Brussels).

interest here is the association of cannibal perversion abroad with feminine deceit (a "pretended" illness) and female psychology: her cannibal appetite, the article asserts, was "like what women with child, and those whose menses are obstructed, *frequently* experience."[120]

An act that in Europe might represent female illness and mental unbalance, as in the Belgian artist Antoine Wiertz's sensational painting of a deranged woman cooking her own child, *Faim, Folie, Crime* (1853), often becomes in the literature of exploration a means of delineating *normative* racial—that is, black female—character (ill. 11). For W. Cooke Taylor, writing in 1840, infanticide, "this fearful slaughter of innocent children," was *the* characteristic perversion of nature to be found commonly among uncivilized, non-Western peoples. And it was a custom, as he represented it, that was significantly perpetuated by the women:

The British government has made great efforts to abolish female infanticide among the Rajpoots in India . . . they have failed more from the resistance of the wives than of the husbands. . . . The mother commits the murder by rubbing poison on her breast, and the infant drinks the potion of death from the source where nature had planted the streams of life.[121]

In the South Pacific, the Reverend John Williams observed, not only was infanticide commonly practiced by women, but it was a neither shameful nor secret act: "We had a servant in our employ for fifteen years, who previously performed infanticide *as her trade.*"[122] So, too, in Schweinfurth's Africa, with the added horror of cannibalism: "The ill-fated little creature," exposed by a slave woman to die in the sun, "was destined to form a dainty dish . . . ready to be consigned to the seething cauldron! I profess that for a moment I was furious. I felt ready to shoot the old hag who sat by without displaying a particle of pity or concern."[123] "Infanticide" served as a powerful indictment of non-European peoples and as a common justification for imperialism. From Africa to Asia, from Fiji to New Zealand, where mothers callously threw their strangled infants "to the dogs or to the pigs,"[124] a defining characteristic of gothic barbarity was often gendered female.

In *Adam Bede*, Hetty Sorrel's stifling of her newborn infant is a woman's crime, which has, however, its countervailing opposite in Dinah Morris's virtue. They are contradictory but coexisting expressions of the feminine. Hetty herself is, of course, both victim and criminal, or rather, her criminality is the result of her seduction and her weak, if passionate, nature. Parallels with contemporary representation of the working class as a whole are obvious, and well focused by an overarching cannibal discourse that creates out of white male middle-class guilt and fear a double, contradictory image of women, the poor, and nonwhites as both man-eaten and man-eaters.

Woman as metaphoric cannibal *victim* is too commonplace in eighteenth- and nineteenth-century literature to require an elaborate proof. The old woman's tale of the cannibalization of the rumps of the harem women by starving Turks in *Candide* gives us woman as actual food, while Candide's beloved, the once-virginal Cunegonde, is food for another kind of appetite. The cliché of the rake of cannibal is an association made explicit in Richardson's *Clarissa*, where Lovelace, like Valmont in *Dangerous Liaisons* and countless others of the species, is a "notorious woman-eater," who belittles the milder rake Belford as a Hottentot "determined . . . to gluttonize on the garbage of other foul feeders."[125] In the marquis de Sade's violently misogynistic fantasies, of course, the metaphoric becomes literal. *Juliette* (1797), among endless scenes of torture and dismemberment, burning of spitted bodies and lapping of blood, includes a particularly graphic tale of cannibal lust, male domination, and, perhaps, class revenge. The tyrannical aristocrat and minister of state Saint-Fond has two lower-class women, first a young girl and then her mother, slowly beheaded while he sodomizes them, taking his pleasure from the spasmodic tightening of their anal muscles around his member as the razor cuts into their spinal cords. It is difficult not to read this piece as, in some sense, an inversion of the Terror. The underclass it is who are here guillotined, while Saint-Fond enjoys the mimicking sensation of having his penis seized but not severed (decapitation/castration?). His victims are then dissected, and their genitals, hung like butcher's meat, are intended for a cannibal feast—a direct, if unintended, parody of the "cannibal feast" of Gillray's sansculottes.[126]

Late-eighteenth- and early-nineteenth-century male fantasies of rape-as-cannibalism have a kind of parallel in the operating theaters and medical school dissection rooms (arenas of exclusively masculine authority). The female body, as Ludmilla Jordanova and Elaine Showalter have observed, was the object, like black bodies in the nineteenth century, of an Enlightenment enterprise of scientific penetration and dissection, a kind of colonial conquest of the mysteries of the vagina.[127] This cannibalism of the dissection room takes us also to the most graphic of nineteenth-century popular images of the woman as victim in accounts of the murder or suicide of the solitary, impoverished, "abandoned" female. Twelve of the sixteen victims for which Burke and Hare were prosecuted were women—poor vagrants and presumed prostitutes. Prostitute suicides might, in any event, legally end up on the dissection tables of London hospitals.[128]

Alain Corbin has argued that there existed in nineteenth-century discourse a strong identification of stinking corpse with prostitute, of the procurement of corpses with the procurement of women, of the danger of corpse contagion with that of venereal infection. In French vernacular, a working-class house of prostitution was a *maison d'abattage* (slaughterhouse).[129] The sadistic, and gothic, implications of such misogynistic associations were realized and confirmed most famously in the "Ripper" murders in London in the late 1880's, but something of the same acting-out of the *abattage* metaphor was dramatically available much earlier in the well-known (to the mid-nineteenth-century English) case of "Bertrand the Ghoul." François Bertrand, a noncommissioned officer in the 1st Infantry, French Army, was tried in 1849 for breaking into graves in Paris and tearing apart the bodies of women and girls.[130]

Early-nineteenth-century gothic fiction characteristically makes explicit what is implied in the "devouring gaze" of the male observer of the unprotected female body, turning male fantasy into a literary literalness—Varney the Vampyre's midnight laceration of virginal flesh and sucking of virginal blood. In Reynold's *Mysteries of London*, the resurrectionist's search for bodies for medical dissection is directly joined with the erotic and sadistic in a story of the robbing of the recent grave of a sixteen-year-old girl. Her coffin is poked with a long iron rod, which the body-snatcher then tastes, under the anxious gaze of an upper-class surgeon—a scene redolent with cannibalism, necrophilia, and voyeurism. "The Body-Snatchers' Song" completes the image of the woman as cannibal victim:

> For the student doth his knife prepare
> To hack all over this form so fair,
>   And sever the virgin limb from limb! [131]

If the cannibalism here seems only vaguely allusive, compare Reynolds's gothic text with an exactly parallel image of the explicit cannibalization of a woman in "The Ballad of the Brig *George*" of 1822. Here an actual event of maritime survival cannibalism was sensationalized for the London public by placing the destruction of a woman's corpse (although five men were also eaten) as the centerpiece of horror:

> Her body then they did dissect
> Most dreadful for to view
> And serv'd it out in pieces
> Amongst the whole ship's crew [132]

The most obvious deployment of these sadistic images in colonial and racial discourse is no doubt the representation of the vulnerable white woman on the frontier, susceptible to being scalped and raped, if not actually cannibalized by ferocious nonwhite males. In the eighteenth century, there was the American staple of the white Englishwoman threatened by demonic Indian braves, who were often also accused of a sadistic and symbolic cannibalism, motivated by revenge and encouraged by their French allies. In the nineteenth century, the cannibal threat moved on to yet more exotic realms. The escape on the northwestern coast of Australia of Eliza Fraser from a cannibal fate in 1836 was sensationalized in London broadsheets and press. [133] This came at a time when the South Pacific was being established in the popular mind as a cannibal field— through the mutually reinforcing stories of early exploration, the *white* cannibalism associated with convicts and sailors, and the appeals of Fiji missionaries.

Of equal interest is the image of the nonwhite female victim within "native" culture as constructed by Westerners in the nineteenth century. The plight of the Indian widow as a justification for white rule in south

Asia finds some resonance in the developing discourse of the cannibal South Pacific. William Mariner's account of the Tonga Islands, published in 1817, tells of four brothers who kill and eat their aunt—although he discounts the crime as a recently learned custom (!) imported from Fiji.[134] Another early account of the Maori treated its readers to a more salacious story of the killing, dismembering, exhuming, and eating of a sixteen-year-old runaway slave girl.[135] It was, however, the flood of accounts from the 1830's to the 1850's of the presumed cannibalism of the Fiji islanders that most securely established the popular cannibal cliché.

Although, as we shall see, some white observers dwelt luridly enough on the rapacious appetite of the female cannibal, Thomas Williams's influential account of the Methodist mission in the Fiji islands does not. He maintains that, although women played an important role in the wild and obscene ceremonies prior to the feast, they seldom themselves tasted *bakolo*, or human flesh. According to Williams, women were, along with tender children, more likely themselves to be eaten. He includes a vivid (inevitably secondhand) tale of a woman who was taken from a besieged town by a savage chief, who had her placed in a large wooden dish and cut up alive, "that none of the blood might be lost." Elsewhere a native man improbably murdered his wife merely in order to eat her, and another chief had a woman of his own village cooked up as a treat for a visiting American seaman.[136] It was a type of sensational story that could not be contained by the Fijian experience, and wandered throughout the missionary-constructed South Pacific: "This horrid cruelty is practised towards those who in civilized communities are objects of the most endearing affection. The husband has preyed upon the body of his wife, and the parent upon the child, in a most revolting manner."[137] And so to other realms. A few years later, the French missionaries Arbousset and Daumas reported that a tribe of Bechuana cannibals in southern Africa "eat their own wives and children, and exchange them with each other."[138]

It is, of course, impossible to tell from this distance in time where gothic fantasy ends in such tales and reality might begin. For our purposes it is sufficient to point out that the rhetorical strategy of establishing the victimization of women served to deepen the unnatural depravity of the observed (masculine) racial order, while reserving a (feminine) area of racial vulnerability to justify intervention and protection. As Mary Douglas has argued in her study of the concepts of pollution and taboo, nineteenth-century Western observers felt compelled to construct primitive societies defined by disorder and anomie, based upon force and appetite and regulated, to the extent that they were "societies" at all, by mere "fear, terror, or dread."[139] This gothic reading of non-European peoples was heightened and further sensationalized, then, by dwelling upon the vulnerability of women as perpetual victims in a demonic world. Of course, such representations involve a projection of Westerners' apprehension at the social and political dissolution of their own urban-industrial system, a system Marx described in terms of cannibalism and vampirism.

At an even deeper level, there is also undoubtedly in these stories of the sadistic devouring of women by nonwhites a sexual as well as social projection of white, European, male desire and obsession. The very fluidity of the woman-as-cannibal-victim genre—its surfacing in the narratives of very different places and peoples—suggests a location as much in the interior of the observer as in the culture of the observed. These stories "travel," like a cannibal joke that was, it appears, first told about a Maori in New Zealand, but subsequently made its way into the table-talk lore of Africa. A chief with two wives is asked by a bishop to "put one of them away" before he can be baptized. He returns and says he has done so. He has eaten her.[140] The mobility of such a tale rests, of course, on the interchangeable nature of the racial primitive anywhere as inherently cannibal. But it also suggests a contemporary male anxiety. This is, after all, what makes it "work" as humor—how to deal with wandering desire, with "too many women," with the difficulty of "putting away" one wife for another.

When cannibal discourse shifted to Africa after mid-century, however, there is generally less emphasis on the female native as cannibal victim. Indeed, Africa as a whole was by some visualized as Amazonian-feminine, where gender relations were reversed in the realm of the cannibal queen. Such a representation conformed to a masculine exploration of her dark, dangerous spaces. If Africa was in some sense female, then her penetration and partition by the white man was itself a form of rape and white cannibalism. H. Rider Haggard seems to suggest as much in the sexual geography of *King Solomon's Mines*, where the mountains beyond the desert are Sheba's Breasts, with the treasure cave further down the road between them. Twenty years earlier, Winwood Reade had deployed another kind of feminized image: "Look at the map of Africa. Does it not resemble a woman with a huge burden on her back, and with her face turned towards America?"[141]

A female Africa was not, however, an invention of the Victorians. There was a literary tradition—most sharply expressed perhaps in the late-eighteenth-century works of those who, like Crabbe, sympathized with the abolition movement—that commonly represented suffering Africa as a mother mourning the loss of her sons, or a maiden the loss of her beloved. Perceptions of Africa as female may have been reinforced by the passivity imposed on males by the condition of slavery. Moreover, the early explorers were often struck by the hairless, feminine beauty of African men, as well as by the gender-reversing fact that women did much of the agricultural labor. For some, the deep beauty of polished ebony provided a sexual and romantic association with nubile African bodies. In *The Prelude*, Wordsworth imagines among the London throng, "Negro Ladies in white muslin gowns."[142] Earlier he had employed a figure of a "white-robed Negro," cruelly deported from France, as feminized image of an oppressed people—"like a lady gay, Yet downcast as a woman fearing blame."[143]

In *Savage Africa* there is a curious passage in which Winwood Reade tells of his hunting and killing a gazelle. The animal is represented graphically as both human and female—"One of those pretty little creatures" with "great startled eyes."[144] When, after shooting "her," he ran up to the body, "flushed with murderous excitement to take her up, she turned upon me those eyes, those tender eyes . . . her poor little body shook convulsively, and then with one low womanish wail, her soul . . . left the body. . . . We had her cutlets dressed *à la papillote*. Exquisite as her beauty, I ate them to indigestion."[145] The reversal here, the white hunter as cannibal, is intended for ironic, almost comic effect, although Reade perhaps reveals more of himself than he intended. Earlier in the same book, he recounts his own sexual attraction to a black girl, whom he impulsively kisses, in language that leaves no doubt about the parallelism of the passages: "She gave a shriek, and bounded from the house like a frightened fawn. . . . The poor child had thought that I was going to dine off her."[146]

> When you're wounded and left on Afghanistan's plains,
> And the women come out to cut up what remains,
> Jest roll to your rifle and blow out your brains. . . .
> —Kipling, "The Young British Soldier"

The counterpoint to the image of woman as cannibal victim is that of the cannibalizing woman; against Haggard's female Africa supinely awaiting penetration in *King Solomon's Mines*, there is juxtaposed the Africa of Haggard's *She*, with its Amazonian threat of reverse imperialism. Here, too, there is pre-Victorian precedent in an imaging of Africa that, in contrast to Crabbe and Wordsworth, dwelt on neither innocence nor victimization, but on danger and entrapment—akin, perhaps to the tradition of the beautiful but syphilitic prostitute. S. M. X. de Golbery's *Travels* of 1803 personified Africa as a woman holding a cornucopia and a scorpion—a promise of fecundity and treasure on the one hand and of poison and death on the other.[147] Similarly, Winwood Reade's Africa combines the attractiveness of the nubile sexuality of his gazelle/black girl and the unnatural threat of the cannibal queen. Like the reciprocating images of Madonna and Magdalene, they are both contradictory and complementary.

Male fantasies of domination coexist with fears of castration, suggested perhaps in the knife-wielding camp followers of *Henry V* or in Kipling's verse above.[148] In the era of revolution and romanticism, the inspiring image of Marianne on the barricades has her debased alter-image in the demonic harridan, a snakey-haired Gorgon in one well-known print,[149] urging men on to acts of barbarism and vengeance. The guillotine was portrayed as a cannibal mistress—later, Dickens's "devouring and insatiate" female monster. If, as Freud maintained, decapitation suggests castration, La Guillotine's blade is emblematic of an explicitly sexual element, of an uneasy middle-class male fear of vulnerability, of woman as masculine aggressor, of woman-as-cannibal. There would, for instance, seem to be some such message in Cruikshank's well-known comic representation of an animated guillotine pursuing the English Establishment. Although above the waist, as it were, the machine appears masculine in its fierce grimace, below, the bleeding hole, through which one can see the grinning teeth of a death's head, is a graphically female sexual image of the entrapping and devouring *vagina dentata* (ill. 12). From this it is but a short step to the Fatal Woman, the beautiful but deadly Medusa or Belle Dame sans Merci, whom Mario Praz has identified as a key component of the nineteenth-century "romantic agony," to the image of the "sexual cannibalism," as he termed it, of Théophile Gautier's Cleopatra as feminine type.[150]

It is of some interest for our purposes that before the cannibal queen emerged as an African racial image, the devouring instrument of the excesses of the Revolution was gendered as female; or that the English bookseller James Caulfield chose as his subject for a sensational engraving of 1798 the story of Mary Aubrey, a Frenchwoman who had dismembered her English husband a century earlier. The story of the tattered women of Paris who marched to Versailles ("ces femme cannibales," as Burke called them, quoting Lally Tollendal)[151] resonated, at least among the English middle class, with such images, as well as with those of the cannibalistic hags who populated their gothic novels.

William Godwin's *Caleb Williams* features one such malignant fury in the robbers' crone, a single example among many: "Not the milk of human kindness, but the feverous blood of savage ferocity seemed to flow from her heart; and her whole figure suggested an idea of unmitigable energy, and an appetite gorged in malevolence." Her ferocity is ex-

Ill. 12. George Cruikshank, "A Radical Reformer" (1819) (British Museum).

plicitly that of the cannibal: "I will thrust my fingers through your ribs, and drink your blood! . . . I will roast you with brimstone, and dash your entrails into your eyes!"[152] Her direct descendent a generation later is the body-snatcher's mother-accomplice in *The Mysteries of London*, a "hideous old woman who considered corpses an article of commerce" and who is called "the mummy" by her son.[153]

Such literary gothic easily crosses into the rhetoric of exploration and race in the early nineteenth century. Observe, for instance, the language of Francis Parkman on the Oregon Trail. A trapper who has taken to wife an Indian woman must feed a "rapacious horde" of her relatives who, "like leeches," "drain all he has." Her brother is "all mouth" with a "ravenous" appetite "in proportion," but it is her ancient mother, "the moving spirit of the establishment," who focuses the cannibal nature of these nonwhites. She is "a hideous old hag of eighty. Human imagination never conceived hobgoblin or witch more ugly than she. You could count all her ribs through the wrinkles of the leathery skin that covered them. Her withered face more resembled an old skull than the countenance of a living being, even to the hollow, darkened sockets, at the bottom of which glittered her little black eyes."[154]

Such masculinized and gothicized old women draw from folktale traditions of the evil crone and sadistic stepmother. They stand in contrast, perhaps, to the cruel but beautiful temptresses, cannibals of the male soul, of the fin de siècle, to Stoker's Lucy Westenra or Haggard's She. These are anticipated, however, not only in the de Sade–inspired exoticism of the French romantics, of especially Gautier and Flaubert, but in many minor pieces of early and mid-century English gothic—as, for instance, in Frederick Marryat's story of a "weir wolf" woman who is *both* beautiful vamp and sadistic stepmother (1839). Like the folktale gypsy lad's widow-bride, she is discovered in the graveyard cannibalizing the corpse of her stepchild, "tearing off large pieces of the flesh, and devouring them with all the avidity of a wolf," and her punishment is decapitation.[155]

If nineteenth-century female gothic drew upon folktale sources of werewolves, vampires, and evil stepmothers, it also had a contemporary, industrial locus. Reynolds invokes the female barbarian in his descriptions of young slum women, in a gendered version of the common nineteenth-century savages-here-at-home representation of urban poverty. "Termagants" fighting each other in the Smithfield stews "lacerate themselves with fists and nails in a fearful manner." Partially naked and disheveled, they have a "wild, ferocious, and savage appearance, such as I never could have expected to encounter in the metropolis of the civilised world." Female poverty is further constructed as primitive savagery in his comment elsewhere on the naked and blackened bodies of female miners, "eating, laughing, chattering" with "no shame—no embarrassment!"[156] There is more here than the savagery of the starving pauper or uneducated and violent plebeian. There is a uniquely female sexual element in a Western tradition that moves back and forth between the metaphorical and the actual, between folktale and modern, between the domestic arena and the colonial—from Burke's "ces femmes cannibales" to an amateur anthropologist's assertion in 1880 that women "have larger teeth than men *relative* to the cranio-facial axis," and that [cannibal] Africans, Fijians, and Australian aborigines had the largest "dental index" of all.[157]

Representations of female cannibalism, white or black, may owe something to an association drawn from the disjointing and cooking kitchen duties of the working-class woman, as well as from the ungovernable bestial/hysterical sexuality that European medicine ascribed to its own womankind: "Those who have been so accustomed to prepare a human body for a meal . . . with as little feeling cut up a dead man, as our cook-maids divide a dead rabbit for a fricassee."[158] Certainly the female murderess, especially when her crime was marital homicide, was invested in popular culture with a particular deviancy—fully the equivalent of the cannibal taboo. When, in 1884, Madame Tussaud's did a waxwork of Captain Dudley of the *Mignonette*, who had eaten his cabin boy, it was exhibited in the Chambre of Horrors together with one of Mrs. Gibbons, who had killed her husband.[159] Finally, to return to the story of Sawney Beane, it is notable that, although Sawney was the head of the cannibal clan, it is his wife and daughters who are portrayed as the most depraved.[160] It will be obvious that the emphasis in the several versions of the story on the dark labyrinth of the clan's refuge, the treasure at its bottom and the dead meat, the cannibalized carcasses, suspended from its roof, provide a sexualized locus of cannibal danger as suggestively female as the "cannibal caves" of Arbusset and Daumas or Haggard's King Solomon's mine. A vivid passage in the most dramatic version of the Sawney Beane tale presents a stark contrast between a woman as idealized victim and the hellish, cave-dwelling fiends of Sawney's clan: "In the Conflict the poor Woman fell from behind him, and was instantly murdered before her Husband's Face; for the Female *Cannibals* cut her Throat, and fell to sucking her Blood with as great a Gust, as if it had been Wine. This done, they ript up her Belly, and pulled out all her Entrails."[161]

In the mid eighteenth century, the sensational story of Pierre Viaud's adventures on the wild American coast, translated into several English versions, offered a singularly colorful and ironic statement of the theme of female appetite. Marooned on a desert island with a Negro slave and a respectable bourgeois woman, Madame la Couture, Viaud faces starvation. Madame la Couture suggests the solution, however, calling to Viaud with "feeble tone of voice" and turning her expressive female eyes, full of "impatience," toward the Negro. This becomes more than a tale of starvation cannibalism at this point, for in her lust for the Negro's flesh, Madame seems to express more than hunger—there is an "eagerness" for the job at hand, and she assists "readily" in holding down the slave and in butchering him.[162]

Even more suggestive of the fury-under-the-skin is the "true story" of Ann Saunders, another survivor of maritime cannibalism, which was sensationalized in the London press and broadsheets. In 1826 the crew and passengers of the *Francis Mary* were forced to cannibalism. But Ann Saunders is represented in a particularly gothic manner. She herself cuts the throat of her betrothed, the ship's cook, and drinks his blood. Possessed of fiercer strength than the men, she performs the part of boat's butcher on the corpses that are eaten. Another version of this story gives her an even more demonic cast: she "shrieked a loud yell . . . and drank his blood." Another woman on board also survived and is supposed to have remarked that the brains of an apprentice were "the [most] delicious thing she had ever tasted."[163] From such elements of the savage white woman in domestic discourse, we can turn to the black cannibal woman of nineteenth-century imperialism.

As in the English use of both the female victim and the gallic virago to distance and demonize events in revolutionary France, colonial discourse in the early nineteenth century emphasizes a double image of native womanhood in order to represent primitivism abroad. There were, of course, elements of this usage from the earliest periods of colonial expansion, but the strategy becomes more insistent in the early nineteenth century as the English domestic ideal of a dependent, childlike femininity became more deeply rooted in romantic, middle-class ideology. Almost all period narratives invoke the condition and character of women to establish the uncivilized character of "native" culture.[164] This can result in a contradictory representation—sometimes in the same text—of the native woman as both victim and savage aggressor. At some level, the nakedness of the female body in these societies, and certainly sexually explicit rituals, played a role, suggesting in the mind of the European male observer the shamelessness of the pauper-slut or the disheveled hysteria of the madwoman.

The image of women as active participants in savage, cannibalistic ritual plays a powerful role in much of the early nineteenth-century discussion of aboriginal life in Australasia. The narratives of Mrs. Fraser's survival among cannibals in the 1830s offer a characteristically sensational contrast between her own passive strength of endurance and the active and malicious strength of the native women, who "appear to be more cruel to those in their power than the men." In his highly colored, illustrated account of "the horrible barbarity of the Cannibals inflicted upon the Captain's Widow," John Curtis stresses aboriginal female "cruelty," while musing that this may result from their own hardhearted treatment at the hands of aboriginal males. He retails a secondhand account of the discovery of a man's thigh in a native woman's bag of provisions.[165] At best, native women were indifferent to the suffering of others. At worst, they encouraged torture and sadism in the cannibal feast— often, like witches on their Sabbath or the women of Paris, abandoning themselves to a wild, dancing participation in the rites of the cannibal orgy, polluting and humiliating those whom the men had killed or captured.

This view is strongly expressed in the Australasian narratives that were so important in Victorian Britain in establishing the cannibal as racial image. Early eyewitness accounts of aboriginal "corrobbories," drinking and dancing rituals, easily slip in the retelling into graphic, if imaginary, descriptions of "feasts upon the dead," where it is the women who "chaunt songs or dirges, and strike upon the thighs with the palms of their hands by way of accompaniment."[166] In Fiji, the overt sexuality of the women's dancing, especially during rituals celebrating the return of war parties with prisoners and the bodies of the slain, was particularly disturbing to missionary observers, and was seen by them as a mere preliminary to a cannibal feast: "I think nothing connected with these sickening scenes is more revolting than the part which the women take."[167] Even when apparently peaceful and pleasant, native life was, in their view, seriously diseased by this usually hidden vice. Cannibalism perverted and unbalanced all other aspects of life like a narcotic addiction or a sexual obsession—both closely associated with female weakness in nineteenth-century European discourse. Then, in the frenzied moment of revenge and appetite, and especially in the wild celebrations of the women, all the inherent anarchy, all that was Dionysian and abandoned in primitive nature, rushed to the surface. Even when they did not directly participate in the eating, it is the women whom the missionaries use to focus the unnaturalness, the explosion of the irrational and the hypersexual, in these societies: "The words of the women's song may not be translated; nor are the obscene gestures of their dance . . . or the foul insults offered to the corpses of the slain, fit to be described."[168]

Conventional Victorian prudery in, not only missionary relations, but exploration and ethnographic accounts of native ritual, served, of course, merely to heighten a prurient reading—to offer a mysterious and deviant sexuality, as veiled as the cannibal deed itself, to the imagination of the expectant European public: "A perfectly full as well as faithful description would be impossible, in the interests of modesty and good taste"; "the first part of the operation [of cutting up the bodies of the slain] must, I am afraid, be left undescribed"; "We do not, and we cannot, tell you all that we know of Feegeean cruelty and crimes"; "the peculiarities attending [the torture] . . . are not only diabolical, but too indelicate to detail"; "The horrid feasting on human flesh which followed would be too shocking for description."[169]

Such language anticipates the "surrogate pornography" that Nancy Stepan has ascribed to late-nineteenth-century anthropology.[170] It also resonates with, and may in fact draw upon, a well-established European fascination with the mixture of violence, licentiousness, and sexual perversity long associated not least in the gothic literary tradition, with the religious customs of the East, and with the Indian subcontinent in particular. Diffusionist theories of the spread and mixture of South Pacific peoples encouraged such a borrowing. G. W. Rusden, for instance, gave credence in his substantial *History of New Zealand* of 1883 to such an interpretation:

> The savage acts of the sect which worshiped Siva and the ferocious Kali were emulated in New Zealand, and the carvings of the Maoris might be adduced to show that the Lingamhari of Hindostan had taught the sea-rovers of the Pacific those obscene rites which defiled the Dionysiac festivals in Greece, and which two thousand years ago were suppressed in Rome with a vigour and a care which demonstrated the conviction of the Senate that the corruption was widespread and the danger terrible.[171]

Others saw in "sensual love of human flesh" as well as in the abandonment to revenge a confirmation of the "childishness" of primitive races everywhere. In words echoing Canning's characterization of the freed Jamaican slave as a kind of Frankenstein's Monster, Arthur Thomson, surgeon-major of the 58th Regiment in New Zealand, averred that the Maori had "the minds of children and the passions of men."[172]

The theme plays differently, though, as one moves around the Pacific. The New Zealanders were commonly thought to be of a superior, lighter-skinned, possibly south Asian race in their origins, and however perverted and childlike, their society was seen to be one of custom, hierarchy, and domestic order. Out among the islands, particularly among the New Guinea headhunters and the Fijian cannibals, who were held by many to be "Negroes," anarchy and appetite were thought to dominate. Accounts of their cannibalism-as-sadistic-sexuality depicts, not so much custom or ritual, as the breakdown of whatever thin social order they may have possessed, with the abandonment of reason, a frenzied insanity lasting as long as there was human flesh to be eaten. Women are used in such stories to force an inevitable association of depraved sexual appetite with the cannibal appetite, much as "abnormal" male sexuality, sodomy, had earlier played a similar role in European stories of the Iroquois and the Aztecs: "On these occasions, the ordinary social restrictions are destroyed, and the unbridled and indiscriminate indulgence of every lust and passion completes the scene of abomination."[173]

The sensational frisson that stories of female participation in cannibal feasts offered a Victorian audience made such tales a tempting device in any account of the exotic, even when far removed from missionary Fiji.

By mid-century, it can creep egregiously into a narrative like that of H. W. Bates's *The Naturalist on the River Amazons*, a work on the whole concerned more with flora, fauna, and geography than with Indian savagery. Mentioning the probable cannibalism, however, of the Majeronas, Bates pauses to tell the story in anecdotal dinner-table style, of "an artless maiden" taken into service in São Paulo, whose ways were "like those of a careless, laughing country wench, such as might be met with any day among the labouring classes in villages in our own country." Yet she related to him "in the coolest manner possible, how she ate a portion of the bodies of the young men whom her tribe had roasted."[174] One gender devouring the other inevitably raises a sexual reading, intended or not, and the reader's unanswered question must follow: which portion "of the bodies of the young men" did she relish most? The text also contains for the European reader a subtext of feminine deceit, of Thackeray's Becky Sharpe as man-eater under a charming surface.

The image of the black female cannibal received perhaps its definitive expression, certainly the most colorful, in Winwood Reade's account, in *Savage Africa*, of a supposed cannibal queen in the heart of central Africa (ill. 13).[175] There had been persistent legends, if not of female cannibalism, at least of Amazonian warriors in West Africa. But Reade's story, taken, he says, on the authority of a Catholic missionary, Father Cavazzi, is presented as fact and, indeed, forms the basis for an extended argument about African sexual identity and character.

Reade's representation of African women is complicated and contradictory. His sympathetic portraits of the beautiful maiden he kissed and of the women he met with generally in Equatorial Africa—"affectionate and caressing, anxious to please," but not particularly "libidinous"—dramatically clashes with that of the "African Messalina," Tembandumba, warrior daughter of a Congolese warrior queen, Mussasa. The mother was "extremely cruel and bloodthirsty" but the daughter is a gothic model of sexual excess and sadism. "A lion in war, she became a tigress in passion; savage in her wantonness—at once voluptuous and bloodthirsty." Matriarchy is secured by the systematic killing of male children. Fierce sexual appetite is served by a "crowd of lovers" (men captured in battle), each of whom she first uses to satiate her lust and then kills "with the cruelest tortures." Their bodies, and those of other captive males who also serve for tribal procreation before being killed, then perform a further service: "The sustenance of her subjects should be the flesh of man; his blood should be their drink."[176] The unnaturalness of the cannibal act is used here to amplify the unnaturalness of matriarchy, which in turn furthers the construction of an inherent perversity in the African race itself.

Ill. 13. W. Winwood Reade, *Savage Africa* (1863):
"The Queen of the Cannibals."

It is obvious that Reade's queen is a fantasy of European romanticism (with a touch of de Sade).[177] She draws directly from the literary type of whom Gautier's Cleopatra was the exemplar—a praying mantis who kills her lover; one night of pleasure, "a supreme orgie," then death.[178] It is an entertaining story in a book full of anecdotal digression. This particular tale of cannibalism and female sexual perversity lies at the center of Reade's racial perception, however—just as the kingdom of Tembandumba lies at the heart of his dark continent. The contrast between the maiden and the cannibal, between the dying gazelle and the killing sadist, Reade suggests, can be understood as universal female contradiction: "It is commonly said that women are always at extremes."[179] Yet this always being at extremes is also the character he has discovered generally in the Negro race. The character of a lesser race is here directly analogous to that of the lesser sex.

The further strategy of the tale of the cannibal queen is, then, to draw attention to a general and perverse inversion of sexual character in Africa. Others before Reade had commented on the apparent reversal of masculine and feminine roles in Africa. Livingstone had drawn attention to stories of female chiefs in the African interior, and two years after Reade's account, he published his own narrative of an expedition to the Zambesi, in which he noted that "it was long ago remarked, that in Africa everything was contrary . . . the women till the land, plant the corn, and build the huts. The men stay at home to sew, spin, weave, and talk."[180] Reade sexualizes this paradox by counterpointing the womanly man to the cannibal queen: "But if the women of Africa are brutal, the men of Africa are feminine." This goes beyond the apparent inversion of work and leisure roles, or aggressive and passive characters. For Reade this sexual reversal is also physiological: the men's "faces are smooth; their breasts are frequently as full as those of European women; their voices are never gruff or deep."[181]

Reade's descriptions of beautiful, even "delicate," African men serve a double purpose here. On the one hand, their character, both physical ("gracefully moulded limbs . . . elegantly formed") and social ("While the women are stupid, sulky, and phlegmatic, the men are vivacious, timid, inquisitive, and garrulous"), makes the black male, clean and meticulous, a naturally "excellent domestic servant." On the other, their feminine natures point to a racial exoticism (analogous to that of the European homosexual) that directly parallels the unnaturalness of the man-eating cannibal queen. The image of the African male as an exotic with an essentially feminine sensuality was hardly uncommon in European romance. The year before Reade published *Savage Africa*, Flaubert, in his bizarre portrait of ancient sensual cruelty, *Salammbô*, had presented the black prince Narr'Havas in such terms: "The Numidian, stroking the ostrich plume which fell down on his shoulder, rolled his eyes like a woman and smiled irritatingly."[182]

The beauty of the African male evokes in Reade himself an ambivalent and troubled response: "While no African's face ever yet reminded me of a man whom I had known in England, I saw again and again faces which reminded me of women." On one occasion a black man he was about to strike ("chastise") "sank on his knees as I raised my stick, clasped his hands, and looking up imploringly towards me, was so like a young lady I had once felt an affection for, that in spite of myself I flung the stick away. . . . I have seen men whose form and features would disgrace no petticoats—not even satin ones at a drawing-room."[183]

On the most obvious level, this simply serves to signify the "otherness" of the non-European, to degrade by association with familiar negative domestic stereotypes and prejudices—with chattering women and effeminate men: "They have also their friendships after the manner of women, embracing one another, sleeping on the same mat, telling one another their secrets, betraying them, and getting terribly jealous of one another."[184] On a deeper level, however, the strategy is more complex. Reade's description, crafted as it is to place the observed African male in a particular relationship to Reade, the white observer, promotes a relationship of dependency that anticipates a yielding, and therefore attractive, character in the black male. As elsewhere in the Victorian empire, a male world of intense homosocial relationships and fantasies, desire and domination, become confused. In 1862 the anthropologist Berthold Seemann advised future tourists in Fiji to forget about the wilder stories of "repulsive" and "bloodthirsty" natives. They could expect the attentions of nearly nude youths in an Edenic idyll: "Let those dark-eyed boys fan you; they do it with pleasure."[185] Reade's own position as both imperialist and narrator remains consistently that of aggressor, a penetrator of African darkness. In this, the challenge posed by the feminized African male is no different from that facing a Lovelace or a Valmont—how to circumvent the defenses of the weaker race/sex: "They [African men] know how to render themselves impenetrable; and if they desire to be perfidious, they wear a mask, which few eyes can see through."[186]

If, in Reade's text, it is the African man whose sexual ambivalence and seduction symbolize the potential the continent offers to the European of a passive servitude, it is the African woman who symbolizes finally the timeless mystery, danger, darkness, disease, and inferiority of the continent and the race. Forgetting perhaps his earlier portrayal of the feminine beauty of young African maidens, his denial of a general libidinousness among African women, or his own admission that Amazonian tyrants like Tembandumba were not "frequently to be met with," Reade reverts to the feminine to focus the animality of the continent, curiously anticipating Freud's later assertion that female sexuality is the "dark continent of the human psyche."[187] African women were "more nearly approaching the brute" than the African male, they were "always a step lower in the scale." Closer to the beast, they were, "according to some authors," excessively lascivious. African women had less shame than men, and he had seen them wash their private parts in public.[188]

This last observation can be compared, for instance, with the testimony of Edward Newman, a Barnsley solicitor, to the Children's Employment Commission in 1842 that he had seen pit girls in the coal mines of England "washing themselves naked below the waist."[189] Both texts fix upon a presumed lack of female modesty to assert a quite parallel racial and class "otherness" or deviancy and (cannibal or proletarian) threat. But the social threat of race and class is also a gendered threat, involving perhaps a specifically male anxiety. Gautier's Cleopatra must enjoy but then kill the beautiful youth who has seen her standing naked at her bath.[190] Freud speculated that it was a boy's first sight of female genitals, "the terror of the Medusa," that inspires fears of his own castration.[191] Some such connection seems suggested in Reade's turning the tables, as it were, by regarding the African custom of clitoridectomy as a kind of female castration that was rendered necessary by the ungovernable sexuality of African women, a (masculine) aggression that commonly, he assures his reader, drifted into lesbianism and produced *elongatio nympharum.*[192]

Furthermore, echoing the association of cannibalism as a disease with feminine physiology found in the *Encyclopedia Britannica* of 1797, Reade brings together disease, skin color, and female sexuality in a gothicized portrayal of abnormality: "I am inclined to believe that the black hue of the negro answers to the livid colour among us; that it is the colour of disease." His argument here turns away from Africa to establish itself in the familiar prejudices of the European tradition that equated menstruation and pregnancy itself with illness. Chief among the proofs that a dark complexion "often results in Europeans from a disordered constitution" was the fact, he says, that "women frequently become brown during pregnancy; there are few cases in which the *mammae* are not encircled by a dark tinge. Cases have been known in which the abdomen has become completely black."[193]

At last, Reade constructs the African continent itself as female gothic: "a Woman whose features, in expression, are sad and noble, but which have been degraded, distorted, and rendered repulsive by disease." In a remarkable extended analogy, he joins the exotic landscape, the miasmal swamps, and deadly diseases that characterized the romantic's vision of Africa as a perverted garden of Eden with the European's misogynistic characterization of the repulsiveness of female odors and, beneath the beauty, female sickness and sexual contamination. Two centuries earlier, the poet Abraham Cowley had represented Africa as Chaos, but the light of civilization flowed "from the old Negro's darksome womb."[194] For Reade, the darksome womb yielded only a poisoned and deformed progeny. Africa is a woman,

> whose breath is perfumed by rich spices and by fragrant gums; yet through all steals the stench of the black mud of the mangroves, and the miasma of the swamps. Whose lap is filled with gold, but beneath lies a black snake. . . . From whose breasts stream milk and honey, mingled with poison and with blood.
>
> Whose head lies dead and cold, and yet is alive. In her horrible womb

heave strange and monstrous embryos. Swarming round her are thousands of her children, whose hideousness inspires disgust, their misery compassion.

She kisses them upon the lips, and with her own breath she strikes them corpses by her side. . . . Thus for ages and ages, this woman has continued to bring forth her children; and to kill them as she attempts to nourish them.[195]

In 1871, *The Times* reported, via the New York press, a story of gothic, racial, and female cannibalism from Jamaica. A Negro woman, "of highly respectable character" was accused of killing and eating 26 children.[196] Such an account inevitably operated on several levels. It used a perversion of feminine nature—nurturing mother turned cannibal—to assert a racial depravity, at a time when colonial rule in Jamaica had been seriously disturbed by black demands for democratic reforms and Governor Edward Eyre's vicious repression of G. W. Gordon's "rebellion." Here, as in the American South after the Civil War, sensational stories of black primitivism served to reestablish the legitimacy of white control. Whatever their basis in fact or fiction, such tales—of Obeah women in Jamaica and Reade's Congo cannibal queen—inevitably manipulated meanings embedded in the culture of the observer. Forty years earlier, in the English industrial city of Manchester, an angry crowd had attacked a house and seriously injured those within because of rumors that a woman there was kidnapping children to use as filling for veal pies.[197] For the English reader, the cannibal torture of children in proletarian Manchester or black Jamaica made the alien unknown recognizable by attaching it to the (gothic) familiar, to the European popular myths of folktale stepmothers, suspect pie sellers, Jewish blood libel, and the sexual sadism of the criminal insane.

DEVIANT CANNIBALS: CONVICTS AND SAILORS

> "You young dog," said the man, licking his lips, "What fat cheeks you ha' got. . . . Darn Me if I couldn't eat em. . . . You get me a file. . . . And you get me wittles. . . . Or I'll have your heart and liver out. . . . You fail, or you go from my words in any partikler, no matter how small it is, and your heart and your liver shall be tore out, roasted and ate."[198]
>
> — The convict Magwitch to Pip

There remain for discussion two notables areas of white cannibalism in early nineteenth-century discourse—those of transported convicts and of becalmed or shipwrecked mariners. Both were principally images of starvation cannibalism, but heightened by the antisocial traditions associated with the criminal and the sailor. Secret brotherhoods with their own mysterious language and signs, criminals and sailors stood outside conventional morality. Both were addicted to drink and prone to violence. Both, as communities of men without women, were associated with sodomy.

Although starvation cannibalism at sea had a well-established history by the early nineteenth century, the tale of the cannibal convict was a relatively recent creation of the post-1788 system of transportation and was formed explicitly on stories of escaped prisoners in the Australian and Tasmanian bush. If the convict cannibal owed something to the common domestic image of the criminal insane and the association of murder and mutilation with at least metaphoric or, in the case of Sawney Beane, actual cannibalism, he also drew much from the association of the locale—the South Pacific—with native abominations, with tales of the cannibalism of the New Zealand Maori, Australian aborigines, and New Guinea and Fiji islanders. Here we have a unique example of the savage abroad juxtaposed directly with the domestic savage, each reinforcing the stereotype of the other in an articulated back-and-forth discourse.

As with women and enslaved blacks, the convict had, like Magwitch, a sympathetic as well as a fiendish face. He was often portrayed as a victim, driven, perhaps, to a life of crime in Britain by starvation, wrenched from home to be sent like cattle to a newly discovered wilderness, and escaping to a hopeless and fatal end in conditions of extreme privation. Another example perhaps of the cannibal cannibalized—in this case, by the law, a devouring system of justice that turned both paupers and criminals into laboring hands in workhouses and prisons and provided for their actual dismemberment in the dissection theaters of teaching hospitals. In fact, convict bodies, like those of the hanged, were preferred to those available from Poor Law establishments: "The Bodies from the Hulks . . . are more prized at the Schools on account of their being for the most part young subjects and better adapted for the display of human structure than the aged inmates of the workhouses."[199] From the official cannibalization of convicts, it was perhaps only a short step in the popular mind to their own dissection of one another. In this, the convict cannibal shared a peculiarity with the sailor, in that in a perverted cannibalism, as it were, he fed almost exclusively on his own kind—that is, on other convicts.

The best-known and most graphic account of convict cannibalism, one that colors much of the image throughout the nineteenth century,[200] was that of Alexander Pearce, an Irishman who escaped from his Tasmanian jailers with six others. The only survivor, he was recaptured but escaped again with another man. Having, it was said, acquired a taste for human flesh from his first experience, he apparently murdered his companion, tore off his private parts and, although not in a starving condition this time, ate his heart and liver. When retaken, in a state of rambling insanity, he had a piece of the body with him and claimed that "human flesh was by far preferable" to fish or pork. Pearce was hanged in Hobart in 1823. Although the model for this genre—and the source for the cannibal Gabbett in Marcus Clarke's classic tale of Australian convicts, *His Natural Life*—Pearce was not unique. In 1832 the convicts Edward Broughton and Mathew Maccavoy were hanged "for the willful Murder of three of their Fellow Transports and eating them as food."[201]

Although these were white men, their crimes were committed on ground that had been associated since Cook's voyages with tales of aboriginal depravity. The two traditions are brought together within the cannibal discourse by stories, which fancifully multiplied after the 1820's, of convicts who escaped and "went native," living in the bush among aborigines, taking wives from among them and, presumably, sharing their taste for human flesh. In 1838 John Curtis repeated in his account of the escape of Mrs Fraser from the cannibals the story of one of the crew, John Baxter, who in his own escape had encountered a convict who lived with natives in the bush, painted his body with ocher, and had taken an aborigine wife.[202] Four years later, the Reverend John Lang reported conversations he claimed a clergyman from a German mission, the Reverend K. W. Schmidt, had had with another escaped convict, Davies, who provided him vivid (and highly suspect) personal accounts of life in the bush, of the ritual procedures the aborigines with whom he had lived followed in their butchery of corpses for cannibalization: he "has often seen a black fellow holding his portion of his fellow-creature's dead body to the fire . . . and drink it [the melting fat] up when he had caught a sufficient quantity to form a draught, with the greatest gusto."[203]

This was a type of tale which strayed as far away as the Fiji Islands, where Thomas Williams related that he knew of an escaped convict, a Swede, appropriately named Savage, who became a headman before being drowned and suffering the inevitable fate of being eaten himself. Another convict—significantly, an Irishman with the ethno-typical name of Paddy Connor—went native and gained, Williams claimed, such a great influence over the Fijian aborigines that his "most inhuman" desires were gratified. These included, apparently, the murder and roasting of those whom he disliked. We can note a difference in the ethnic coding of the white native here—the Swede, who had "redeeming traits," was ultimately himself eaten; the Irishman "was thoroughly Fijianized" and "depraved" and populated the island with 50 of his half-breed children.[204]

Finally, we should note the close association of the convict cannibal with the sexual—here, with Paddy, the fecundity of the Irish; with others, a sexuality directed like their appetites toward other convicts, often in a discourse picturing the young, passive, and soft recent arrival as victim to the lusts of older, hardened, aggressive prisoners. The resonance between cannibalism and a sexual appetite constructed as unnatural is obvious. There was, in fact, a well-known (if largely outside polite discourse) sodomitic subculture in the convict settlements from the earliest days of transportation. Often the overseers themselves were rumored commonly to abuse their authority in demanding sexual favors. Soldier guards and prison governors perforce tolerated irregularities that their system was inadequate to control, and that in any event doubtless worked to establish a useful hierarchical order within the camps. Later, of course, the common knowledge of sexual behavior among convicts was but another aspect of the transportation system that "legitimate" settlers strove to overcome in their drive for respectability.[205] In 1846 Gladstone sacked the governor of Van Diemen's Land (Tasmania) for failing to deal with the "problem." A full parliamentary inquiry followed.[206]

The association of cannibalism with sodomy in the confined, single-sex, sadistic, unnatural world of the convict received its most sensational form in Marcus Clarke's novel *His Natural Life*, published in 1870. However much Clarke's story derives from the actual horrors of the system, his telling of it is strongly indebted to the gothic literary tradition. His central themes—unjust confinement and sadistic persecution—are clichés of the genre. Also resonating with the gothic tradition were the analogies contemporaries often drew between Catholic religious houses and prisons. Both were unproductive "seminaries of vice." Governor Thomas Brisbane observed, "The Convict-Barracks of New South Wales remind me of the monasteries of Spain."[207]

Clarke's cannibal convict, Gabbett, is a gigantic Frankenstein's monster (as he had come to be represented), a habitual criminal with a lunatic's brain, like "one of those monstrous and savage apes that haunt the solitudes of the African forests."[208] In his first two escapes, he returns alone, and Rufus, the novel's hero, finds the partially devoured body of one of his victims, a younger man whom he has murdered. Back in the camp, Gabbett torments and, it is strongly implied in one of the most graphic episodes of the novel, rapes a young man "of about twenty years of age, thin, fair and delicate," afterward referred to as Miss Nancy.[209]

The sodomy of the convict cannibal resonates with the supposed sodomy of the cannibal Iroquois, the cannibal Aztecs, and the cannibal Battas. Such racial association seems to have been recognized and further encouraged in the way Clarke and others present the convict "Ring" as a "secret society," "complete with elaborate initiation ceremonies, distinguishing tattoos . . . and a communal chant."[210] Indeed, the commander of the First Fleet, Arthur Philips, fantasized an actual, if forced, identity-by-incorporation of the European sodomist and the racial cannibal: "I would wish to confine the [murderer and sodomist] until an opportunity offered of delivering him to the natives of New Zealand, and let them eat him."[211]

But the convict's perversions also struck a common chord with popular notions of the sailor, with *his* tattoos, chants, and sexual license, with whoring in port and sodomy at sea. Like the convicts they transported, sailors were a race apart, a marginal, floating, polyglot society, distrusted by Henry Mayhew in his study of the London poor.

> The faces of the sailors were vacant, stupid, and beery. I could not help thinking one man I saw at the Prussian Eagle a perfect *Caliban* in his way. There was an expression of owlish cunning about his heavy-looking features that, uniting with the drunken leer sitting on his *huge mouth*, made him look but a "very indifferent monster."
>
> I noticed a sprinkling of coloured men and a few thorough negroes scattered here and there.[212]

There can be little doubt that tales of maritime cannibalism, which often portrayed the cabin boy as most at risk, involved a confusion of desire and appetite that had strong sexual overtones. Common tales of ship's boys who were actually girls—as in the ballad "The Female Cabin Boy"—invoke a sexual ambiguity that depended upon the androgyny of youth in a world without women. A. W. B. Simpson cites numerous nineteenth-century stories of the maritime cannibalization of boys, from that of the barque *Francis Spaight* in 1835, or the *Earl Moira* in 1838, down to the *Euxine* in 1874, the *Cospatrick* in 1875, and the *Mignonette*.[213] The abused body of the cabin boy, emblem of victimized innocence, became the common ground for both a sexual and a cannibal depravity, the locus for the homologous activities of unnatural eating and deviant sexual intercourse, where the domination of the cannibal over his prisoner-victim merged with that of the aggressive sodomist over his passive object.

Both cannibalism and homosexuality were often represented in the nineteenth century as acts, like masturbation, that became addictive. Once enjoyed, they demanded an excessive indulgence, which debilitated the reasoning faculties. W. Cooke Taylor offers a highly eroticized description of the "danger" of acquiring a cannibal appetite, which strongly suggests just such a linkage:

> Nothing is more certain, than that a depraved and unnatural appetite, when once formed, has a tendency, not only to continue, but to in-

crease. . . . A friend, whose name I am not at liberty to mention, has favoured me with notes of a conversation with a man, who, under pressure of famine at sea, had eaten a part of one of his companions . . . after the lapse of many years, he never thought upon the subject without finding desire strangely mixed with loathing; and finally, that it was this instinctive feeling which rendered him most reluctant to allude to the subject.[214]

Or, as St. Johnston says of the Aztecs—he retells W. H. Prescott's story of the sacrifice of an unblemished and beautiful youth—"the appalling appetite only grew by what it fed upon . . . a morbid and overmastering craving."[215] In the literature of cannibalism, sexual taboo—especially sodomy—seems often to be close to the surface, whether it is Crusoe's longing for a male slave in his "idyll without benefit of women"[216] or the African explorer H. H. Johnston's curious late-Victorian suggestion that in a distant overpopulated future, statesmen might sanction "a certain limited consumption of the effete and unfit by the young and vigorous members of the commonwealth,"[217] an anticipation of H. G. Wells's theme in *The Time Machine*, where the Morlocks subsist upon the effeminate Eloi.

Samuel Johnson once remarked that being in a ship was like being in jail, with the chance of being drowned (and commonly with worse company than one could expect in a jail).[218] The association of the convicts transported to Australia with the sailors who took them there was facilitated in the popular mind by the often told stories of mutinies, of convicts themselves pressed into service, of drunken and criminal depredations of sailors in port. Behind the Victorian attempt to romanticize and sentimentalize the common seaman, there lay a long tradition of the sailor as no better than criminal, often suspected of a deviant sexual as well as an unnatural gastronomic appetite. In London, during the Ripper panic of 1888, sailors, along with other suspect marginals, such as Jewish immigrants, were singled out for questioning.[219] Both convict and sailor focused the most extreme fears of the dregs of society, the most pauperized classes, which, as we have seen, had often, in the shape of the ravening mob, been accused by respectability of cannibal instincts. Both, however, were also often portrayed as victims. It is perhaps no coincidence that the most sensational representation of the sailor as victim, Samuel Plimsol's campaign to improve the conditions of the merchant marine, occurred at a time when the "custom of the sea" (as maritime cannibalism was known) was under mounting attack as demeaning to the Victorian image of the manly stoical sailor-hero.

How much of the survival cannibalism of sailors is myth and how much reality is largely irrelevant here. Suffice it that the tradition was long established, as A. W. B. Simpson has demonstrated, before the no-

torious case of the *Mignonette* in the 1880's, which in some sense celebrated the close of a custom more appropriate to the age of sail than to
that of steam.[220] Although maritime cannibalism was but one variety of
"starvation cannibalism," as opposed to the cannibalism of desire and
volition associated with the mad, the deviant, and the racial Other, there
is nevertheless often an element of ambivalence to such stories, where
extreme stress exposes something buried in the sailor's nature. In reading the many accounts of eighteenth- and nineteenth-century maritime
cannibalism, from the *Nottingham Galley* in 1710 to the *Mignonette*, it
is important to observe how the event unfolds—who among the crew
suggests "the last fearful expedient," and who the victims of choice are.
As with the convict Pearce, some sailors had more than one experience
of this and were portrayed as more likely to anticipate the ultimate recourse before necessity drove them to it. Their shared knowledge, a loss
of innocence, was part of the custom of the sea, which helped to construct the sailor as deviant or at least separate from those on shore who
had not participated in this awful, secret rite of taboo-breaking.

Here, in these tales of one variety of white cannibalism, I shall focus
on two aspects that directly invoke a racial element. The first concerns
the older maritime stories, essentially an Atlantic tradition, and the way
in which they relate white cannibalism to the nonwhite—to Amerindians and Negro slaves. The second takes us into the nineteenth century
and the association of the cannibal seaman with the unfolding discourse
on Polynesian custom. In the transition, we shall observe a significant
reconstruction and redirection of the survival story.

In the eighteenth century, the crews of English and American ships
were likely to be racially and ethnically mixed. Non-Anglo-Saxons—
Irish, Spanish, half-breeds, Negro or mulatto slaves or freedmen—were
commonly found in ships' crews. It is remarkable how often, even when
lots were drawn, they were the first victims of survival cannibalism. In
his discussion of these stories, Simpson noted that the first to go were
often the obvious victims—the lowliest of the crew.[221] The abandonment of black slaves to their fate on foundering or becalmed slave ships
had been a common indictment of the trade. In 1737 the *Gentleman's
Magazine* reported such an occurrence in the loss of the slaver *Mary*.
The crew, who first sacrificed the Negroes to the sea, survived by devouring several of their own number—including, first perhaps, those
who were least English, two Portuguese and an Irishman. In 1759 there
was a report of the English crew of the *Dolphin* drawing lots and, inevitably, eating the only Spaniard on board. The best-known of these stories, however, was that of the *Peggy* in 1765, where the lot predictably
fell on the only Negro crew member. "Used with utmost economy," the

body lasted ten days. Similarly, as noted, the story of Pierre Viaud, shipwrecked in 1766, involvèd the slaughter, without drawing lots, of his Negro slave.[222]

Two related observations may be made here. First, there is the obvious connection between the slave economy, the African as commodity, and the commodification of the Negro's actual body parts, "used with the utmost economy" in a white cannibal feast. As Pierre Viaud attempted to rationalize the murder of his slave, "This animal is my entire property; I have bought him, for my own use."[223] Second, however, there is a kind of inversion, already seen in the case of women and paupers, whereby a threatening identity may coexist with a contradictory one of vulnerability and victimization. Here on these ships plying the Atlantic, it was the savage who was cannibalized, for each of these types—the pauper Irishman, the Spanish papist, and the Negro—were represented in contemporary gothic literature as types of dangerous depravity. That the Anglo-Saxon sailor should become like them, and they his victims is a form of ironic reversal.

In the nineteenth century, however, there was a change in the discourse on maritime cannibalism, reflecting a progressive racialization of anthropophagy. For Pierre Viaud, the distinction between savage and civilized rested not so much on racial distinction as on the human condition. Starvation was sufficient to weaken his own intellect and subordinate his own, European, humanity to a basic need for survival: "My reason was impaired, my mind sympathized with the weakness of my body . . . distracted beyond the power of reason."[224] Victorians required something more powerful and essential, in line with the emotional and biological, as well as intellectual, distinctions they were determined to draw between black and white.

In the first place, the multicultural nature of ships' crews became analogous in the nineteenth century to a kind of miscegenation, and the white sailor, by association (and perhaps sexual liaison) with racial aliens both on ship and in exotic ports of call, absorbed some element of their strange, deviant ways. This is particularly marked as, often, the tales of maritime cannibalism move their locus from the Atlantic to the South Pacific and are interwoven with the developing discourse on Australasian and Fijian cannibalism. John Baxter, a survivor, like Mrs Fraser, of the *Stirling Castle* disaster, regaled the Lord Mayor of London in 1837 with stories of both their own intention to resort to cannibalism (by the drawing of lots) and an aboriginal cannibal feast.[225]

As with the escaped convict, there is an element of "going native" in the popular nineteenth-century image of the South Seas sailor that strongly colors even his survival cannibalism. In Edgar Allan Poe's *Nar-*

rative of Arthur Gordon Pym (1838), the gothic horrors of brutal mutiny, sadistic murder, and the "last horrible extremity" are interwoven with the peculiarly racial savagery of both nonwhite crew members and islanders who are "among the most barbarous, subtle, and bloodthirsty wretches that ever contaminated the face of the globe." As a significant prelude to the survival cannibalism of the protagonist, we are presented with the metaphoric cannibalism of "the most horrible butchery" practiced by the ship's cook, a Negro and "in all respects a perfect demon." In such a place and among such a crew Arthur Pym, a white youth from New England, is introduced to survival cannibalism—that is, across a *racial* boundary—by an ambiguous friend/foe, the half-breed Dirk Peters, who then accompanies him into the mysterious and inverted world of savage South Pacific islanders, who tear "to pieces" the bodies of the crew, and whose teeth are black, not white.[226]

The same confusion of racial boundary (often with the familiar inversion of the cannibal cannibalized) can later be seen in the cannibal tales of the American West, from the Donner Party, where it is the two Indian guides who are first eaten, to "Liver-Eating" Johnson and Dapick Absarcka, "the Crow Killer." In 1853 the American journal *Harper's* published an account of Fiji that described an exotic world of cannibal feasts, "the stern spectacle of a race in decay," and Europeans who, like a tattooed Cockney the author met there, had reverted to the savage. As for Queequeg on Ahab's *Pequod*, the tattoo becomes a nautical symbol of a possibly cannibalistic primitivism. The author of the *Harper's* story recalled from his own youth a "strange sailor" who wandered through New England villages showing children "strange tattooing indelibly marked" on his brawny chest: "None of his tales so wrought upon us as those about the Feejees . . . of human victims roasted alive and eaten with horrid delight." Here the older tradition of the "custom of the sea" takes on a new element of racial gothic in the association of the sailor with the actual realm of the Fijian cannibal: "He always denied ever having partaken in this horrid repast; but sometimes when something particularly to his appetite was presented to him, he would give a horrid grin, and mutter, half-audibly, 'This is as good as man!'"[227]

Already a race apart, "to be numbered neither with the living nor the dead," according to one eighteenth-century cleric, sailors bore signs of their difference—their earrings, tattoos and flogging scars, their cursing and their pidgin—that made them both exotic and threatening: the men of the *Bounty* were much tattooed.[228] The strategy of portraying the sailor as a kind of half-breed exotic, however, ultimately conflicted with the Victorian need to sentimentalize the sailor as the white, Christian, and patriotic guardian of the British nation. Cannibal tales retold in the issues of *All the Year Round* in the 1870's and 1880's illustrate the difficulties and contradictions involved. The story of a white sailor's survival cannibalism in 1872 is too temptingly sensational to avoid, but, instead of a tattooed old salt, we have a simple English youth, sharply distinguished from the stereotypical native, the "wild South Sea Islander, with face painted vermilion" who could be expected to have "a brass ring through his hideous nose, and the thigh-bone of a man stuck horizontally through his matted hair." Marooned on the shore of New Holland with another sailor, the lad merely eats his deceased black cook—a characteristic comic reversal.[229] As we shall see, the humorous, rather than gothic, mode of this story is a common late-nineteenth-century strategy, one that trivializes the cannibal threat and removes it from serious discussion. The same article also offers another version of the often repeated tale of the *Peggy* of 1765, with a twist appropriate to the late-nineteenth-century effort to reconstruct the masculine, imperial image of the Briton abroad. The captain of the ship, we are assured, did not partake of the body of the Negro whom the crew had, in their lack of self-discipline, killed. The captain's singular conduct is explained, not only by his class, but by ethnicity as well: he was, we are told, the only Englishman on board.[230]

To bring the sailor's image in line with the national and, increasingly, racial ideal necessitated either skeptical denial of much of the tradition of white cannibalism or displacing the "custom of the sea" downwards to a criminal and lower-class irregularity, one that ought to be prosecuted at law. Perhaps the most remarkable and instructive example of the passionate denial of a possible case of survival cannibalism can be found in the pages of Dickens's *Household Words* in December 1854. Here issues of race and class were both deployed in shifting an allegation of cannibalism away from white English sailors.

Sir John Franklin, naval officer, arctic explorer, and one-time lieutenant-governor of Van Diemen's Land (where he "did much to humanize the convicts"), led an expedition to attempt a Northwest passage in 1845. He vanished, and no word was heard of the fate of his ships and men until Dr. John Rae, a surgeon of the Hudson's Bay Company, found convincing evidence in 1854 of their deaths from exposure and starvation. His report to the Admiralty also alluded to the disturbing possibility of cannibalism at at least one camp discovered by Eskimo: "From the mutilated state of the corpses and the contents of the kettles, it is evident that our wretched countrymen had been driven to the last resource."[231] The imputation of cannibalism, even as a last resource, greatly disturbed relatives of Franklin and his men in England, and led Dickens to defend their "honour" in the pages of *Household Words*, and, more obliquely, in his sentimental production in 1859 of "The Frozen Deep." His arguments are of some interest here.[232]

Dickens's rebuttal was based on a skepticism that William Arens might applaud. Rae's information was second or thirdhand. His Eskimo interpreter had to translate confused stories into a language that he perhaps did not fully understand. Such an informant might well "be under a strong temptation to exaggerate" in providing sensational information to a superior. Franklin had been in conditions of extreme privation on earlier expeditions but the idea of cannibalism did not apparently ever arise among his white crew members. Finally and categorically: "No statement of cannibalism, whether on the deep or on the dry land, is to be admitted suppositiously, or inferentially, or on any but the most direct and positive evidence: no, not even as occurring among savage people, against whom it was in earlier times too often a pretence for cruelty and plunder."[233] But in spite of the apparent repudiation of cannibalism on what at first appear to be the familiar grounds of eighteenth-century rational skepticism—insufficient evidence, the confusion of myth with reality, and so on—Dickens's central objective is to defend an ethnocentric construction of the white, manly, British sailor-patriot: "The noble conduct and example of such men . . . outweighs by the whole universe the chatter of a gross handful of uncivilised people, with a domesticity of blood and blubber."[234]

Remarkably, Dickens turned from his passionate disbelief in the cannibalism of the Franklin expedition crew to imply, not only the untrustworthiness of the Eskimo informants, but their own possible involvement in the deaths of the white men: "No man can, with any show of reason, undertake to affirm that this sad remnant of Franklin's gallant band were not set upon and slain by Esquimaux themselves. . . . We believe every savage to be in his heart covetous, treacherous, and cruel."[235] Although English allegations of Eskimo cannibalism date from the very first contact—Frobisher assumed them to be "Anthropophagi" on "no perfect intelligence" about their customs[236]—there had been little in the subsequent history of the Canadian north to sustain such ideas. Any disappearance in the far north, however, inevitably raised suspicions of a "savage," little-seen, and little-known people. When James Knight's expedition of 1719 to find the northwest passage was never heard from again, there were claims that Eskimo had killed, if not eaten, them. While Dickens does not accuse the Eskimo outright of a cannibal deed, he opens the possibility—alluding to an earlier expedition of Franklin's where the only member of the group to suggest cannibalism was an American Indian, an Iroquois, who was shot.

Although Dr. Rae defended his version of the fate of the expedition in

The Times, and at least one early account accepted his report without question,[237] Eskimo savagery subsequently crept into the popular knowledge of the event. Remarkably, it was Rae's own expertise, his intimate knowledge of the people and the region, that was turned against him. Accused of "going native" and of lacking "good form" in his preference for Eskimo methods of travel and dress, he raised both distrust and jealousy in London at the Royal Geographic Society and the Admiralty.[238] As late as 1880, Admiral George W. Henry Richards could write to *The Times*, following his own explorations, that there was "grave suspicion" that natives in the Arctic had cut apart the bodies of the Franklin men. That whites might have resorted to cannibalism, "I am at a loss to conceive how it can have been suggested."[239] A few years later, a cheap religious "true story" of the expedition could assume that the men were "probably" murdered by the Eskimo.[240]

Dickens's attempt to reconstruct the honor of the British seaman reached beyond the issue of who ate whom in the Arctic. In a survey of the tradition of maritime cannibalism, he took pains to separate the modern Victorian navy from past "custom" in a way that involves strategies both of class and of race.[241] Where there appear to have been confirmed accounts of maritime cannibalism, as in the case of the *Peggy*, he assumes that either the perpetrators were insane (a crewman who ate the Negro on the *Peggy* "went mad") or "of an inferior class." In the famous case of the *Medusa*, he similarly found a partial explanation for cannibalism in the ill-discipline of the kind of rabble that he suggests characterized French naval recruitment: few among the *Medusa*'s crew were "of decency, education, and purpose enough, even to oppose the maniacs. . . . They were the scum of all countries, the refuse of the prisons." He employs class, a Burkean allusion to the era of the Revolution, and national stereotype to construct an alter-image to that of the British sailor: "And is it with the scourged and branded sweepings of the gallows in France, in their debased condition of eight-and-thirty years ago, that we shall compare the flower of the trained adventurous spirit of the English Navy . . . ?"[242]

Dr. Rae replied from the perspective of actual experience that he "doubted the character" of the British Arctic crews that Dickens praised. Dickens, however, was unassailable by mere experiential fact. His images sprang from within, from a mid-Victorian determination to establish firm boundaries of character and race, and his passion is raised precisely because of the threat Rae's report suggested to these boundaries, that they might be permeable or illusory. This seems confirmed in his last word on the *Medusa*, that the hideous conditions on the raft brought out in some a manifestly racial depravity, while such conditions, he strongly suggests, would have elicited from the Briton stoicism and, in the last extremity, a noble and uncomplaining death like that of a soldier in the line. Perhaps like Parisian women led on by a termagant hag, the drunken plebeian French sailors of the *Medusa* were "headed by 'an Asiatic . . . of colossal stature, with short curled hair, and extremely large nose, an enormous mouth, a sallow complexion, and a hideous air.'"[243]

Here we can observe a postrevolutionary conflation of the European savage with his nonwhite counterpart, of class with race, that seems to go beyond Lee Sterrenburg's view that Victorians constructed the working class as appetite. There is more here than Burke's cannibalism of the sansculottes. Burke's cannibalism was the ferocity of the uncivilized. Dickens's is an inherent defect, signified by physical difference. If Burke's analogy had employed "race," it was closer to the older ambiguity of race-as-culture. Dickens's vision is informed by something harder, more inescapably biological, that is physiologically and mentally abnormal. It reminds us that the cannibal metaphor itself had come to be embedded in a more general concept—that of race. As the idea of race changed, so did one of its most emotive signifiers, man-eating.

It was this rigidification of the concept of racial identity that worked more than anything else to undermine the acceptability of the European "custom of the sea." The same year that Dickens challenged Dr. Rae's report on the Franklin expedition, the third volume of a new edition of the *Encyclopedia Britannica* appeared with an essay on "Cannibalism." This supplanted, as the main reference for man-eating, the much shorter article on Anthropophagi," which had been carried forward more or less in its original, if abbreviated, form since 1797, a change that itself suggests a racialization of the concept of man-eating.[244] Although the term *cannibal*, specifically deriving from practices in the Caribbean reported by Columbus, had long been in common usage, the encyclopedia's preference for *anthropophagi* hitherto reflected the eighteenth-century scholarly strategy of locating the tradition first in the stories of the ancients—that is, in the European past. The eighth edition, however, recounts a "Cannibalism" that begins with the Caribbean and closes with the Fiji islanders.

Whereas the eighteenth-century philosophic observer had searched for universals of human nature, and, like William Marsden among the Battas of Sumatra, found forms of cannibal custom that could be seen to be analogous to European culture—the ceremony of justice, the desire for public humiliation of enemies and deviants[245]—the diversity of cannibal practice that the mid-Victorian *Britannica* depicts is entirely within the nonwhite field. Instead of universals of custom and social function, we have peculiarities of racial "taste" related in a style that might be called "wry gothic": "Considerable diversities of taste, however, prevailed among the savages in different parts of the world, as to the most delicate portions of the human frame. Among the South Sea Islanders, the palm of the hand, especially of a young girl, was looked upon as the most dainty morsel; while the New Zealanders gave a decided preference to the foot."[246] Finally, the cannibal is given a phenotypical identity. The original cannibals, the Caribs, are portrayed, like the "Negro Fijians" of missionary and exploration literature, as a kind of universal African: "They are, in general, downcast and given up to idleness and day-dreams. They have dark-olive complexions and flat brows and nostrils."[247]

The next edition, that of 1876, recruited the well-known anthropologist E. B. Tylor to rewrite the entry on cannibalism. Tylor's essay follows the course of late-Victorian evolutionary social science.[248] He enumerates a quasi-scientific catalogue of "causes" (fury, morbid affection, magic, habit, etc.), each of which is identified with examples drawn exclusively from nonwhite cultures. Cannibalism is now sited in a primitive stage of human development—returning to a universal construction, but one that locates the nonwhite "primitive," culturally, if not exactly biologically, in a prehistoric past.[249] Although the ethnologist may carefully speak here of "culture," the late-Victorian reader inevitably leapt to conclusions shaped by Darwinist biology. We have already seen hints of a biologically determined cannibalism in Clarke's 1870 representation of the man-eating convict Gabbett, a "giant" with "slavering mouth" and "slowly grinding jaws" like "one of those monstrous and savage apes that haunt the solitudes of the African forests."[250] From this it is but a short step to the casual assumption of an early twentieth-century Haggard-imitator like Charles Gilson that cannibals are physiologically—that is, racially—identifiable as "bestial, gorilla-like creatures, with exceptionally powerful jaws and teeth like fangs."[251]

Dickens's angry dismissal of the possibly of the Franklin expedition's having had final recourse to cannibalism anticipates such a racial reading—canibalism as the realm of the nonwhite—as well as a class reading which placed any instances of white cannibalism that might be proved in the category of madness and criminality, an essentially lower-class abnormality. It is a logical consequence of such a representation that the decision of the Falmouth authorities in 1884 should have charged the survivors of the *Mignonette* with murder. In its commentary on the *Mignonette* affair, the *Spectator* vigorously assaulted "the hideous tradition of the sea," saying: "There is no good race of cannibals, and never will be; and no race which, when it has once risen to the possession of full consciousness, is not instinctively ashamed of the practice, and debased by having resort to it."[252] This racialization of the "custom of the sea" went hand in hand with an effort to raise and separate the British sailor from the dangerous proletarian residuum of Mayhew's whoring, deceitful beggars. A decade before the *Mignonette*, the story of David Webster, awarded the Albert Medal, Second Class, advanced just such an enterprise.

David Webster had been the second mate of the collier *Arracan* out of Greenock. His defense, pistol in hand, of the ship's boy Horner from the fate that ship's boy Parker of the *Mignonette* later suffered—being eaten by a starving crew—evoked a lengthy editorial (published in the *Spectator* and reprinted in *The Times*) defending Webster as heroic model of British manhood and merchant marine officer. Webster's bravery would help break up, it was claimed, "one of the most utterly wicked traditions of our Merchant Marine . . . a peculiarly dastardly and selfish form of assassination." The rhetorical question is posed: why cannot the starving seaman stoically turn his face to the wall and die like poor starving widows, or as "thousands of Irish died" in the Famine? "The seamen of the *Arracan* had no more right to eat Horner at sea than they would have to eat their [ship's] owner at home. Their duty was to . . . die quietly like men."[253]

From the Gothic to the Comic: Medical Science and the Cannibal Joke

> It is disgusting to talk of anatomy as a science,
> whilst it is cultivated by means of practices which
> would disgrace a nation of cannibals.
>
> — 'The Lancet', 1832[254]

> Burke's the butcher, Hare's the thief,
> Knox the boy that buys the beef.
>
> — Popular ballad, ca. 1832[255]

Finally, there was a domestic, if metaphoric, cannibalism, well located in the early nineteenth century, that in some sense ties the separate anthropophagic discourses of the pauper, the woman, the criminal, and the nonwhite together. All were themselves the subjects of the comparative anatomist and under his knife provided a postmortem ritualized spectacle in the operating theaters of London and Paris—a kind of cannibal feast.

A gothic representation of the locus of the surgical, dissecting act as a "theater of blood," a "charnel house," and an abattoir was compelling to the early nineteenth-century romantic mind. When the young Hector

Berlioz fled from the dissection theater of the Hospice de la Pitié in 1822, he described his experience in the language of the sensational gothic novelist:

> The sight of that horrid human charnel-house, those scattered limbs, those grimacing heads, those half-cracked skulls, the bloody cesspool in which we walked, the revolting odor pouring out, the swarms of birds fighting over scraps of lung, the rats in their corner gnawing on bloody vertebra, filled me with such dread that, jumping from the amphitheater window, I took flight and ran home all out of breath, as though death and all her hideous procession were at my heels.[256]

The image of the surgeon as, not merely a creature of such surroundings, but himself sadistic cannibal was encouraged by a double representation. First, from outside the profession, there was that of the humanitarian opponents of practices that appeared to subordinate the patient, alive or dead, to the research interests of the scientist, to substitute self-interest and necrophilia for benevolence. Second, from within, there was that self-imposed hardening of the heart, the cultivation in medical schools of "clinical detachment"—leading inevitably among young male students to the irreverence of the practical joke and an abusive handling of the dead, which had both sexual and cannibalistic overtones. These two are roughly paralleled in the discourse on "real" man-eating by the missionary image of cannibalism as depravity and abomination on the one hand and the detached raconteur's deployment of sometimes obscene cannibal humor on the other.

The growing professionalization of medical training and the fashionableness of comparative anatomy[257] ensured that the market for cadavers, sensationalized both by the Burke and Hare murders of 1828 and gothic fiction, was well established in the popular Victorian mind. To service the medical schools, corpses were imported from abroad, "trussed in sacks, roped up like hams . . . dismembered and sold in pieces, or measured and sold by the inch."[258] Such objectification of the body as a commodity, although resonating with contemporary political economy, was no doubt an inevitable aspect of modern medical education. Nevertheless, like G. W. M. Reynolds's representation of the resurrectionist, it helped entrench in popular culture a gothic image of the surgeon and medical student as bizarrely inhumane.[259] At the same time, reforming crusaders within the medical profession itself could deploy an essentially gothic representation of their less-advanced colleagues. Southwood Smith's defense of anatomical dissection cautions the public that just those they most trust, the older men with the largest practices, are those they should fear most.

Ignorant physicians and surgeons are the most deadly enemies of the community: the plague itself is not so destructive; its ravages are at distant intervals . . . theirs are constant, silent, secret; and it is while they are looked up to as saviours, with the confidence of hope, that they give speed to the purposes of disease and certainty to the stroke of death.[260]

That this is at some level a projection onto his enemies of charges that were popularly leveled at the reformers themselves, is suggested in Southwood Smith's own unintended association in this text of the advances of the contemporary anatomist with "the partial knowledge of anatomy" accidentally acquired in ages past by "the priest in immolating his victim," the augur "pursuing his divinations," and the torturer.[261]

Subsequently, the antivivisection movement deployed similar images of the surgeon as depraved, and used much the same language that one can find in the contemporaneous missionary discourse on Fijian cannibalism. Instead of working to prevent disease, the researching medical profession and the medical schools, "speculators in blood and torture," seemed engaged both in an organized assault on the dignity of the human body and in "groveling in the entrails of animals."[262] The researching scientist-doctor as an inherently gothic type resurfaces, of course, in late-Victorian fiction—for example, in Stevenson's Dr. Jekyll and Wells's Dr. Moreau. This was a representation that still drew from (and itself manipulated) a suspicious popular culture. During the Ripper panic of 1888 "one of the strongest rumours . . . was that the Terror was a medical student or doctor."[263]

The cannibal metaphor was a compelling one in the popular attack on the medical profession. Lord Carnarvon, addressing in 1837 a meeting of the Society for the Prevention of Cruelty to Animals, called the medical schools charnel houses where degraded practices took place comparable to those of the (cannibal) "savages of Scythia." Bodies trussed like hams for sale also, at least in the dissection classes of Joshua Brookes, smelled like hams, owing to a niter solution he used to arrest the deterioration of tissues.[264] Elsewhere the notorious stink of decay associated with dissection classes exactly parallels the missionary or explorer's language of the "revolting and intolerable stench" of the cannibal village. Nor do the analogies stop there. William Marsden invokes European anatomical practice in his observation that the cannibal Battas of Sumatra dissected and devoured parts of their capital criminals as a form of "ignominious punishment." Schweinfurth portrayed the cannibalism of Africa as a kind of pauper and criminal dissection: "In short, all who with ourselves would be consigned to the knife of the anatomist would here [in Africa] be disposed of by this melancholy destiny."[265]

If the unclothed body of the anatomy lesson suggests the unclothed body of the primitive, the "punishment" of the pauper, the prostitute, and the criminal at home by dissection is curiously analogous to the punishment of sepoy troops after the Mutiny, for instance, whose bodies, strapped to the cannon mouth, were blown apart. Like the last native man and woman of Tasmania, whose bodies ended up on display, the American Indians whose skulls reside in the Smithsonian, or the body of the "Hottentot Venus," whose remains can still be found preserved in Paris, the convict cannibal Pearce, like the body-snatching murderer William Burke, was not only hanged but anatomized, and his skull too found its way into a phrenologist's collection.[266]

Here the literal deconstruction of the body is a prelude to the reconstruction of the racial, female, criminal, and pauper Other as physiologically aberrant. Africa itself was, in the words of Francis Galton, "dissected and laid bare" by Stanley, whose killing of "a few hundred barbarians . . . many of whom are professed cannibals" was "a small matter."[267] It is a curious fact that Winwood Reade was moved to visit Africa by a chance meeting with a young surgeon, whose descriptions of "that wonderful land" fired his imagination.[268] Upon return from visiting "the cannibal Fans," Reade himself entered a London hospital as a medical student, having been inspired with a passion for science by Darwin's *Origin of Species*. It was with a surgeon's eye that he later accompanied the British assault on the Ashanti in 1874, and his account (Wolseley called Reade "a very cool and daring man")[269] draws together the imperial assault on the cannibal continent with an actual dissection tutorial provided by the bodies of the wounded natives he observed. His friend Surgeon-Major Gore (*sic!*) was, after one engagement, "in a tremble of delight, having had an object lesson in anatomy." An Ashanti warrior had been cut down by a blow from a sword, laying bare his still heaving diaphragm: "As human vivisection is not yet allowed even in the Paris schools, this spectacle was quite unique." The two were equally delighted at finding a skull and matching jawbone "as white and polished as any specimen in the Museum of the College of Surgeons."[270]

After William Burke's body was dissected in Edinburgh before an audience of ticket holders in 1829, it was viewed by nearly 2,000 students, who had been involved in a near riot at their exclusion from the entertaining event.[271] As dissection, in the decades following the passage of the Anatomy Act a few years later, moved for the average student from the realm of theater and observation to ordinary, "hands-on" participation, easily accessible bodies became a staple of medical school humor. Student pranks (and the body parts they were based upon) inevitably escaped from the realm of the medical school into an already anxious community: on one occasion in London, there was public outrage when a student dropped a leg down a chimney near the anatomy theater and it fell into a housewife's stewpot.[272] Nor is cadaver humor a peculiarly English phenomenon. In Paris in 1842, a student was summoned to appear before the academic council for having exhibited a child's arm on a vaudeville stage.[273] It is also likely that such joking almost inevitably takes a cannibalic form. With anatomical dissection a commonly required part of the medical curriculum, this particular kind of irreverence among medical students became a Victorian cliché. One humorous sketch of medical student life published in 1861 offers a selection of dissection-room pranks, including the sending in a fish-basket of "two gastrocnemii muscles, with the tendo Achilles cut short" to the house-surgeon "as a pair of soles."[274] In 1867 *The Lancet* investigated a case of medical student cannibalism of a corpse that had been sensationalized in the press as an act of gothic depravity, but that turned out to be a juvenile escapade. A lab assistant at St. Thomas's Hospital cooked and ate a small piece of human flesh "out of bravado." The journal was relieved that the offender—who was dismissed—was a lower-class youth, not one of the St. Thomas's medical students who were "gentlemen both by birth and education."[275]

Dissection-room humor often has a cannibal association even when it does not directly involve the consumption of human flesh. As in the "sin-eater" or "corpse cake" folk traditions, eating in the vicinity of the corpse necessarily suggests cannibalism, and it is a common literary device, as well as a risible aspect of student hospital life: "The dissection-room is his favourite resort for refreshment, and he broils sprats and red herrings on the fire-shovel."[276] When Dr. J. F. Handley told Edwin Chadwick's sanitary committee in 1842 that he had "relished many a biscuit and glass of wine in Mr. Grainger's dissecting-room when ten dead bodies were lying on the tables under dissection," it was to make use of just this mode, although as a risible introduction to his serious charge that the living conditions of poor families he had visited were "exceedingly nauseous," and that *their* smell *did* deprive him of his appetite. The subtext here of the equivalence of corpse and pauper, of the poor as passive objects for upper-class dissection, is as obvious as it was no doubt unintended.[277]

Dickens made much use of this kind of humor. Bob Sawyer, who looks "like a dissipated Robinson Crusoe," and Ben Allen, stereotypical drinking and joking medical students, horrify Mr Pickwick by discussing dissection over their dinner of oysters and fowl:

"Nothing like dissecting, to give one an appetite. . . ."
"By the bye, Bob," said Mr Allen, "have you finished that leg yet?"

"Nearly," replied Sawyer, helping himself to half a fowl as he spoke. "It's a very muscular one for a child's."[278]

Our Mutual Friend, which begins grimly enough with Gaffer Hexam dredging corpses from the Thames to loot them, provides a comic-gothic scene in Mr Venus's taxidermy shop, full of skeletal remains acquired from hospitals. A meeting there with Wegg—whose own amputated leg has preceded him—inevitably involves the consumption of a meal surrounded by both human and animal body parts, including Indian and African infants preserved in glass jars, while human teeth find their way into the coffee pot.[279] And in *Bleak House* we move from the dissection-as-cannibalism joke to actual, if comic-ironic, cannibalism when the two law clerks, Snagsby and Weevle, unknowingly taste the "rather greasy" airborne remains of the legal stationer Krook's spontaneously combusting body.[280]

Although the effect is still comic, Dickens has moved his cannibalism here, as later in *Our Mutual Friend*,[281] away from the entertaining medical school prank to corroborate a larger and gravely serious metaphor—of a cannibalistic world in which lawyers, Poor Law guardians, bureaucrats, and the rich, generally, live through the destruction and consumption of others. Poor Joe the Crossing Sweeper is a double victim of cannibalism, although he is not "one of Mrs Jellyby's Tockahoopo Indians" or "Borrioboola-Gha" blacks, "not a genuine foreign-grown savage; he is the ordinary home-made article."[282] Both cannibal victim and (unwitting) cannibal, Joe has his life, his potential, sucked out of him by the respectable world, while his physical death is a result of his own ingestion of the contagion of their bodies from the cemetery effluent that seeps into his basement world at Tom-All-Alone's.[283]

Finally, like the gothic uses of cannibalism, comic cannibalism also quite often has a sexual undertone. Mr Pickwick perhaps senses this when he warns Bob Sawyer and Ben Allen (whose raw oysters may already carry some sexual resonance), "Hush, hush, gentlemen, pray . . . I hear the ladies." The obscenity of naked body parts—of either sex—manipulated by irreverent young men leads naturally to the ribaldry of some medical school pranks and to the actual suspicions, often voiced at the time, that bodies, particularly those of young women, were not safe from violation in hospital dissection rooms: "Who, even among the practitioners of medicine, does not shudder at the contemplation that the remains of . . . wife, sister, or daughter, may be exposed to the rude gaze and perhaps to the *indecent jests* of unfeeling men."[284] It is clear that the strong repugnance of the missionary for the obscene handling of the dead by Fijian women inverts this fear. As so often in the racial discourse of

Europeans abroad, the distorting mirror they hold reverses and enlarges the image—and what is familiarly disturbing at home becomes doubly unnatural in the realm of the racial cannibal. In England, although traditions of the "pollution barrier" of the corpse may have encouraged a popular view of the old women who handled them as unclean, corpse-*profanation* is largely a masculine sphere, and inevitably finds its way, not only into gothic fiction, but into the Victorian other world of pornography. H. S. Ashbee, as "Pisanus Fraxi," gives, in his famous compendium of male sexual fantasies, one such eyewitness account of necrophilia at St. Bartholomew's Hospital in 1830.[285]

Coarse ribaldry and a peculiar and ironic sense of humor are characteristics associated with the sailor as well as the medical student. Unsurprisingly, therefore, comic and satirical versions of maritime cannibalism appear in nineteenth-century literature, from Byron's *Don Juan*, where the shipwrecked men draw lots and dine on Pedrillo, to Thackeray's "Little Billee" and W. S. Gilbert's "The Yarn of the Nancy Bell." These were often, especially as the century advanced, associated with racial cannibal jokes. In a poem from *Punch* in 1865, the comic story moves from sailors who propose cannibalism ("eating the skipper / With winegar, mustard and pipper") to the South Seas kingdom of the "Lumbagees."[286] And Gilbert's "Yarn of the Nancy Bell," which has the entire crew disappear into the mouth of a single surviving sailor, who perforce becomes the crew, is paralleled by his "King Borria Bungalee Boo," where it is black cannibals whose identities vanish into each other's mouths and are merged.[287]

It is possible to see the comic cannibal sailor as an anticipation of the racial cannibal joke that flourished in the last part of the century.[288] It may be, however, that already by mid-century, the genres are too complexly confused for such a linear association. As we have seen elsewhere, there is likely to have been influence back and forth, a metaphorical give-and-take between nautical/domestic and racial humor. Moreover, there are other domestic comic sources that bring us even closer to the comic cannibal image, which reached a kind of apogee in the last decades of the century. There would seem to be a direct relationship between the humorous representation of the domestic Negro servant, an image borrowed from America and the Caribbean, and that of the Fijian or Congolese savage abroad. In 1861 Dickens's *All the Year Round* published a story of black cannibals suggested by that year's Ethnological Society *Transactions*. Here the savage is represented as speaking with the kind of southern plantation dialect already familiar in the nigger slave joke: "I no eat him, for my cook done spoil him; he no put nuff pepper on him," and is invested with the comic laziness of the same genre—cannibalism flourished, we are told, because the natives were too lazy to fish and hunt.[289] There may even be some resonance between the mid-Victorian music-hall icon "Bones," the singing and dancing black-face minstrel, and a humorous portrayal of cannibal ritual as rhythmic cavorting before an unseen white audience peering through the bushes.

In fact, in Western popular culture, the dancing cannibal and the nigger minstrel have much in common. They both seem to involve a progressive humorization of stereotypes that initially at least carried some purposeful seriousness of meaning—the horror inspired by the unchristian savage on the one hand and a sympathetic abolitionist pity on the other. In both cases there was a distancing, a "fetishizing," as the popular images of the dancing cannibal and the nigger minstrel drew further and further away from their originals and became entertaining theatrical substitutes created by and for a white audience.[290] In this sense, they became more "real" than the originals from which they were drawn, and went to define in the popular mind an essential quality of the racial Other that was then reimposed on the original. In 1884 a writer in the *Saturday Review*, a London weekly, depicted just this process, telling of "genuine darkeys" in a recently performed "nigger minstrel" show who were lighter and more varied in skin color than the audience expected, and who had therefore been "blacked up" to resemble (white) professional minstrels. "It may show," he says, "how the accepted type comes in time to seem preferable to the real thing."[291]

Cannibalism as racial joke borrowed extensively from a domestic tradition of folktales (often containing a grim humor and irony), maritime stories, and American "nigger humor," as well as from dissection pranks.[292] It also often employed a familiar literary technique, that of ironic reversal. The fate of Robert Southey's surgeon who rifled graves, "made candles of dead men's fat," and "bottled babes unborn"—that of the cannibal cannibalized—points up just this form of humor:

> And my Prentices now will surely come
> And carve me bone from bone,
> And I who have rifled the dead man's grave
> Shall never have rest in my own.[293]

The often obscene ribaldry that characterized both racial and medical humor suggests a specific domestic context—the middle-class male-bonded social world of the Victorian professional and gentleman, the urbanity of the gentlemen's club or dinner table, where prurient humor over cigars and port so disturbed Ralph Waldo Emerson. The skeleton displayed in the front window of the Anthropological Society in London in the 1860's suggests those in Mr Venus's shop, and evokes medical school humor as well as "Savage Africa." Calling themselves "the Cannibal Club" and gaveling their meetings to order with a mace in the form of an African's head [294] were the kind of juvenile jokes that reflected the sustained immaturity of the English all-male social world (whether an anatomy class or a Pall Mall club), as well as anticipating a general late-Victorian fashion for racial cannibal humor. The proceedings of such societies seem to have inspired a style of reportage in *The Times* and other metropolitan papers that was wryly amusing. A reviewer of a volume of the *Transactions* of the Ethnological Society in 1866 ends with a revealing, comic comparison: "The old lady, who watches her neighbours eating their dinner on the other side of the street, is an ethnologist . . . as well as the *savant* who watches a cannibal eating his dinner on the Fiji Islands." [295] Here the ostensible butt of humor is the prying old woman, but the underlying subject of derision is also the anthropologist—who is merely a nosy-parker abroad.

Important elements of the "Joke-technique" that Freud identified—substitution, displacement, the reversal of opposites [296]—provide a useful approach to cannibal humor, as they do to the genre of race and ethnic joke generally. So how might one "read" medical school pranks and relate them to the racial cannibal joke? Clearly, the house surgeon's proffered meal of fillet of human muscle has at least two ulterior objects. The most obvious is that it subverts, in fact, reverses, the student-faculty relationship by subjecting the surgeon to a "test" of his anatomical knowledge. It is unnecessary that he actually be fooled by the substitution—although presumably this would provide an additional, delicious dimension. Secondly, and more deeply, it clearly targets a highly emotional, disturbing aspect of medical school education—that for his own professional survival, the student requires the literal death and dismemberment of others. The most available metaphor for this is cannibalism. It follows that the attempt to turn the surgeon into an unwitting actual cannibal is an example of displacement—transfering their own guilt to another, and displacing their disgust at groveling in gore into the "fun" of the practical joke.

If we turn to the racial cannibal joke, we see something quite similar. Obviously, any such humorous trivialization of the black assists in assuaging any lingering guilt the European might feel at his own cannibalization of the colonized. But there are other strategies beneath the surface. Alfred St. Johnston tells of a missionary forced to eat part of a white man, "an exquisite joke." [297] But what is the motive for this kind of reversal? If making the missionary/anthropologist ludicrous serves to deny the authority of the probing moralist, such a device may indicate an intensifying fear of self-exposure among a Victorian middle class dedicated to the privacy of self and family, fearful of any loss of respectability, and suffering some degree of status-anxiety. It was a fear that found expression in popular unease at the "disrespectful" exposure of the human body in teaching hospitals, and in a general distrust of doctors and medical schools—so evident in the assault on the authority of the medical profession that was mobilized by the anti–Contagious Diseases Acts and antivivisection campaigns. At some level, it seems clear that the ethnologist behind the bushes straining for a view of the cannibal act becomes comic[298] *because* the prying old woman behind her curtains peering into the privacy of the house opposite is no longer an acceptable form of social discipline.

As with the old woman and the anthropologist, one of the devices of late-Victorian cannibal humor is to point up a kind of risible comparability of opposites, of civilized and savage—for instance between the reader/consumer of cannibal stories and the originals they portray: "Let the reader, as he is sipping his soup this evening, ponder over the wonderful varieties of dinner which are going on, perhaps at the same moment, in the barbarian world . . . a Fijian chief . . . is about to sit down to a much-anticipated banquet of 'long pig.'"[299]

In the Reverend Thomas Williams's account of Fiji, the arrangements for the cannibal meal (which Williams, of course, never actually observed himself) are described in careful detail, down to the dishes and cutlery, and the text is illustrated with pictures of "cannibal forks"—looking much like any fork, made sinister (and, unintentionally, comic perhaps) by this very familiarity (ill. 14).[300] In fact, much was written after mid-century in popular texts on cannibalism about cannibal "etiquette"—emphasizing the ironic conjunction of depraved savage appetite with a niceness, even fastidiousness, of ritual. It is an extension of the view that cannibalism was often a kind of gourmandizing, a preference rather than either bestial madness or necessity. Cannibalism in Fiji, the Reverend Williams claimed, was "regarded by the mass as a refinement."[301] Such straining for homologous detail ("The head of the eater is thrown back, somewhat after the fashion of an Italian eating macaroni")[302] inevitably begs for comic representation. A characteristic example is an item in *The Times* titled "How to Cook a Man," which uses a quite detailed and grisly description of the torture and presumed cannibalization of French soldiers in the South Pacific to subvert missionary horror into amusement: "If any one of us looks forward to being eaten by cannibals. . . . It is a comfort to know that the savages who may devour him are by no means devoid of refinement in their culinary disposition."[303]

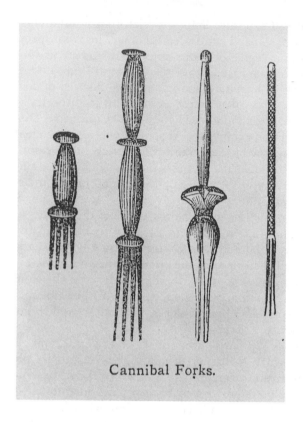

Cannibal Forks.

Ill. 14. Thomas Williams, *Fiji* (1860): "Cannibal Forks."

The urbane, postevangelical approach to cannibal representation, substituting humorous detachment for gothic empathy, may reflect, then, a strategy appropriate to the times. To dwell on the actual dangers and abominations of nonwhites abroad, as the missionaries did, was, in a sense, to admit that out there the world was still theirs, that the Other had a realm of his own. This is a rhetoric appropriate to the early period of imperial conquest, a rationalization for penetration. As the late-Victorian imperial enterprise gained ground, however, and with it the anthropologist's conquest of the "native's" own past and present, the native as threat and object for conversion yielded to the native as servant and object of derision. When the anthropologist Berthold Seemann published light accounts of his experiences in Fiji in 1862, he attempted to displace the earlier, missionary-driven representation of the natives as cannibal savages, not by denying their cannibal past, which he fully accepted,[304] but by humorizing the European's own gothic dreams of blood and terror: "For breakfast there were, as our jokes have it, missionary pies and a cold shoulder of clergyman on the sideboard."[305] Two years earlier, in a description of the Fijian cannibals written for "boy-readers," Thomas Mayne Reid had included, as no missionary text would have done, a humorous song, "King of the Cannibal Islands."[306]

It became necessary to trivialize what had earlier been represented as a dangerous challenge—the cannibal nature of the colonized. This shift was effected, not only by a change in authorial representation of the cannibal, but by a popular reading that sought, and found, a comic message even where not intended. Williams's cannibal fork was meant to induce horror, but with a note of humor behind the repugnance. The title of the Reverend Oscar Michelsen's memoir of missionary work among the Tonga islanders, published in 1893, might have been received seriously a half a century earlier, but by the 1890's *Cannibals Won for Christ* would have been more likely to provoke laughter and Wildean derision.

There lurks in the strategy of the racial cannibal joke a need to distance the white observer from the black object. Just as the comic "nigger servant" (like his counterpart the comic/thieving/incompetent Irish servant in England) was a product of the close domestic relations of the southern household, the cannibal joke emerged out of the growing density of white-black relations in the late-Victorian empire. Whites feared for the loss of their own privacy, that their own penetrating gaze would be returned. Something of this obsession can be seen in a powerful passage from the memoirs of the Reverend John Hunt, a Methodist missionary in Fiji, a mid-Victorian text that unintentionally demonstrates the closeness of the horrific and, subsequent, comic representations of the cannibal. Like missionaries elsewhere, the Hunts lived in a European-style house, an island in a threatening sea of the black unknowable. The natives would not permit them to have a fence or window-bars and were often found standing without, peering inside. The house is a refuge, a private place, but like Crusoe's cave, one that is constantly under threat of exposure: "Once, when Mrs. Hunt was bending over her dying babe, she looked up to see dark, savage faces, laughing and mocking her anguish."[307]

In this context, it is appropriate to note the role that the cannibal's "stare" (like the stare of the insane or the meaningful stare of the harlot) plays in the literature on the primitive. The missionary John Williams observed that the influence of religion upon the savage "is manifested, not only in the character, but even in the countenance, by changing the wild and vacant stare of the savage into the mild expression of the Christian."[308]

The European's unease at a direct, probing eye-contact—like that between equals, not like that between master and servant—indicates his concern to protect his thoughts, his privacy, and (since direct looks invoke the sexual)[309] perhaps his privates. This is often disguised by a European "reading" of the savage's look as hunger and himself as potential food. Richard Burton said that he commonly found that in Africa, "'A hungry look hung upon them all,'—and amongst cannibals one always fancies oneself considered in the light of butcher's meat."[310] Winwood Reade's disturbed (or aroused) view of women washing themselves at some level suggests a fear that he himself might be exposed—the observer observed—just as his belief in the "need" for female circumcision as a solution to their brazenness may have been suggested by his own fears of castration at the hands of the cannibal queen. Missionary- and anthropologist-constructed "knowledge" of the cannibal worked like a European man's carnal knowledge of a woman—as an empowering gaze and act, which must not be returned.

It is no coincidence that cannibalism was demoted to something "weird" and humorous at the same time that Western intellectuals were discovering a primitive darkness within themselves and within their own society's past. By the turn of the century, Joseph Conrad, James Frazer, and Sigmund Freud each turned to the cannibal tradition as a sensational means of exploring the private, hidden nature of the European: Conrad, in *Heart of Darkness*, of course, and more directly in *Falk*, a story of maritime cannibalism, while both Frazer and Freud employed a presumed present-day cannibalism among primitives as evidence for their theories, respectively, of the origin of Western religion and of infantile oral sadism.[311] These theories demote the cannibal abroad by making him no longer a uniquely demonic force but *merely* an atavistic signifier of a buried universal. That is, they shift the cannibal out of his own realm and into that of the European. This, it will be seen, is also the strategy of the reversing and displacing cannibal joke. By humorizing the inherent aggression and sexuality of the cannibal act, the joke both reduces the importance of the racial Other and assuages the European's own fears of cultural and personal degeneration. One might even argue, along Freudian lines, that ultimately the cannibal joke, on this deeper level at least, is not about the cannibal at all, nor even about race, but about an interior anxiety that, displaced and turned into jest, might be avoided, not engaged.

To a very large degree, the nineteenth-century middle-class Englishman imagined the cannibal realm of the black by projecting upon it the gothic images he found most disturbing in his own world. This served him well in the era of imperial expansion in shifting responsibility for the ugliness of white brutality: "Man-eating of the grossest kind is found more or less from one end of Africa to the other."[312] Firmly established in the realm of the cannibal queen, these representations could then become both gothic and comic capital for reinvestment at home in shoring up a threatened middle-class masculine self-confidence by first demonizing and then making ludicrous certain challenges to it. The man-eating feminist, the homosexual aesthete, the starving Paddy, and the alien Jew—each previously constructed as a kind of cannibal unnatural— commonly jostle each other as comic caricatures in the pages of late-Victorian humor magazines.

Meanwhile, profiting from the perceived success of the colonial enterprise in achieving the desired subordination of the racial Other abroad, the Victorian gentleman could become a tourist among them, a raconteur collecting stories, like a white hunter collecting trophies, or an anthropologist collecting skulls—safe in the sense that the monstrous had become merely the amusingly curious. As Winwood Reade explained from the library of the Conservative Club in Pall Mall,

> I make, of course, no pretensions to the title of Explorer. If I have any merit, it is that of having been the first young man about town to make a *bona fide* tour in Western Africa; to travel in that agreeable and salubrious country with no special object, and at his own expense; to *flâner* in the virgin forest; to flirt with pretty savages; and to smoke his cigar among cannibals.[313]

CHAPTER 3

Vampire Gothic and
Late-Victorian Identity

Zarxas [the barbarian] ran up, knocked him down and plunged a
dagger into his throat; pulling it out, he flung himself upon the
wound — and with his mouth glued to it, with grunts of joy and
spasms which shook him from head to foot, he pumped out the
blood with all his might; then he quietly sat down on the corpse,
lifted up his face and threw back his head to breathe more freely,
like a deer which has just drunk from a stream.

— Flaubert, Salammbô (1862)[1]

The savage cannibal and the gothic vampire, a species of cannibal, have much in common. Their sharp teeth and bloody mouths signify
an uncontrollable hunger infused with a deviant sexual sadism. Both are
types of the primitive: the vampire appropriates the vitality, the lifeblood, of his victim, just as the cannibal wished, it was thought, to absorb the physical strength and courage of the enemy upon whose body
he feasted. Together they share a kind of unholy communion, taking the
body and blood of the innocent and transmuting them into their own
identities. That which the cannibal performs by the machinery of his
digestive system, the vampire accomplishes by a supernatural parasit-
ism and pollution.

However much a construction of the shadowland between myth and
reality, the cannibal, with his filed teeth and his weird tattoos, is a creation of this world, a tangible and threatening (or comic) presence with a
geographical location on the frontier of empire. The vampire's realm is
one of myth and fiction, and lies on the other side of another frontier,
that of the supernatural and the nightmare. The cannibal is "out there,"
located in the place and time of colonial conquest; the vampire, here
among us in folk superstition and literary imagination. Both, however, are projections of nameless fears, and the closeness of the two in
nineteenth-century discourse is a further indication of just how much
the image of the cannibal deed as a racial and primitive "fact" was indebted to the overarching gothic imagination.

These two types, the "real" and the imagined, share much in the language of their narrations and in their proximity in folktale and myth as
types of the demonic and the sadistic. The unifying image is that of

blood, and its often metaphoric derivatives (blood lust, blood thirst, blood guilt, blood-letting, blood-sucking). "The blood is the life," as Dracula's Renfield says, and wherever the cannibal narrative emphasizes a reveling in the frenzied consumption of human blood, a vampiric association is close to the surface. When Sawney Beane's clan drag down their prey, "cut her Throat, and [fall] to sucking her Blood with as great a Gust, as if it had been Wine," they are vampires as well as cannibals, as are the *buveurs du sang* of revolutionary Paris or the barbarians of Flaubert's fantasy of ancient Carthage, or Ann Saunders cutting the throat of her betrothed to drink his blood in the cannibal South Pacific, or the Maori chiefs of New Zealand who, it was said, "sucked living blood from flowing veins."[2]

It also tells us something when we find that those who are heavily invested in presenting cannibalism as a racial characteristic are themselves also drawn to the fictional vampire. Richard Burton, who entertained his English audience with wry accounts of cannibalism in Africa, who was also a virulent anti-Semite, was fascinated by Hindu fairy tales of vampirism, and published his own translation of *Vikram and the Vampire; or, Tales of Hindu Devilry* in 1870. And Dickens's *Household Words*, which hinted at Eskimo cannibalizing of the Franklin expedition, shortly afterwards published an article on "Vampyre" superstitions.[3]

Perhaps an equally important, if less obvious, connective idiom than their teeth, is the gaze or stare of cannibal and vampire. Conan Doyle's Sherlock Holmes, a kind of ethnologist of the criminal world, claimed an ability "by a momentary expression, a twitch of a muscle or *a glance of an eye*, to fathom a man's inmost thoughts."[4] Eyes are windows of the soul, which the missionary proposed to save by decannibalizing the savage, and which the vampire has already traded for an eternal body. The hungry gaze of the cannibal terrifies his object; that of the vampire mesmerizes and entices. That of the Jew, another species of bloodsucker, is veiled and calculating, perhaps hypnotic, and a sign of pathological difference.[5] That of the aggressive homosexual, another devouring unnatural, with, like the vampire, a double life, invites one to share a different (forbidden but alluring) communion.

While the history of prejudice may show certain long-term, underlying continuities in the West, in the rhetorical association of, say, Jews and homosexuals with impurity, conspiracy, secret invasion, and corruption, the historian's task is to explore particular cultural contexts, as well as to search for "turning points," periods when the discourse has been amplified, subverted, or redirected. The thesis here is that the late nineteenth century saw a significant redeployment of racial gothic in

Britain and western Europe generally, focused by what is now commonly recognized as a kind of panic over sexual, racial, and social identities—in Elaine Showalter's well-known characterization, a fear of cultural and gender "anarchy." In this, the vampire and its close relations among the living, the homosexual, the Jew, and the racial half-breed, take prominent place as creatures of the void, without authenticity, trapped between two worlds.

Identity and the Gothic Revival

> And the moral of that is [the Duchess said to Alice]—"Be what you would seem to be."
>
> —Lewis Carroll, Alice's Adventures in Wonderland (1865)

> These monsters used to make my father laugh. They were compounded of parts of monkeys, parrots, squirrels, fish, and hedgehogs, dried and stitched together with great neatness and startling effect.
>
> —Joseph Sheridan Le Fanu, "Carmilla" (1872)

> I [Dr. Henry Jekyll] hazard the guess that man will be ultimately known for a mere polity of multifarious, incongruous and independent denizens.
>
> —R. L. Stevenson, The Strange Case of Dr. Jekyll and Mr. Hyde (1886)

Late-nineteenth-century gothic should not be seen merely as a response to contemporary fears of social and biological "degeneration."[6] It in fact reexpresses a much more general anxiety about self and self-control, a cliché of the bourgeois mentality. In the first gothic manifestation, it was the struggle of the hero to gain control over his life that most closely attached gothic to the central moral problem of establishing a liberal market economy and a meritocratic political society based on personal responsibility. What brought it back to life and made it so compelling for the late Victorians was not only the neo-Malthusian and social Darwinist racist constructions of social, cultural, and biological degeneration, nor even the advances in psychological theory that drew attention to clinical cases of compulsive behavior and multiple personalities. At some level, these theories themselves reflect much more general misgivings, about self-control and rationality. Moreover, just as the image of the educated, middle-class white male as the basic building block of liberal economics and politics was being undermined by theories of social and biological determinism, his world also seemed threatened by a convergence toward the end of the century of the analogous challenges of the "new woman," the effeminate aesthete, the socialist and anarchist proletarian, the alien Jew, and the nonwhite subjects of his "new imperialism" in Africa and Asia.[7]

If the earlier gothic was often occupied with the *liberation* of the physical self from unjust imprisonment and degradation, the late-nineteenth-century stories frequently revolve around the *preservation* of one's individual identity, the conscious self, from disintegrating internal conflict, as in Dr. Jekyll's doomed attempt to suppress Hyde, or from alien pollution, as in the infection that Dracula brings to the English. Torture, chains, and dungeons are at last supplanted by the threat of the decay and dissolution of one's own personality. In *Dracula*, the several first-person narratives that make up the novel can be seen as representative of this struggle to preserve the individual.[8] Indeed, one character, the scientist Seward, attempts to secure a part of his own personality from death itself by recording his voice on phonograph cylinders. This suggests the anxieties, not of an aspiring but thwarted middle class, but of an established and entrenched property- and status-possessing bourgeoisie that feared dispossession—not the 1790's but the 1890's.

Anxieties about self-identity and the preservation of individuality provoked a more intense awareness of the "unnatural" in human relationships—that is, of sexual perversion and racial "miscegenation," which often implied the subversion or even reversal of the assumed-to-be-natural power-relationships of class, gender, and race. The vampire myth offered an uneasy middle-class readership both sexuality and "bad blood" as subversions to be feared and blamed for cultural failure. It is no mere coincidence that there should have been a minor boom in sensational stories of supernatural and psychological vampirism in the troubled last third of the century, when the issues of "unfair" economic competition, immigration of "the unfit," and race degeneration featured prominently in both the sensational and the quality press.[9]

The typical late-nineteenth-century gothic story revolves around the problem of confused, vulnerable, or secret identities, fear of exposure, evil masquerading as respectability, or respectability built upon a hidden corruption. It may be instructive here to compare two political cartoons that offer early and late gothic representations of the Irish problem. "The Irish Frankenstein" (ill. 4) dates from the end of the early period of gothic and presents the Irish people themselves as monstrous, raised up for his own purposes by Daniel O'Connell. In contrast, Sir John Tenniel's "The Irish Vampire" of 1885 (ill. 15) casts the Irish as victim in the prostrate form of the female body of Hibernia, while it is Charles Stewart Parnell, the middle-class, propertied, and respectable leader who has become the monster—the vampire bat. This shift seems to indicate a late-nineteenth-century preoccupation with the confused identity and inner

THE IRISH "VAMPIRE." *Parnell*

Ill. 15. "The Irish 'Vampire'" (*Punch,* 24 Oct. 1885).

contradictions of middle-class respectability itself. Parnell is monstrous precisely because he confuses his own social position as Anglo-Irish, Protestant landowner and member of the parliamentary ruling class. Like Parnell, Stevenson's Jekyll/Hyde, Wilde's Dorian Gray, and Conrad's Kurtz are types of the male establishment (a doctor, a leisured gentleman, a colonial merchant) who have gone wrong or "gone native."

It has been argued that the fear of publicity and public censure—the loss of reputation and probity—was a powerful, perhaps the most powerful, disciplining element in nineteenth-century liberal bourgeois culture.[10] The threatened revelation of dreadful secrets is a cliché of the gothic, but that other popular late-nineteenth-century genre, the detective story, which received its classic definition from Sir Arthur Conan Doyle, is also closely dependent on the same obsession with hidden realities[11]—in particular, with disguises and the exposure of false or multiple identities. "The Man with the Twisted Lip" lives in two worlds—that of a beggar and a respectable man of property—just as surely as Dorian Gray or Jekyll, and is tormented by a similar fear of shameful exposure.[12]

INTERPRETING DRACULA

As is the case with *Frankenstein*, Bram Stoker's *Dracula* has been the subject of a substantial reevaluation in recent years.[13] Neither was considered part of the critical canon before the dawn of deconstructionism, although a quasi-Marxist reading that invoked buried images of class heralded a richly rewarding, if at times superficial and tendentious, reexamination of such minor classics of popular literary culture. If Frankenstein's Monster was a dangerous proletarian, the transformation of the peasant vampire of tradition into an aristocrat at the hands of Polidori and Byron, a representation later confirmed by the popular and sensational *Varney, the Vampyre* (1847?), was representative of the ambiguous attitude of the middling classes to the feudal element in an industrializing and democratizing society.[14] In this vein, one might argue that the peculiar combination of the fated and the nostalgic with the repulsive and the threatening elements in the vampire-as-aristocrat mirrors the conflicted identity-search of the bourgeois himself—straining to justify his virtuous independence while at the same time affecting the gentlemanly, pseudo-gentry culture of a dead or at least dying and anachronistic landed and polite society. Like the vampire's victim, the bourgeois both hated and longed for the embrace of his class enemy.

Subsequently, however, criticism has been pushed away from considerations of the historical formation of class toward the psychological eternalities of sex. Dealing as it does with the inner realm of nightmare and anxiety, gothic has often attracted the interest of psychoanalysts, and there is ample treatment of the vampire myth and its supposedly buried oral sadistic and oedipal or pre-oedipal messages.[15] This highly conjectural approach has been congenial to an often feminist deconstructionism, which, again as with *Frankenstein*, has turned away from the immediate economic and social context of the author's own particular experience in favor of a deeper, psychological-sexual reading of text dominated by the binary issues of gender. The overt sexuality of the vampire story has always been obvious, with the exchange of blood as metaphor for sexual intercourse.•

• It has been argued that Dracula's vampire consorts are representations of male fear of the sexually aggressive woman,[16] although Christopher Craft has gone beyond this to reveal the "abrogation of gender codes"

involved both in the female vampire—equipped with piercing instruments—and in a Dracula who himself sucks as well as bites, exemplify-
ing the threatening sexual ambiguity of the orifice with teeth. His important essay led to further exploration of the theme of suppressed
homosexual anxiety in Stoker's novel.[17] This search for sexual meaning
has yielded significant insights, although it has remained largely limited
either to an examination of text or, in Phyllis Roth's biography of Bram
Stoker, to relatively narrow speculation about the psychological makeup
of the author.

On a different track, Steven Arata has focused on one aspect of Bruce
Hatlen's insight that the feminist critique has tended to ignore the degree to which the "view of women encoded in the book is inextricably
bound up with certain attitudes toward the cultural, racial, and social
'other'."[18] Arata develops the idea of a general fin de siècle fear of "reverse colonization." In his analysis, Dracula is an inversion of the European tourist and imperialist and follows the lines of European conquest
back to its source.[19] In London, Dracula intends, like Haggard's She, to
use his primitive force to conquer the conquerors. This has the virtue of
locating the novel within a historical experience, the new imperial consciousness of the late-nineteenth-century British, without, however,
making much effort to show how Stoker's own experiences and interests
might plausibly have led to such fears of reverse colonization.

Arata's identification of Dracula with the racial outsider was a step in
the right direction, but in trying to link the most powerful hidden aspects of the tale with empire, he has displaced a deeper and more obvious
domestic source in Western popular culture—the nationless Jew as
bloodsucker (literal and allusive), sexual threat, and corrupter of Christian morality. In the 1880's and 1890's, the Jewish "problem" was prominently and powerfully developed in the press attacks on financial corruption and alien immigration.

This section attempts to advance beyond interpretations based on either gender ambiguity or fears of reverse colonization, while bringing
elements of them together. It also attempts to return to the biography
and social context of Bram Stoker, and of his late-Victorian audience.

Stoker and the Homosocial

> Reticence . . . is the highest quality of art; that which can be and
> is its chief and crowning glory.
>
> — Bram Stoker, "The Censorship of Fiction" (1908)[20]

Bram Stoker's last book was a collection of essays on historical, or
quasi-historical, examples of hidden identities, of people *pretending* to

be what they were not.[21] In exploring the lives of "famous impostors," culminating in a section on gender fraud—that is, cross-dressing—he employs a kind of argument that paradoxically serves to reestablish firm boundaries at a time of threat to racial, cultural, and sexual identity. By and large, these are stories that suggest clever impersonation rather than inherent ambiguity. The threat of the actual mutability of identity could thus safely be set aside. It will be seen that a version of this strategy can often be found in the rhetoric of racism. The assimilated Jew was still first of all a Jew, and the black who passed for white (who might have been four-fifths "white") was underneath, in essentials, still a Negro. The idea of the sexual "imposter" also played a role in denying the validity of homoeroticism and the reality of the homosexual personality. Here the popular image of the homosexual as a man devoted to intrigue, disguise, and secret signs of recognition was a necessary corollary to the common assertion that the "real" individual was physiologically determined, and that homosexuality itself was an elaborate self-deception.[22]

Ironically, Stoker's life ended with the wild dissolution of personal identity in dementia praecox (schizophrenia), a condition that may or may not have been the result of the terminal stage of syphilis.[23] From his earliest years, however, there had been ambiguity and conflict over just what he was. Like many middling Victorians, he had had to construct himself, as an outsider in London, without substantial resources of family or personal wealth.[24] The personality that crumbled away in 1912 had a slippery foundation, and the very heartiness of his character indicates the emotional effort he put into stabilizing its façade.

The Stokers were modestly respectable Protestants in Dublin. His mother came from a traditional Irish peasant background; his father's origins are obscure, but he held a civil service position at Dublin Castle that provided enough status and income to allow Bram to attend Trinity College, Dublin, and the family to associate with others of some provincial standing. His father was elderly, however, and was forced into retirement, and, for economy's sake, a life abroad, before Stoker was himself established in a career. Although he had some social advantages, Bram's situation was thus nevertheless ambiguous—as a Protestant in a Catholic country, as the son of a modest bureaucrat (retired and living on his pension) among the sons of the landed ascendancy, and as a young man who was more drawn to literature and the stage than to law and the civil service position his father had managed to secure for him. Like others, he looked to make his way in the larger world of London, and he jumped at Henry Irving's offer of a place as his manager at the Lyceum in 1878. Here there was further social ambiguity, that of an educated but financially not very well endowed Irishman in the capital following the equally anomalous careers, only on the verge of professionalism, of a writer of fiction and a theater manager.

The suggestion that Stoker's Irishness, specifically his family's Protestantism in Catholic Dublin, might in some complicated way underlie his attraction to the gothic finds corroboration, perhaps, in the lives of other writers from what R. F. Foster has called the "fractured and uncertain" background of a "declining elite."[25] Stoker's precursors in "Irish Gothic," Charles Robert Maturin (*Melmoth*) and Joseph Sheridan Le Fanu ("Carmilla") were Protestants who had, like Stoker, attended Trinity College. Of his contemporaries, Oscar Wilde, whose *The Picture of Dorian Gray* (1891) is constructed around an essentially gothic theme, and Lafcadio Hearn, a "master of horror" inspired, like Yeats, by the "terrible" in Celtic folklore, were also marginalized Irish Protestants, whose preoccupations with the occult and the gothic "surely mirror a sense of displacement, a loss of social and psychological integration, and an escapism."[26] Wilde and Hearn, who shared an interest in symbolism and "decadents," were both, like Robert Louis Stevenson, expatriate wanderers (Wilde assumed the name of Maturin's gothic hero, Melmoth, in his own terrible years of continental exile). Abandoned by his Greek mother and raised by a Roman Catholic great-aunt, Hearn, however, traveled farthest. He was a nomad who after leaving Ireland in 1869 lived in no place more than a few years—Cincinnati, New Orleans, the West Indies, New York, and then Japan, where he married a Japanese. He continued his wanderings in a narrower realm, to Yokohama, Matsue, Kumamoto, Kobe, and Tokyo, where he was buried with Buddhist rites in 1904. As one posthumous critic put it, he had been "half Greek, half Celt, whole gypsy, masquerading as an Oriental."[27]

If Stoker's modest, surefooted, and successful journey from Dublin to London seems much less dramatic than the self-imposed exile of Hearn, Wilde, or Stevenson, his personal relationships were perhaps as complicated and ambiguous as theirs. Stoker's close connection with Irving in fact makes a central issue of the role of the homosocial in his life, even allowing for the unguarded, pre-Freudian language of intimacy common to friendships of the time. The argument here is not that Stoker was homosexual, but that his homosocial relationships were of an intensity that may have been troubling and certainly encouraged him to compensate with an exaggerated heartiness in his dealing with men, and with a degree of homophobic coding in the construction of his most famous literary creation, Count Dracula.

Stoker was physically imposing—large-framed, tall, with, after college, a bristling red beard. At Trinity from 1864 to 1870, he was apparently never a shy boy, rather a gregarious extrovert who enjoyed sport, especially wrestling and football, and who took an active role in debate at the Trinity Philosophical Society. In 1867, however, at age nineteen, there were two experiences, much reflected upon, that pushed him in rather surprising directions. The first of these was his first sight of Irving, then twenty-nine, in the role of Captain Absolute at the Theatre Royal, Dublin: "What I saw, to my amazement and delight, was a patrician figure as real as the person of one's dreams, and endowed with the same poetic grace."[28] The experience of Irving's poetry in motion was followed a few months later by the discovery of the work of the American poet Walt Whitman, whose *Leaves of Grass* was at the time the subject of much undergraduate snickering over its veiled homoeroticism: "We all talked of Walt Whitman and the new poetry with scorn—especially those of us who had not seen the book. . . . I took the book with me into the Park and . . . from that hour I became a lover of Walt Whitman."[29] Stoker also became then and later Whitman's passionate public defender. This placed him within a small circle of Whitman devotees at Trinity, and their struggle to secure acceptance for the poet is paradoxically important in understanding the mechanisms of "homosexual panic."[30]

The young Stoker responded enthusiastically to Whitman's invocation of the creative joy of male companionship, and may have from the first associated its message with his own intense feelings about Irving—certainly he did so later, after their relationship had been established, when he presented Irving with a two-volume edition of Whitman's works.[31] Surely Whitman affirmed for him the "loving and understanding friendship" that developed, and revealed to him "something of those root-forces which had so strange an influence on both Irving's life and my own, though at the first I was absolutely unconscious of even their existence."[32]

In Stoker's defense of the poet, however, he was compelled to argue, self-defensively one assumes, against suspect passages, interpreting them as either nonessential or expressing a "higher" meaning: "We had quite a fight over it with our companions who used to assail us with shafts of their humour on all occasions. Somehow, we learned, I think, a good deal in having perpetually to argue without being able to deny—in so far as quotation went at all events—the premises of our opponents."[33]

It seems likely that Stoker's exaggerated heartiness, his throwing himself into rough sport, had a double meaning in this context. On the one hand, it was an acting out of Whitman's blessing of a close physicality among men; on the other, a defensive means of ensuring that "the premises of our opponents" about Whitman's homosexuality would not be extended to himself. That Stoker was self-conscious about the "moral issue" in Whitman seems confirmed in his later advice to the poet to make judicious cuts of offending passages for a new popular edition. "I ventured to speak to him what was in my mind as to certain excisions in his work. I said: 'If you will only allow your friends to do this—they will only want to cut a hundred lines in all—your books will go into every house in America. Is that not worth the sacrifice?'"[34]

Stoker in fact enjoyed over a number of years a passionate, if mostly distant and epistolary, attachment to the much older Whitman. He wrote intense letters, unanswered until he sent one, some years after he had left Trinity, in which, he later recalled, "I poured out my heart. I had long wished to do so but was, somehow, ashamed or diffident—the qualities are much alike."[35] He had written, with unrestrained admiration and intimacy: "How sweet a thing it is for a strong healthy man with a woman's eyes and a child's wishes to feel he can speak so to a man who can be if he wishes father, and brother and wife to his soul."[36]

"You did well to write me so unconventionally, so fresh, and so affectionately too," Whitman replied, and there followed, not only a correspondence that lasted until Whitman's death, but three visits by Stoker to Whitman in America. "I found him all that I had ever dreamed of, or wished for in him."[37] On being introduced to Irving and Stoker for the first time, Whitman for his part recorded, "Best of all was meeting Bram Stoker, the Irish boy who had written so uninhibitedly."[38]

A year after leaving Trinity, Stoker met Irving for the first time in his dressing room at the Theatre Royal, where Irving was playing Hamlet. His idolatry found its way into the reviews he wrote for the Dublin press, and an invitation followed to attend a small gathering at Irving's hotel. Here the actor's dramatic rendering of Thomas Hood's "The Dream of Aram" so touched Stoker that he broke down in tears and hysterics, "the thunderous outlet" of "pent-up feelings." Irving rushed to his bedroom and returned with a photo of himself inscribed "God bless you!" It is interesting that when, in his biography of Irving, Stoker tells of this emotional event—the climactic occasion that established the closest personal relationship of his life—he does so in a way that attempts, in the passage immediately following, to draw attention to the manliness of his own character. "I was as men go a strong man, strong in many ways. . . . I had played for years in the University football team. . . . I was physically immensely strong. . . . When, therefore, after his recitation I became hysterical, it was distinctly a surprise to my friends." This apologia then allows him—surely this is its underlying strategy—to pour out his feelings of intense attachment without danger of "misinterpretation." He can then continue: Irving's "pleasure in realizing that [my] capacity for receiving emotion was something akin in forcefulness to his power of

creating it. . . . Soul had looked into soul! From that hour began a friendship as profound, as close, as lasting as can be between two men . . . the
sight of his picture before me, with those loving words . . . *unmans me
once again* as I write."[39]

Stoker was as much in Irving's company as possible over the next few
years, and "the hope grew in me that a time might yet come when he
and I might work together to one end that we both believed in and held
precious in the secret chamber of our hearts."[40] The chance came in
1878, when Irving unexpectedly asked Stoker to become his business
manager at the Lyceum. Stoker immediately resigned from his minor
civil service post in Dublin, put his affairs in order, and got married. His
marriage to Florence Balcombe was moved forward a year, presumably
as a part of a general sorting out of the details of his new life in London.
Irving was "mightily surprised when he found that I had a wife,"[41] but
apparently Florence was not allowed to impinge on work at the theater.
They took no honeymoon, and she figures hardly at all in Stoker's expan-
sive, gossipy biography of Irving—a source that otherwise contains
much about Stoker's own life. The marriage produced one child the next
year, but, if it did not fail outright like Irving's marriage, it seems quickly
to have taken second place to Stoker's more intense relationships at the
theater. Indeed, it is Irving who is spoken of in the biography in terms
explicitly suggesting a marital familiarity: "Irving and I were so much
together that after a few years we could almost read a thought of the
other; we could certainly read a glance or an expression. I have sometimes seen the same capacity in a husband and wife who have lived together for long."[42] Nor was their connection, at least on Stoker's part,
without an element of jealousy, of competition with others for Irving's
approbation.[43]

The biography, otherwise full of dropped names, anecdotes, and asides
about well-known people, contains another, perhaps revealing, omis-
sion. Florence Balcombe's first, rejected, suitor had been Oscar Wilde. In
Dublin, Stoker knew Sir William and Lady Wilde, and after his marriage
to Florence, Oscar continued to see them socially as an occasional dinner
guest at Stoker's house in Cheyne Walk—even after, to the disapproval
of Society, Wilde began to accept invitations without his wife. The copy
of *Salome* he sent to Florence in 1893 was inscribed "with kind regards
to Bram."[44] Yet there is no mention at all of Wilde, family friend, fellow
Irishman and Trinity scholar, and successful playwright, in *Irving*. This
is not simply a matter of Stoker's delicacy in approaching a subject who
was, by the date of the biography's publication in 1906, a public scandal.
His friendship with Ellen Terry, whose three marriages and extramarital
relations were the subject of common gossip, is prominently displayed

in the book, and her character is defended. Stoker was no prude, and the world of the theater in which he was immersed was full of the sexually unconventional and ambiguous. Clearly, it was the prospect of Wilde's name (and the homosexuality with which it had become inextricably bound) *in conjunction* with passages such as those quoted above about the intensity of Stoker's own relationship with Irving that deterred him. This is probably more than Stoker's reluctance to risk the public suspicions that a declared friendship with Wilde might have incurred after the trial of 1895. Like his desire to see Whitman publish a "safe" version of his poems, it involved his own effort to defend, to himself, his close homosocial attachments as something other than sexual. Wilde's affectations and very public flouting of conventional morality brought into doubt the whole structure of a "higher" relationship between men that Stoker used to rationalize his life with Irving. If Stoker did not, that we know, join in the public ostracization and condemnation of Wilde, the gothic novel that took shape in the two years after the Wilde trial clearly drew something from a need to secure the identity of, in Dr. van Helsing's words, "real men." "We men are determined—nay, are we not pledged?—to destroy this monster."[45]

THE STAGE, THE SELF, AND
THE DISGUISED PERSONALITY

> But how can a man know himself if he mistrusts his own identity, and if he puts aside his special gifts in order to render himself an imperfect similitude of some one else?
> — Henry Irving[46]

Where but on the stage is the confusion of reality, the proliferation of personalities, so well expressed, and the self so problematic? Stoker was associated with the theater most of his adult life: first as a journalist drama critic in Dublin, then as Henry Irving's manager in London, and finally as his biographer. Irving's grandly expressed "philosophy of acting," paraphrased approvingly by Stoker, itself drew upon the paradox of the stage—that the actor must know by experience "endless variants and combinations" of human types, but for a successful performance must project as purely and simply as possible only one: "If a character have in itself opposing qualities which cannot be reconciled, then it can never have that unity which makes for strength."[47] This belief, however, that the actor should throw himself wholly into a role, in effect become the person portrayed, implicitly involved, as Irving himself called it, a "dual consciousness"—where the actor renounced Diderot's "emotional distance," but underneath at some level remained a professional player pursuing the tricks of his trade.[48]

The dilemma of the actor's identity suggests Stoker's own situation. Although a strong, robust figure who projected authority and assurance, he spent much of his life playing a willing and self-denying Jonathan to Irving's David. Stoker's professional role was a highly dependent, derivative, and ambiguous one—and shifted with time from that of observer and critic to facilitator and passive participant to, finally, eulogizer. Where he did have a voice of his own, in his sensational stories of the supernatural, he is nevertheless concerned to present apparent contradictions, irreconcilable "opposing qualities," as signs of the pathological, the unnatural, or the dishonest. A conventional late-Victorian gentleman in most respects, he vigorously affirmed the platitudes of his class and time and saw human character in terms of the "strength and unity" of the Victorian code of gentlemanly behavior. But he was also strongly attracted to the world of stage names (Irving had changed his from his family name of Brodribb), a world built on mimicry and amorality, in which honesty was the honesty of portrayal of one of an "endless variety" of emotions and identities. Characteristically, he was both part of and separate from this world: he was not an actor himself, but a go-between, a half-breed, a mere intermediary between audience and performer. He found himself both behind the scenes and in the stalls.

The stage was traditionally associated with loose morality, and many Victorian actors were concerned to project themselves as respectable professionals, to reconstruct their public identities within the conventional idiom of a morally acceptable market economy, where skill, effort, and self-discipline might bring the rewards of both economic benefit and social acceptability. Stoker worked to promote professionalism in the theater, to emphasize the hard work and dedication of actors, and to erase the traditional association of the stage with scandal and immorality.[49] Although this echoed a concern of Irving's, it was also a defensive gesture that expressed Stoker's own ambiguity about his association with such a world. This is an important point, because it indicates the key to Stoker's very similar responses to other areas of prejudice and stereotype, in which denial may suggest a similar inner conflict of attraction and repulsion or embarrassment.

The theater was undeniably a locus for the sexual: the prostitutes who thronged the entre-act refreshment areas, the actresses whose private lives flouted conventional morality, the aesthete devotees of opera and the stage who found in the theater a world that resonated with their own socially imposed game of masks. The stage was also the locus of the sexually ambiguous. Aside from the trousered roles that Ellen Terry played so well,[50] the use of makeup invoked gender ambiguity, especially for males. Like many who feel themselves privileged to get an insider's view of the profession, Stoker found the world of greasepaint thrilling, and claimed that the exaggerated makeup of the Victorian stage was essential (in *Personal Reminiscences of Henry Irving*, he relates a story about a young actor who disastrously attempted to play a role "naturally"). If makeup was a boundary and identity-confusing (and of course feminizing) component of the trade that strongly attracted Stoker, it was also, especially in an age where outward appearances in dress and self-cultivation mattered so enormously, a metaphor for the morally suspect. A prostitute's rouged cheeks and red lips were badges of shame—but what if the innocent also wore these "chains of the devil"? Makeup confused the business of "reading" character, so important in the nineteenth-century metropolis. In an interesting passage, Stoker tells of the great actor's use of a few strokes of the grease pencil on Stoker's own seven-year-old son to turn the "pretty" child into a sneering Mephistopheles.[51]

G. L. Mosse has noted the striking similarity of the late-nineteenth-century discourse about homosexual freemasonry and conspiracy, on the one hand, and that of the Jewish "state within a state," on the other. Both the secret sodomist and the assimilated Jew can be seen as actors slipping like Dracula into respectable society, with the aid of the anonymity of a metropolis that screens the all-important facts of private life.[52] In each case, there is mystery and an inhering ambiguity. Where is the boundary between the homosocial and the homoerotic, the dandy and the sodomite, the poseur and the immoralist? When does the process of assimilation turn a foreign Jew into an Englishman, what racial characteristics remain embedded in the descent of generations?

It is clear that Dracula is an actor—the hammy campness of his twentieth-century Hollywood portrayals arises directly from the inherent theatricality of a character who must conceal his real nature, and whose outward form can mutate at will. In some sense, he may even be a projection of Henry Irving, whose ability to transform himself into his roles was legendary. Stoker saw *Dracula* as potentially at least a piece for the stage, and he may have intended Irving to play the part—just as earlier he had unsuccessfully tried to persuade Irving to take the role of the Wandering Jew—a juxtaposition that has significance in the context of a long tradition associating the Jew with the demonic and the sexually degenerate.[53]

HOMOPHOBIA AND GOTHIC HOMOEROTICISM

It may be that the gothic genre, in its often lubricious search for the unnatural, in its manipulation of buried fears and desires, and in its dependence on secrecy, disguise, and fear of exposure, has always carried with it important homosexual and transsexual elements.[54] Eve Sedgwick has argued that the gothic was "the first novelistic form in England to have close, relatively visible links to male homosexuality" (many of the early gothic classics involve the persecution of younger by older males) and a surprising number of the early gothic authors were themselves "probably homosexual" (Walpole, Beckford, Lewis).[55]

It is now appreciated that the image of the homosexual in western Europe underwent a complex transformation in the nineteenth century.[56] Although the humanitarian assault on capital punishment resulted in the tacit abandonment in England and Wales of the death penalty for buggery after 1837 (abolished in 1861), the effect of this liberalization appears to have been an actual increase in the number of prosecutions for this and other forms of indecency. In 1885 Labouchere's clause of the Criminal Law Amendment Act in fact criminalized a range of homosexual behavior that had previously not been prosecutable. Repression of dangerous sexuality was an important aspect of the drive for respectability, and it seems likely that there was throughout the century an attenuation of areas of popular culture where before there had been some tolerance for "mollies" or "Mary-Annes," and that the late-nineteenth-century bourgeoisie, as well as the working class of pub, music hall, and football ground, became more intensely homophobic than before—driven by a need to distance the wide range of intense male homosocial relationships from "the unspeakable" effeminacy of the aristocrat.[57]

Although Stoker did not introduce homosexual or transsexual characters directly into his fiction, he did devote a section of his book on impostors to "true" or plausible stories of women living as men and men living as women. Titillation and sensationalism mark his retelling of such tales as that of the chevalier/chevalière d'Eon, who was presented to Marie Antoinette at her request in female dress, although characteristically he tacks on a defense of d'Eon as "a real man," with "les organs masculins parfaitement formés," disgracefully forced by the whim of the monarch to play the role of transvestite.[58]

Hidden—that is, disguised—sexual identity is perhaps a more common theme in early, rather than late gothic. It finds its way, for example, into both Lewis's *The Monk* and Maturin's *Melmoth* in the form of a similar tale of a woman disguised as a novice in order to be with her lover.[59] The effect, of course, depended on the long-popular suspicions of monastic sexuality and the unnatural community of men without women. The device of the disguise allows the author to achieve something of the sensational frisson of same-sex passion, while in the end returning the reader to the acceptable world of heterosexuality.

The preoccupation of much early gothic literature with exploiting popular prejudice against the unnatural world of the convent or monastery led inevitably to an emphasis on the perversity of intense same-sex relations. This continued to lie at the heart of much of the genre, even after it had turned away from its early anti-Catholic roots. In William Godwin's *Caleb Williams*, the sadistic enslavement of novice to monk is suggested in secular terms in Caleb's tortuous escape from Falkland's influence. This association serves to heighten the already densely homophobic character of a radical literature that stigmatized aristocratic patronage as destructive of manliness and the aristocrat as a species of effeminate sodomist.[60] Curiously intense, contradictory forces of same-sex repulsion and attraction are a hallmark of many of the classic works of gothic fiction: Frankenstein and his creature, Jekyll and Hyde, Wilde's Dorian (who was once "about to join the Roman Catholic communion")[61] and Basil. In Sheridan Le Fanu's tale of vampirism, "Carmilla," the relationship is between a young girl and an aggressive older woman, but here as well, as with Stoker's Harker and Dracula, the effect of the vampirism motif requires an attractive, innocent, and passive—that is, "feminine"—seducee, male or female, and an older, dominant, and "masculine" seducer, male or female.

While, as in Heathcliff's subjugation of Catherine, psychological vampirism is almost a commonplace of nineteenth-century romances of heterosexual passion, the gothic, in its search for the sensational, often sought to supplant the theme of unexceptionable male dominance of passive femininity with same-sex eroticism, or at least reversed sex roles. Both happen in Stoker's *Dracula*: Dracula's seduction of Harker and the vampirized woman Lucy's transformation into an aggressive, preying threat who in her victimization of small children, as much as in her attempts to penetrate the neck of her lover, has renounced maternal, nurturing, and sexually passive femininity. These buried themes of moral corruption and gender inversion would previously have most readily signified to the Protestant British mind an unnatural Roman Catholicism, but here wander away from this nearly exhausted locus in order to confirm more powerful late-Victorian prejudices—homophobia and anti-Semitism.

Finally, it should be noted that folk vampirism associated a strongly unpleasant odor with the vampire. This finds its way into Stoker's representation of Count Dracula, whose resting places are full of a stench strongly suggesting decomposition and defecation—to a Victorian reader, the airborne infections of cemetery effluvia and bad drains. In this context, it is also relevant to note the metaphoric significance of the piles of gold coins also found in Dracula's lair. Heaped "in a corner," "stained," and covered with dirt,[62] they suggest that cliché of nineteenth-century fiction, the association of wealth with feces. Strong odors may also introduce a hint of sexual perversion.[63] Like his anemia, the vampire's fetid breath and rank body odor may suggest the marks of masturbation, a vice often associated with the developing homosexual.[64] An intimation of fecal odor in the vampire's lair, "a deathly, sickly odour," may also suggest the sodomist.[65] Certainly, association with the fifteenth-century Walachian tyrant Vlad the Impaler, notorious for the staking of victims through their fundaments (displaced in the literary vampire by impalement through the heart), reinforces such an interpretation. One must note as well the resonance between the darkness that surrounds the vampire's crimes, his fear of light, and the darkness associated with the anal, as well as the necessarily hidden nature of homosexual contact. It may even be significant that Dracula's crypt/lair is in the basement of the castle, in its bowels.[66]

Whatever the specific significance, it is clear that in an age in which the bourgeois was perpetually nervous about caste, body odor, which hardly figures at all in polite discourse, emerged in the literature of terror as yet another aspect of nightmarish social dread, associated with sexual perversion, lack of bodily hygiene, and disdain for polite self-control. If one also considers the strong body odor associated in racist discourse with the animalistic African or with the unpleasant odors associated with the Jew (the *foetor judaicus*), as well as that ascribed to prostitutes (owing, it was thought, to the retention of semen) and to menstruating women, it is clear that scent played a role in drawing together or bridging a surprising number of nineteenth-century middle-class prejudices. The discourses of racism, homophobia, misogyny, class hatred, and religious bigotry were all corroborated by this most penetrating of the physical senses.

"DRACULA" AND MALE SEXUALITY

Feminist criticism in the past decade or so has attempted to move the center of this classic of gothic fiction away from the demonic being of the title to his female collaborators and victims, to see in the novel primarily a text about the threat of female aggression.[67] It has been observed that for much of the novel Dracula himself is off-stage, while the real demon at the center of events is the vampirized Lucy Westenra, and that her highly sexualized murder reveals the brutally misogynistic heart of the story.

It is clear that throughout his terror fiction Stoker was, in fact, preoccupied with defending "natural" gender roles by associating the transgression of the boundaries of gender-defined character with danger, madness, and the supernatural. This results in much heavy-handed rendering of women who threaten to preempt the leading role. The devouring, emasculating woman, reinforced by a vivid sexualized imagery, achieves its ultimate expression, no doubt, in *The Lair of the White Worm* with the Lady Arabella, a snake-demon who drags men down into her well-hole. Critics have been quick to seize upon the obvious—that Lady Arabella's well-hole, like the mouth of Lucy Westenra, is a *vagina dentata*. Certainly Stoker's writing is full of images that depend on sexual association for their vividness—such as the "obscene clefts" into which deadly serpents glide in "The Castle of the King." But it is necessary to see that in such a jumble of images, one has both the obscenity of the cleft and the threat of the snake, and that the danger of the masculine woman lies in her masculinity rather than her femininity—that Lady Arabella has, after all, been transformed into a serpent, an image of the male member. Having been injected, as it were, with the virus of maleness, the female vampires could be said to have become unnatural men. Therein lies their danger, and it may therefore be that there is more at work here than mere misogyny. This requires a somewhat different kind of analysis than that involved in the image of Stoker as characteristic woman-hater—with a dominant mother, pre-oedipal fixations, a frigid wife, and a fear of and revulsion from the prostitutes who may have infected him with syphilis.[68] Instead, it will be useful to take as our starting point Stoker's preoccupation with defending a robust "natural" male heterosexuality because of his misgivings about his own homosocial relationships. Following Craft's interpretation, Marjorie Howes, drawing from a textual rather than biographical reading, has concluded that "fundamental ambivalences" motivating *Dracula* "revolve around . . . male homosexuality," and that "the fear that the self contains a subversive side . . . combines with a drive to banish the corrupt self."[69] Consideration of Stoker's life, it will be seen, substantially confirms and amplifies this view, while suggesting perhaps a greater complexity of construction and motivation.

In an article in the *Nineteenth Century* in 1908, Stoker asserted that "the only emotions which in the long run harm are those arising from sex impulse, and when we have realised this we have put a finger on the actual part of danger."[70] This not only gives the lie to the remarkable assertion that Stoker was unaware of the erotic nature of Whitman's poetry, Le Fanu's "Carmilla," or his own creations,[71] but leads us to query wherein in fact lay the "danger"? The passage, with its hint of masturbatory guilt ("a finger on the actual part of danger"), would seem to associate "harm" with his own uncontrollable sexuality. Buried within Stoker's "misogyny" is, in fact, a fear, not of women, but of male sexuality wandering from its natural location (into women) and seizing upon unnatural objects (other men). In "The Man from Shorrox," Stoker tells a story of a commercial traveler in Ireland who insists on the best room in a small hotel, goes to bed in the dark, and awakes in horror in the morning to discover that he is sharing the bed with a corpse. Significantly, the corpse is male. Here the horror of pollution from the dead is reinforced by that of unwittingly having gone to bed with another man. That the other man is lifeless may suggest the taboo of necrophilia, but perhaps also the sterility of homosexuality. It is an early and interesting example of his route into the fiction of the unnatural.

Finally, there has been insufficient recognition of the way in which the literary representation of the vampire in the years prior to *Dracula* had become overtly that of a sexual inversion. There is not merely the implied lesbianism of Sheridan Le Fanu's Carmilla, nor the homosexual overtones of Stevenson's Jekyll and Hyde and Wilde's *Dorian Gray*, but what might almost be called a genre, in which vampirism is the undisguised same-sex sensual exploitation of youth by age. It seems likely that Stoker, with his appetite for researching the vampire legend, would have been fully aware of this emerging fashion for homosexual gothic. For instance, in 1885 Carl Heinrich Ulrichs's "Manor" offered such a story, set in the Faroe Islands, of a sailor's love for a youth. After death, the sailor returns as vampire to suck the blood of his beloved.[72] If Ulrichs's tale, published in Leipzig, escaped Stoker's attention, that of Count Stenbock, published in London in 1894 while Stoker was laboring on his own vampire, would not have. Stenbock's tale, set in a castle in Styria, revolves around the destructive love of an aristocrat, Count Vardalek, for a doomed, faunlike boy with "large, wild, *gazelle*-like" eyes. The count, tall, imposing, and multilingual, is a "cosmopolitan, a wanderer on the face of the earth," with a "soft and insinuating" voice.[73]

The central danger in *Dracula* is Dracula. Although feminist criticism has generally been of great service in locating the cultural significance of the gothic, its perspective has at times been a relatively narrow and perhaps distorting one. In the case of *Dracula*, one must return to the vampire as image of the aggressive male, dangerous because his sexuality can be directed anywhere—toward men as well as women. Stoker was fascinated by the sexual danger exuded by strong men. He described Sir Richard Burton in terms that make this clear: "The man rivetted my attention. He was dark, and forceful, and masterful, and ruthless. . . . He is steel! He would go through you like a sword! . . . As he spoke the upper lip rose and his canine tooth showed its full length like the gleam of a dagger."[74] Why should Burton be described here—Stoker is recollecting intimate meetings, in railway carriages and at small dinners, which involved Irving as well—in terms that clearly associate the explorer with both sexual aggression and the vampire?[75] One answer lies in the need Stoker felt to juxtapose Irving and Burton, to portray the unequivocally sexual attractions of a man like Burton in terms quite different from those he reserved for Irving, those "thin, ascetic" features and "manners of exquisite gentleness" made Stoker's platonic relationship with him defensible.[76] In the same way, Dracula becomes the rogue male, is the "unnatural" threat absolving the close social relations of "normal" men. His seduction of Harker can be restored to the important position it deserves in the story,[77] just as Dracula's own murder at its conclusion, and not Lucy's destruction, marks its resolution. In fact, Dracula draws upon an older construction than that of the late nineteenth century's effeminate "homosexual" degenerate. This is the image of the aggressive, sadistic sodomist, who, like one of the sexual tyrants in de Sade's fantasies, threatens to seize any object—man, woman, or child—in a frenzied search for orgasmic release.

Dracula opens with the young Jonathan Harker's journey through eastern Europe to the count's castle. Like Stoker when he accepted Irving's offer to leave Dublin for London, he is young, a Protestant, trained in the law, and recently engaged to be married. He has, like Stoker, been engaged to arrange the business affairs of an older man. Harker falls under the count's mesmerizing influence, and under that of the three vampire women, who nearly succeed in exploiting his feminine passivity ("I closed my eyes in a languorous ecstasy and waited")[78] in a seduction resonating with incipient fellatio ("Lower and lower went her head as the lips went below the range of my mouth and chin")[79] before the count himself intervenes to save Harker for himself. "Back, I tell you all! This man belongs to me! . . . I promise you that when I am done with him, you shall kiss him at your will."[80] The overtly sexual nature of the assault of the three vampire women serves here to prepare the reader for the idea of the sexual element in the count's own threat, as does the suggestion, immediately following this passage, that, when the fainting Harker awakens, back in his bed, it was the count who carried him there and, "hurried in his task," undressed him.[81]

On one level, at least, the threat of moral contagion, of the unnatural sexualizing of innocence, that this passage projects can be associated with the insatiable and corrupting appetite of male sexual desire focused on other men—and on children. At this stage in the story, before Dracula has announced his intention to make "your girls that you all love" in England his, it is, apparently, the children of the village upon whom he habitually preys. It is this threat of child molestation and the corruption of his own innocence to which Harker responds as he views the count prostrate in a state of slaked desire.

This was the being I was helping to transfer to London, where, perhaps for centuries to come, he might, amongst its teeming millions, satiate his lust for blood, and create a new and ever-widening circle of demi-demons to batten on the helpless. The very thought drove me mad. A terrible desire came upon me to rid the world of such a monster.[82]

The significance of the Harker episode that opens the novel has been effectively drawn by Christopher Craft, and it is no longer possible to argue, as one critic did some years ago, that the novel is "rigidly hetero-sexual" in its framework, or that Dracula's interest in the young man is "ultimately trivial."[83] And although Craft associates Stoker's fear of "the fluidity of gender roles" with contemporary discussion by Havelock Ellis and others of "inversion," rather than, more pointedly, with Stoker's own personal experience, he is surely right to propose that in the novel "an implicitly homoerotic desire achieves representation as a monstrous heterosexuality, as a demonic inversion of normal gender relations."[84]

It remains to consider other intense male relationships in the novel. One, that of the older Dr. van Helsing and his protégé, Dr. Seward, is not free of erotic overtones. Once, we are told, when van Helsing suffered a gangrenous knife wound, Seward sucked it clean. But this connection, like that generally of the four men banded together to save Lucy and punish Dracula, is intended as a representation of the "higher," non-erotic, validly homosocial. Seward's relationship with Renfield, the zoo-phagic madman whom he has imprisoned in his house, however, raises in a more ambiguous way the problem of the uncertain boundary be-tween the homosocial and homosexual. Seward, we are told, suffers from "inner torment" and ineffectuality, and it is he who would take a "savage delight" in helping van Helsing behead Lucy. In "keeping" Renfield, Seward is tempted to immoral experimentation. As Ellis Hanson has ob-served, Renfield is a kind of "homosexual hysteric" with "a gloriously oral-sadistic diagnosis; 'zoophagous.'"[85] He is, of course, a direct conduit of Dracula's pollution, and the suggested relationship between the count and his creature is clearly sadomasochistic. Invited into Renfield's bed-room, Dracula kills him in a struggling embrace.

It has been remarked that the problem of Lucy Westenra, which domi-nates the central section of the novel—first the attempt to save her from Dracula's nightly depredations, and then the need, as she becomes bes-tial herself after death, to hunt her down and destroy her—is a device that serves to bring together the novel's main male characters in bonds of friendship and selfless duty.[86] It has been further argued that the male bonding of van Helsing, Seward, the aristocrat Godalming, and the American Morris carries a suggestion of homosexual desire, especially in the transfusion story, where they each attempt to save Lucy by injecting her with their blood (concealing a homoerotic desire to pool—that is, share—semen).[87] Without denying such an interpretation at some level of the text, we can appreciate that Stoker's more obvious strategy here is to suggest that the union of the four, grounded in a determinedly unsexual homosocial ideal, is the positive mirror-image of the dangerous and destructively sexualized union exemplified in the Dracula-Harker or Dracula-Renfield connection.

Finally, there is the important theme of male hysteria in the novel— the emotional vulnerability of men, and its meaning in a world where gender boundaries are being contested.[88] Stoker portrays, at one time or another, feminine-like weaknesses in several of his male characters, who are nonetheless "real men." As innocent youth, Harker is, of course, the least mature and therefore the weakest of the men. But variously the others too have their breakdowns. Arthur, Lord Godalming, collapses before Mina in a well-drawn picture of grief that unmans him—much as, it seems fair to point out, Irving's death later affected Stoker himself (who collapsed after the funeral). "He [Arthur] grew quite hysterical, and raising his open hands, beat his palms together in a perfect agony of grief."[89] But it is Dr. van Helsing who most surprises us with his emotional instability: "The moment we [Seward and van Helsing] were alone in the carriage he gave way to a regular fit of hysterics. . . . He laughed till he cried and I had to draw down the blinds lest anyone should see us and misjudge."[90] This is a revealing passage, for van Helsing is the stern realist, the guiding hand directing the antivampire confederacy. The intent here seems to have less to do with portraying men as sharing with women a capacity for public emotion—so at odds with the stiff-upper-lipped imperial ideal—than with representing male emotion as "different": "I tried to be stern with him, as one is to a woman under the circumstances; but it had no effect. Men and women are so different in manifestations of nervous strength or weakness."[91] This passage, in fact, recalls Stoker's own hysteria at his first meeting with Irving, and his need to portray this—to himself as well as to others— in terms that do not suggest the effeminate male, to avoid being "misjudged."

In 1887 the Gaiety Theatre in the Strand mounted a burlesque called *Frankenstein; or, The Vampire's Victim* with the popular comic actor Fred Leslie in the role of the Creature.[92] Gothic horror was reduced to farce by the cobbling together of the two types of monster story, by the cross-dressing of both men and women—a pantomime and music-hall idiom,[93] and by Leslie's parodying of Oscar Wilde. He made his entrance dressed as Galatea,[94] while Dr. Frankenstein was played by Nellie Farren in trousers. In subsequent scenes, the Creature, flamboyantly dressed,

Ill. 16. Fred Leslie as the Creature in
The Vampire's Victim, Gaiety Theatre,
London, 1887 (Mander and Mitchenson
Theatre Collection).

with a sunflower in his buttonhole to suggest the aesthete and dandy
Wilde (ill. 16), acquires a vampire mate called "Mary Ann." *Mary-Anne*
was of course a common London slang word for homosexual, and Leslie
played the innuendo to the hilt. The press referred to his solo satirizing
of Wilde as his "special police number."[95]
  Aestheticism had been mocked on the stage before this—most popularly in 1881 in Gilbert and Sullivan's *Patience*—but the association
here, if only in burlesque form, of gothic monstrosity with gender ambiguity and homosexuality seems particularly confirming of the analysis
sketched out above. Additionally, however, there was interpolated an
element of nationalism and racism, a jumble of prejudiced music-hall

clichés, jingoistic asides, xenophobia directed at Germans, and allusions, in particular, to Haggard's Africa: "(Boy hands telegram) 'What's this?' (Reads) 'Handed in at the Witch's Head, near King Solomon's Mines. No sign of Mary Ann in South Africa. Is it a She? Love to Stead. Rider Haggard.'"[96]

The Vampire as Racial Other

In *Dracula*, an association of sexual perversion with Jewish pollution, even if only at a subliminal level, locates the work in the mainstream of late-nineteenth-century European prejudice in general and, in particular, within a quite specific racial discourse.

At first glance, the assertion that the vampire's threat is at some level a racial one—a conclusion encouraged by the immigrant Dracula's avowed wish to seduce "the girls that you all love"—would appear to contradict that of the vampire as (ancient) sodomist and/or (newly constructed) effete, homosexual degenerate. Yet Dracula's ultimate goal is a large one—not the girls only, but "through them you and others shall yet be mine." As Christopher Craft has argued, there may be here a "process of substitution by which 'the girls that you all love' mediate and displace a more direct communion among males."[97] Along these lines, there may be some significance in Conan Doyle's late (post-*Dracula*) tale of "The Sussex Vampire." Here guilt is displaced from the "obvious" vampire suspect, a dark Peruvian woman married to an Englishman, to the real villain—her English stepson, a fifteen-year-old crippled youth, "pale-faced and fair-haired, with excitable light blue eyes," who has an unnaturally close attachment to his father ("He rushed forward and threw his arms round his neck with the abandon of a loving girl. . . . Ferguson gently disengaged himself from the embrace with some little show of embarrassment"), whose affection is, as Holmes explains, "a distorted love, a maniacal exaggerated love."[98]

Late-Victorian homophobia and racism, of course, come to share much under the surface. The racial fiend is often a sexual threat and the sexual "pervert," a racial (that is, eugenic) menace. In the first place, both the racial outsider, black, Asian, or Jew, and the homosexual are by tradition highly sexed. They are in theory mastered by their lubricious and bestial natures. Moreover, the fear of race-mixing, of "miscegenation," which allows racial others to pass for whites and continue secretly to infect their blood, resonates with that of the disguised homosexual, who threatens a secret moral pollution damaging to both the fecundity and the vigor of the race.

Association of the, often exotic, racial outsider with dark cruelty and perversity, with the supernatural and mysterious, with the secret rites of witchcraft and sexual taboo, is common in the gothic, and can be associated generally with other representations in the genre of the psychological, sexual, and cultural outsider.[99] While the threatening image is often that of the Negro—as in "Carmilla," where we meet "a hideous black woman,"[100] the racial outsider may also, especially in early gothic, wear an Asian face. In Sue's *The Wandering Jew* of 1845, a work with which Stoker was very familiar, there is an elaborate subplot involving an Indian thug, who represents the beautiful cruelty of the East, "where the gigantic vampire bat sucks the blood of its victims whilst it prolongs their sleep."[101]

It is, however, the threat of the transference of racial danger to Europe itself that has seized the attention of those critics who have seen fear of "reverse colonization" in the deployment of the vampire myth. It is an apprehension expressed explicitly—although only to be dismissed by a "scientific" Sherlock Holmes—in Conan Doyle's "The Sussex Vampire": "We had thought it [vampirism] was some wild tale of foreign parts. And yet here in the very heart of the English Sussex. . . ."[102] Infection from abroad can, of course, be indirect—that is, through the corruption of the European, who brings back to the heart of empire a moral disease contracted abroad. But in its most tangible form, it is the literary representation of an actual assault, the threatened invasion of the alien him- or herself, that directly appeals to the heart of racial prejudice. Already in 1845, Sue's novel raised this danger by portraying his murderous thug as part of a racial conspiracy to dominate the white world: "'Exile will widen our dominions. Brother, you shall have America!' he said to the negro. 'Brothers, I will take Europe!'"[103]

If, as I maintain below, the racial threat in Stoker's *Dracula* can best be associated with the Jew rather than the black or Asian, one must remember that Jew, Asian, and black shared a rhetorical opprobrium that, although each possessed in the literature of prejudice uniquely repulsive elements, tied them together. All were slaves to tradition or superstition, all were marked by a peculiar odor, all were sexual threats. It is not difficult to present Dracula as representative of a generalized non-European, although it may be going too far to suggest, as one critic has done, that although Dracula's skin is white, his clothing is significantly black.[104] This degree of subtlety is unnecessary if the racial threat posed by Dracula is that of the Jew rather than the nonwhite.

THE EMPIRE, BLACKNESS, AND THE WANDERING IMAGE OF THE JEW

Like Dracula, "the Jew" can take a variety of forms. He can be both eternal threat and eternal victim, Judas and the Wandering Jew Ahasuerus, capitalist and sweated proletarian, masculine roué and feminized homosexual, white and black. In a sense, the question of whether Dracula at some level represents the colonial Other or the domestic Jew is moot. This is not merely because each is a type of generalized "Other," but because, as the realm of European conquest spread in the eighteenth and nineteenth centuries, the gothic image of the Jew traveled with it. The "blackness" of the Jew—the anti-Semitic assertion that Jews possessed, in Robert Knox's words, an "African character,"[105] and more specifically that they were, as Houston Stewart Chamberlain claimed, a "mongrel" race with Negro blood—is an aspect of racist discourse made familiar by the work of Sander Gilman, G. L. Mosse, and others.[106] What is not so well understood is the way the "Jewishness" of the black figured in colonial discourse.

Jews were, of course, an actual and visible presence in the late-nineteenth-century Empire, from South African entrepreneurs who rose to great fortune like Alfred Beit and Barney Barnato to lesser actors in the "New Babylon" of the Witwatersrand—Alois Nellmapius, Sammy Marks, and the convicted "white slaver" Joe Silver,[107] down to the petty traders, dealers and outfitters, hoteliers and hucksters of frontier society everywhere. European Jews, like those from other trading cultures, the Lebanese or, on the east coast of Africa, Indian middlemen, were drawn by the commercial and lending opportunities of the army camp and the colonial town. Moreover, by the end of the century, the great exodus from eastern Europe provided an augmentation of often very poor and more ethnically distinctive Jews. Throughout the rough and squalid ports and river stations of the fin de siècle empire, there was also an international prostitution network, which was, in popular culture at least, commonly seen (or imagined) to be a characteristically Jewish enterprise. Prominent among the colonial whores who serviced the sexual needs especially of those British who were reluctant to take "native" mistresses were Polish-Jewish women.[108]

The Jew in the empire, already "the flower of a Negroid root,"[109] provided another service as well. The stereotypical character and physiognomy of "the Jew" surfaces surprisingly frequently in the language used to describe nonwhite peoples from the Arctic to the Tropics. Writing of an Eskimo he encountered at Spafarief Inlet, Berthold Seemann makes an association that, of course, goes deeper than appearances: he "possessed to a remarkable degree the hooked nose and large black eyes peculiar to the Hebrew."[110] Nor, commenting on the avariciousness of a central African tribe, could Livingstone resist invoking the language and tone of Shylock and his lost ducats. When a bride who had cost ten goats died unexpectedly, "Not a syllable of regret for the beautiful young creature does one hear, but for the goats: 'Oh, our ten goats!'—they cannot grieve too much—'Our ten goats—oh! oh!'"[111]

What really focuses, however, the association of black and Jew are the inherently gothic themes of blood sacrifice, self-mutilation, and cannibalism, and it is in the realm of sadism and the cannibal that the Jewishness of the savage flourishes best, from the sixteenth-century Dominican priest Durán's theorizing that the Aztecs were "the children of Israel"[112] to a remarkably dense nineteenth-century representation of South Pacific religion, custom, and physiognomy as Jewish.

Familiarity with the biblical story of the women who, in the days of Elisha, in time of famine devoured their own children (2 Kings 6:29), made a Jewish association with the "revelling in human flesh" of the Pacific islanders tempting.[113] In New Zealand, Surgeon-Major Thomson commented on the "Jewish style of features" of the Maori. His further remarks on their exaggerated grief, their laceration of their flesh, continue the theme, as "analogous to a similar custom among the Jews."[114] An earlier visitor, John Nicholas, who also noted the similarity between ancient Hebrew grieving and Maori practice, remarked upon the keenness with which the Maori traded with his ship: they were "very noisy merchants, and as keen in enhancing their commodities as the most crafty Jews on the Royal Exchange."[115]

Such homologies were greatly encouraged by the common, if bizarre, belief that a wandering "lost tribe" of Israel, passing through Asia and thus into the Pacific had actually contributed Semitic blood to the islanders' racial inheritance. The missionary the Reverend Richard Taylor thought the Pacific custom of taboo very like "the Mosaic law relating to uncleanliness," and this, together with the fondness of the natives for reciting genealogies, helped establish in his mind the likelihood of a Jewish migration in ancient times to the cannibal islands, where they "fell to their lowest state of degradation, given up to the fiercest passions."[116] Taylor also had peculiar theories about the affinity of Maori and Semitic languages, but one reads much the same drift of diffusionist logic elsewhere. For instance, without actually spelling out a "lost tribe" solution, the Reverend Michael Russell took note of the curious fact that "the posterity of Jacob displayed in their idolatrous worship an affinity to the ignorant hordes who now occupy the islands of the Pacific."[117] In 1838 Edgar Allan Poe employed suggestions of diffusionist mystery in his tale of maritime and South Pacific terror, *The Narrative of Arthur Gordon Pym*; there are "hieroglyphs" in caves and the king of the savage islanders is called "*Tsalemon* or *Psalemoun*."[118]

The particularly grotesque descriptions of a cannibalism of appetite and frenzy in Fiji seem, however, to have encouraged the most determined associations with Jewish custom and appearance. The Reverend Thomas Williams, having noted the "Hebrew usage" suggested by the behavior of Fijian women in greeting returning war parties, made an even more vivid linkage in his account of Fijian singing: "They assemble nightly for recitation exercises, and enliven their daily tasks by frequent snatches of songs, sung to a sort of plaintive chant, limited to a few notes, and always in a minor key. Some have thought it to resemble the singing in a Jewish synagogue."[119]

Another missionary, John Hunt, carried the association further, inevitably linking the trading shrewdness of some of the islanders with Jewish commercial practices—they were "the Jews of Fiji; and Jews many of them are in many respects. . . . In war, the Fijians are anything but brave."[120] Even the urbane Alfred St. Johnston, writing late in the century, when theories of an actual migration of lost tribes had been discredited, could not resist a (comic) judaicizing of Fijian "cannibals": "I found them [Fijian women] pleasant enough, and in the course of the day have taught the cannibal one, who is of a distinctly Jewish type, with fine hook nose and large nostrils (this information I 'throw out' for the benefit of anyone interested in the Lost Tribes Question), how to cook a potato."[121]

St. Johnston also, however, brings us to the probable deep source of such association—not only in diffusionist theories, but in the gothic imagination, in a domestic cannibal tradition that traveled to the Pacific in the minds of European observers. In an article in the *Gentleman's Magazine*, he discusses cannibalism generally as a "real" practice, but ends with the myth of the blood libel, noting that "the Russian, Polish, and indeed all the Slave [*sic*] races, credit the Jews with the use of this rite to this day. . . . They believe that at Passover a child is killed and eaten with many dark and unheard-of observances." Although he calls this an "absurd tradition," he reminds the reader that it had nevertheless figured in recent criminal trials in Hungary.[122]

And so back to the gothic tradition. William Mariner's account of the South Pacific makes mention of another association that brings the cannibal into the realm of the Jew. The Fijians, he noted, were circumcised, "according to the Jewish rite."[123] By the end of the century, Herbert Spencer had erected an evolutionary sociology on such parallels: Jewish circumcision was a survival of a stage when primitive cannibalism had given way to a symbolic mutilation, when society moved from a sadistic and fatal trophy-taking to a lesser blood-offering. In Fiji, he claimed, one could see a kind of missing link—where both an earlier cannibalism and its successor, circumcision "in the Jewish manner," survived side by side.[124] If the painful and bloody rituals of cicatrization and tattooing in Africa and the Pacific were available parallels to a Jewish "self-mutilation," there may lurk another, more hidden association, which draws us not merely into an essentially gothic discourse, but into the realm of the vampire. Sander Gilman has argued that the ritual of *met-sitsah*, the sucking of the infant's penis by the *mohel* in the orthodox Jewish rite of circumcision to staunch the bleeding was extensively discussed as a possible route of transmission of the syphilis, which Jews in particular were thought to harbor.[125] We may note the sexual and vampiric, as well as pathogenic associations of such blood-sucking, and the combination of all three—infection, unnatural sexuality, and blood lust—in Stoker's Dracula.

The stereotypical Jew was deeply entrenched in European popular culture and can be expected to have been buried deeply in the mentality of the nineteenth-century British missionary, explorer, and colonist. Employed frequently and casually by analogy and metaphor to further darken the image of the nonwhite abroad, it itself absorbed some of that Other's blackness in the process of association—another example of the mutually reinforcing back-and-forth flow of a pejorative and gothicized discourse.

DRACULA AS JEW

> *The last I saw of Count Dracula was his kissing his hand to me,*
> *with a red light of triumph in his eyes, and with a smile that*
> *Judas in hell might be proud of.*[126]

As Bryan Cheyette has recently reminded us, the extent to which a racialized image of the Jew permeated nineteenth-century mainstream culture in liberal Britain has been largely neglected.[127] "The Jew" was propelled to the fore of public discussion in the 1880's and after by eastern European pogroms and immigration in much the way that the abolition debate had exalted negative and positive stereotypes of the Negro a hundred years earlier. Previously, the image of the threatening, wandering Jew had played a relatively minor role in British popular culture, compared to the thickness of the equivalent representation in the folk traditions of Germany and eastern Europe.[128] But sensational press accounts of alien immigrants in London, like blood-libel stories in Hungary or fear of the plague in Hamburg, heightened public apprehension. In the context of fin de siècle anxieties over Britain's imperial strength, the wealthy, assimilated Jew could be readily gothicized, to become, in Cheyette's perceptive phrase, "a dark double of Empire," "a degenerate 'chosen' race," compared to the "civilizing" imperial race (ill. 17).[129]

If a plausible case can be made for Frankenstein's Monster as escaped Jamaican slave, a parallel argument for seeing Stoker's Count Dracula as the eternal Jew seems obvious and compelling.[130] Until recently, such a connection, seemingly obvious, excited little comment or exploration. In 1991, Jules Zanger, noting the convergence of the Dreyfus affair, the

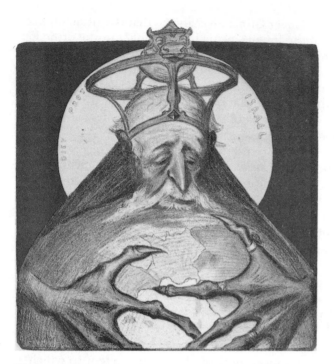

Ill. 17. C. Léandre, "The House of Rothschild" (1898),
from Eduard Fuchs, *Die Juden in der Karikatur* (British
Library).

mesmeric character Svengali in the popular London stage production of
Trilby, and *Dracula* in the mid 1890's, made a tentative and brief exploration of anti-Semitic messages possibly buried in Stoker's text.[131] While
it seems unlikely to me that Stoker drew directly from Svengali for his
Dracula—he began his book well before the play appeared—both drew
from the same tradition of the "penetrating glance" and secret knowledge of the eternal, alien Jew. To a historian's mind, making the case
requires more, however, than a deconstructionist assault on the text.[132]
We must ask what Stoker's own sources and ideas on the subject of the
European Jew may have been, and what the nature of the public discussion of the alien "problem" contemporaneous with the writing of
Dracula was, before proceeding to consider ways in which the story of
the vampire itself can be said to demonstrate Jewish—that is, anti-
Semitic—coding.

    The thinness of the biographical record makes it difficult to assess the
extent to which Bram Stoker may have been influenced in his Dublin
years by Irish anti-Semitic traditions. There was at least polite prejudice

in Dublin, as in London, society. It is not inconceivable that Stoker himself, christened Abraham, with a foreign-sounding surname, suffered from some degree of peer prejudice in childhood, or that he was sensitive that on this score he might be "misjudged." Jews as such, though, have no role in his early stories dealing with Irish life, although there may be a hint of Jewish avarice in his portrait of the money-lending Gombeen man in *The Snake's Pass:* "an' he would take the blood out of yer body if he could sell it or use it anyhow."[133]

As Irving's business manager, Stoker was familiar with London Jewry in his work at the Lyceum in arranging financial backing for Irving's productions, in his dealings with the press to get plays well reviewed, and in his hiring and firing of actors, actresses, and musicians. Prominent Jews, such as J. M. Levy, owner and editor of the *Daily Telegraph*, numbered among Irving's admirers and friends and were seen socially by Stoker and his wife. There is no indication that Stoker or Irving were anti-Semitic in any public or vulgar way, and among Stoker's own records of guests at "first night" dinners he arranged at the Lyceum, one finds the names of many prominent and wealthy Jews, from the Rothschilds to the socially more dubious Barney Barnato.[134] Social mixing with wealthy Jews, of course, hardly precludes a casual acceptance of stereotype or the anti-Semitism of the smoking-room kind.

Irving did not play Shylock until after a trip to the Middle East in 1879. The experience of seeing the Jew "in what seemed his own land and in his own dress" convinced him that he could bring to the part a more genuine understanding.[135] Although the result was a more dignified and sympathetic characterization than was often seen on the London stage—winning both the applause of some Anglo-Jews and attacks from anti-Semites like Lord Houghton—nevertheless, it can be argued that this more "natural" portrayal actually served more effectively to remove Shylock from a distanced caricature and locate him as a contemporary and actual presence. As Houghton observed, the theatrical Jew of stage myth was transformed by Irving into a "gentleman of the Hebrew persuasion, with the manners of Rothschild."[136] At the same time, Irving adopted a way of emphasizing the first words Shylock speaks ("Three thousand ducats—well") so that it should immediately communicate "the harsh note of the usurer's voice."[137] Moreover, his own magical combination of makeup and facial contortion produced, in fact, a racial and ethnic Shylock of convincing effect: "the lips thickened, with the red of the lower lip curling out and over after the manner of the typical Hebraic countenance . . . the bridge of his nose . . . rose into the Jewish aquiline . . . the eyes became veiled and glassy with introspection—eyes which at times could and did flash like lurid fire."[138]

Eyes that flash, red lips, and aquiline nose are characteristics Stoker gave Count Dracula. This association is not far-fetched. Stoker's friend Hall Caine recorded that at the time their imaginations "constantly revolved" about the supernatural subjects of both the Wandering Jew and the "Demon Lover" as possible roles for Irving.[139] Irving's success with Shylock—it was a part he played "thousands of times"—apparently led Stoker to hope to persuade him to perform a dramatic version of Eugène Sue's "really excellent"[140] novel *The Wandering Jew*. Whether or not Stoker wanted Irving to take the Jew's role (or the more gothic one of the Jesuit Rodin, or, possibly, both),[141] he was especially taken with Sue's association of the Jew's curse with the advance of the cholera, an idea that "seemed to be a dramatic inspiration and had prehensile grasp."[142] Stoker's fascination with the legend of the Jew Ahasuerus, condemned by God to roam the earth until the Second Coming because of his refusal to succor Christ on his way to the Crucifixion, led him to research the story (as he would also research the vampire legend in the British Museum) through its Renaissance and medieval sources, and, oddly, to include it in his book on famous impostors.[143] It became, Hall Caine later recalled, "one of Bram's pet themes."[144] His awareness that the story was hard to suppress in an age of "Jew-baiting"[145] may have led him to hope that a stage version, at a time when there was a tangible increase in anti-Jewish feeling in London owing to Ashkenazi immigration, would be a popular success—although it is fair to point out that neither Stoker nor Irving saw themselves as anti-Jewish. Irving was, indeed, deeply troubled by stories of pogroms in eastern Europe.[146] It is also true that the Sue version of the legend, in line with the nineteenth-century evolution of Ahasuerus into rebel and romantic wanderer,[147] places the Jew in a favorable light, making him a tragic, almost heroic figure, who manages to foil the nefarious schemes of the story's real enemies of humanity, the Jesuits.

There were nineteenth-century English versions of the Wandering Jew before the Sue novel appeared in translation in 1846.[148] Maturin invokes the tale in the title and theme of *Melmoth the Wanderer*, and Lewis includes a cameo appearance, as it were, of the Jew himself in *The Monk*. Stoker was probably familiar with these novels. He certainly knew the rendition of the Wandering Jew presented in the Reverend George Croly's *Salathiel* in 1828. Croly was an eccentric well known to Stoker's father in Dublin.[149] But presumably it was a version of the Sue story adapted for the stage that inspired Stoker to see the story as a promising thing for the Lyceum. There had been a number of dramatizations since the story's revival in London in a 21-scene production of 1873.[150] In the stage directions of George Lander's version (which call for a Wandering Jew with long jet-black hair and jet-black eyebrows, dressed in a long black robe), for example, it is not fanciful to see some version of Stoker's representation of Dracula—an association that may also be suggested in the Jew's declamation, "A curse has fallen on all who inherit my blood!"[151]

Before turning to what resonances there may be between Sue's story and *Dracula*, however, it is necessary to consider another of Stoker's intense male friendships, that with the minor novelist Hall Caine: "friendship which is not a jilt sure to desert us . . . our friendship has needed no solder of sweet words to bind it."[152] Caine was deeply interested in the historical Jew. He wrote one popular novel about a Jewish family set in Morocco, *The Scapegoat*, and planned another on the Jewish ghetto in Cracow. Both projects were assiduously researched, Caine actually going to Morocco and to Russia for local color.

Like Stoker, his near contemporary, Hall Caine was an outsider—born on the Isle of Man—who sought his career in London through journalism and sentimental novels. He became Stoker's closest friend, next to Irving, whom he also knew familiarly, and in 1893 he dedicated his story of a Manx sea-dog, *Capt'n Davy's Honeymoon*, to Stoker. The character of Davy, portrayed with "the heavy manners of a bear [but] the big soft heart of the baby of a girl" was, he claimed, shaped on that of his friend: "Capt'n Davy without his ruggedness and without his folly, but with his simplicity, his unselfishness and his honour—Bram Stoker!"[153] Stoker returned the favor in 1897, dedicating *Dracula* to "Hommy Beg"— Caine's childhood Manx nickname.

Caine's fascination with the Jew was a complex affair. In Morocco, he "so steeped himself in the knowledge of Jewish life and ideas and ritual" that his friends, says Stoker, "almost accepted him as an authority on the subject."[154] The preface to *The Scapegoat* gives thanks to the chief rabbi in London and to other Jewish scholars for information they had provided on Sephardic Jewry. And yet the result was a characteristically confused racialism, in which there are good and bad stereotypical blacks, Muslims, and Jews. Although, like Stoker, one supposes, Caine saw himself as relatively free from prejudice, and his work as an effort to portray the Jew with a human and sympathetic face, nevertheless the work insistently racializes human character. Muslims are represented as corrupt and sensual fanatics, and the majority of the Jewish community, if not evil, are represented as intolerant, unforgiving, and "absorbed in getting and spending." Significantly, the greatest evil in the book, the Muslim governor of Tetuan, has Negro blood, while the pale, blue-eyed Jewish heroine, Naomi, is half-English.[155] Both Jew and Muslim are presented as ancient types, as unchanged over the centuries—the novel is set in the mid nineteenth century—as Dracula with his Boyar blood. Such hereditary stasis was changeable, for good or ill, only by infusion of the blood of another race.

This ambivalence toward the Jew is even more apparent in Caine's

musings to Stoker about his experiences in Russia and the terrible pogroms then much in the newspapers. Like liberals generally, Irving and
Stoker were inclined to view the forced exodus from the east as a terrible
"persecution." Caine returned however with the Russian official version, and "explained it all to me fully":

> The Jew tavern-keeper was also the local usurer, and would make a certain
> advance [to the peasant who sold his grain for drink] on the man's labour
> for the coming year. When that credit had ended, since he never could get
> even, he would pledge the labour of his children. Thus after a time the
> children, practically sold to labour, would be taken away to the cities there
> to be put to work without remuneration. It was practically slavery. Then
> the Russian Government, recognizing the impossibility of dealing with
> such a state of affairs, undertook to drive out the Jews altogether.[156]

This account, it will be seen, manages to couple the metaphoric vampirism of the usurer with the Jew's medieval reputation for child-stealing,
something that Stoker's vampires also engage in.

Public discussion of the Jewish "problem" in late-nineteenth-century
Britain was focused within three interconnected areas of discourse. First,
there was that surrounding the social issue—unemployment, sweating,
and the role of the Jew as both exploiter and impoverished, undercutting
workman. The second involved the politics of immigration—and raised
the image of an "invasion" of "aliens" who retained their own language
and institutions, colonizing areas of towns and displacing native Englishmen and women. The third involved a heightened imperial patrio-
tism and apprehension of an approaching Armageddon in which a fifth
column of foreigners might be a national danger, and in which Jews, in
particular, were singled out as unpatriotic and physically degenerate, not
a manly or imperial race. This latter fear was reinforced, of course, by
the press attention given to the Dreyfus affair.

In the same year that saw the publication of *Dracula*, the novelist Robert H. Sherard brought out a collection of essays on *The White Slaves of
England*.[157] Writing on the slipper-makers and tailors of Leeds, he blames
the low wages that were driving many English out of the trade on the
unfair competition of recently immigrated Jews. His visit to a Jewish
slipper factory in the dead of night, when it was gas-lit and going strong,
evokes an essentially gothic image.[158] This exercise was but a modest
example of what had become a commonplace in the sensationalist press
of the 1880's and 1890's—the encoding of the urban social problem as a
Jewish problem. Beatrice Potter's analysis for Charles Booth of the poor
East London Jewish community instills a kind of primitive exoticism
into her subject that resonates with much in the gothic literary tradi-

tion. She observes their alien ceremonies from behind the trellis of the women's gallery: "the heat and odour. . . . A low, monotonous, but musical-intoned recital of Hebrew prayers . . . this rhythmical cadence of numerous voices, the swaying to and fro . . . you may imagine yourself in a far-off Eastern land."[159]

This discourse is best exemplified, however, in the writings of Arnold White, who published extensively, appeared before parliamentary committees, and was a frequent and aggressive public speaker on the need for strict controls on immigration. White preached progressive, even radical, solutions to urban environmental degradation and poverty, but grounded his case in anti-Semitism, which he clearly hoped would provide a popular basis for a non-Marxist national and patriotic socialism. Although White, like the slum clergyman Canon Barnett and many others, could claim in his more guarded moments that he was only attacking a certain type of Jew, not Jews as a race, in fact the rhetoric he employed vividly represented the threat as a racial one. In the 1880's, the term *alien* came, in the coded discourse of the social problem, to mean specifically the eastern European, Ashkenazi Jew. It is a word that itself carries a sense of invasion, danger, and mystery. White in fact employed a gothicized image of the Jew, and spoke darkly of their "tainted constitutions," of their "brains charged with a subtle mischief, and languishing or extinct morality." They would "transmit a terrible inheritance of evil to the next generation, there to taint once more a whole community."[160]

There was, of course, a long-established tradition, on the Left as well as Right, in which the Jew was emblematic of exploitation and cosmopolitan wealth. Dracula's heaps of hoarded gold have a direct as well as metaphoric relevance here. Moreover, money is vividly associated with the vampire in the important confrontation scene where Dracula tells his pursuers that "you and others shall yet be mine—my creatures, to do my bidding and to be my jackals." When Harker lunges at Dracula's heart with his great Kukri knife, gold coins and banknotes flow out of the slashed coat rather than blood.[161] With or without the Jew, capitalism begged a vampire metaphor. As early as 1733, we find this employed in an assault on foreign (Dutch) financiers: "Our Merchants, indeed, bring Money into their Country, but, it is said, there is another Set of Men amongst us who have as great an Address in sending it out again to foreign Countries without any Returns for it, which defeats the industry of the Merchant. These are the *Vampires* of the Publick, and Riflers of the Kingdom."[162] Engels spoke of "the vampire property-holding class" in *The Condition of the Working Class in England*, and Marx employed gothic imagery when he spoke of capital itself as "dead labour which,

vampire-like, lives only by sucking living labour."[163] And in popular
parlance generally, unscrupulous company promoters and (often Jewish)
stock-jobbers were "vampires," "bloodsuckers," "wolves," and "vul-
tures"—gothic imagery that had a peculiar aptness when, in the 1880's,
the manager of the London Burial Company embezzled some £300,000.[164]

   In the nineteenth century, the image of the Jew as threat was appropriated and intensified by the writers of gothic fiction and then redeployed
in the political-economic rhetoric of socialists and the xenophobic bigotry of proto-fascists like White. In Maturin's *Melmoth*, we find an aged
"converso" Jew, apparently assimilated, but in reality living a secret existence in the hidden rooms and passages beneath his house. Here in this
cryptlike subterranean maze, he hordes, not money but that which lifeless coin may signify. There are open coffins with skeletons, instruments
"anatomical," and "human and brute abortions, all in their states of
anomalous and deformed construction, not preserved in spirits, but
standing in the ghastly nakedness of their white diminutive bones."[165]
There was always a metaphoric vampirism in the traditional image of
the Jew as usurer, as bloodsucker. This is reinforced by the ancient
charge of occult practices involving the blood of Christian children. The
popular story of the Wandering Jew, even when the Jew is presented in a
favorable light, does not escape the vampire association. He cannot die,
and he brings the plague. Indeed, the contradictory composite image of
the Jew as both victim and doom-bringer directly parallels the contradictory anti-Semitic representation of the Jew as both degraded, sweated
proletarian and capitalist exploiter.

   White and others committed to the social question in the 1880's and
1890's persistently gothicized the problem of the alien immigrant. The
danger was painted in language that drew directly upon that of gothic
monstrosity and infective danger: White wrote of the Jew as a social
"contagion," a "pollution" that threatened to "penetrate" the lives of the
poor.[166] He applauded American anti-Chinese legislation with the curious insistence that "they habitually desecrate graveyards by the removal
of bodies therefrom."[167] In England, the problem was the "asiatic" Jew,
and he attached the Jewish immigration problem to the larger racial
rhetoric that constructed a threat of "reverse colonization": "Whether
the decline of the British empire will be dated from the time when Barbarians were first introduced into her workshops, is a matter for the historian of the future." Although Jews "come here *for the most part* not
because they have an inborn desire to colonise England" (the qualifica-
tion is significant), the English had, just as did the citizens of British
Columbia or of the Australasian colonies, a need to preserve "the welfare
of their own blood, race, and language."[168] Nor was White averse to call-

ing up the possibility of direct popular action if government were too slow to meet the threat—a "*Judenhasse* [hatred of Jews] in the heart of London." Given the gothicization of the image of the Jew, it will come as no surprise to recognize in that familiar scene of twentieth-century film gothic, the villagers in arms in pursuit of creature/vampire/were-wolf, the translation of *Judenhetze* (Jew hunt) into *Monsterhetze*.[169]

It remains to examine *Dracula* in the light of Stoker's reading of Sue's *The Wandering Jew* as well as the public discussion of the alien problem and the Dreyfus case. The most obvious connection is that of deathless-ness—like the vampire, the wandering Jew suffers the curse of immor-tality.[170] In the rhetorical idea of "the eternal Jew," this deathlessness characterizes the entire race, condemned to eternal diaspora, unevolv-ing, an enduring primitive presence in Western society. In Sue's novel, of course, though the Jew brings in his wake God's curse in the form of cholera, the subversive threat is actually transferred to another deathless tribe—the order of Jesuits, whose unnatural union is perpetuated from generation to generation. Jewlike, the Jesuits have insinuated them-selves into every level of society. M. Rodin is the real vampire of the story. Dressed in rusty black, he possesses a visage that is "absolutely colorless" and has "a death-like immobility." He "might have been mis-taken for a corpse."[171] As with Dracula's distant control of Renfield or Lucy, Rodin exercises his malign influence from a distance, through the web of clandestine informants that tie together the worldwide con-spiracy. Furthermore, like both Jew and vampire, the Jesuit is especially associated with the abuse of innocence, with the capture and infection of children.

In *Dracula*, there is another tribe of eternal wanderers, associated with superstition and clandestine threat, and with child abduction—the Gypsies. Harker notes that the Gypsies who serve the count are but part of a worldwide order, "Almost outside all law."[172] The count's departure from his castle is facilitated by these people, Jewlike in their stateless-ness; his return, by the only Jew directly represented as such in the novel, Hildesheim, a money-hungry agent of the count's, with a nose "like a sheep."[173] Both Gypsy and Jew, of course, recall the count's own obscurely asiatic origins. They are all primitive types associated with the tribalism of a premodern era, models of "arrested development" and "incomplete moral evolution."[174] Specifically, van Helsing's character-ization of the vampire's childlike, undeveloped mind suggests the charge that the traditional Jew was representative of a premodern—that is, Old Testament—level of primitive moral development. It has been noted that the story of Dracula is itself an inversion of the Resurrection story—how Dracula reverses the Eucharist and drinks the blood of the faithful.[175]

This association of the count with the Antichrist lends further weight to the association of Jew with vampire, and of the moral world of the primitive boyar with that of the vengeful, blood-sacrifice-demanding God of the Old Testament. Dracula's pitiful acolyte Renfield has, as Dr. Seward notes, taken the scriptural phrase "For the blood is the life" literally.[176] He had abandoned the metaphoric blood sacrifice of the Protestant service for a more ancient, cannibalistic superstition.

The terror that Dracula inspires lies in the mobility of his threat, in his ability to change forms, to travel and to influence people at a distance. The danger has no fixed location, and its victims may be male or female, adult or child, foreign or English. It is this that lifts a conventional gothic tale of a haunted castle into something with a wider resonance—into a metaphor for the generalized fear of strangers, outsiders, and the dark "Other." This fear may be linked to a perceived national—that is, racial—vulnerability, as Steven Arata has argued, or, more generally, to a powerful late-nineteenth-century identity crisis. Dracula destroys his victims' "real" selves and gives them others, versions of his own "race."[177] That Dracula is in some sense coded as racial threat is obvious: we may note his strong, if ambivalent, sexuality; his offensive odor; his corruption of the blood of his victims. But if this is true, what kind of racial threat does he suggest? Here it is necessary to remind ourselves that Dracula immigrates to England and becomes the invisible threat within. It is reasonable to associate him, therefore, with the most tangible alien immigrant threat of the time, the eastern European Jew, rather than a more generalized and metaphoric image of the unspecific colonial "Other." As a member of an assimilated "white" race already familiarly part of European culture, Dracula can "pass": "I am content if I am like the rest, so that no man stops if he sees me, or pause in his speaking if he hear my words, to say, 'Ha, ha! a stranger!'"[178]

> Singly, in twos, and in threes—like the rats of Hamelin—from
> all sorts of cellars, garrets, and butcher shops, the [slum Jewish]
> finishers still at work came forth.[179]

The association of Dracula-as-immigrant with the eastern European Jew is strongly suggested in the count's eastern European origin. By the turn of the century, almost 90 percent of Rumanian emigrants were Jewish.[180] Moreover, his mode of travel, on a Russian ship loaded with a cargo of filth—that is, the soil from Dracula's vault—has some significance. From the Middle Ages on, wandering Jews, like vampires and rats, had been associated with plague, and as recently as 1892, reappearance of cholera in Hamburg had been blamed on the arrival of Polish Jews there.[181] Jews bound for England often left from German or Baltic ports in overcrowded and unsanitary ships for the northeastern coast of England, and when Dracula's (Russian) ship of the dead slips into Whitby harbor, it is arguably a representation of lively contemporary fears that continental diseases would be brought into England by unclean immigrants from the shtetl. These fears were shared even by the defenders of Anglo-Jewry, who, often from Sephardic backgrounds themselves, found the Yiddish-speaking Ashkenazim an alien and disturbing presence that complicated the question of their own identity.

The extent to which the Jew of whatever background was able to assimilate to English society was, of course, itself a basis for anti-Semitic anxiety. To be told that the children of the immigrants "enter the schools Russians and Poles, and emerge often almost indistinguishable from English children"[182] turned the threat from one of an alien culture to that of the disguised, surreptitious threat of alien "blood." The "problem" of the Jew who was indistinguishable, like Dracula on the London streets, from the English raised acutely the problem of identity. In his book *The Modern Jew*, Arnold White posed the question "What is a Jew?" and answered that the "peculiar characteristics usually associated with the Hebrew community are not religious, but racial." They possessed a "complex and mysterious power denied to any other living race."[183]

The mysterious mesmerizing power exercised by the vampire in *Varney* or "Carmilla" or *Dracula* is clearly sexual—one that compels and lures the intended from her or his betrothed, or child from parent. And as a dangerous sexuality, it brings infection, and like syphilis may suggest what was seen to be a peculiarly Jewish threat of social and sexual pollution. The close and unsanitary quarters of immigrant ships were often associated with both excrement and promiscuity, with the supposed indifference of the alien Jews occupying them to either personal hygiene or moral decency. The passage itself was but an introduction to the immorality of life in the London slums, where "moral contagion" was associated with the Jew: "These people exist—and even to a certain extent thrive—in an atmosphere and amid surroundings which to the more highly-developed Englishman and Englishwoman mean disease and death."[184] The image of the Jew as "unnatural" and immoral competitor, both as a laborer and as a businessman was joined, like that of the Jew as both usurer and compulsive gambler, to contradictory images of sexual depravity—as both habitual client and owner of brothels, as profiteer from the "white slave trade" in underage girls, and, within another anti-Semitic discourse, as cowardly homosexual degenerate.[185] In fact, Dracula's ambiguous rogue male sexuality conforms to the contradictory image of the Jewish moral threat—one that threatened the race directly by taking "your girls that you all love" and indirectly by corrupting with unnatural desire an English youth like Jonathan Harker, who returns to his Mina drained and impotent. Like Dracula, the Jew as corrupter was usually an image of male immorality, and Arnold White looked to "the growth of the woman's movement" in Britain "for the healthiest antidote to Jewish materialism," because women, he thought, were the guardians of family and morality.[186]

There was, of course, another sensational contemporary representation of the urban night-stalking threat, suffused with a violent and deviant sexuality, "Jack the Ripper," the "fiend in human shape."[187] Walter Dew, who had been a young detective at the time, later recalled that "people allowed their imaginations to run riot. There was talk of black magic and vampires, especially among the superstitious foreigners."[188] The world of London prostitution, with its social diseases, its violence, its hidden places, and the dependence of the prostitute on her male seducer/exploiter, resonates with the world of the vampire. Jack's knives were his teeth, and if he left his victims their blood, there was a suggestion of cannibalism in his selective removal of internal organs. His victims, prostitutes, were also, like Stoker's Lucy Westenra, themselves carriers of both moral and physical corruption, and were, like Lucy, destroyed by violent and savage dismemberment.

If Jack, like Hyde or Dracula, is an elemental evil, he was also constructed by the police and the public as a familiar evil—the eastern Jew. Sander Gilman has persuasively established this connection in an essay that reminds us that the police concluded that "Jack" was most likely a low-class East End Jew, protected by his kind, a ritual butcher of Christian, if fallen, women. The official description, of a dark figure speaking in a "foreign accent," was apparently concocted entirely on the basis of the anti-Semitic assumptions of Sir Robert Anderson, his colleagues in the force, and the sensational press. A high proportion of the 130 men whom the police questioned in the case were Jews.[189]

Finally, the Jew as vampire-fiend (with an ambiguous sexuality) was also available to Stoker explicitly in at least one fin de siècle precursor to *Dracula*, a story to which, like that of Stenbock's homosexual vampire, Stoker would have been exposed as he researched his own tale. Julien Osgood Field published his "Kiss of Judas" in *Pall Mall* in July 1893. It was republished the next year as a part of a collection of tales.[190] The vampire in this story, a repulsive, dirty, yellowed recluse, is no aristocrat, but Isaac Lebedenko, a young Moldavian Jew ("a medical student or doctor, the captain thought"). He speaks "lisping French" and carries with him the "sickening smell of animal musk." Like the Wandering Jew, he also carries a curse—that of the children of Judas who must eternally prowl the world. They can (like Dracula) adopt any shape. When killed, they return in another form—often as a lovely woman whose embrace is fatal, the kiss of Judas.[191]

If these connections seem speculative, there is after all some evidence that Stoker was himself concerned with the "problem," in his own world of literature and stage, of Jewish materialism and immorality. There would seem to be an anti-Semitic undertone in a public attack he made on the "corruption" of modern literature, which perverted "the principles and lives of the young of this country": "They found art wholesome, they made it morbid; they found it pure, they left it sullied." Here Stoker defends literary censorship in terms that come as no surprise, given his readiness to suppress embarrassing passages in Whitman. While he is not explicit about the source of the threat he had most in mind, his argument is signposted with anti-Semitic tags. Those who "tried to deprave where others had striven to elevate" did so out of "selfish greed." And finally, "in the language of the pulpit they have 'crucified Christ afresh'."[192]

FROM FRANKENSTEIN TO DRACULA: SCIENCE AND THE DEATH OF MONSTERS

"Well," said I, "for real cold-blooded horror, commend me to your men of science."[193]

Mary Shelley's story was about a birth, a creation that ultimately wanders into the mist, an embarrassment that obligingly takes itself away. Stoker's creature comes to us not as a symbol of birth, however misconceived, but of death. He comes, sui generis, out of the mist into the modern world, as Eugène Sue's Wandering Jew, who cannot die, comes into the world from that same frozen Arctic into which Frankenstein's creature had disappeared.[194] Frankenstein creates life from death. Dracula perpetuates a form of life-in-death, but ultimately his crypt becomes an abattoir. The destruction of the vampire, unlike the end of earlier gothic creatures—often doomed and tragic figures fated for *self*-destruction—must be prepared for and accomplished by resolute men of science.

The stitching together and the cutting apart of bodies, like the blood and the stench of the vampire's lair, suggest the locus of the nineteenth-century surgeon—the operating/dissection theater, and behind this the ambiguous image of the Faustian medical researcher, the doctor who both brings life into the world and presides over its dissolution, who is both mystery-solving diagnostician and guardian of public health.[195] Frankenstein's laboratory is a charnel house and evokes the anatomy student's investigations performed on the corpses of the pauper, the prostitute, the criminal, the black—and the Jew. Jewish bodies, we are told in a memoir of 1896, had been valued in the schools because of the orthodox custom of early burial, assuring the resurrectionist of "the best and freshest subjects."[196]

Dracula's own destruction by the men of medicine who pursue him is of some interest here. If·the vampire that closes the nineteenth-century gothic genre is a projection of dangerously constructed racial and sexual "Others" in an era of anxiety and self-doubt,· then it follows that the mode and agency by which Dracula is dispatched may also be of significance in understanding how society was psychologically prepared to deal with the tangible monsters it appeared to face. Steven Arata has gone to the heart of this matter in observing that, if Dracula stands for an entire race, his death "becomes a fantasized genocide."[197]

In 1990 there was a well-publicized outbreak of anti-Semitism in France, which took the form of the desecration of Jewish graveyards. One such incident in Carpentras is reported to have involved the impaling of the body of a recently deceased Jewish man. Whether fact or fiction, the story takes us back to the medieval punishment by staking of certain offenders, such as suicides, and of course to the Dracula myth. When, during the height of the Dreyfus affair, the Jew-baiting journal *La Libre Parole* raised a subscription for the widow of Colonel Henry, a suicide who had played a key role in contriving the evidence against Dreyfus, one of the subscribers advocated the impaling, not, of course, of Henry, but of all Jews.[198] In England, it was homosexuals who in the quite similar explosion of public fear and hatred in the wake of the Wilde trial became the social vampires most deserving of a ritual extermination. "I have helped to cut up and destroy sharks," wrote the marquess of Queensberry after Wilde was convicted. "I had no sympathy for them."[199]

The fate of Stoker's Dracula, brutal execution by an outraged community of men, is a fantasy that parallels the contemporaneous destruction of Oscar Wilde and Alfred Dreyfus at the hands of those who saw themselves as the moral guardians of their nations. It also, of course, anticipates the mass destruction of both European Jews and sexual deviants at the hands of Nazi racial hygienists. The teutonic Dr. van Helsing's surgical assault on the supine, immobile, and vulnerable form of Dracula, in a ritual murder outside conventional morality, without the sanction of law and due process, for the sake of the health of the nation, its youth, and its womenfolk, found a kind of realization 45 years later in the operating theater of Dr. Joseph Mengele.

CHAPTER 4

The Half-Breed as
Gothic Unnatural

Although *Dracula* remains in popular culture the defining fictional vampire, Bram Stoker's novel was only a single, if powerful, manifestation of a widespread late-nineteenth-century revival of an earlier Romantic archetype.[1] An obsessive image at the fin de siècle, the vampire can be found in painting, poetry, and novels as well as in political and social discourse generally. The year *Dracula* was published in London, 1897, Philip Burne-Jones, artist son of the great Victorian painter, exhibited his own *Vampire*, a seductress, which inspired a poem by Kipling on hard-hearted women: "a rag and a bone and a hank of hair / (We called her the woman who did not care), / But the fool he called her his lady fair." Although, as we have seen, Stoker's tale of vampirism, like many of the earlier stories, involves a threatening, if ambivalent, masculinity, the female vampire, allusive or otherwise, can be said to dominate much late-Victorian representation, which drew much from the "exotic aestheticism" of, particularly French, romanticism, from the vampiric women of Gautier, Flaubert, Mérimée, and Baudelaire.[2] *Dracula* itself nearly surrenders to this mode in its vivid portrayal of Lucy Westenra as monster before wrenching itself back to the source of corruption, an alien male.

From Sheridan Le Fanu's "Carmilla" to the "vamp" of the 1890's, the specifically contemporary fears that lay behind the gothicizing of the female as blood-sucking temptress and unnaturally masculinized threat have been well treated in Elaine Showalter's *Sexual Anarchy*. That such images resonate with an intensifying race prejudice, as well as expressing the striking misogyny of the time, is clear. Winwood Reade's cannibal queen in the heart of the Congo was a manly woman whose blackness reinforced the same fear of castration that we find in dangerous white seductresses like Haggard's She-Who-Must-Be-Obeyed and Stoker's Arabella. But there is also lurking in the vampire the powerful suggestion of an explicitly racial obsession—that of the "half-breed." Both vampire and half-breed are creatures who transgress boundaries and are caught between two worlds. Both are hidden threats—disguised presences bringing pollution of the blood. Both may be able to "pass" among the unsuspecting, although both bear hidden signs of their difference, which the wary may read.

These themes are remarkably drawn together, in fact, in a long-forgotten novel by Florence Marryat, daughter of a better-known novelist father, Captain Frederick Marryat.[3] One of her own gothic tales, *The Blood of the Vampire*, was born in the shadow of Stoker's story, appearing the same year as *Dracula*. Florence Marryat was a prolific minor novelist, whose Roman Catholicism and spiritualism conspired with her gender to ensure, whatever merits her prose might have possessed, a generally condescending tone in her male critics and a dismissive reference in the *Dictionary of National Biography*. *The Blood of the Vampire* is, nevertheless, an interesting work, in some ways as complicated in its message as Stoker's lumbering "classic." It is also a striking culmination of an explicitly racial gothic, and demonstrates the force of some of the connections that we have sought to establish.

The Blood of the Vampire is the story of nineteen-year-old Harriet Brandt, an orphaned heiress from Jamaica, who, fresh from an Ursuline convent, has come to Belgium with a sickly younger friend. At a seaside resort, she is befriended by a respectable upper-class Englishwoman, although she ultimately attaches herself to the entourage of a vulgar "baroness," a lower-class Londoner who has married an ennobled German shoe manufacturer. Harriet is a mysterious child-woman, with a kind of voluptuous innocence, dark, heavily lidded eyes, and a full mouth, "large with lips of a deep blood colour." Clearly a sexual threat—she mesmerizes adolescent boys, young men already engaged, and confirmed bachelors—the carnal hunger she inspires is matched by her own almost bestial physical appetite: "She riveted all her attention upon the contents of her plate. Miss Leyton thought that she had never seen any young person devour her food with so much avidity and enjoyment . . . as if she feared someone might deprive her of it."[4]

As with her physical hunger, Harriet has a compulsive need for companionship, male or female. With a suggestion of Le Fanu's lesbian vampire Carmilla, Harriet feeds on her intimacy with women as well as men: "She had crept closer and closer to Mrs. Pullen as she spoke, and now encircled her waist with her arm, and leaned her head upon her shoulder.

It was not a position that Margaret liked."[5] She yearns, in fact, for affection in a manner that suggests "young unsophisticated girls [who] had taken unaccountable affections for members of their own sex."[6] Intimacy, masculine or feminine, with Harriet is invariably followed, however, by a gradual loss of vitality and ultimately by sickness and death. There is here no overt vampirism, but a kind of invisible contagion, and the girl herself is innocent of the destruction she causes, an unwitting agent of evil who is also its victim. This is an ambiguous double representation, which we have already encountered in the image of the cannibal, the enslaved Negro, and Mary Shelley's Monster. Harriet does not have to "become" evil through a transformation like Jekyll into Hyde or saintly Lucy Westenra into demonic Lucy the vampire. She is innocent in her evil and carries its contagion around within her like a hereditary disease.

Indeed, as in Ibsen's *Ghosts* and Zola's *Nana*, the explanation that unfolds depends upon the familiar late-nineteenth-century problem of the fatal inheritance and the reduction of issues of social evil and aberration to biological determinism. Here, however, the fatal inheritance is not merely that of illness or the inherited character of dissolute and criminal parents, but of "racial" character as well. For Harriet is the daughter, we discover, not only of a vicious, sadistic, mad white father, but of a half-breed, Obeah-dealing mother as well. A beautiful and innocent child, she carries within her a mingled misinheritance of criminal madness *and* black blood.[7]

The central, most emotive threat of the novel is, in fact, that of racial pollution, although this is partly disguised by its being so tightly intertwined with the images of female seduction and the gothic. The novel self-consciously draws together elements of the Frankenstein myth with that of a cannibalic vampirism. Harriet's Jamaican father is a Swiss physician, expelled for experimenting on patients even from the Swiss hospital laboratories, "renowned for being the most foremost in Vivisection and other branches of science that gratify the curiosity and harden the heart."[8] In the exotic secrecy of his Jamaican plantation, Helvetia, he performed hideous experiments on ex-slaves until they rose up in revolt, murdered him and his "half-caste mistress," "with appropriate atrocity," and burned down his house.

Shelley's Frankenstein began the nineteenth century with a monster suggestive, I have argued, of the Jamaican slave. At the century's end, Florence Marryat confirms and makes explicit the allusive implications of Shelley's plot by locating the origins of her gothic threat in the actual region of racial conflict. The difference in the stories, the overt invocation of racial pollution as gothic danger in Marryat's tale, reflects the shifting, reifying nature of "race" itself in the course of the century. Another difference, the shift in gender of the racial monster from male to female is also significant, suggesting as it does the late-Victorian obsession with an unnatural feminist challenge. That the author is a woman is not problematic—Marryat, it is clear, has in some sense internalized the male opposition from which she herself suffered professionally and projected it onto her creation.

In this novel, the horror of the mad scientist father, whose physical appearance is hardly mentioned, is in fact diminished and ultimately displaced by Marryat's vivid and detailed descriptions of the form and character of Harriet's mother: "She was a fiend, a fitting match for Henry Brandt! . . . A fat, flabby half-caste, who hardly ever moved out of her chair but sat eating all day long."[9]

> I can see her now, with her sensual mouth, her greedy eyes, her low forehead and half-formed brain, and her lust for blood . . . she thirsted for blood, she loved the sight, and smell of it, she would taste it on the tip of her finger when it came in her way . . . a sensual, self-loving, crafty and bloodthirsty half-caste.[10]

Marryat's introduction of the supernatural, the vampire bat's bite suffered by Harriet's fiend-mother while pregnant, is in fact nearly superfluous. The hereditary dice are already loaded, and the knowing doctor in London who unravels the mystery has easily typed Harriet as a *"dangerous* acquaintance" (i.e., sexual partner) because she "is a quadroon, and she shews it distinctly. . . . I can tell you by the way she eats her food, and the way she uses her eyes, that she had inherited her half-caste mother's greedy and sensual disposition."[11]

At the heart of this gothicization of the half-Negro is the idea of abnormal appetite, greatly focused in the rhetoric of race prejudice by the nineteenth century's long obsession with cannibalism. Cannibalism, with its association with self-destruction, madness, and sexual incorporation, with the abuse of children and, in the inverting world of the gothic unnatural, with women as both victims and devourers, is explicitly invoked by Marryat. In Brussels, Harriet visits the house of the painter Antoine Wiertz, a museum, and is absorbed by his pictures of "Napoleon in Hell" being fed the bloody limbs of his victims and "of the mother in a time of famine devouring her child" (ill. 11): "'I *like* them!' replied Harriet, moving her tongue slowly over her lips, 'they interest me!'"[12]

Harriet is "not fit to marry into any decent English family," not because of her unsuspected vampirism, but because she is a quadroon. Her vampirism only works to intensify this "problem," and that which signifies her vampirism, her large mouth with its "restless," "twitching" lips, is also a more readable sign of her racial and racial-sexual nature, an orifice that suggests not only black appetite—that is, cannibalism—but black sexuality as well. When Dr. Phillips warns Harriet against further fatal liaisons with white men, and she asks whether it was her love that killed them, he replies, "You will have, in fact, *sucked them dry.*"[13]

What serves to tie the racial fears of the story to the larger issues of fin de siècle identity and social anxiety that one sees in gothic generally, and particularly in the sister genre of the mystery or detective story, is apprehension of those who can "pass," who can move with impunity across boundaries of class, gender, race, or ethnicity. Marryat's novel is full of false or secret identities, of pretension and fraud. Harriet's passing for white is only the most dangerous instance of these. The "baroness" who takes her in is a vulgar social climber, who has moved out of her own very low world by marriage and money into one that is itself only pseudo-genteel. But, as the doctor notes of Harriet, there are always "signs" that give away those attempting to pass, and the baroness's social pretensions fool no one except an innocent outsider like Harriet. The baroness is more successful, however, in her role as fraudulent spiritualist, a pretended channel for the spirits of the dead, who pass back and forth between their world and ours. With the help of a failed actor (another type that, as we have seen, is defined by inauthentic multiple identities), she hosts false séances for gullible but "well-dressed" men and women.

Nor is "passing" in the novel only a device of the "Other," of a dangerous penetration of the authentic and superior by the low, false, and alien. In Marryat's anarchic world, boundaries are crossed in both directions. She gives us in Anthony Pennell an establishment figure who subverts both class and profession. A barrister-turned-novelist, he is also an upper-class socialist who has written about "the People." In fact, like Jack London, he has "passed" for a pauper, having "gone and lived amongst them; shared their filthy dens in Whitechapel, partaken of their unappetizing food in Stratford; and watched them at their labour in Homerton." Pennell, also represented as *both* aesthete and athletic hearty, "could pass anywhere, without fear of a hand being lifted up against him."[14]

In the end, Marryat returns to and parallels Mary Shelley's tale of a monster who wants to pass but cannot. Frankenstein's Monster and Harriet are both innocent of the crimes they commit—that is, they are themselves victims of their perversely created natures. They are both unnaturals—the Monster's construction has violated the tabooed boundary of death itself and confuses animate and inanimate, life and death. Harriet's making is the result of "miscegenation," the violation of another boundary. Both creatures are enslaved by their perverted, unnaturally constructed bodies. Their only ultimate recourse is self-destruction. Harriet takes chloral hydrate knowing, like Frankenstein's Monster, that she is forever destined to destroy those whom she loves, and her suicide note echoes his wail against his fate: "My parents made me unfit to live."[15]

If Florence Marryat's representation of the half-breed as gothic unnatural reflects what had become very nearly a convention by the end of the century, her tale carries within it elements of an earlier, more sympathetic image, that of the innocent, if fated, child of *mésalliance*. The half-breed monster of late-Victorian popular culture, the creature that, in popular wisdom, inherits the worst aspects of each of the incompatible worlds from which it has sprung, had often received a more generous reading earlier when "race" itself was still a loose and shifting, as much cultural as biological, concept.

In the Caribbean, where there had long been a complicated racial and social hierarchy based on degrees of relationship, the mixed race had an ambivalent, but often positive, place in colonial representations of the slave and ex-slave. The commonest association was that between a high proportion of "white" blood and intelligence, diligence, and morality. Although mainland American discourse largely lacked the language finely to distinguish degrees of racial mixture, even so sympathetic a work as Harriet Beecher Stowe's *Uncle Tom's Cabin* mirrors such opinion in its implication that the color spectrum on her southern plantation ran from intelligent and generous near-white (George Harris or the quadroon Emmeline, "a similacrum of white femininity") to vicious and degraded dark black (Sambo and Quimbo).[16] In England, however, the issue of degrees of whiteness was still less compelling, and the complex language of racial identity known in the West Indies, the maroons, quadroons, sambos, octoroons, and so on, was commonly collapsed into the simple issue of "black blood."

We have seen that the idea of a secret racial contamination occasionally found its way into early Victorian literature as a device to establish a naturalistic explanation for moral depravity and aberration. This anxiety over bad blood drew no doubt as much from middle-class fears of social as racial derogation. Focused by the Anthropological Society of London in the 1860's and transmitted via moral panic to late-Victorians obsessed with identity, an increasingly negative and overt deployment of the theme of miscegenation encouraged the view that any degree of "pollution" was ineradicable and fatal to cultural progress. But there was another literary tradition only gradually displaced in popular culture—that of a more benign racism, in which cross-breeding improved the Negro without necessarily threatening the white. This reflects the more sanguine opinion, common at the beginning of the century, that traces of blackness were likely to disappear over time into the larger pool of more vigorous "white" blood.

Consequently, the half-breed could be viewed sympathetically, not as a racial danger to whites, but as a superior class of Negro, touched by the saving grace of white blood; or, alternatively, as an object of sympathy, a "victim of class and colour," unfairly rejected, martyred, by both worlds. Either way the half-breed was here the true inheritor of the image of the ex-slave crafted by the evangelical abolitionist. An eternal victim raised from the bestial, not merely by evangelical exhortation, by the blood of the lamb, but by the actual blood of the white paternalist.

In 1846 the Royal Victoria Theatre in London presented a play, *The Black Doctor*, that had a successful run with Ira Aldridge, a popular American black actor, in the title role. It was a tragedy in five acts, originally written for the Paris stage by Auguste Anicet Bourgeois, and set in the French West Indies and in revolutionary Paris. It is the tale of a mulatto freed-slave doctor who saves an aristocratic heiress from illness in the Caribbean and subsequently falls in love with her. There is a secret marriage, but she is sent away to Paris, first to a convent and then to the Bastille, where her pursuing lover rescues her at last—only to fall victim himself to the fury of the Parisian mob. In a final tableau of "grief, despair and death," "pure love immolates itself to save its object." Fabian dies confessing to the crowd that the white woman, his master's daughter, is his wife.[17]

While French attitudes toward interracial marriage were famously more relaxed than those of the British,[18] the play's success on the London stage serves perhaps as a warning against anticipating the characteristic late-Victorian panic over "bad blood." At worst, one can say that there was a popular ambivalence, in France as well as in England, toward mixed-race people before mid-century; at best, a certain sentimental, sympathetic tradition, expressed in such popular mid-century novels of Thomas Mayne Reid as *The Quadroon* (1856), *Oçeola* (1859), and *The Wild Huntress* (1861).[19]

One can certainly find, although not as densely present as in late-nineteenth-century fiction, negative representations of the half-breed, often as a social-cum-racial outcast, in the romantic period. For example, another French import, which appeared in London the same year as *The Black Doctor*, Eugène Sue's popular gothic romance *The Wandering Jew*, presents a dramatic alternative to tragic Fabian in its portrayal of a demonic half-caste. The immorality of Faringhea the Thug is signified by a phenotypical muddiness.[20] He has a face "of a dead yellow, that tint peculiar to those who spring from the union of the white race with the East." His is the evil of the outsider; he can dispatch white and nonwhite alike with no qualm of conscience, because he is alien to both communities; he is neither one thing nor another, and "shabbily dressed in European clothes" his appearance signifies the unnaturalness of his kind.[21]

These contrasting types, the tragic nobility of Fabian and the Caliban-like demonism of Faringhea, are images of the masculine. The female half-breed offers another pair of contrasting images—the childlike victim and the temptress, with the former image predominating in the early nineteenth century, the latter by the fin de siècle. In his gothic novel *Melmoth*, Maturin presents the female half-caste as a child of nature, the orphan Immalee, around whom there was "a mingled light of innocence and majesty."[22]

The "tragic octoroon," an Anglo-American stereotype before the Civil War, was usually a beautiful girl with only the slightest trace of Negro blood and no dialect; a conventional victim, threatened by the slave owner's lust. These stories lie somewhere between melodrama and the gothic, but often the latter predominates, with the narrative depending on self-discovery of a shameful secret (black blood), persecution, and entrapment, and ending in despair and suicide. They involve, as one critic has noted, "the stuff of nightmare."[23] It may be significant of shifting popular attitudes that after a successful run in New York, Dion Boucicault's sentimental dramatization of Reid's *The Octaroon* had a very different reception at the Adelphi in London in 1861, and was greeted there with catcalls and rude scenes. The story involved the tragic love of a white man for a one-eighth negro slave girl. Boucicault himself complained that he felt "strangely bewildered at such a change in feeling." It has been suggested that the change may have reflected popular sympathy for the South in the American Civil War,[24] although it is as likely that the audience were protesting the tragic ending (the octoroon heroine takes poison).

The beauty and innocence of the fated mixed-race heroine are, of course, a male fantasy, inevitably seeking to invest the object of desire with an exciting element of forbidden fruit. Behind the innocence (her whiteness) lies the temptation of the sexually exotic (her blackness). Such confusion of two "discursive networks," may, as Peter Hulme has argued, be inherent in the European reading of the uncivilized since at least the Columbian voyages.[25] But with the revival of religious enthusiasm, particularly in Protestant Britain, an obsessive middle-class preoccupation with abstinence and imprudence encouraged an explicitly sexual reading of the duality of primitive innocence and cunning—the carnality of the childlike savage. For Victorians, this contradiction also asserted itself in domestic readings of the problem of female sexuality generally, and of the fecklessly reproducing, but mentally immature, proletariat. This increasingly overlaid the reading of the "savage" abroad and reinforced a sexualized primitive that, in the context of an empire where sexual temptation was available to an ever-widening number of middle-class men,[26] substantially heightened the likelihood of a gothic rendering of the half-caste female.

The projection of male inner conflict and guilt in an age of increasing sexual suppression, frustration, and moral anxiety is graphically demonstrated in Tennyson's "Locksley Hall" (1842):

> Ah, for some retreat
> Deep in yonder shining Orient . . .
> I shall take some savage woman, she shall rear my dusky race.
> Iron-jointed, supple-sinew'd, they shall dive and they shall run.

But the temptation to race-mixing in "Summer isles of Eden" must be resisted. It would lock white progress into "a cycle of Cathay" by chaining the free-roving masculine to the sensual bed of the feminine—"I *know* my words are wild."

> I to herd with narrow foreheads, vacant of our glorious gains,
> Like a beast with lower pleasures, like a beast with lower pains?
> Mated with a squalid savage. . . .

Tennyson's shift in the same text from a representation of interracial union as escape into Edenic bliss ("the passions cramp'd no longer") to one that vividly associates the connection of the civilized and the savage, the white and the black, with the perversion of bestiality, provides a dialogue similar to that in "In Memoriam," where gendered Nature *herself* is first an (illusory) benefactress, only to be revealed as (in reality) a blind destroyer.[27]

This passage in "Locksley Hall" also suggests—in fact, depends upon—a male memory of coition itself. A fantasized release, an ejaculation "deep in yonder shining Orient," is followed directly by loss of interest and shame. Passion spent, there is a characteristic spurning of the former object of desire as degrading. Here, in the fantasy of interracial union, sexual guilt, and self-loathing can be rationalized and projected outward onto a savage, black, feminine temptress. The racial blackness of the woman also functions, of course, to absolve the white, idealized, unsexed domestic angel, to help resolve that inherent contradiction in the Victorian construction of woman as both (black) Magdalene and (white) Madonna.

The debate within "Locksley Hall" resolves itself against the union of races, through a jarring reconstruction of the mere savage into threatening beast-woman, of a convenient refuge into a dangerous trap. This anticipates the consistently sterner and less ambivalent representation of "miscegenation" and the "half-breed" that dominates in much late-Victorian fiction, as well as in social and scientific discourse. It was paralleled and reinforced by a shift in popular perceptions of the actual role of those of mixed race in the empire after mid-century.

Shadows

> . . . and a race of devils would be propagated upon the earth who might make the very existence of man a condition precarious and full of terror. Had I a right, for my own benefit, to inflict this curse upon everlasting generations? [28]

In 1831 there was a meeting in the Town Hall of Calcutta of those members of the Eurasian (or, as they preferred, "East Indian") community who had petitioned against what they felt to be a rising prejudice against them, and particularly against their exclusion from military and government office. One of those (mostly aggrieved merchants and professionals) attending, a Mr. J. Welsh, seized upon the obvious irony: "It is absurd to see our rulers starting at shadows of their own creation." [29] Although unintended no doubt, his image of the half-caste as shadow—as an inescapable, following/pursuing, guilt-inducing, distortion of its creator—has a kind of spectral, gothic quality. It suggests not only the unjust denial of paternity and responsibility of the plantation master who, having fathered children upon his black mistresses, nevertheless "feels that he is connecting himself with one of an inferior and servile caste, [that there] is something of degradation in the act." [30] It also recalls exactly the dilemma confronting Frankenstein vis-à-vis *his* creation.

In fact, the Frankenstein association—that is, not only a gothic rendering of the half-breed as a warped "creation" expressive of the sexual guilt of the creator, but an actual patterning of a language of description on Shelley's own gothic prose—surfaces now and then throughout the long nineteenth century. For example, Walt Whitman's youthful exploration of a gothic mixed-race theme, "The Half-Breed" (1845), offers a deformed Irish-Indian hunchback who, malignantly evil but "not very bright," evokes language that appears to be lifted almost verbatim from Mary Shelley: "This strange and hideous creature. . . . I almost shrieked with horror at the monstrous abortion! . . . Scorned and abhorred by man, woman, and child, the half-breed . . . fled." [31]

We witness here a double process by which the "pure-blood" nonwhite becomes romanticised (like Whitman's noble, stoic, and doomed brave, Arrow-Tip, in the story above) and safely relegated to the past as a vanishing Mohican, or to the reservation or kraal, while the half-breed it is who becomes the threatening creature of the boundary between white and nonwhite, a living sign, an emblem of shame. Either innocent and sympathetic or deformed and demonic, half-breeds were visible reminders of what came to be felt in the nineteenth century to be a white fall from grace. In suggesting that slave owners deliberately impregnated slave women to increase capital assets, Harriet Martineau may have believed that the half-breed was another kind of emblem—that of a perverted self-interest,[32] but the more prevalent Victorian view was that half-breeds signified, not rationality, but its reverse—loss of (white) self-control. The half-breed child was the product of an act of passion, a perpetual witness against the weak or dissolute natures that created them. As the French missionaries Arbousset and Daumas declared in 1846: "Wherever Europeans have carried their civilization and their industry, there they have also carried their vices. . . . In every country colonized by Europeans we find a mixed race,—a living testimony to the sin of their fathers."[33]

While such an observation draws from well-established Christian moral discourse about the bastard progeny of illicit union, it can only take on its powerful, mid-nineteenth-century connotation of degradation in the context of developing ideas about "race" and the presumed boundaries of biological affinity. It depends upon a heightened sense of the sexual "unnaturalness" of interracial union, especially resonating with the language generated in the nineteenth century to stigmatize sexual misconduct like masturbation and sodomy as "acts" of social and biological as well as moral "degradation."

That an unflattering representation of the half-breed may reflect at some level a (male) projection of the guilt of the colonizer and sexual exploiter is a well-established theme.[34] Where, earlier, liaisons with native women among traders, officials, and military men had often been blessed by marriage or at least a customary social approval and even official encouragement, by the early nineteenth century, Ronald Hyam has argued, racial inter*marriage* in much of the British Empire "was virtually at an end."[35] It was assaulted by Protestant missionaries, by the growing number of memsahib, and by an officialdom increasingly bothered by the need to displace the half-caste in order to find jobs for the superfluous sons of the English middling and upper classes. "Instead of stable unions, native women were reduced to the status of temporary mistresses and even prostitutes,"[36] and their progeny, the half-breed, took on the added stigma of prostitute's bastard. There were, of course, rogues and eccentrics, like the seventh earl of Stamford and the fourth Baron Gardner, whose interracial marriages may have scandalized polite society, but these were increasingly the exceptions that confirmed a more rigid proscription.[37]

It may well be true, as Hyam provocatively suggests, that interracial sex outside the acceptable bonds of marriage and customary cohabitation need not "automatically" be seen as an act of imperial, racial, and masculine domination, that it may generate an "admiration and affection" across racial barriers that is "healthy" and "cannot always be dismissed as merely self-interested." But his own evidence of the growing stigmatization of interracial union by the white missionary and official establishment, of the substitution of "parergal" (that is, recreational and often commercial) sex for the real intimacy of cohabitation, would argue otherwise. The fact that by the end of the century, the empire had become, in his own words, "as much a system of prostitution networks as it was (in Kipling's famous phrase) a web of submarine cables" seems eloquently to confirm that "sex is at the very heart of racism." And yet, Hyam's animus against feminist and gay deconstruction, his odd dismissal of all exploration of the connections between the domestic construction of gender and sexuality and a wider imperialism, substantially inhibits an otherwise valuable study.[38]

To suggest that the pejorative nineteenth-century image of the half-breed in large part arose from middle-class male guilt in a era of sexual repression, when an essentially masculine enterprise of imperialism abroad was too obviously often a matter of literal, as well as metaphoric, rape, does not, of course, deny the importance of other contributing and reinforcing factors. Language itself both reveals and itself shapes the processes by which stereotypes are reified into social fact. Although words borrowed from the Spanish Caribbean, such as *mulatto* and *mestizo*, had much earlier currency, both *half-breed* and its approximate synonym *half-caste* appear to have entered English common usage in the course of the late eighteenth century.[39] The two terms were nearly interchangeable by the early nineteenth century, but the former continued to have a particular American resonance—often associated with "crosses" between native Americans and Europeans or Negroes. *Half-caste* had its apparent origin in India and, although its meaning is primarily interracial, may imply social and religious differences more strongly than the sexual element of animal husbandry that *half-breed* evokes and that provides a bridge of sorts to the post-Darwinian language of racial "hybridization."

It will be clear that language employed to define interracial genealogy inevitably also fixes the fluidity of individual character. The progeny of parents of different "races"—already arbitrary abstractions—become not merely something different, but are themselves confined by the very words used to name them. The terms *half-breed* and *half-caste* are double, hyphenated constructions. Like these words, persons of mixed race became in nineteenth-century English discourse hyphenated beings—or, more accurately, were themselves hyphens. *The* half-breed, not *a* half-breed or some particular kind of half-breed, became itself a reified object, although one ordinarily defined, not as a new and autonomously valid whole, but merely as a link. The term resonates with other linguistic inadequacies and incompletes—with *half-wit* and *half-dead*, with *half-naked* and *half-truth*, and, of course, with *half-civilized*. The half-breed is, by the word that defines him or her, not a true or authentic being, not a member of a race for which there is a word. In this may lie some explanation of the long and insistent effort, by slave-holding racists in the eighteenth-century Caribbean and antebellum America, and by nineteenth-century anthropologists, to deny the fertility of the mulatto, the full ability of the half-breed to replicate his or her self, for a shadow cannot cast a shadow.

And yet the word *half-breed* itself would originally—that is, in the late eighteenth century—have drawn some of its associative meaning from the analogy it suggests with animal husbandry, with the breeding practices of, particularly, the English agricultural revolution. The resonance here was at least in part a positive one. Of course, it also served generally to associate mixed-race humanity, the progeny of slaves, with the world of beasts rather than mankind. The most common analogy drawn from agricultural breeding practice was that of the mule (*mulatto* itself may be derived from the Spanish word for mule), a useful but ill-tempered and, of course, infertile, beast, fit for its task but awkward to handle.

Nevertheless, this eighteenth-century association with an essentially positive practice—with, that is, the production of improved strains of sheep and cattle—correlates well enough with a positive contemporary reading of the uses and virtues of the half-breed in at least some colonial contexts—in West Africa, for instance, where the mulatto might be able to resist diseases deadly to the white man, or Hudson's Bay, where the "country-born" might combine the fur-trapping skills of the Red Indian with the Calvinist virtues of the Scot. Nor were improvements only to be expected from mixtures of primitive with "white" blood. In 1839 Sir John Bowring argued that the Chinese, emigrating throughout the western Pacific, were "wonderfully advancing the work of civilization" by intermarrying with, for instance, Indian women in the Philippines. Their "mestizo descendants . . . form incomparably the most promising" part of the population, were more handsome, rose to become the most prosperous merchants and landed proprietors, and occupied most of the lower offices of government.[40]

Associative meanings, however, do not remain fixed, but shift with time and context. Earlier, the presumed infertility of the racial hybrid had been insisted upon by racists like Edward Long to deepen the "difference" of the slave and justify his state. In the nineteenth century, a modified form of this fantasy of racial incompatibility was appropriated by the developing sciences of biology and anthropology in a way that suggests a number of underlying, if unarticulated and perhaps subconscious motives—not the least of which is undoubtedly a kind of wish-fulfillment.[41]

One might note in passing that this obsessive insistence on the infertility of the racial hybrid resonates strongly with a charge laid against the homosexual in European culture—that such unions were unproductive and therefore, especially in a world dominated by the language of political economy and the reproductive imperatives of the financial and industrial system, by definition unnatural, inefficient, and fated. At some level, it also seems likely that apprehension of domestic social change, of challenges to the boundaries of class and status, was involved. The words *miscegenation* and *misalliance* (respectively signifying biological and social mismatching) sound vaguely similar and at times seem nearly interchangeable in late-nineteenth-century metaphoric usage.[42] More obviously, social changes in the empire, examined below, served at precisely this time to marginalize and devalue those of mixed-race parentage. This clearly encouraged the evolution of a less-favorable reading of the human "hybrid," not as an improved (and useful) species but as a curious, unstable, and inconvenient, perhaps dangerous, anomaly. Through the course of the nineteenth century, there was a progressive shift toward an essentially negative reading of the half-breed as biological unnatural, and away from the more positive one grounded in animal husbandry.

After mid-century, the tendency to view races as the near-equivalent of separate species was encouraged, no doubt, by a popular reading of Darwin's *Origin of Species* (although Darwin himself has little to say in *Origin* on the subject of human difference) and the rush to apply evolutionary concepts to ethnology generally. In 1864 the French anthropologist Paul Broca's loose and impressionistic speculations on human hybridity were published in Britain under the aegis of the Anthropological Society of London. *On the Phenomena of Hybridity in the Genus Homo* owes perhaps as much to the racism of Gobineau as to Darwin, but its use of animal analogy locates it within an evolutionary discourse that approached the study of variation in mankind through the lower animal world.[43]

In Broca's view, half-breeds ("mongrels") were a "eugenesic" type—that is, although able to reproduce, they were marked by a diminished degree of fertility. This biological shortcoming served to confirm "common knowledge" of the moral, intellectual, and physical failings of the half-breed that Broca cites: a lack of "vigour or moral energy," and a tendency to produce "stammerers, [the] blind, hunchbacks, and idiots," as well as criminals.[44] It will be evident here how closely his language parallels that often used to describe the effect of habitual masturbation. The masturbator and, at one remove, the half-breed both suffer from the physiological effects of a shameful and unnatural sexual indulgence.

Broca's "eugenesic" parallel in the animal world was, significantly, the cross between dog and wolf. It will be seen that this choice depends at least as much on an implied character analogy (like the choice of the mule) as it does on a biological parallel. The dog is an owned and mastered thing, fawning, loyal, and grateful; the wolf is a red-eyed savage and threatening creature of folk myth, and the cross is suggestive, not of a tamed wolf, but of a demonized dog. As in the literature of the half-breed generally, such analogies have negligible scientific importance, of course, but considerable emotive significance. It is a comparison that elicits an essentially gothic response. The wolf or half-wolf became, in fact, a common trope for the threatening half-breed in the nineteenth century.

Seeing the half-breed as a lone wolf, isolated from both communities that gave him birth, needless to say, suggests a familiar form of gothic monstrosity. Although not as common in nineteenth-century British literature as the cannibal and the vampire, the werewolf obviously shares much with them as a type of the demonic with a human face. Like them (and like the half-breed), he is a confusion of identities. Ideas of the werewolf and the vampire were closely connected in Slavonic folk traditions, while cannibalism is an often explicit theme in stories of the werewolf as ghoul—as in the female "weir-wolf" who devours her dead stepchildren in Frederick Marryat's *The Phantom Ship* of 1839.[45] In 1847 G. W. M. Reynolds published his own werewolf potboiler, *Wagner, the Wehrwolf*, in serial form. As in *Varney, the Vampyre*, which appeared the same year, the monster is a sympathetic, even tragic character, liberated ultimately by his own death (one notes the difference from Marryat's purely demonic *female* werewolf). As in the polar representations of the half-breed, the werewolf texts offer contradictory, binary images of the creature as demonic *and* tragic, criminal *and* victim.

Not itself a work of fiction (although he later wrote novels), the Reverend Sabine Baring-Gould's compilation *The Book of Werewolves* (1865) was clearly designed to appeal to the popular taste for cheap sensationalism, a fact he attempts unconvincingly to suppress by sermonizing against "popular superstitions." Then a young rural curate, he intended to go on to publish a series that would include vampires and the Wandering Jew.[46] What is of most interest to us here, however, is the manner in which Baring-Gould attempts to establish a social and biological basis for his folktales of the grotesque—that is, how he allows himself freely to associate werewolf gothic with its plausible "sources" in actual life. Beyond the obvious historical "explanations" (that medieval peasants feared wolves, etc.), he locates his tales of lycanthropy in actual perversion, with behavior he associates with quite specific and hardly extinct forms of deviancy: "Under the veil of mythology lies a solid reality . . . an innate craving for blood implanted in *certain natures*, restrained under ordinary circumstances."[47]

In the first place, both the superstitious beliefs and the behavior upon which they were founded are to be seen as un-English, almost entirely continental—French, Eastern European, or, finally, "Oriental" ("Eastern superstition attributes to certain individuals a passion for unearthing corpses and mangling them. . . . There is every probability that these ghouls were no mere creations of the imagination, but were actual resurrectionists").[48] This distancing strategy is contradicted almost immediately by his argument, however, which searches the domestic and contemporary realm for the most compelling analogues to the monstrous in folk-superstition. He finds his own werewolves at home, as it were, in the cannibalic blood lust of the insane, in the uncontrolled libidiousness of the masturbator, and, finally, in feminine hysteria and pregnancy.

The "real" werewolf "may be found howling dismally in some padded room of a Hanwell or a Bedlam." Such berserkerlike hallucinations, he claims, lead "in most cases to cannibalism."[49] Such "a morbid craving for human blood," of course, takes us by a predictable association to other cravings, desires that are clearly sexual, and are not confined to the raving mad: "It is positively true that there are many to whom the sight of suffering causes genuine pleasure, and in whom the passion to kill or torture is as strong as any other passion"—boys watching a dying pig or sheep "with hearts beating fast with pleasure, and eyes sparkling with delight." But the "propensity" is "widely diffused," in (the language is unintentionally significant) "those who have never had the opportunity of gratifying it, and those who gratify it habitually."[50] Here a line of argument that began with the cruelty of children has drifted, by an unconscious association, it would seem, into the obsessive area of mid-Victorian discourse on the danger of uncontrolled sexual gratification, and of masturbatory self-abuse in particular: "A relaxation of the moral check, a shock to the controlling intellect, an abnormal condition of body, are sufficient to allow the passion to assert itself."[51]

If in both sexes the fascination for blood is closely related to sexual urges—a touch or a glance in either case can "fire the magazine of passion"[52]—the *cruelty* of the werewolf is finally located (as cruelty is often gendered) in the feminine, in the "highly strung nervous temperament" of young women who enjoy threading flies with sewing needles, or in the "abnormal condition of body" during pregnancy when the female "appetite" becomes "diseased." Here the reader is treated to a curious digression—a number of stories presented as medical fact of pregnant wives killing their husbands and sons and eating parts of them,[53] before we are returned, in following chapters, to tales of *foreign* werewolflike perversions—of Bertrand the French ghoul, of Swiatek the Galician cannibal, of Oriental grave-robbers and corpse-manglers.

The half-breed man, as we shall see, was often represented as somehow feminine in his emotional/biological instability. In this, he seems to share something of Baring-Gould's construction of the "real life" sources of "werewolf" perversion. Like Hyde within Jekyll, the wolf-feminine exists within the man. The parallels with subsequent evolutionary and psychological theory, with male hysteria and a fin-de-siècle panic over human degeneration, are obvious.[54] The resonance of the racial half-breed with this form of gothic monstrosity is inescapable, and already available, perhaps, in Marryat's presentation of *his* (female) werewolf as that "great rarity," a *white* wolf.

A few months after Broca's work was published, the sensational story of "A Half-Wolf at Large," obliquely suggesting just this kind of gothicizing of the half-breed cross, appeared in *The Times*. This report of an unnatural animal although a "true story," can be read as a kind of werewolf or vampire tale, and its language (sheep were "seized" by "the brute") is essentially anthropomorphic. A large animal brought to Harrogate by a traveling menagerie had been exhibited as half-wolf, half-dog. It escaped and lived by raiding local farms until it was trapped and shot. "How well it fared by this process its fat carcass afforded the best proof. The sheep were nearly all seized by the neck, which the brute tore open and sucked the blood until satiated, leaving the carcass of the sheep unmutilated except at the neck."[55]

This is not a study in intellectual history, and the story of the use of hybridization in anthropological thought in France and Britain has been well treated elsewhere.[56] However, evolutionary discourse about "missing links" and surviving anomalies that straddled the boundaries of species worked its way well down into popular culture, and the half-breed absorbed a new resonance, which was strikingly negative. Whatever eighteenth-century associations there may have been with breeding up (and these would have been weak and ambiguous in any event), after the

1860's, the associations most available became either the "dead ends" found in the fossil record or creatures like flightless birds or the duck-billed platypus that seemed to be obsolescent half-species doomed to die out or to survive merely as ludicrous evidence of nature's confusion, of experiments gone wrong. It was not only in the work of the racist propagandist Robert Knox that the "human hybrid" was now seen as "a degradation of humanity . . . rejected by nature."[57]

If *half-breed* implied inadequacy, incompleteness, and failure, *miscegenation* (an American neologism of 1864, appropriate to the post-Darwinian racial discourse) suggested through its pseudo-scientific resonance that the act of engendering such creatures was itself not merely individually culpable and shameful but a biological confusion, an error that set in train the process of racial degeneration. Earlier, opinions had differed. W. Cooke Taylor could argue in 1840 that quite the reverse was true, that want of "renovation" through exogamous marriage caused both social and, as with African "Pigmies," biological deformity: "Barbarism is not a state of nature, but a perversion of nature by isolation of a type and a lack of 'intermixture.'[58] In 1845 Ralph Waldo Emerson could expand on the evolutionary possibilities that might flow from a racial melting pot:

> Well, as in the old burning of the Temple at Corinth, by the melting and admixture of silver and gold and other metals a new compound more precious than any, called the Corinthian brass, was formed: so in this continent,—asylum of all nations,—the energy of Irish, Germans, Swedes, Poles, and cossacks, and all the European tribes—of the Africans, and of the Polynesians,—will construct a new race, a new religion, a new state, a new literature, which will be as vigorous as the new Europe which came out of the smelting-pot of the Dark Ages, or that which earlier emerged from the Pelasgic and Etruscan barbarism. *La Nature aime les croisements.*[59]

This vision of progress through amalgamation, in America at best an eccentric and uncertain voice, the quavering echo of an earlier abolitionist utopianism, was a hope that was utterly drowned by a late-Victorian fear of mongrelization and degeneration.[60] Emerson himself, after reading Robert Knox in the 1850's (and in the context, perhaps, of the beginning of that great migration to America of poor, malnourished, and often diseased Irish and southern Europeans), was persuaded that hybrids were not after all likely to be vigorous, but rather tended to degeneration.[61] As Gertrude Himmelfarb has observed, only a month after the publication of *Origin*, John Brown's raid at Harper's Ferry gave *The Times* of London an opportunity to expand on the popular "lessons" to be drawn from evolutionary debate (if not legitimately from Darwin's own careful speculations). Invoking the kind of moral panic that became common in the late-Victorian press, the leader writer warned that the abolitionists in America were threatening to turn the South into a kind of racial laboratory, where the mixture of races would tend "not to the elevation of the black, but to the degradation of the white man."[62]

A Spreading Realm

White-black marriages and children from mixed-race unions were not unknown in eighteenth-century England, and the attention they drew seems commonly to have been that of the curious rather than the fearful. Where there was a sharp color difference—a light-skinned child born of dark parents or a black child of seemingly white parents, or where a child's skin was mottled or hair a surprising texture or color, he or she was in danger of being regarded, like an albino, as a freak. Indeed, the period's fascination, scientific and otherwise, with actual cases of "albino Negroes" probably tells us something about the popular attitude toward the light-skinned mulatto—who could similarly be regarded as a living paradox, a blackamoor washed white.[63]

Regarded as anomalies or freaks, and on occasion exhibited as such, light-skinned Negroes did not, however, much disturb the public in Britain—either as a social or racial danger or, for that matter, as objects of sympathy. In the late 1740's, a very fair "white" child born to a plantation slave mother in Virginia was brought to London to be shown at the Royal Society, but on "finding that one of the sailors had debauched the girl and given her the pox," she was returned to America. Nineteen years later, a similar case of a "White Negro," a young male, was in fact exhibited at the Royal Society.[64] It may be significant that neither of these cases of "white-looking" progeny of "black" parents were treated as probable evidence of a secret miscegenation—the reading they would almost certainly have been given in the mid nineteenth century—but as curious examples of haphazard variation.

The ever-present danger of black revolt in the Caribbean, well focused by sensational press accounts of the maroon wars of the 1790's in Jamaica and the bloody revolution in Haiti, made the issue of the half-breed or mulatto infinitely more problematical for whites in the islands. Where did his or her loyalties lie? Such doubts paralleled the difficulty of reading the racial identity of the half-breed. In effect, was he or she half-white or half-black? In Jamaica, the loyalty of freed-slave mulattoes and their descendants, especially those who held property, was often contrasted with the deeper blackness of the most recalcitrant and dangerous—the recently enslaved and escaped slaves who had fled to the interior. Like the half-caste Eurasian in India, the freed mulatto in Jamaica was expected to be loyal to his white progenitors, but there inevitably lurked the fear of an ever-buried racial affinity in the other direction—an affinity that would be read as treason and ingratitude.

An interesting pre-Victorian view of the mulatto can be found in the gothic novelist "Monk" Lewis's account of visits to his own estates in Jamaica immediately following the conclusion of the French wars. Lewis himself was a species of hyphen, a man of ambiguous identity. That is (leaving aside the issue of his probable homosexuality), he was a cosmopolitan and liberal, a man of continental and British literary reputation, but who also, by inheritance, was an (absentee) slaveholder and plantation proprietor, and his account of Jamaica bridges in a sense the predictable prejudices of the Jamaican landowner and the more distanced humanitarianism of the London salon.

Lewis's construction of the half-breed is itself an ambiguous affair. He lays out the complicated language of color difference and caste separation for us and implicates the mulattoes themselves in the system of color prejudice: "Nor can the separation of castes in India be more rigidly observed, than that of complexional shades among the Creoles."[65] The anecdotes about mulattoes that he tells communicate a general sympathy, however, touched by an element of romance that draws from an inevitable (for an eighteenth-century man of letters) association of mixed-race alliance with the familiar tale of Inkle and Yarico.[66] He dwells on the sultry beauty of a "sambo" manumitted slave, Mary Wiggins:

> I really think that her form and features were the most *statue-like* that I ever met with: her complexion had no yellow in it, and yet was not brown enough to be dark—it was more of an ash-dove colour than anything else; her teeth were admirable, both for colour and shape; her eyes equally mild and bright; and her face merely broad enough to give it all possible softness and grandness of contour: her air and countenance would have suited Yarico . . . Mary Wiggins and an old Cotton-tree are the most picturesque objects that I have seen for these twenty years.[67]

Other mulattoes, if less picturesque, are also described positively. Nicholas, a mulatto carpenter, had a "clean appearance and intelligent countenance" and was "a very interesting person, both from his good looks and gentle manners."[68]

And yet the underlying object here is, at least in part, to prepare us for his much darker, gothic image of black Negro treachery, of an especially feminine cruelty and callousness—in, as we have seen, his tales of poisoning and revenge, which he took from the standard planter lore of the lurking bestial nature of even the most trusted blacks. In the mulatto male, however, this feminine element inherent in the half-breed became softness, gentleness (as in Nicholas the carpenter), and ultimately effeminacy:

> There was . . . a mulatto, about thirty years of age, named Bob, who had been almost deprived of the use of his limbs by the horrible cocoa-bay [disease], and had never done the least work since he was fifteen. He was so gentle and humble, and so fearful, from the consciousness of his total inability of soliciting my notice, that I could not help pitying the poor fellow; and whenever he came in my way I always sought to encourage him by little presents, and other trifling marks of favour.[69]

Between Lewis's first and second voyages, Bob dies, longing, we are told, for "Massa" to return.

Lewis's construction of the mulatto in Jamaica has a certain resonance with later images, as we have seen, of African Negroes as feminine men and masculine women. He includes several anecdotes of maiming and fighting among Negro women and oddly observes that "they are deficient in one of the most requisite points of female beauty. . . . Young or old, I have not yet seen such a thing as a *bosom.*"[70] But ultimately it is the effeminacy of the male mulatto that he projects onto the half-breed generally: "Mulattoes . . . are almost universally weak and effeminate persons, and thus their children are very difficult to rear."[71]

There is of course more at work here than a possible self-revelation, some reflection of Lewis's own attraction to a dependent, feminine male. Mixed-race people were by definition creatures of contradiction, however amiable and attractive. The half-breed was often seen as emotionally unstable and perhaps ultimately an untrustworthy compound: as in the "weaker sex," a fawning affection might slide unpredictably into the jealous rage of the impotent or the scorned. And when mulatto married mulatto, the instability—a kind of dementia of conflicting identities—was compounded. As Arbousset and Daumas later observed of the intermarrying community of mulatto "Bastaards" (or "Basters") in southern Africa, anger could arouse in them the character of the "true" Hottentot—"treacherous, malicious, and passionate,—and he gives himself up to unrestrained rage and revenge. . . . [But his] habits are, in general, gentle and peaceful."[72] For Lewis, the children of mulatto-mulatto unions pass beyond the system of nomenclature into the realm of the unpredictable, the total loss of boundary, and they are as "difficult to rear" as the mule is to lead.

Lewis, master of the gothic romance, has combined the elements of threat and dependency, beauty and abnormality, gentleness and savagery into a creature of his own particular making—a feminized mulatto race whose deviancy is both attractive and threatening. As a novelist, he has a feeling for the telling descriptive detail, the pointed anecdote, and the metaphoric incident. His journal is not a mere travelogue but an imaginative text, where descriptions of the commonplace slide into tales of horror, of poisonings and bludgeonings, of heads on stakes in the lush, Edenic countryside. A striking and, it seems to me, clearly significant digression may be found in his recollection of having, out of mere curiosity, bisected a centipede and placed it in a jar to see whether either half might regenerate. The severed head remained quiet, but the tail continued to twitch for several days, prompting a flippant, if curious, observation: "The tail was evidently much more lively and full of motion than the head: perhaps the centipede was a female."[73]

Lewis's little joke here can be given a double meaning. More obviously it scores off of the commonplace that women were sexual, hysterical creatures without male intelligence. But this is Jamaica, and the centipede in a jar (a dangerous, poisonous thing confined and, like the slave subjects of Marryat's Henry Brandt, subjected to sadistic torture) can surely be read as a metaphor for the Negro slave, especially since Lewis has already given us tales of female slaves who poisoned their masters. The centipede's tail, its female part, contains the sting. Does the black's womb also contain the thing that threatens to poison the white race?

It was in this fearfully imagined realm, this corrupted Eden, of course, that the racial half-breed as an essentially gothic type took its characteristic form. The half-breed as image in British domestic culture did not develop out of the commonplace mixed-race reality in the streets of London or Liverpool. This was not only because it was among the beleaguered and fearful whites of Jamaica that racist discourse flourished most aggressively, to be carried to England like a contagion in the minds of returning planter-nabobs, but also because the fanciful, deeply pejorative nineteenth-century *British* literary image of the half-breed, the myths about half-breed character and biology, and the gothic language used to construct them, flourished upon distance and unfamiliarity. The shaping of the literary image required, not only the importation of the raw material of exploration narrative and plantation anecdote, but the free flow of a distanced imagination that made *the* half-breed more a shadow of the mind than a social reality in a specific place and time. He or she became a composite of projected anxieties, as one professedly sympathetic commentator, writing from London at the end of the century, made graphically plain in his catalogue of "crossed race" weaknesses:

The bad or weak qualities . . . are a latent vanity as strong as that of a Southern Frenchman, indolence rising in middle age almost to a passion, and in all directions a lack, after a certain amount of provocation, of reasonable self-control. This is a point at which every man with dark blood in his veins is liable to allow his reason to cease to rule him, and to act like a gambler when the fever has overcome his brains. He acts for a time as if he were *"possessed."* [74]

"Vanity," "passion," lack of "self-control"—these were precisely the flaws of character that the white imperialist himself was admonished to overcome, the suppression of which was in fact fundamental in the reconstruction of the idealized upper-class male as selfless stoic in the second half of the century. Clearly, the search for the image of the half-breed begins, not with the savage black temptress and the product of her womb, but with the white man himself. It was resentment of the white who rejected his kind, who fled from the civilized community to live among barbaric savages, that seems first to have given birth to an image of bizarre anomaly, a white man gone native, himself in fact become a half-caste, a monstrous self-transformation, a Crusoe mastered by Friday. This unnatural being fathered children, and it was his perverting image that was communicated to them. They were, at least originally it would seem, reflections of *his* cross-boundary transgression.

In the early accounts of the Spanish conquest of the Caribbean, we find something of this—in, for instance, Bernal Díaz's story of the Spaniard Gonzalo Guerrero, captured by Indians, who refused to be liberated eight years later. Stephen Greenblatt has argued that such cases threatened the "blockage" by which Europeans denied the obvious homologies between the "savages" and the Europeans' own savagery against them. Guerrero's case threatened to collapse the civilized European self into that of the Other, and it therefore elicited a predictable horror. [75] This is a convincing interpretation as far as it goes, but one that may have difficulty accommodating the whole record.

Sometime after Díaz's account, the French Protestant Jean de Lery wrote similarly of discovering, to his "great regret," fellow Frenchmen who had gone native in Brazil. Although, like Díaz, he expressed dismay that European men had "polluted themselves by all sorts of loose and base behavior," even indulging in cannibalism, he appears to have viewed the collapsing of separate identities as merely an instructive confirmation of the universality of sin. The white man's deviancy abroad, his going native, was brought back home. Like Montaigne, de Lery uses New World savagery as a text from which to deliver a homily on the "brutal action" of Europeans, who, even in Europe, "not content with having cruelly put to death their enemies, have been unable to slake their bloodthirst except by eating their livers and their hearts." [76]

Guerrero, who married an Indian and had several children, is described by Díaz as bearing the stigmata of his deviancy—his face was tattooed and his ears were pierced. In a white man, these were already readable signs. They located him in the same medieval and Renaissance traditions that "marked," physically or in dress, the criminal, the leper, the heretic, the madman, the Gypsy, and the Jew. That is, he—as well as the natives he consorted with—could be "read" in an Old as well as a New World context.

We have seen the signifying power of the tattoo in the eighteenth and nineteenth centuries, transferred first from the Caribbean native to the white cannibal sailor, and then, in the new borderlands between white and black in the South Pacific, from the fierce Maori to escaped convicts, sailors, and traders who "went native" on the other side of the world. Here, in much of the nineteenth-century discussion of the significance of the antipodean tattoo (and it was a popular topic), there was a search for associations that, like the diffusionist theories of the Wandering Tribes, enabled the uncomfortably alien South Pacific to be drawn into a familiar field of representation.

If Joseph Banks and Captain Cook (who introduced the Polynesian word *tattow* into English) were more bemused than troubled at a custom they associated merely with "superstition,"[77] the Victorians came to read tattoos as signs with a darker message. Darwin on *The Beagle*, although he discovered an almost seductive attractiveness in the sinuous tattoos of the Tahitian men, was disturbed by the fiercer facial markings (which "puzzle and mislead") of the New Zealanders; they not only gave a "disagreeable expression to the countenance," but were accompanied by "a twinkling in the eye which cannot indicate anything but cunning and ferocity."[78] J. S. Polack, in a discussion of the manners and customs of the New Zealanders published in 1840, found both the tattoo and the process of tattooing deeply disturbing. He saw in them, not merely the curious and exotic practice of a primitive people, but an outward sign of an inner immorality, expressed in the biblical imagery of the evangelical: "The mark in the forehead of Cain has been likened by some commentators to puncturing, and the imitations made by his children, as the origin of tattooing."[79] The painful and bloody process of tattooing and cicatrization itself provided an irresistible opportunity to gothicize, to associate primitive custom with sadistic/sexual fantasy via a familiar and sensational vocabulary: "The process of puncturing is attended with intense pain, the victim to this curious fashion, lies recumbent, wincing and writhing at every stroke given by the operator, the body quivering under the torments inflicted. . . . The blood gushes forth at every stroke."[80] A few years earlier, Augustus Earle had observed Maori "cutting their flesh as a cook would score pork for roasting. . . . All were streaming with tears and blood."[81]

Thus located within a traditional, domestic, and gothic field, as well as within that of the primitive Other, the tattoo and the ornamental scar signified rather more than simply "going native." Europeans who had "disfigured themselves with these barbarous embellishments" to "disgusting effect"[82] had not merely gone over to a lesser culture. They had also exteriorized an inner deviancy.

The image of the half-breed drew heavily on the deviancy associated with whites who went native, as well as on the entrenched popular "knowledge" of that other Edenic realm of fierce Caribs and Guerrero's disfiguration, of Defoe's imaginary cannibals, and of maroon marauders in the mountains of Jamaica. In the South Pacific, there was a fresh recombination or renewal of reciprocating images of white and black, of white aberration and the half-breed typicality it helped to construct.

In fact, the domesticated black of the Caribbean plantation was in danger of losing his gothic character, although apologists for the peculiar institution struggled to keep memories of slave rebellion and demonic atrocity fresh. The Jamaican uprising of 1831 did not, for instance, elicit quite the same degree of empathetic horror in Britain, if press accounts are any indication, that the maroon wars of 1795–96 had done (nor that Gordon's "revolt" was to do, with much slenderer basis, in 1865). Moreover, the free and slave mulatto played an often positive role in these accounts, being associated more often with the white master than with the more "full-blooded" black rebels.

The first half of the nineteenth century, however, saw the gestation and infancy of a reconstructed half-breed threat. What happened between Frankenstein's Jamaican monster of 1816 and the reinvented, generalized racial danger following mid-century was not only the construction and general acceptance of a harder, more concrete idea of race, but a spreading imperial realm. Within this wider sphere, a more intimate and often violent contact with strange and resisting peoples required *their* otherness to be understood as a universalized blackness. One result of this was to displace whatever elements remained of the notion that the half-breed's threat derived from the deviant white. The half-breed came to be viewed as "essentially" black, and his danger as that of the hidden pollution of "pure" white blood with bad blood / black blood. Or, as Lafcadio Hearn observed of Martinique mulattos in 1890, "the old African element . . . has now become itself the modifying instead of the modifiable race element in the western tropics."[83]

It may be instructive to consider one area where such a shift in reading the half-breed occurred most strikingly. This was, unlike the Caribbean or American South, a fresh region of racial ambiguity ready for an imaginative reinvention, a new Columbian penetration.

In the South Pacific, the half-breed could be viewed as the product of a much more vicious and exploitative relationship between deviant white and wild savage than was true of the common view of the Jamaican or southern plantation, where, at least among the worldly, there appeared to be a kind of, albeit regrettable, naturalness in the settled, domestic concubinage of the black slave girl to her white paternal master. In the popular (and governmental) mind, the coarse whalers and sealers, sex-starved sailors, escaped convicts, and unscrupulous traders who went native in the South Pacific islands and along the coast of New Zealand and Australia were deviant marginals, marauders, and outcasts, who, it was claimed, seized and discarded native women to suit their lusts. Augustus Earle blamed "Beach Rangers," low whites, whalers who had deserted to avoid just punishment for their "crimes," and escaped convicts, for infusing into Maori life "a tinge of vulgarity, of which the native women retain the largest portion. In many instances, they quite spoil their good looks, by half adopting the [gaudy] European costume" the sailors gave them and becoming "the most grotesque objects imaginable."[84] These white men were read as the social analogs, not, as the Jamaican planter was often read in Britain, of the landed gentry, but of the dangerous classes of urban criminals and beggars—something the transportation system itself served to entrench.[85]

Drawing from this contemporary representation of brutal whites who took native "wives," Robert Hughes has painted a sensational picture of lawlessness, of pillage, murder, and exploitation, committed by a desperate fringe of white marauders who, themselves devoid of all morality, slaughtered aboriginal males and took their women for sex and survival lore.[86] Hughes relies of course on the accounts of captured white men seeking to ingratiate themselves by telling authorities what they wanted to hear, and on government sources, on the records of those who viewed these men in any event as moral savages, as, by definition, "the most desperate and lawless of mankind," prepared to commit "every species of crime."[87]

Without denying the brutality of many of the men who took native wives, especially the sealers, we can trace the language used by contemporaries to generalize about them as a whole (as, almost, a race apart) to a well-established European discourse. That is, any possibility of real intimacy, any validity in these mixed-race unions, was blocked by their own presumed social deviancy. The "taking" of black wives and the fathering of "the offspring of these poor Creatures and their oppressors" is read as merely further evidence of their immorality. To many observers, as to Governor Darling, these "riffraff with their black slave-harems" were threatening to infect the New World with their "half-wild tribal communities,"[88] with half-breed progeny whose wildness derived at least as much from the white male rogue as from the black female—often constructed for this purpose as victim.

Another influential source of the threatening half-breed, at least at the metaphoric level, can be traced in Australia to white society. This is the image of the emancipist—the free man with an ineradicable convict past—and, especially, his children, the second-generation "native" or "Currency," who attempted to rise above their origins. The snobbery aimed at this class, and their own recognition of their otherness made them a powerful, if disguised, equivalent of the racial half-breed. The language Louisa Anne Meredith used to justify "the prejudice against them," for instance, to describe the parvenu, rich, social-climbing vulgarity of the successful emancipist, has a strikingly familiar ring: his "daughters dress in the extreme of fashion and finery," he himself rolls home "in his gay carriage . . . with face, hands and apparel as dirty and slovenly as any common mechanic." His son may be seen "with a dozen costly rings on his coarse fingers, and chains, and shirt-pins, glistening with gems, buying yet more expensive jewelry, yet without stock or stockings to his feet."[89] The social snobbery here has already an element of racial association—in the language of anti-Semitism commonly deployed at home to describe the rich Jew. In the course of the nineteenth century, it flowed into new realms. The vulgar Jewlike emancipist (sometimes in fact a Jew, like Ikey Solomon), in a new world itself defined as a racial borderland, is a precursor of a racial type—the postabolition landowning mulattoes of Jamaica, the uppity blacks of the Reconstruction South, or, as we shall see, the Eurasian minority in India.

In England, the representation of the convict "stain" in Australia, and the problem of the ticket-of-leave man, like Magwitch, trying to "pass" among respectable society, is directly and obviously analogous to the emerging "problem" of the racial half-breed. As the Victorian world became ever more race- and class-conscious, there arose the image of a new generation of mixed-blood persons, often with resources of their own, no longer fixed or anchored by slavery or poverty in their own realm—the Caribbean plantation or Canadian trading post or the suburbs of Calcutta—but a mobile population spreading like the empire itself and, ultimately, threatening to return "home."

Away from the Australian "System," both the whites who went native and mixed-race unions could generally be represented in calmer language, without the cruder gothic elements that served to link the criminal convict or rapacious sealer and his aborigine bride in a monstrous embrace. In John Savage's description of New Zealand at the beginning of the nineteenth century, we are offered natives who are not the natural victims of demonic whites. Rather, the Maori were seen as a warrior caste, infinitely superior, although presumed cannibals, to the pitiful aborigines of Tasmania and Australia, and to the whites among them as well—whom Savage presents as weak of character, cowardly, and dependent.

A story Savage tells of a white man in New Zealand who has gone native nevertheless follows a familiar line of representation. He is like many others of his kind, "profligate" fellows, often fugitives or those put ashore for mutiny or "improper conduct" (sodomy?), who have fled into the interior, taken native wives, adopted the manners and customs of the Maori, and fathered mixed-race children. Although "spoken well of by the natives," he brings a kind of destruction, a pollution, with him, and the sign of this fatal gift can be read in the faces of his children. Savage tells of one whom he has seen, a child of dark skin but fair hair, which unnatural combination is matched by an aberrant character:

> The difference between this child and those of the unmixed native is very remarkable: the native child looks full in your face with perfect confidence; this half-bred child is all bashfulness, and when you attempt to caress it, clings to its mother with marks of apprehension and distrust . . . it is by no means superior to the native, and there is no reason to suppose that it will excel in qualities of the mind.[90]

Savage, who took a full-blooded young Maori back to England, idealizes this Eden and the native in a predictably Rousseauian manner. In his account, the white man represents the vices of civilization, the savage (*pace* his cannibalism) the virtues of the natural life. The half-breed bears the enduring curse of an infection that is real as well as metaphoric. The venereal diseases the white men bring to their native partners will undermine the race, and "in all probability," a few generations of children of diseased parents will produce "a puny . . . miserable and disgusting" people, which will in no respect resemble "the hardy inhabitants of the island, previously to their unhappy communications with civilized man."[91]

Inevitably, the widening and deepening of European contact, the establishment of permanent white settlements, of naval stations, garrisons, and ultimately colonists, required a different mode of representation. When Richard Cruise, a regimental officer stationed for ten months in New Zealand, published his memoir in 1823, we have a significant shift in perspective. Like Savage, he has little good to say about the European sailors who bring venereal diseases to the island, but he is not concerned that their progeny, the half-breeds, will undermine a noble, Edenic world. The half-breed children he describes are not unnatural natives (like Savage's black faces with the odd stigma of blond hair) but near-whites—"fair" and "pretty," "quite English" in appearance.[92] Presumably *their* effect on the native race would be an ennobling one, but this is unlikely to happen.

Considering the "extensive intercourse" between European sailors and native women, Cruise can only explain the very small number of half-breed children he observes by assuming that their mothers kill them.[93] That is, he shifts the reader away from the culpable European male—who brings disease and casually abandons the women he has debauched and the children he has fathered—to the black women, Savage's erstwhile victims, who now themselves become criminal in their recourse to both abortion and infanticide. Child-killing was, of course, a staple of the gothic and had overtones of cannibalism and ritual murder. It is an accusation that, whatever the reality of social custom among the wide variety of "primitive" cultures to which the charge was laid, suggests a prejudice well grounded in domestic British culture.[94] Some years later, an Englishwoman, Mrs. Flannagan, writing about the Antiguans, in a travel book full of murder and Obeah poisonings, accuses black Caribbean women of commonly practicing infanticide—"especially since emancipation" gave them the liberty to do so. It was, Mrs. Flannagan reflected, "one of those unnatural offences which shews too clearly our fallen state."[95]

It is worth noting, whatever the actual incidence of infanticide in New Zealand ports of call (and here Cruise, like Mrs. Flannagan, is too ready to draw an analogy with the practices of prostitutes in English naval towns), that it is only the Englishlike half-breed children whom he notices. There were no doubt many others who were blacker and escaped his attention. One unconscious result in his text is that the "murder" of the half-breed thereby becomes the murder of the near-white, not of near-black, children.

Some twenty years later, after the immigration of settlers had begun in earnest and the islands were a contested ground between an increasingly marginalized black and a dominant resident white population, Edward Shortland, employed by the colonial government as a "Protector of Aborigines" kept a journal, which he expanded and published in London in 1851.[96] Shortland was a sympathetic observer of the Maori, as one would expect, and his representation of the native population is calm and factual. Seeking to counter the sensational claims of a writer in the *Edinburgh Review* that the Maori were doomed to extinction owing to both inbreeding and cannibalism, he portrays them as unthreatening, and likely to survive as a kind of enduring anomaly—like, he says, the Celts of Wales—within a basically Anglo-Saxon realm. The half-breeds, in his account, have been thoroughly domesticated. No longer the unwanted children of prostitute-native mothers, they represent, perhaps, a potential blending away of the original Maori race (not, significantly, a threat to the purity of the white race), but in fact their numbers are "trifling," and their circumstances respectable.[97]

Shortland presents an undemonized view of native, half-breed, and white alike (his sailors "live on very good terms" with their native "wives," and some of them actually have church weddings). If probably an eccentric view, parallel with that of the radical abolitionist in America, it nevertheless expresses a calmness appropriate to the optimism of the year of the Crystal Palace, and to a period in imperial race relations unmarked as yet by social Darwinism, the Indian Mutiny, the scientific speculations of the Anthropological Society, or moral panic over white degeneration.

We may conclude with the first substantial "history" of New Zealand, that published in 1859 by Arthur Thomson, a surgeon major who had served in the islands, and whose account is marked by some of the respect a military men might feel for a fierce opponent, if not by Shortland's aborigine protection views. Thomson's Maori, however, are firmly and pejoratively placed in a framework of evolutionary racial progress. In a neat inversion of the moral message of Savage's invocation of Rousseau, Thomson's work is significantly subtitled *Past and Present — Savage and Civilized.*[98] For Thomson, the only hope of survival for the Maori lies, paradoxically, in their interbreeding with the more vigorous white population. It is the pure-blood Maori who now bear the stigmata of degeneration, although half-breeds inadequately strengthened with white blood might share these gothic signs of debility: "Two-headed children, and other monstrosities, have been witnessed. Persons blind from disease and age are not infrequent. Five albinos have been seen, two of them were half-castes. The unpleasant tongues of stammerers are heard in villages. Flat feet are common."[99]

Thomson embraces what I have argued was an early understanding, derived from animal husbandry, of the half-breed as an improvement, a step up, just as his observation that the infertility and physical abnormalities of the Maori are traceable to an ever-greater inbreeding among them makes use of negative images drawn from the same source. "Breeders of dogs, horses, sheep, and fowls, know that these animals, after several generations of close intermixture, degenerate in those physical qualities for which they had been originally celebrated, and unless crossed with a new breed die out."[100]

Thomson's account of New Zealand's future in fact accomplishes naturally—that is, biologically—what many settlers no doubt anticipated accomplishing by other means: the genocide of the pure-blooded Maori race.

In this process, the half-breed occupies a complicated and somewhat contradictory position. On the one hand, Thomson sees the mixed race as the salvation of the Maori from "scrofula and sterility," and he quotes a missionary who has nothing but praise for this "new race of civilised mixed people, which shall be better for the world." Thomson establishes the half-breed in his text as a kind of paragon—"a noble and beautiful race, and they only require education to develop the force and power of their minds." And yet, in the last analysis, it is an unstable, transitory thing. Here, where the image of the half-breed has apparently been freed from all traces of a gothicized, demonic representation, has reached what may be called the apogee of its status before being regothicized in the second half of the century, it nonetheless remains incomplete, a hyphen.

Thomson believed that all barriers to intermarriage should be lifted and writes ecstatically in an extended passage on historic European amalgamations of conquered and conqueror that seems free of race bias. But the end result will not be a beautiful, vigorous new race but the utter absorption of the Maori into the Anglo-Saxon. "In the third generation, the nut-brown skin, the black eye, and the raven hair generally disappear . . . the less numerous shall be lost in that of the greater number . . . the features of the Maori race will disappear." Only in this way, through the virtual extermination of the Maori via the half-breed will Gibbon's famous vision of a Hume of the Southern Hemisphere springing from the "cannibal races" be realized.[101]

In an illustration accompanying this panegyric, we are given a view, an engraving from a photograph, of a Maori girl with her half-caste nephew and niece by her side, elaborately dressed in European clothing. She is dark and they, the coming generation, look white—a common strategy in mixed-race illustration straining for a favorable representation (ill. 18).[102] Thomson's text in fact accomplishes its positive image of the half-breed by treating it as an improved part of the Maori community—that is, as whiter blacks. In this way, he avoids the problem of the reversed image—of the half-breed as a darker European. His half-castes live inside the frame of a Europeanized black world. It requires only a slight shift of perspective, however, to turn white smugness into white fear, to take the half-breeds out of one frame and put them into another, that which the white in the empire was constructing for himself alone.

In 1872 the government settled some 70 Tasmanian "half-castes" on Cape Barren Island, where, on land reserved for their farms and pastures, they increased and prospered. But an early optimism soured, and in 1894 Bishop Montgomery "believed now it had been a mistake to concentrate the 'half-castes' into a township that had brought its own special evils. They had developed a 'settled hatred' for himself, the schoolmaster, and

Ill. 18(a). A. S. Thomson, *The Story of New Zealand* (1859): "New Zealand Girl with Her Half-Caste Nephew and Niece."

the constable, and had expressed a wish not to become 'like white people'."[103] It is clear that the insistence of the Cape Barren mixed-race people on their "difference" was a response to the prejudice and resentment with which they (and their reserved land) were increasingly regarded by the island's "whites." As we shall see, this pattern conformed to a changing environment elsewhere in the empire.

The Half-Breed and Rebellion: Three Studies

The shadowy image, in late-Victorian popular culture, of the half-breed as a racial and moral threat draws from a tradition in which the mixed-race person was often represented as an ambivalent creature torn

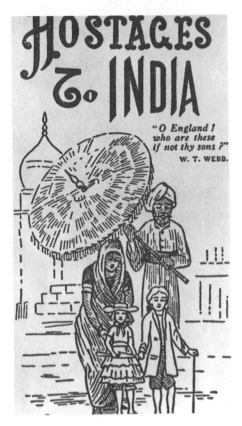

Ill. 18(b). H. A. Stark, *Hostages to India* (1936).

between different cultures and loyalties, an outcast, a misfit, and a biological unnatural. In the colonial empire, he had long been an object of condescension, when loyal and useful, and of fear and hatred when rebellious. After mid-century, whatever positive aspects of representation there may have been were overwhelmed by what one can call a kind of moral panic. This popular reading, particularly well inscribed in late-Victorian gothic literature as in popular discourse generally, was, of course, itself the product of a complex conjunction of social forces, both domestic and imperial.

Here I shall briefly examine how the image of the half-breed or half-caste "played" in three imperial theaters: India before and after 1857, Jamaica during the Gordon "rebellion" of 1865, and the Canadian West during the Riel or Métis rebellions of 1870 and 1885. These will serve to illustrate a striking shift away from the view that half-breeds were at least useful tools in the spread of British rule and culture toward one that construed them to be, at best, marginal and irrelevant, and at worst dangerous instruments of pollution and sedition.

In each of these areas, mixed-race people, the Eurasian or half-caste in India, the mulatto in Jamaica, and the half-breed in Hudson's Bay and western Canada, had played a largely positive role by mediating between European and non-European, bridging cultural distance, transmitting vital knowledge upwards and a model of submissiveness downwards. They were living symbols of a kind of interdependency and intimacy between outsider and native, master and slave. No doubt, as in India and Canada, the scarcity of white women in the early period of conquest made at least concubinage inevitable, but such connection was also extremely useful well beyond the early period of an essentially masculine colonial penetration. And the mixed race that flowed from such unions itself became an important resource—as translators, overseers, middlemen generally, and, importantly, providers of early warning of unrest to a perpetually anxious white minority.

INDIA

In India, the Eurasian community had emerged by the late eighteenth century as a useful collaborating class (to use Ronald Hyam's phrase), one that was growing in numbers and prosperity. Intermarriage and the keeping of Indian mistresses had in fact been encouraged by the British administration. "Anglo-Indians" (or "Indo-Britons" or "East Indians") as they were first called—the Victorians, significantly perhaps, preferred "Eurasian" or "half-caste"—secured an increasing number of lower and middle-level administrative and military positions, as well as prospering as commercial and financial middlemen, in a way familiar from other European empires in Asia, Africa, and Latin America. But during the 1790's there was a sharp reversal of official attitude, anticipating a similar about-face elsewhere in the British Empire. Anglo-Indians were prohibited from holding civil or combatant military office in 1791. Intermarriage came to be officially frowned upon, although many officials, such as Lord Metcalf (governor-general, 1835–36), continued to take Indian mistresses and produce half-caste children. In 1835 intermarriage was explicitly forbidden to company employees.[104]

It has been argued that this change reflects fears generated in the era of revolution by the shock waves of the violent rebellion in Haiti, by the increasing numbers of Protestant missionaries, who abhorred concubinage, and by an administrative determination to impose a permanent and formal Raj, to administer directly rather than working through native structures. The first half of the century—down to the Mutiny—

saw the growth of prejudice generally.[105] Thereafter, in the wake of the panic over the 1857 rebellion, and because of the increasing number of Englishwomen in India, the role of the Eurasians became even more circumscribed. They became an increasingly endogamous, marginalized community.

In fact, the loyalty of Eurasians seemed guaranteed by the low position they held in the caste system, inasmuch as they were despised by Hindus as "unclean"—although this was an argument at times deployed against them, as it seemed to limit their usefulness as go-betweens.[106] In William Huggins's *Sketches of India* (1824), the half-caste is presented in mostly positive terms as a necessary security against the doubtful loyalty of the sepoy troops; mostly "European" in language, dress, and religion, Eurasians would "form a medium . . . and, acting as a centre between two extremes, would preserve an equipoise, both harmonious and consistent."[107]

Nevertheless, there was, in spite of (or perhaps in some way because of) their undoubted desire for acceptance as mostly Christian Indo-*Britons*, a clear erosion of sympathy for the Eurasians and a growing condescension among the white establishment in the generation before the Mutiny. One indication of just how the image of the Eurasian shifted from that of a (potential) pillar of the Indian Empire to that of a despised and marginal class, or even a potential threat, can be seen already in the early-nineteenth-century rhetoric of the evangelical Lord Teignmouth (who, as Sir John Shore, had served in India as governor-general [1793–98]). He exhorted the Eurasian community to renounce the alien half of its identity, its "Indo-Asiatic habits"—sloth, selfishness, gross sensuality, falsehood, and deceit. By dwelling upon their vulnerability to "the infection of Asiatic vices," "the grave of everything excellent in the human mind," he established their difference in language heavily indebted to the gothic as well as evangelical image of a morbid sexuality. His emphasis on the sensual/Asian side of their nature as the chief source of infection, however much it might grow out of the particular representation of the Asian, conforms to suspicions elsewhere, as we have seen, of the lack of self-control and feminine nature of the half-breed generally: "*Sensuality*, which in taste, in smell, in touch, will seek a thousand unworthy gratifications, almost unknown to the sensualist in Europe, and which, stupifying the immortal mind, literally entombs it in the body."[108]

It is also true that in India, as in the South Pacific, the half-caste often came to be associated, not only with the vices of the "native," but with those of the particularly debased European "stock" from which he or she sprang ("the worst of both races"). This was a representation that gained ground in the nineteenth century as the act of "miscegenation" itself came to be seen as evidence of moral weakness on the part of the white, Christian male. The idealized masculinity of the Victorians demanded sexual abstinence, a romantic loyalty to "the girl at home," and a conception of "manly duty" that required firmness toward and social distance from the objects of imperial rule: "The great defect in the character of men brought up in India . . . is the want of self-reliance, self-independence, a certain hardness of character that I may call backbone."[109] The moral weakness of the European sensualist and of the unrespectable "poor white" generally in India was thus projected onto their half-caste progeny, a denigration that was all the stronger when the "white" side of the alliance was not British, but of another culture (Portuguese, Dutch, or Jewish) already stigmatized in patriotic convention.[110] In India (and, as we shall see, in Canada) a sharp distinction had long been available between half-castes with "British" blood, and those with an inferior mixture.

Catholic Portuguese and "Asiatic" Jews (as we have seen, Portuguese and Jew were also associated with the slave trade and white degeneracy in Africa) were of particular utility in a developing discourse on the supposed long-term effects of race-mixing. It comes as no surprise that vestiges in India of an ancient Semitic migration should have been seized upon by some commentators as another colorful, romantic, and instructive case of the wandering Jew. While some might view the survival of "Black Jews" in India as further evidence of the primitive tenacity and stubborn exclusivity of "the Jew" everywhere, others found a quite different, but similarly prejudicial, moral.[111] What survived was (inevitably) only a corrupted, vestigial religion and culture, and a bloodline that had offered little resistance to the overwhelming degenerative influence of the Asian majority. Here there was a sort of multiplying effect as the Jews' Asiatic nature was drawn out and magnified by the exotic people among whom they came to live.

As with the half-caste community in general, the Jews of India (although they were a tiny minority) had earlier been looked upon favorably.[112] Christian missionaries thought they would be easier to convert than Hindus and Muslims; Bene Israel sepoy troops had remained loyal during the Mutiny; and some administrators, like Sir Bartle Frere, governor of Bombay, continued into the 1860's to see at least the richer (usually Baghdadi) Jews as "a most valuable link between us and the natives—oriental in origin and appreciation—but English in their objects and associations, and, almost of necessity, loyal."[113]

Opinion generally about the usefulness of the half-caste eroded toward the end of the century, and in any event the dark, Marathi-speaking, impoverished, Indianized Jews of the Cochin coast were hardly to be associated with, say, the wealthy and educated Sassoons of Bombay. The observations of one British visitor at the turn of the century, the biographer and novelist Henry Bruce, illustrate a reaction perhaps typical of travelers who sought out "the Jews of India" only to find an essentially Indian community. Bruce found the Jews of "Jew Town" near "Mantachery" (*sic*) on the Malabar coast a disappointment—although they were "White Jews" rather than the even more debased "Black Jews," whom he "had no wish to see." Living along a "squalid lane," they were "content to vegetate" in "a twilight comfort, which must be intensely unhealthy and depressing. In the doorways I saw some children's faces, with the Jewish prettiness, but so dark that I could not believe that they called themselves white." In fact, he concludes that, although they continued to practice some form of the Jewish religion in their "common little synogogue" (where prayers were sung with a "screeching" and "hideous discord"), they had physically ("with eyes showing the mystery but not the genius of the race, with refined anaemic faces") and culturally degenerated by "cruel intermarrying." Proof of this lay in their susceptibility to the diseases of the poorest class of Hindu, and, even more important, in their own repellently "fatalistic" attitude to diseases the European would dread.[114] It will be clear how, in Bruce's text, his indictment of the Asianization of the Jew—and its overt strategy is to excoriate Asian, not Jewish, life—nevertheless rests surreptitiously on a quite familiar structure of Western anti-Semitism: on smells ("the place somehow suggests the odour of stale mutton"), on the alien "discord" of orthodox Jewish services, and on the susceptibility of the Jew to disease.[115]

Portuguese-Indian mixed blood nevertheless received much the same treatment from those British drawn to search for historical evidence of the effects of racial amalgamation. In Bengal, long-established communities of Indo-Portuguese "Feringhees" ("earth-coloured Europeans") played an important role in the nineteenth-century assault on the idea of the half-caste. Even William Huggins, who in the 1820's, like Surgeon-General W. J. Moore fifty years later, saw in the Indo-Briton a future bulwark of the empire, held the Portuguese half-caste in contempt, presenting him as poor, "insignificant," and despised by both white and black. He "eats with his fingers," was "dark as the Indian," and, generally, did "not display a trace" of his European descent.[116] "Not of a very pure type," and practicing a "debased" form of a Christianity (Roman Catholicism) that British prejudice had already invested with a primitive, deceitful, and superstitious character, the Feringhee was easily dismissed as a discredited type of hybrid, a biological and social dead-end: "Their study has a melancholy interest."[117] The Bengal Feringhees, one commentator claimed, had been established by half-caste priests from

Goa, themselves "renouned for their superstition, ignorance and selfishness." The weakness of the European stock, thus undermined by an unmanly religion and the Portuguese character ("lazy, treacherous, effeminate, and passionate to excess" in the words of the *Edinburgh Review*)[118] had proved incapable of countering the natural defects of the Asian, and the Feringhee "approximates much more to the native races than the Eurasian [Indo-Briton] does. Like the worst examples of the latter, he is wanting in energy and ambition."[119]

This discourse among the Orientalists of the monthly and weekly reviews found its more sensational parallel in the fiction of the century, in Sue's evil half-caste Thug, "Faringhea," in *The Wandering Jew* (1845–46), whose murders suggest a perverted sensuality, and in Thackeray's not-so-comic portrayal of Colonel Jowler's half-caste wife in *The Tremendous Adventures of Major Gahagan* (1838): "She was a hideous, bloated, yellow creature, with a beard, black teeth, and red eyes: she was fat, lying, and stingy—she hated and was hated by all the world."[120]

With the progressive removal of Eurasians from the military, another aspect of their character could be transformed in a way resonating with their construction as unmanly sensualists. As the community prospered from its somewhat privileged commercial position, it became commonplace to deride its affectation, its love of "luxury and fashion": Eurasians displayed "conceit," a "love of finery and display," and an "aversion to work."[121] In place of the image of the fighting men of Skinner's Horse, we have the Eurasian as parvenu. In a Raj that was ever more self-consciously a stage for the invention of tradition, for military display and the affirmation of the white as essentially a creature of duty and stoicism, the image of the Eurasian as greedy, self-indulgent, and vain came to operate rather like that of the prosperous Jew in Bismarck's Reich—as a negative image that helped define the real patriot.

Ironically, in their calls for a reformed and revitalized Indo-British community that would be able to command respect and privilege, Eurasian spokesmen themselves seem to have accepted much of this indictment, and this was not only true of the evangelicals among them.[122] From its foundation in 1879, the Eurasian and Anglo-Indian Association of Southern India hoped to get the more modest of their people to abandon the affectation and false snobbery of the suburban communities they clung to, and embrace "'humble labor', sobriety, and economy" in the countryside. In the cities, where the Eurasian struggled to maintain a shabby-genteel style of life through borrowing and dependence on the government, "It would be . . . surprising if [they] were not what they are—hot-house plants, passing phenomena like the figures in a kaleidoscope."[123]

By the late-Victorian period, this representation had become the defining one—well entrenched by the gossipy domestic snobbery of the clubs and drawing rooms of the late-imperial Raj. Inevitably, it was an image to which fin de siècle anthropology gave a gloss of scientific approval, rationalizing Eurasian exclusion from the military with statistical "evidence" of physical and mental debility. In 1898 Edgar Thurston (superintendent of the Madras Government Museum) compared a sample of poor Eurasians unfavorably with the physique of the "average Sepoy."[124] The poor Eurasians he examined were thin-chested and (not surprisingly) badly nourished. He also noted something else: "The Eurasian body being enveloped in clothes, it was not til they stripped before me, for the purpose of anthropometry, that I became aware how prevalent is the practice of tattooing among the male members of the community."[125] And there was yet another "sign" of difference. The dark color of their "pudenda" was "very conspicuous in many cases which came under observation."[126] These "observations" are, of course, packed with meaning; from beneath his or her European clothes the half-caste emerges, not as a near-European, but as a secret "Other."

The next year, the prestigious London medical journal the *Lancet* published a piece from its "special correspondent" in India that, although advocating the granting of full privileges to the Anglo-Indian community as bearers of "the blood of the ruling race," echoed Thurston's misgivings about the biological inadequacy of the Eurasian: "It is said that the cross between East Indian and the European is less satisfactory than that of the European with the negro; and that both are very far inferior to the product of a mixture [in reference to the Russian Empire] of Turanian and European blood. These differences are doubtless of vast importance."[127]

In general, the image of the vulgar parvenu involves a kind of social dishonesty—a pretending to be what one is not—that resonates with a biological dishonesty, a pretension to "whiteness," and attempt to "pass": "It is a matter of common knowledge, that among the better-placed and wealthier Eurasians, when there is no trace, or perhaps a slight one, of the racial mixture, the rule is to *pose* as Europeans. . . . There are cases of course where the speech or a nameless something indicates the *alien*, even when the appearance may be otherwise."[128] This is essentially the image presented in 1938 by Dennis Kincaid in his well-known history of British life in India. His Eurasians are, significantly, defined by their exaggerated European dress: the men are "smarter" than their white counterparts, with "large signet rings and gold-headed canes," while the women commit the "solecism" of overdressing: "They had started well enough in the current fashion but the wearers could not resist an extra rose here, another purple bow there, a love-knot, several gold chains and two or three huge brooches."[129] Dress is, of course, only a sign of underlying character, and his Eurasians are marked by an "almost masochistic obsequiousness," by "nervous giggles and gawky bows," and (in a projection characteristic of the literature of prejudice) by their own snobbery, a "pathological ferocity" aimed at those less white than themselves.[130]

The Mutiny, which galvanized the inherent prejudice of the British into a paranoiac racism, served inevitably to heighten uncertainty about the inherent orientation of the Eurasian, however much the actual events appeared to establish their loyalty to and dependence upon the European Raj. Tales of Eurasian loyalty during the Mutiny were common,[131] and afterwards Lord Canning asserted that "the Eurasian class have a special claim upon us."[132] And yet, if loyal, the Eurasians were hardly a dependable resource—relatively few in number, seen to be dependent on white rule for their social and economic position, and often perceived as physically "poor weakly-looking persons, very sallow and unhealthy in their appearance, and very small in stature" (Lord Ellenborough in 1853).[133] When, in 1874, Surgeon-Major W. J. Moore asserted that "it may some day be found, that Eurasian regiments and Eurasian loyalty will be the great bond of union between England and India," this belief, like his view that the Eurasian community was a rapidly increasing "composit race," had already become a minority and eccentric opinion among the British generally, and certainly among the rulers of the Raj.[134]

One popular type of story of Eurasian loyalty, that of the brave half-caste boy, in a way confirms the marginalization of the Eurasian. If the drummer boys in the sepoy regiments of 1857 were the "only sure guard" officers' families at the cantonments could look to,[135] their young innocence, impotence, and sad fate only served to feminize the image of the half-caste as a whole. Another ambivalent reading is suggested by the story of George Brendish, a mixed-race youth who valiantly stood by his telegraph key in Delhi sending out news of the sepoy rebellion while chaos erupted around him.[136] Brendish's story, however, offers a very modest example of half-caste usefulness. He was, after all, not in uniform, did not wield a weapon, and, in any event, represented in such texts more the universalized "plucky boy" than a Eurasian. By the end of the century, in one popular account at least, his identity had simply been altered to that of an "*English* boy that saved the Punjab."[137] Furthermore, his sphere of usefulness is significant. Like the telegraph he operated, he was merely passing on information; he is a hyphen that connects. However bravely Brendish performed his duty, his ultimate flight from that narrow telegraph office suggests, moreover, the general breakdown of communication between Indian and Briton and the end of the utility of the half-caste as communicator. The inscription at the base of the memorial obelisk unveiled by Lord Curzon in 1902 to mark the site of the Delhi Telegraph Office simply ignores the Eurasian hero and boasts, "The Electric Telegraph Saved India."

However loyal Eurasians might appear to be in accounts of the Mutiny, the general, swift, and surprising collapse of authority in 1857 significantly degraded the apparent usefulness of the half-caste. In a future where continued rule was thought to depend more on military force and a distanced and autocratic vice-regal display than on suasion, education, and direct communication, the Eurasian's usefulness as intermediary and communicator counted for much less. Earlier, it had been a commonplace that, as the president of the Central School of Bombay had told the Select Committee on East Indian Affairs in 1829, the "proper place for the East Indians . . . is to become a useful and connecting link between the Europeans and natives." Although they were "a shade inferior to the Europeans," their knowledge of native languages (and their relative cheapness) suited them for government employment.[138] It is significant that in the second half of the century a common disparaging term for the half-caste in India, "Chi-Chi," also came to refer to their manner of speech. What had once been to their advantage—their bridging of languages—was now used against them. In the words of the novelist Henry Bruce, "This lamentable accent [Chi-Chi] of those brought up speaking English in India, who are chiefly Eurasians, is . . . largely a general slovenliness in pronunciation, with curious false stresses . . . a foolish abundance of accent, which [is] not unallied to character."[139] In the late-Victorian reading, the language of the half-breed everywhere, the pidgin or sing-song of cross-racial communication, became merely a degraded form of English, the stuff of racial parody. The telegraph boy of 1857 was a useful tool for transmitting the language of others. The Chi-Chi, however, is like the Yiddish-speaking Jew. He has taken the language of others and deformed it.

Inevitably, stories of loyal half-castes during the Mutiny stress their Englishness, whereas discussion of Indo-Briton failings both before and afterward emphasize their Asian characters. That British reaction to the Mutiny itself made intimate liaisons between Indian and white even less respectable is clear. Stories on stage and in novels of the rape of white women by sepoy troops (almost entirely without foundation) served dramatically to invert, Nancy Paxton has argued,[140] the traditional representation of the Indian as victim to one of villain. The sensationalization of rape across racial boundaries, long a staple of anti-Negro rhetoric, served also to heighten negative reading of the half-caste. There is some evidence of this even in the case of the philo-Indian G. O. Trevelyan, who, in his effort to discredit the stories of rape, charged that Miss Wheeler, the one woman who could be proved to have been abducted, appeared to have gone willingly, and later married her abductor. He significantly concluded that she was herself in all likelihood "by no means of pure English blood."[141]

From the 1860's on, even a discreet concubinage became increasingly less acceptable for British officers, owing to the shock of the Mutiny, the increasing numbers of middle-class white women who either accompanied their husbands to India or successfully went out to find husbands there, and the establishment of a system of regulated prostitution to service the common soldier. While the memsahib as determining factor behind worsening colonial race relations has rightly been subjected to some recent criticism,[142] it is probably true that the extension of regulated prostitution stigmatized "normal" interracial unions and their progeny. Subsequently, the half-caste, whatever his or her antecedents, was bound to be associated with a "social evil."

The fixing of the non-European as a sexual commodity in the spreading prostitution networks of the Victorian Raj was paralleled by a progressive objectification of the half-caste according to his or her degree of "blackness." Edgar Thurston observed at the end of the century that, although there was no equivalent in India of the Jamaican nomenclature of racial hierarchy, the "proportion of black blood" in the veins of Eurasians had come to be "commonly" indicated "as in the case of cotton, jute, coffee, and other crops" in fractions of a rupee—"the European pure breed being represented by Rs. 0-0-0, and the native pure breed by 16 annas (= 1 rupee) . . . eight annas [were] half and half."[143] Such designation not only suggests blackness as commodity, but curiously appears to invert the earlier system by which approximation to whiteness was privileged.

Finally, and inevitably, the reification of "the" Eurasian worked its way into the popular literature of the prewar empire. Sympathetic representations, as in "Aleph Bey's" *That Eurasian* of 1895,[144] usually dwell on the half-caste as a perpetual and passive victim, as much an essentialized object as the more common representation of the half-caste as an active threat—as, for instance, in Henry Bruce's violently antipathetic tale *The Eurasian* (1913).[145] This latter work was a kind of culmination of the negative images of the century, woven together in the sensational/popular style, with touches of the gothic, which was characteristic of such ephemera. It is the story of a Eurasian clerk, Robert Slow, who, obsessed by his belief that he is the illegitimate son of the province's governor, marries an innocent but foolish English servant-girl and gradually and fatally subsides into his Hindu nature. He is a "weakling," unmanly, and therefore "the truest sort of Eurasian." [146]

The District Collector, Mr. Atkins, vainly tries to discourage the white girl, Cherry, from making a fatal mistake:

> Because he hasn't a chance in nature, my girl! Because he connects with a world full of corruptions and of obscure dangers, which is antipathetic to ours! Because, in short, he's a Eurasian, a mixture! . . . The Eurasian as such is a man of streaks, all striped, like a barber's pole. He's not a whole man. Many mixtures are good, but not this one. The only certainty about a Eurasian is his uncertainty. [147]

But Cherry marries Robert Slow anyway, and must live with him in his squalid native house near the bazar, where she "became familiar with that cruelist of Eastern sights, the blue-eyed, tawney-haired bazar child." [148]

The light-colored, blue-eyed Eurasian was commonly seen to be a kind of biological fraud; Bruce's half-caste Robert Slow is also living a lie— the illusion that his mother was a noble Maratha lady (she was a prostitute) and his father the provincial governor (he was a common young lieutenant)—and what respectability he has in his junior post is destroyed by a "secret vice," which gains control as he sinks into the native side of his nature. He becomes a "ganja fiend." He has given up wearing boots, "no longer even the man of streaks, the striped barber's pole which Mr. Atkins had predicated. He was all Indian now." For Cherry, the white woman who has abandoned her own kind, there can only be a miserable entrapment among people she despises. She has a "puny," "yellow" daughter who "would perpetuate the faults, and the grotesque weaknesses, of its father. There was no escaping the doom of mixed blood." Her "little alien eyes . . . were pools of shadow." [149]

Bruce's conclusion returns to the familiar Victorian theme of the ultimate instability of the half-caste and his suspect loyalties, but focused by the contemporary fin de siècle obsession with decline, degeneration, and loss of empire. Robert Slow's self-destructive rage at his own dispossession, his constitutional and emotional weaknesses, and, finally, his Asiatic abandonment to narcotic illusions draw him into a Hindu conspiracy to "bring down the Empire." Now thoroughly Indian, disguised in a long white cloth and "crazed" with ganja, he assassinates the governor of the Northern Provinces—his father, as he thought—stabbing him "deep in at the throat, twisting [the blade] round savagely several times."[150]

JAMAICA

Eight years after the Indian Mutiny, an "uprising" of blacks confined largely to the parish of St. Thomas-in-the-East in Jamaica triggered a savage campaign of retribution throughout the island. Fueled by Governor Eyre's own exaggerated despatches and the hysterical accounts published in the Jamaican press, English newspapers, including the quality press like *The Times*, indulged their public in a sensationalism of gory gothic detail not seen since the news of the Cawnpore massacre during the Indian rebellion.[151] But where the Eurasian community in India had been portrayed as loyal, if largely ineffective, in the great crisis, the Jamaican mulatto received a more ambiguous reading. Most mixed-race Jamaicans, especially those with some property and standing, in fact feared that they themselves might be the target of any general uprising, and they appear for the most part therefore to have sided with the white plantation class. But in postabolition Jamaica, there were "rogues" whose allegiance seemed to be shifting from white to black, who saw themselves as advocates of the rights of the freed slave and looked to become leaders of the majority mixed-race and Negro community. Prominent among these was the self-taught illegitimate mulatto George William Gordon, the son of a white planter and a Negro slave, and himself married to an Irishwoman. And it was on Gordon, summarily hanged by Governor Eyre as the diabolical instigator of atrocity, whom the press first seized in lurid accounts of massacre and torture.

What is of interest here is neither the well-known controversy that quickly arose in England over the constitutionality of Eyre's too-vigorous suppression of the outbreak, and his use of courts-martial, nor the fact that Gordon and his fate attracted a sizable and prominent movement in his posthumous defense. Rather it is necessary to examine how the first descriptions of the rebellion make use of a language that might be called traditional Caribbean gothic, and the extent to which Gordon's presumed treason was explained in terms of his half-breed nature.

An understanding of the Jamaican accounts of the rising, and of the reports in the English press based upon them, requires not merely that one recognize in them a white, panic-inspired coloring of what were admittedly gruesome events. Nor is it only a matter of selectivity—of the press's lack of interest, at least in the beginning, in the much more widespread sadistic mutilation, casual murder, and arbitrary destruction committed by the forces of law and order. Whatever their factual base, the accounts of "diabolical" (it is a word used time and again) black atrocities depend heavily on a traditional representation of savage rage and demonic ritual, which we saw already fully developed in Bryan Edwards's day. Moreover, by 1865 such reportage would also have been able to draw upon, and would certainly have been read in the light of, a popular domestic gothic literature of terror, as well as the highly fantasized tales of depravity on the unfolding imperial frontier in Africa and the South Pacific. The fascination in the press with the grisly anatomical details of Jamaican mutilation resonated strongly with similar preoccupations with the dissection theater and the cannibal feast.

The first reports in the London press in November 1865 centered on the mutilation of the bodies of the victims of the rising at Morant Bay. These were mostly men in positions of local authority—the custos (chief magistrate), Baron von Ketelhodt, the curate, a Reverend Herschell, and Lieutenant Hall of the Volunteers, although a black assemblyman and building contractor, Charles Price, was also killed.[152] *The Times* spared no detail. As in the tales of South Pacific cannibals, it is often the women who are represented as most ferocious in mutilation. A black woman cut out the curate's tongue "while his heart yet beat," and, in an image of savage frenzy that could as well come out of a popular account of the harridans of revolutionary Paris, "held it up in triumph." According to the same account, Price's body was "ripped open by women" and his entrails dragged out. A few days later, the point was reiterated: the bodies "were fearfully mutilated by the women, who were as infuriated as demons."[153]

The fate of Baron von Ketelhodt, the most prominent victim, and a personal friend of Governor Eyre's, took a prominent place. According to one version in *The Times*, the mob hunted him down "like dogs" (the story of the Harrogate "wolf-dog" had appeared in the same paper six days earlier). His fingers were, we are told, "disjointed . . . leaving them hanging by some small teguments." Laughing, his killers, like crazed medical students indulging in a macabre joke, "dangled them about with a jeer—'Now, you write no more lies to the Queen against us.'"[154]

Eyre's dispatch, reported verbatim in *The Times* some days later, added to the gory detail in ways that reinforce a cannibalic reading of the massacre. There was, he had heard, an attempt to skin the curate. Lieutenant Hall was "literally burned alive." Others had had their eyes "scooped out" or their heads "cleft open and the brains taken out." Indeed, another correspondent makes cannibalism explicit, telling of "murderous orgies" in a chapel, where these brains were mixed with gunpowder and rum and consumed. "We have been," the writer warns, "petting panthers."[155]

There may very well have been some such highly symbolic mutilation—of tongues that spoke and fingers that wrote against the rights of
black men and women, but the representation of these deeds is inevitably that of savage frenzy rather than pointed design. The descriptive
text serves to disguise a ritual and political dissection with one that is a
mere preliminary to cannibalism, just as it deflects attention from the
actual expression of political and economic grievance to a fantasized
gothic realm of black rage and bestial lust. There were hints of sexual
mutilation by black women, and it was commonly asserted that the
black men were driven by carnal appetite: "They determined . . . after
killing all the [white] males and children, to share the women among
themselves."[156]

In fact, the gothic language of cannibalism took on a moving, fluid
course of its own. Beyond its specific role in demonizing the racial Other
in Jamaica, it slipped generally into public discussion of the "affair" and
established its metaphoric currency on both sides of the debate. A dinner
for Eyre in Southampton on 12 August 1866 was placarded with posters
deriding the event as "the feast of blood" and a "Banquet of Death,"
while, very much on the pro-Eyre side, Jane Carlyle could write to her
husband of an anti-Eyre friend as someone who "would have had Eyre
cut into small pieces, and eaten raw."[157]

The Jamaican terror evoked a double message. On the one hand, it
simply replicated the familiar tradition of Obeah superstition and licentious black demonism in the lush environment of a corrupted Eden
found in the literature of Caribbean slave revolt. The tales of the revolts
of 1745, the 1790's, and 1831 are out of much the same mold. On the
other, it signified something that was perceived as increasingly problematic in the empire at large—the confrontation between white and black
as, no longer merely a conflict between civilized and savage, but a racial,
in its new sense, incompatibility. As W. F. Finlason explained in his
"History" of Gordon's rebellion, "A negro rebellion is necessarily, sooner
or later, a war of *extermination*."[158] The Jamaican rebellion has to be
read, then, in this wider context—of, for instance, Maori who were reported to have reverted to cannibalism during the continuing rebellion
in New Zealand that had broken out in 1860, or, for that matter, of Irish
outrages in the United Kingdom: "Like the Irish . . . there was a constant
and inevitable tendency to retrograde toward barbarism. . . . They [the
Jamaican freed slaves] appear to have reached at last the same stage as
the Irishman."[159] Eyre himself had previously served in New Zealand
and Australia, where, although sympathetic generally to the plight of the
aborigine, he had been immersed in the missionary-developed lore of a

lurid cannibalism in the islands. It is in this context that we should read his revealing comment that the Jamaican women "were even more brutal and barbarous than the men," "*as usual on such occasions.*"[160]

But the most available resonance was, of course, that with the presumed sexual and sadistic depravity of the Indian Mutiny.[161] An actual Indian connection was perhaps implied in allusions in the press to the fact that since 1860, Indian "coolies" had been introduced into the West Indies as laborers. Although there was no suggestion that these had been involved in the revolt, this created the sense of a general mobility of racial threat throughout the empire. (If not as submerged by numbers as in India, the white establishment in Jamaica was also a small minority—perhaps, as *The Times* asserted, in a ratio of 1 to 32 nonwhites.)[162] Eyre's dispatch of 20 October, which received very wide publicity in the English press, drew the obvious comparison: "The whole outrage could only be paralleled by the atrocities of the Indian mutiny."[163]

As in India, property-owning, respectable mixed-race people rushed to affirm their loyalty to the white establishment during the crisis, but public attention was inevitably focused on Gordon as *mulatto* troublemaker and, inasmuch as he was himself a propertied (if self-made) member of the House of Assembly, as class traitor as well.[164] Gordon had long been a thorn in the governor's side, and Eyre took advantage of the violence in St. Thomas's hastily to seize, prosecute, and execute him as "the chief cause and origin of the whole rebellion."[165] Before Gordon's cause was taken up by Exeter Hall (he was also a lay Baptist preacher), correspondents from Jamaica and the English press that reproduced their reports simply echoed Eyre's representation of Gordon's "deep-dyed wickedness."

What is of interest is the way these reports commonly turn from Gordon's undoubted political radicalism, his previous use of revolution-threatening language, which was no more seditious than that deployed by contemporary working-class leaders demanding franchise reform in England, to what they construct as Gordon's *secret* character. In this, his presumed "hypocrisy"—in serving the Crown as legislator and magistrate while fomenting treason, in preaching love in his Baptist chapel while inspiring race hatred abroad, and in enjoying his own wealth and comparative privilege while encouraging the propertyless to seize the wealth of others—is explained by invoking a deep contradiction in his inherent character: "Mr. G. W. Gordon," *The Times* reported, "was a singular compound of opposites. . . . Such a mixture of strange contradictions leads to a suspicion that he could not have been a man of sound mind."[166] It is clear that the buried message here goes beyond speculation about Gordon's own aberrant psychology. It draws directly from, and helps reinforce, the common image of the unstable, contradictory character of the half-breed generally.

The heated debate in England over Gordon as either victim or villain conforms to the wider and much older problem of racial construction, the view of the half-breed generally as both victim and villain, a "compound of opposites." The 1860's were, however, an important period of transition, a working out of the contradiction in which, in effect, villain comes to predominate over victim. Public discussion of the Jamaican affair coincided with that on Reconstruction in the American South. In America, the mulatto had long been seen as an ambivalent figure, perhaps less loyal, certainly problematic in the slaveholder's desire to maintain the "natural" boundaries between free white and slave black, and it was the extreme apologists for the peculiar institution who, like Henry Hughes of Mississippi, employed the starkest gothic language: "Impurity of races is against the law of nature. Mulattoes are monsters."[167] But the issue of intermarriage had earlier provoked violent public demonstrations well beyond the Old South, and in many states there was heated controversy, like that in Indiana over legislation forbidding "amalgamation." After the war, new state laws prohibiting interracial marriage were upheld in the courts.[168]

At some level, the emergence during and after the Civil War of "maverick" mulatto leaders drawn from an often urban free mulatto class as spokesmen for the freed black majority in the South served further to establish the identity, North and South, of those with "a single drop" of "Negro blood" as essentially black.[169] Like Gordon in Jamaica, they were seen to have shifted their alliances from white to black in an increasingly hostile environment. The reading of the mulatto as essentially black (beneath a misleadingly light skin) allows the full play of gothic stereotype without the restraining element of the half-breed as victim, as trapped between two unfriendly worlds. It also allows the mulatto to be seen more distinctly as a threat to white blood rather than a conduit of whiteness to African blood.

The denser connections between America and Britain after midcentury, the focus the Civil War gave generally to American affairs in the English press, the ever-growing number of British visitors to the United States, and the resonance between the problems of the postabolition West Indies and the postwar United States facilitated an exchange of attitudes that can be seen in the obvious parallels, for instance, between the "scientific" discourse of London anthropologists and the bigotry of white American legislators. Writing during the American war, an anonymous reviewer for the London *Anthropological Review* took the American writer of what appeared to be an abolitionist and pro-intermarriage tract (it was in fact a hoax to discredit the Republican Party) to task for promulgating an "absurd" doctrine of miscegenation, in order to advance an entirely "specious racial equality." Such "licentious absurdities" could have only been written by "a Mulatto or a Mulatress."[170]

In the years following Gordon's execution, the image of the West Indian mulatto became ever more problematic. As Bernard Semmel has suggested, spreading sympathy for Governor Eyre in England should be read in the context of deep middle-class misgivings over working-class enfranchisement in 1867.[171] Eyre was portrayed as a loyal servant of the Crown broken for his manly determination in putting down a "black rabble." Prosecutions of servicemen sent to England for trial and of Eyre himself (1867–68) failed because juries refused, against the instructions of the bench, to indict them. At the same time, the case mounted by the defending barristers, well reported in the metropolitan and local press, kept alive the most lurid details of the early reports of atrocity, the wildly exaggerated stories of murder, rape, and mutilation, and of Gordon's probable culpability.

It was in this context that the issue of the character of the mulatto generally and in the Caribbean in particular was taken up in the pages of the *Anthropological Review* and elsewhere. Shortly before a grand jury refused, finally, to indict Eyre in June 1868, Charles Ottley Napier Groom (later, Groom Napier), an amateur ethnologist with West Indian connections, read a paper before the Anthropological Society (most of whose members were, of course, strong supporters of the governor) that examined some 40 case studies of "coloured" (mixed-race) people of West Indian origin. While he detailed an instance or two of "noble characters," cases of dissipation, disease, and immorality were "far more common." Such "evidence" built upon and confirmed earlier suspicions of those, such as the anatomist Sir William Lawrence, who had argued as early as 1822 that crossing "brought about a physical and moral 'deterioration' of the European" even where the "black blood" appeared to have entirely disappeared in subsequent generations.[172]

Groom's most colorful example, the centerpiece of his presentation, was an educated young man who had become a successful West Indian merchant (Gordon had made his money as a merchant). This "child of quadroons" was "vain and proud," "addicted to display and frippery," with "the manners of a French hairdresser or man-milliner." As often in the literature of the half-breed, the mulatto is depicted as living a double life, an inherent hypocrisy.[173] He looks respectable but only his careful concealment, his "prudence," prevents public scandal.

Groom leaves little doubt about the particular secret that parallels the mulatto's racial unnaturalness: "Like coloured men in general he is more than half a woman, without the tenderness and chasteness which become the better examples of European females." Reproducing the by now familiar discourse of gender reversal, he completes the image by observing that the mulatto women he has observed "have the strong passions which in Europe are characteristic of the male sex." In general, this might not be a bad thing from the point of view of the white employer, as Groom himself later explained in an extended study (1870) of "human types." Mulattoes often made good servants because they had "little sympathy with [i.e., were not sexually attracted to] the opposite sex."[174]

Finally, there is significance in the fact that both Groom and a number of the commentators on his paper dwell on a presumed predilection of the mulatto for the crime of forgery. This deceit, the attempt to "pass" bad checks, suggests the light-skinned Negro's attempt to "pass" as white, as it does generally the notion of the half-breed character as a kind of biological fraud. In the context of Groom's portrayal of the man-milliner merchant, it also suggests that the homosexual is an equivalent kind of self-forgery.[175]

CANADA

> *Half-idiot, half-devil.*
> — *Walt Whitman, 1845*
>
> *Half Indian, half white man, and half devil.*
> — *Francis Parkman, 1849*[176]

Five years after Gordon was hanged in Jamaica, Colonel Garnet Wolseley, deputy quartermaster general in British North America, faced the task of putting down another rebellion inspired by a half-breed rebel. A French-Indian (Métis) miller's son, Louis Riel,[177] had led a rising in the Red River valley against the authority of the new Canadian confederation, seized Fort Garry (now Winnipeg), and was proclaimed president of a Métis republic in November 1869. En route across a thousand miles of difficult terrain, Wolseley had plenty of time to consider how he might deal with "vermin of [Riel's] kidney." His inclination was to apply the same summary justice Gordon had received: "I should like to hang him from the highest tree in the place." The tribulations of Governor Eyre seem, however, to have been in his mind, and he wrote to his wife from Fort Alexander that he hoped Riel would have "bolted"—as indeed he did—for "my treatment of him might not be approved by the civil powers."[178] He need not have worried. The Red River expedition, Wolseley's first independent command, was to begin the making of his extraordinary reputation.[179]

In the fur-trading areas of the Canadian north and west, interracial relationships, living *à la façon du pays*, had been reluctantly accepted as inevitable and largely beneficial by the officials of the Hudson's Bay Company and, after the conquest of 1763, was especially encouraged by its competitor the North West Company. Emulation of the French *coureurs du bois* in this respect was seen in the eighteenth century as essential to overcome language barriers and establish the necessary goodwill with Indian trappers and traders. As in India, however, what had been customary in the late eighteenth century became progressively less acceptable with the arrival of Protestant missionaries and European women.

Liaisons with Native American women were never, however, regarded in Canada with the same guilty repugnance as those with Negro women in Jamaica or the American South. What had to be viewed in slave societies as concubinage—the unequal exploitation of black servant by white master—in Canada was seen to be a more equal and necessary arrangement. In settlements like Red River, interracial domesticity had evolved into stable "marriages" (whether or not recognized by the Church). But whereas the half-caste community in India was seen to be a thing of the white administration, sheltering in and profiting from the protection of the Raj, in Canada the half-breed world was a more independent one, associated with the fringes, the frontier, of an expanding empire, and, increasingly, seen as an anomalous survival of an earlier, more primitive, if heroic, period of history. Nevertheless, negative representation of the half-breed in Canada shared something with that of the Caribbean mulatto and the half-caste of Asia.

In most areas, mixed-bloods were treated as Indians rather than being enculturated as whites. Only on the fringe of the Great Plains, in the valleys of the Saskatchewan, Red, and Assiniboine rivers, and especially at Red River Settlement, did a mixed race "emerge as a distinct sociocultural entity."[180] As elsewhere in the empire, the relationships that gave birth to a community of mixed-race people were almost entirely white male and nonwhite female connections, and inevitably the language of prejudice drew some reinforcement from (masculine) European attitudes of gender inequality. If the half-breed was in Canada not directly and explicitly feminized in popular discourse the way we have observed in representations of the impotent and dependent Eurasian or the obsequious/treacherous mulatto, gender prejudice was certainly interwoven into the image of the North American half-breed in important ways.

Although the language used to describe the half-breed here lacked the words for the complicated degrees of relationship used in the Caribbean, something of this can be found in the terminology of full-, half-, or quarter-blood. Significantly, this normally refers to the degree of Indian, rather than white, parentage—as in "her mother was a full-blood Cree." Among the English-speaking population, there was a tendency to view part-blood males as "essentially" Indian, while daughters (as inherently more submissive) were thought to absorb the qualities of their civilized halves more readily. In those settled areas where Scots and English fur traders who took Indian wives established families, it was more often their half-blood daughters, rather than their sons, who were instrumental in perpetuating the mixed-race line—who, that is, were more likely to stay within the community and marry. Mixed-blood wives came early in the nineteenth century to be regarded by English and Scots settlers as more desirable—in appearance and manner—than full-blood Indian women, now no longer as useful as in the earlier days when whites had had to live at the sufferance of the native inhabitants, and the latter were increasingly associated with mere prostitution.[181]

For English observers and writers, it was often assumed that, whatever the sex of the offspring, the product of Anglo-Saxon fathers and Indian mothers was likely to result in a subordination of the "weaknesses" of the mother's blood by the "energy and 'push' characteristic of their sires." As a medical doctor with experience in northwestern Canada put it to the Anthropological Institute of London in 1875, "Their mother's blood has not, as a rule, imparted that restlessness, slovenliness, impatience of control, wild liberty, superstition, and, when roused, the fiendish hatred and temper, that might have been anticipated."[182] The image of the half-breed as dangerous rather than compliant was more likely to be applied, not to the "country-born" descendants of English or Scots who received a British Protestant education, but to the alien-speaking, resentfully dispossessed, Catholic French-Indian community. Traditional prejudice against French culture, religion, and "immorality" conspired with racist views of the Native American to produce an intensified image of gothic instability and danger. This negative-image half-breed in fact served to enforce a positive reading of English or Scots mixed-race unions: the one was an obstacle to progress, the other a facilitator of white conquest. The one led to anarchy and rebellion, the other to law and order. In these representations, Frenchness is assimilated to the Indian, and the result is a compound of (Indian) childishness and savagery with (French) cowardice and treachery. Francis Parkman observed in his popular adventure-history of *The Oregon Trail* that mountain men "were a mongrel race; yet the French blood seemed to predominate: in a few, indeed, might be seen the black snaky eye of the Indian half-breed, and one and all, they seemed to aim at assimilating themselves to their savage associates."[183]

In Wolseley's letters, we have an opposition between a loyal, sober

Scots-Indian half-breed in charge of an isolated post and the drunken, idle, treacherous, but ultimately weak-willed Métis.[184] Here it is the xenophobic English (and Anglo-American) construction of the Catholic continental foreigner as unmanly that underlies and bears most of the weight of the notion of the half-breed as a dangerous unnatural. In the English-native compound, the feminine Indian element is seen as ultimately complementary and subordinate to the masculine English or Scottish element. With the Métis it is otherwise. As with the Feringhees of India, the inherent weaknesses of the native have been compounded rather than counteracted by the European addition; the result is a half-breed constructed of an alternative femininity—not subordinate and loyal but hysterical and vengeful—and that in fact draws as much from Romish French nature as from childish Indian character. Catholicism, a "womanish" religion of superstition and devious, unmanly priests, has, as we have seen, a central place in the gothic. In nineteenth-century discourse about the half-breed, it can emerge as a means of magnifying the presumed limitations of certain kinds of strategically important non-English mixed-race people. The Roman Catholic Métis in western Canada have their counterparts, not only in the Indo-Portuguese half-castes of the Raj (more snobbishly despised than their Anglo-Indian counterparts), but similarly in the Portuguese-Africans whom Livingstone and others blamed for the peculiarly horrific nature of the interior slave trade.[185] In one of his first pieces of prose to appear in print, Walt Whitman's malignantly vengeful half-breed Bodo is significantly the offspring of an Indian "squaw" and an Irish Catholic monk.[186]

The Métis are more problematic than the country-born of Indian-English/Scots mixed blood because of their "difference"—their language, their dress, their religion, and their self-awareness as a "New Nation." Here we might note the way the half-breed's speech, "Bungay"—a rapidly uttered mixture of mostly Canadian French with Indian words and some broad Scots and Irish brogue, dismissed by the English as a "polyglot jabber,"[187] signifies, as a nonlanguage outside a recognized cultural system, the inauthenticity of the mixed race. Bungay parallels the Chi-Chi of the Eurasian and the Creole of the Jamaican mulatto as a sign of half-breed character that both diminishes and separates. Similarly, the dress of the Métis plainsman, the combination of European shirt and trousers with the worked and beaded leather of the "savage," proclaimed a confusion of cultures that both disturbed and intrigued the European observer, but that ultimately encouraged a dismissive "reading" of the Métis in line with that of other "half-civilized" colonized peoples throughout the areas of European domination. As an American explorer early in the century had explained, their wearing "the garb of the

savage . . . has something which partakes of the ridiculous, as well as
the disgusting. . . . The awkward and constraining appearance of those
Frenchmen who had exchanged their usual dress for the breech-cloth
and blanket, was as risible as that of the Indian who assumes the tight-
bodied coat of the white man."[188]

Métis separateness, their independence, depended, firstly, on the profits of the buffalo hunt and, secondly, on their claim as original settlers to
land in the river valleys. As the one declined, owing to dwindling herds,
the other became more essential. Defiance was ingrained in Métis character, and the coming of the Land Survey in the late 1860's appeared to
threaten their tenure and with it the coherence of their community.
What is of concern here is not, however, the reality of Métis culture and
the Riel affair in its actual context, but the characterization of the Métis
and their leader by Anglo-Canadian and British observers, and the ways
in which such images may draw upon the kind of obsessions that we
have seen at work in other instances of half-breed gothic.

A negative representation of the Métis had to work against the Victorian idealization of the stoic nobility of the rugged, independent, and
self-sufficient outdoorsman. Unlike the enervating steamy tropics, the
Canadian wilderness itself was often portrayed as an environment that
strengthened character and turned weak emigrants into "real men." To
the romance of the West, there was also attached some sympathy for
what could be portrayed as a proud people "of great intelligence and energy of character" struggling against being handed over to become, as
Robert Fowler, an aborigine-protectionist Tory M.P. in London, put it, "a
colony of a colony."[189]

In opposition to such an available construction of Métis character
was deployed an effective amalgam of traditional francophobia and anti-
Catholicism, amplified in the popular accounts of the actual events of
"rebellion" in 1869–70 and 1885 by what had become the inevitable
gothic racism of half-breed discourse. If the image of the Métis as bloodthirsty monsters never quite achieved the degree of vilification of the
murderers of Morant Bay, nevertheless the press accounts resonate with
those of mulatto treachery as they do with portrayal of half-breed instability generally. As in the case of Jamaica, the most virulent, hysterical accounts appeared in the colonial papers, and were transmitted by
uncritical correspondents back to Britain. A thousand miles from Red
River, the Toronto press created a threat that owed at least as much to
well-established popular traditions of the half-breed (and the Red Indian)
as to the thin and biased information it received from the English-
speaking community around Fort Garry.

This gothic tradition extends back to the supposed demonic depravity of the Indian allies of the French during the long contest for North America in the late seventeenth and eighteenth centuries. Tales of ferocious revenge, torture, scalpings, and cannibalism had entered popular "memory" of this history in a highly romanticized form, to be revived and reinforced in the nineteenth century by dramatic narratives of conflict on the American plains. In fictional literature, the Red Indian as bronzed stoic often has an alter-image, always close to the surface, in the demonic rogue-brave. The popular French novelist Olivier Gloux ("Gustave Aimard"), whose many "Indian Tales" were translated and published in London in the 1860's and 1870's, makes a free use of such contrasting images, and their gothic associations, which can be found throughout the genre. In a characteristic novel, The Red River Half-Breed, he offers a malign Crow, a fraudulent guide who pretends to befriend white travelers, only to lure them to their doom: "This red nigger's turned 'bad'!" He was a "monster"; his savage companion braves were "wolves," "beasts of rapine and slaughter," who displayed a "goulish merriment" in their indiscriminant murders: "Dead bodies, gashed and unlimbed, strewed the late virgin-white expanse." The imagery is that of literary gothic, and when the heroine believes an Indian corpse has revived, "a ghastly phantom," she draws a predictable parallel: "So do the vampires spring to life when the moon bathes them in radiance."[190]

The Métis could easily be portrayed as the corporeal amalgamation of a peculiarly Indian sadism and French treachery. Such a representation was already available in British accounts of the vicious competition between the Hudson's Bay and North West trading companies in western Canada at the turn of the century. The North West Company had encouraged Métis violence in the Red River region; and shortly after their "New Nation" flag was unfurled in 1816, the "Seven Oaks Massacre," in which the governor of Rupert's Land and twenty of his men were slaughtered, seemed to confirm the unnatural ferocity of a half-breed race. The bodies of the dead, it was said, were stripped and dismembered "in an orgy of mutilation."[191]

The growth of permanent settlements in the area, owing both to the immigration of ever-increasing numbers of Scots and English and to the establishment of a more settled and propertied Métis community, had the effect over time of submerging the more gothic aspects of British representation of French-Indian depravity, although at times of crisis and conflict a demonic characterization of even the most acculturated Métis was readily available. In 1839, at the time of the Papineau Rebellion in the East, Métis (and many of the English settlers as well) organized their own protests to air western grievances. These were represented, however, in at least one account as merely a reversion to primitivism: "The war song and war-dance were commenced in the fashion of the Indians. The whole half-breed race of French extraction were in motion . . . we were struck by their savage appearance. They resembled more a troop of furies than human beings, all occupied in the Indian dance."[192]

Generally, however, there was a shift in representation of the Métis from alien and demonic (although lurking fears were never entirely displaced) to feckless, familiar, and despised. This roughly parallels the Victorian deployment of ideas of race and ethnicity that were grounded essentially in class prejudice, and that in the colonies often reflected the powerful need on the part of white settlers to establish their own respectability in the moral dubiety of the frontier town. This is certainly the reading offered by Alexander Ross in his account of the colony published in London in 1856. Significantly, Ross is unable to draw a boundary in his descriptions between the settled Métis and the Gypsylike "wanderers," white men with tanned skin and half-breeds alike, who have gone native and speak "an almost unintelligible jargon of the English, French and Indian languages." All are "mongrel settlers," whose children are "permitted to grow up in ignorance and thoughtless levity—a perfect model of savage life and manners, taught them by their wandering and degenerate parents."[193] In language resonating with the middle-class assault on Poor Law dependency in Britain, Ross charges the half-breed with improvidence, with "idleness and wild freedom," and in hard times with dependence on the charity of the Company. Although he calls them a "gypsy-like class," the rhetoric he deploys would seem to draw as much upon the tradition of the Irishman (also, like the Métis, Catholic) in domestic Britain. "While enjoying a sort of licentious freedom, they [the Métis] are generous, warm-hearted and brave, and left to themselves quiet and orderly. They are, unhappily, as unsteady as the wind in all their habits, fickle in their dispositions, credulous in their faith, and clannish in their affections."[194] Significantly, it would later be claimed that Riel, whose father was part Irish, received the support of Irish Fenians in Chicago.

Although Ross does not mention the fact in his history of the Red River settlement, he had in his earlier career as a fur hunter married an Okanagan. His own children were thus half-breeds, and two of his sons married half-breeds.[195] It seems reasonable to assume that his histories of the region, and especially his representations of the half-breed, are shaped in ways that excuse, deny, or project his own transgression. Ross had moved from an early "wild freedom" into a comfortable and settled respectability at Red River. His narrative of these early years, *The Fur Hunters of the Far West*, sounds many of the themes he later repeated in *Red River*, but with a difference. At Red River, the "problem" of the half-breed lay in his or her fitness as near-white for domestic, settled life. In the earlier, "heroic" period, it lay in the inauthenticity of the half-breed as near-Indian:

> [They] resemble almost in every respect the pure Indian; with this difference, that they are more designing, more daring, and more dissolute. They are insolent, thoughtless, and improvident; licentious in their habits; unrestrained in their desires; sullen in their disposition; proud, restless, clannish, and fond of flattery. They alternatively associate with the whites and the Indians, and thereby become falsely enlightened.[196]

Such a construction contains revealing strategies. In the first place, Ross's assault on half-breed character is essentially a representation of the weaknesses of the half-breed male, an image of vice that draws heavily on his deeply negative portrayal of those whites who have gone native, of French Canadian men who have escaped to live "in comparative idleness" and have "become more depraved, more designing, and more subtle than the worst of Indians," "young men of vicious and indolent habits . . . lost to all ties of kindred, blood, country, and Christianity." Ross's half-blood women, however, are surprisingly attractive. Many "are as fair as the generality of European ladies; the mixture of blood being so many degrees removed from the savage as hardly to leave any trace, while, at the same time, their delicacy of form, their light and nimble movements, and the penetrating expression of the 'bright black eye,' combine to render them objects of no ordinary interest." They have a "singular talent for imitation."[197] Such views were not, of course, unique to Ross, although they do suggest the rationalizations of those who, as he had done, themselves crossed the racial boundary. One gets a quite similar treatment in, for instance, the fin de siècle observations of Lafcadio Hearn on mixed-race women ("humble and submissive") in the French West Indies: "Said a creole once, in my hearing:—'The gens-de-couleur are just like the *tourlouroux*: one must pick out the females and leave the males alone.'" Hearn himself had briefly been married to a mulatto and was in his wanderings something of a sexual gourmand, seeking out colored prostitutes. The *tourlouroux* was "a sort of land-crab;—the female is selected for food, and, properly cooked, makes a delicious dish;—the male is almost worthless."[198]

The idealization of the half-breed woman rested on a European view of an alluring female weakness, the "childishness" of the "naïf" in Hearn's words,[199] that which made her pliant to white masculine will. For Ross, the half-breed maiden naturally absorbs more of the positive character of her white side than her male counterpart, whose stubbornness reveals the worst of his Indian half. And yet, surely, this also speaks to Ross's need to expiate and palliate his own guilt. Others followed another course and were ready enough to create a female monster, a squaw-wife of stupidity, passion, and appetite.[200] Secondly, Ross's image of the half-breed male is almost exclusively that of the French-Indian cross. This enables him to deploy a language heavily indebted to a traditional patriotic and chauvinist francophobia, while at the same time avoiding his own history and the problem of the character of his own "half-Indian" progeny.[201]

Ross's picture of the Métis—an affable if unstable and potentially dangerous race, easily deluded by "designing and disaffected demagogues"[202]—helps us to read the accounts of the Riel rebellions of 1869–70 and 1885. Briefly, the first rising was construed as an act of anarchy on the part of a childlike people inspired by a self-serving demagogue. The second affair, involving as it did the reemergence from American exile of Louis Riel in alliance with disaffected western Indians, was represented in darker colors as the mad treason of a ruined man prepared to unleash the demonic forces of race war. In both, gothic elements (as well as farce) are to be found in the popular accounts, but it is the ultimate tragedy of 1885 that perhaps offers the closest comparison with the mulatto Gordon, whose fate Riel shared—dying ultimately, not for articulating the grievances of his own kind, but for a devil's alliance with the full-blooded racial Other.

Like the dissection of the corpse of the custos in Jamaica, the rebellion of 1869–70 provided a central gothic incident that helped to focus the reports of the rebellion as "desperate, depraved and devilish." This was the execution by the Métis rebels of an Irish-Canadian (and Orangeman), Thomas Scott, at Fort Garry on 4 March 1870. Before the highly colored reports of this incident appeared in the Toronto press, there had been some sympathy among English-speakers—as well as, of course, in Quebec, where Riel became a folk hero—for the resistance of the Red River settlers to forced incorporation into the Canadian union. Scott's "murder" was reported in gruesome detail. He had been shot by firing squad, then dispatched by a coup de grâce through the head and put in a coffin. Five hours later, the story went, his groans from within the coffin drew his assailants' attention, and he had to be more definitively "finished off" by two Métis soldiers. There was a final gothic twist: when the coffin was exhumed a year later, the body had disappeared.[203]

Scott's death was instrumental in enabling an imaginative construction of the rebellion as half-breed depravity. Freed from the actual event, accounts of the affair in Toronto or in London could follow a line of explanation drawing on language and concepts that signified a tradition of representation rather than whatever was actually occurring in the Red River valley. Already the press had seized upon a familiar gothic theme in the supposed influence of Roman Catholic priests in fomenting rebellion. The Toronto correspondent for *The Times* of London believed that the clergy exercised "almost absolute control" over the Métis rebels and had inspired the revolt to save their parishes from the influx of Protestant immigrants.[204] Two days later, this characterization was deepened when *The Times* reprinted a letter from the Toronto *Globe* that named a "deranged," "half-breed priest," the Reverend M. Richot (who was arrested in Ottawa after Scott was executed). Father Richot, it was reported, spoke of the Métis community as having "been reared by the wolf."[205]

The sending of an army detachment under Wolseley, and its long arduous journey through difficult territory, allowed another theme to be deployed. There was, in the event, no pitched, heroic engagement between the British force and the Métis rebels—who had fled when Wolseley finally arrived at Fort Garry. But the story of the trek itself provided an important means of transferring the virtues of stoicism and rugged self-sufficiency from the Métis woodsman and plainsman to Wolseley's column. That is, what was most positive in the traditional representation of the half-breed was here co-opted, as it were, for the British. The army's progress through the wilderness was symbolic of order and efficiency even under the most adverse conditions, while the "drunken half-breeds" bickering and falling out among themselves behind the walls of Fort Garry came, in the popular telling, to symbolize its opposite—anarchy and cowardice.

The man whose career profited most from this expedition, Colonel Wolseley, himself presented just this kind of opposition in his own rendering of the event in his memoirs. Here Scott's trial and murder are carried out, not only by "a mock Court-Martial of . . . drunken half-breeds," but in the presence of a French-speaking priest, who absolves them of the crime "on the spot."[206] In Wolseley's rendition, as in many of the press accounts, the rough, violent, and abusive Protestant Irish laborer Scott becomes a respectable Englishman, whose murder is thereby made more clearly to demand condemnation and retribution. The strategy of another curious misrepresentation in Wolseley's memoir is more obscure. He presents Riel as "a pure French Canadian," although with half-breed relatives.[207] This serves, I believe, simply further to focus on the Frenchness of the half-breed as the true source of evil. We have seen that Wolseley found praise for a Scots-Indian half-breed. If it is the French (and Catholic) component that degrades the Métis, then Riel must be all French, as he is all villain—like the priests. As the historian George F. G. Stanley has observed, "both Scott and Riel ceased to be men, human beings with human frailties; they became political symbols."[208]

Wolseley's reading of the rebellion as that of a weak-willed, childlike race tempted to evil by a demonic celibate clergy—the rebel flag, he claimed, had been sewn together by the nuns of a nearby convent—parallels a common reading in England. Evangelicals in Parliament and elsewhere spoke of the malign influence of Catholic priests and of the need for an assisted Protestant English immigration to western Canada.[209] This revival of anti-Catholic gothic in the wilderness of western Canada coincided with a surge in anti-Catholicism in Britain in the late 1860's and early 1870's. The year 1870 saw both the surprising success of Charles Newdegate's motion in the House of Commons for an inquiry into the presumed immorality of convents and monasteries, and the promulgation of papal infallibility by the Vatican Council.[210]

When Riel reemerged in the mid 1880's, however, the new rebellion played in a different context. As earlier with the murder of Scott, reports made use of an event to sensationalize the revolt—the defeat of local police, represented as a "massacre," at Duck Lake—and by a highly charged and gothic rendering of anticipated Red Indian sadism. But, perhaps in part because of the rise of French Canadian politicians in Quebec dedicated to working within a more mature union, and because of the clear marginality of any conceivable Métis threat in a western Canada linked to the East by railway and flushed with a growing European immigration, the representation of Riel's own character shifts from one side of his double nature to the other. His fated campaign appears, not exactly as farce, but as hopeless and as primitive as that of the dying tribes of plains Indians with whom he was now identified. Significantly, it was not Riel's ability to raise a powerful, dangerous response among the Métis that had the focus of public attention, but his treacherous association with the race enemy, the primitive and savage Indians. In the press his French-Catholicism no longer served to explain aberration of moral character. "Half-Indian in blood," he had become "wholly Indian in character and sympathies . . . one of themselves." He instigated, *The Times* asserted, "to rise with him whole tribes of savage Indians, as ready for massacre now as they were in the days of Montcalm."[211]

After the battle of Batoche, where the British Gatling gun scattered the Indian and Métis forces that Riel had been able to gather to him, General Middleton claimed that his victory would "have dispelled the idea that half-breeds and Indians can withstand the attack of resolute whites."[212] It is significant that, as elsewhere in the empire, the half-breeds are here displaced in importance as a unique people. Inherently unstable, biologically anomalous, and "eugenesically" fated, they had either become impotent and marginal, like the Eurasians of India and the Basters of southern Africa, or were being absorbed for good or ill into one of the two cultures that had created them. While earlier there had been a general optimism among British observers that the half-breed would ultimately be absorbed into the dominant white culture, in the second half of the century, a certain pessimism gained force. The half-breed was still an unstable compound, but one that, it was increasingly thought by some amateur anthropologists like A. P. Reid, would tend toward its baser element: "There is rather a tendency toward the Indian type taken as a whole. . . . The more distant from first and second classes the nearer approach to the race of the primitive mother."[213]

In defeat, Riel, leader of the Métis, had to float free from his representation as the spokesman for this failed and unstable community and instead, like Dr. Jekyll, decline into the primitive side of his own duality. *The Times* reported that when captured, Riel had "let his hair grow long, and is dressed more shabbily than most half-breeds." He was "beyond hope of mercy" and, *The Times* professed to know, had been abandoned by loyal French Canadians as "wholly Indian."[214]

Full Circle

It will be clear that beginning largely as an act of imagination, the image of the half-breed, like that of the cannibal, took on a confirming, corroborating reality in popular readings of imperial events in the nineteenth century. Mixed-race people were floated free from their special places on the red map of empire, invested by means of a spurious empiricism with a common character, and then drawn back into the world of literary fantasy in the 1880's and 1890's as powerfully reified abstractions.

The half-breed as free-floating sign had, of course, a literal counterpart, in an empire pulled ever closer together by steam and prosperity, in the actual mobility of the children of mixed-race unions. While panic about "reverse colonization" was arguably a late-Victorian or Edwardian obsession, people who were obviously of a mixed race, sent to England for education or apprenticeship, would earlier have faced some degree of social difficulty. In a hierarchy of prejudice, the Afro-Caribbean mulatto, followed by the Eurasian with lascar or dark Asian (Hindu rather than Muslim, say) blood, was at the bottom. The relatively few North American half-breeds in Britain, on the other hand, no doubt benefited from the romanticization of the Red Indian and from the absence of strong phenotypical differences, especially in those of only quarter-blood or less. Nevertheless, those with inadequate means and without familial networks of support risked a fate that confirmed popular suspicions about their inadequacies. John Sutherland, for example, a Canadian half-breed sent to London to study, but marooned there by the death of his stepfather in North America, fell ill in his penury, threw himself on the charity of his landlady, and died in distress without the means for his own burial. His married benefactress and perhaps lover, herself thrown out of lodgings with him and her children, had to appeal to the parish for relief: "Having kept the corpse until so offensive as to endanger the health of the family, we have been compelled to apply to the parochial authorities for the means of burial."[215]

By mid-century the social position in white society of clearly marked half-castes, even those with resources, had probably deteriorated substantially, thanks in part to the spread of pseudo-scientific ideas about racial difference and human character. Characteristic of evolving popular opinion, perhaps, is the view of a retired Hudson's Bay clerk, John Todd, in 1843:

> Well have you observed that all attempts to make gentlemen of them [North American half-breeds], have hitherto proved a failure. The fact is that there is something radically wrong about them all as is evidently shown from mental science[;] I mean Phrenology, the truths of which I have lately convinced myself from extensive personal observation.[216]

Out in the empire, mixed-race people were, of course, a common and mobile element, especially in coastal and administrative and market towns, where they were inevitably seen as "the Jews" of the local economy (as Livingstone described a mixed-race tribe in Angola).[217] Occasionally, "difficulties" with the natives, frightening and surprising uprisings, ambushes, resistance that seemed inspired by a knowledge of white ways unexpected of "savages," was explained by the presumed treachery of the half-breed, or its emotional and symbolic equivalent, the white man who had gone native. In New Zealand, the surprisingly effective resistance of the Maori at mid-century, for instance at the battle of Puketakauere in 1860, was explained by the presumed collaboration of low-class army deserters, Australian convicts, Irish Fenians, or even French missionaries—whose presence was simply deduced from the way in which the Maori had made use of European arms and tactics.[218]

In the scores of "little wars" of the Victorian empire that provided the stock material for the boys' adventure stories of the late nineteenth century, degraded whites and half-castes were often given a role that established them as a treacherous, free-floating threat wherever white and nonwhite collided. James Cowan, who claimed to have written down the memoirs of a New Zealand half-caste "deserter from civilization" in 1903, saw this as a commonplace part of the imperial system: "Renegades of every European nationality have been found living with and fighting for native tribes in Africa and America and the Islands of Polynesia."[219] Cowan's tale is presented as "a true story of adventure." In the person of the half-breed Kimble Bent, it bridges—like Edgar Allan Poe's earlier fictional half-breed sailor Dirk Peters[220]—two worlds of this study. His mother was "a half-caste Red Indian girl, of the Musqua tribe . . . of the St. Croix River." Bent ran away from home to be a sailor, joined the British army, and finally deserted in New Zealand, where he claimed to have become "Pakeha-Maori," completely assimilating their customs and language and witnessing the revival of cannibalism among the savage Hauhaus during the Titokowaru war of 1868–69.[221] Art and life bear the same message: neither Poe's Peters—who is both a howling demon with long eyeteeth *and* Arthur Gordon Pym's savior—nor Kimble Bent have exactly definable or fixed loyalties; they are ambiguous in both character and blood, and range from the borderland wilderness that produced them to another "contact zone" half a world away.

More significant, of course, than any such physical mobility is the fluidity of the half-breed as a readily available image, a concept that not only asserts the homologous nature of mixed-race people everywhere, but extends itself by affinity and metaphor into analogous types of problematic identities, such as the European who "goes native" or the "full-blood" native who "apes" the European.

Three years after settling the Riel business, Wolseley, now General Sir Garnet Wolseley, was given command of an expedition to punish the Ashanti of the Gold Coast hinterland. In francophone West Africa, owing to the wide acceptance in the eighteenth century of *métissage*, whereby French residents, like the Portuguese further south, commonly took African mistresses, there were well-established, assimilated communities of mulattoes (called *métis*).[222] In the Gold Coast, the English had been less interested in the interior or in long-term settled domesticity, and depended upon the coastal Fanté people for their trading contacts. These go-betweens, both the "gentle," "effeminate" Fanté and the Cape Coast mulattoes, were despised by Wolseley in language that parallels his contempt for the Métis of the Red River valley. The Fanté lacked the virtue of courage; the urban mulattoes, that of authenticity: "Only fancy *Ladies* with cards here; their complexions vary from the colour of an old saddle to that of a Spaniard. Three ladies paid me a visit yesterday, all got up in swell hats that smacked of Bond Street."[223]

Here the unnaturalness of the mulatto is signified and deepened by the inappropriate European clothing of the English-speaking town black. In contrast, the fierce Ashanti was a "real" African, a fitting opponent, who had humiliated both the weak and untrustworthy Fanté levies and a mulatto regiment sent from the West Indies: "The more I see of these Fantes the more I feel convinced they ought to be the slaves of the Ashantees."[224]

It is clear that Wolseley extended his detestation of the unnatural half-breed to the full-blooded Africans on the coast who had adopted European manners and speech. They had crossed racial boundaries like their counterparts, Europeans who had gone native, and were degraded and inherently unstable and untrustworthy. The colonial chaplain, "the very blackest of negroes," had received a university education in England but was corruptly incompetent in performing his duties and, when dying, Wolseley claimed, had "sent for the chief 'fetish man': So much for our educated West African converts."[225] And so back to the actual half-breed: at Koomassee, "We found the half-caste Mr. Dawson at liberty. He had sent me several written but cringing and un-English messages during the day entreating me to stop."[226]

Wolseley's unflattering view of the West African mulatto and his extension of this characterization to "civilised" natives, often stigmatized by their wearing of inappropriate or shabby, discarded European clothing, is of course a commonplace in the English literature of African conquest. Winwood Reade, who (like the young novelist G. A. Henty) accompanied Wolseley to Koomassee, has in his *Savage Africa* little good to say, especially of Portuguese mulattoes—a people who "inherited the vices of both races," whose yellow features betray "a low and cunning," "half-civilised" nature. Inevitably, such stories depend upon an element of European class snobbery—a "half-civilised negro," for instance, who wears a cambric handkerchief but blows his nose with his fingers. And of European ethnic prejudice transposed to the tropics: the tendency to view the half-breed as a metaphoric Jew receives here an actual, corporal confirmation in Reade's pointed retelling of the familiar story of Portuguese Jews forcibly transported to São Thomé and married to Africans from Angola: "From this union arose a mixed race, which the Portuguese firmly perpetuated."[227] Perhaps there is a resonance here with the anti-Semitic Richard Burton's exactly contemporary view that the African mulatto, "the worst class of all," was "everywhere, like wealth, *irritamenta malorem*."[228]

FICTION AND THE USES OF THE HALF-BREED

Wolseley at Koomassee, despising equally the feminine weakness of the Fanté and the pathetic cringing half-caste in the Ashanti compound, takes us back to England, to a Victorian fictional literature of imperial adventure stories that made much play with the superiority of the full-blooded, "authentic," if fierce, native over the degraded metaphoric or actual half-caste of the coastal towns, just as it developed the image of the drunken and criminal Cockney gone native in Polynesia.

In his influential study, *Rule of Darkness*, Patrick Brantlinger has drawn attention to "imperial gothic," to the use of the gothic elements of atavism, the occult, the grotesque and a sadistic, near pornographic preoccupation with death itself in late-Victorian imperialist adventure fiction. He has located this genre in the milieu of cultural malaise, in the obsessive contemporary anxieties over the decline of religion, the psychologists' exploration of the irrational, and threats to Western civilization generally from both without and within. Gothic romance and adventure romance share, he asserts, an impulse "to submerge language, reason, selfhood in 'the destructive element' of death." An often grotesque dissolution of the individual in such literature becomes an allegorical death of race, culture, and nation through a threatened conquest by or reversion to barbarism.[229]

Brantlinger, and other literary scholars interested in representations of empire, have drawn together suggestive elements of the works of imperial fiction of, especially, Haggard, Kipling, and Conrad, and connected them convincingly to resonating themes in the gothic revival—in Stevenson's *Dr. Jekyll and Mr. Hyde*, Stoker's *Dracula*, and Wells's *The Island of Dr. Moreau*.[230] At the same time, important work on gender and identity by Elaine Showalter, Ludmilla Jordanova, Ruth Harris, and Judith Walkowitz, among others, has also seen in the gothic a reflection of the challenges posed by the "new woman" to Victorian masculinity.[231] Together, such cultural studies have well established an intimate relationship between domestic anxieties, the imperial realm, and the gothic sensibility in fictional representation.

This study has attempted to bring an, at first, buried aspect of the gothic, the long eighteenth- and nineteenth-century preoccupation with racial difference, to the fore. Imperial gothic is to a large extent racial gothic. This should not be seen as merely a response, conditioned by certain contemporary domestic anxieties and obsessions, to the knowledge of other cultures made available by the late-nineteenth-century expansion of empire. Brantlinger is right to reach back to Ballantyne at mid-century or earlier to Captain Marryat's patriotic tales, well before the fin de siècle malaise focused the dangers of degeneration—not, however, because these are sources or precursors of the later full-blown "imperial gothic," but because they point to the concurrent gothicization of racial knowledge throughout the century. That is, a gothic imagination itself shaped the language, images, and rhetoric of imperial narration and anthropological, scientific, and popular discourse from the beginning. It shaped the understanding of the "reality" of the abstraction of race. When Rider Haggard et al. invest racial difference, interracial relations, and the half-breed with a gothic reading, it is not merely a borrowing from another genre inspired by obsessions characteristic of the time. The language of race was inherently, perhaps from its very inception, a gothic language. A hundred-year tradition of reportage—of demonic Caribbean uprisings, sadistic cannibalism, and unnatural miscegenation—inevitably culminated in a literature of "imperial gothic."

At the end of the century, the racial monster returns to its literary home. In an eruption of race panic, the half-breed and miscegenation emerge to take center stage, as in Florence Marryat's tale of the vampire mulatto, in a gothic revival that explicitly and centrally deploys "race-mixing" and its abnormal product as symbols of sexual, social, and national degeneration. While those literary scholars who have explored imperial gothic have recognized the role of race generally and the half-breed in particular in aspects of the work of the favored authors of the new canon, they have not, I believe, sufficiently emphasized its centrality, nor indeed, its omnipresence.

Certainly, Haggard, Kipling, and Stevenson made play with the half-breed as villain and "cross-breeding" as a dangerous unnaturalness.[232] In "Beyond the Pale" (1888), Kipling employed a fully gothic representation of the dangers of miscegenation, making use of what we have seen to be a long-established representation of the non-European woman as both seductress and victim (with overtones of the convent/purdah as prison and of cannibalic sadism).[233] In a passage of horror, Bisesa, the young Muslim widow, has her hands severed from her body and her white lover is deeply wounded in the groin. Kipling's moral is explicit: "A man should, whatever happens, keep to his own caste, race and breed. Let the White go to the White, and the Black to the Black."[234]

It is important, however, to see racial gothic at the hands of major writers like Kipling as drawing from what had become a common language of representation—one extending far down into ephemeral popular literature, and outward well beyond fiction. Gothicized *racial* representation drew from and reinforced other areas of prejudice and fear. In Britain at least, the fear of transgressing racial boundaries, of race-mixing as pollution, and of the danger and instability of the half-breed, saturated the whole system by which the unfamiliar and threatening—whether pauper, criminal, madman, feminist, or homosexual—was represented in late-nineteenth-century literature.[235]

The familiar work of fin de siècle gothic that most obviously demands a racial reading is H. G. Wells's *The Island of Dr. Moreau*. In his important analysis of gothic literature, David Punter sees Moreau's island as "a Gothic vision of empire," and Moreau's failed attempt to form beast-men obedient to his own moral and social ideas as the image of "white imperialism in its decline."[236] More recently, Elaine Showalter has seen the island as a "mythological place where men can be freed from the constraints of Victorian morality . . . [to] explore their secret selves within the framework of what they can safely call the 'primitive'." Such fin de siècle "male quest" romances often, she maintains, contain an underlying cannibal theme that signifies "the final breakdown of civilised ethics."[237]

I would go further. In Moreau's creatures created from the beasts of the island, Wells offers new Calibans, the equivalent of plantation mulattoes, lifted directly from the long tradition of the *unstable* half-breed likely to decline into the primitive side of his nature. Wells's interest in this particular problem seems confirmed in a story he published the following year (1897), "Pollock and the Porroh Man." It is a tale of a white man enmeshed, via his own miscegenation with a black concubine, in the demonic half-breed world of Sierra Leone. The evil at the heart of the story is a cannibal witch with "a faint Caucasian tint in his composition," but we also have a half-breed servant called Shakespeare, a half-breed Arab merchant dealing in preserved heads, and (*vide* the São Thomé tradition) a Portuguese Jew.[238]

Wells's movement from the allusive to the racially explicit is thoroughly in keeping with the emergence of the half-breed threat as an *overt* device in turn-of-the-century popular gothic. When one shifts analysis downward from "literature," that is from the important canonical writers like Conrad and Kipling, or even the popular minor classics of, say, Stevenson, Wells, and Haggard, into the world of mere ephemera to which Florence Marryat's myriad works belong, half-breed gothic is densely commonplace.

Fanny Van de Grift Stevenson, R. L. Stevenson's American-born wife, who accompanied him in his wanderings around the Pacific in his last years, and who nurtured her own literary ambitions, had a "childhood bent for horror tales."[239] While Stevenson contemplated turning his South Pacific experiences into a kind of ethnological study, Fanny's reading of their life there demanded a sensationalized combination of the exotic and the gothic, which, she thought, a European and American public expected: "Think," she wrote in exasperation to Sidney Colvin, "of a small treatise on the Polynesian races being offered to people who are dying to hear about Ori a Ori, the 'making of brothers' with cannibals, the strange stories they told, and the extraordinary adventures that befell us!"[240]

Fanny in fact published her own half-breed romance in 1891, a tale called "The Half-White," set in Hawaii, where a Roman Catholic aesthete falls in love with a half-caste girl. A priest, who has himself contracted leprosy from a native woman,[241] warns that the sin of miscegenational "self-indulgence" "shall pursue the innocent to the third and the fourth generations."[242] Stevenson's half-breed girl is the female victim familiar in racial discourse—the innocent, if possibly tainted, object of desire. Her counterpart, the evil half-caste seductress, may be found in another half-breed story by another woman, Annie Linden. "The Half-Caste" appeared in the *Pall Mall Magazine* the year after Marryat's *Blood of the Vampire*. It is set on a coral island in the Dutch South Pacific and tells the story of Fia, a black-eyed half-caste with "almost white skin" who is sent away for a European education, but who, however finely dressed in European fashion, is entirely mastered by her lustful passionate and devouring nature. She has "love affairs with coffee clerks and post-office officials, and all manner of half-caste men" before seducing a young missionary, leading him to his death, and running away with a sailor.[243] As punishment for miscegenation, Stevenson offers hereditary disease; Linden, humiliation and death.

One last story of race-mixing in the tropics provides a concluding view of the half-breed as gothic type at the end of the nineteenth century. James Rodway, a Wiltshire weaver's son, had emigrated as an apothecary's apprentice to British Guiana in 1870, where he became an amateur naturalist, museum curator, and historian of the colony. In 1898 he published a romantic novel with gothic undertones that, although he had himself married a "Creole" from Demerara, dwells on the danger of seduction that young emigrant white men faced in the tropics. Kate Reedon, the native-born wife whom he married shortly after arriving in the colony, and who bore him eleven children, may have been from an entirely "white" Guianan family,[244] although it was commonly thought that such Creole lines inevitably carried traces of "black blood." It would not, in any event, have been impossible—or even unusual—for Rodway to have published a violently negative representation of the half breed while having himself "crossed the line." As we have seen, Alexander Ross at Red River did so. Lafcadio Hearn, who had contracted an illegal (and brief) "marriage" with a mulatto ex-slave in Ohio,[245] and who later married and had children by a Japanese woman in Tokyo, in the very year of his second marriage published an attack on "half-breed" people in the West Indies as "the greatest error" of slavery, "an all-powerful element of discord," a people who were prone to "mutinous obstinacy." "Fierce with resentment, sullen, distrustful, and daring," mixed races were perpetual creatures of contradiction, of "treachery and resolve, duplicity and courage." Although Hearn admitted that their women often possessed "grace and charm," the half-breed in general was susceptible to "cruelty, perfidy, and ingratitude."[246]

One can only speculate on the buried motives here of the white author. Some, like Ross, had earlier been able to "save" a positive image of the half-breed female by separating her from the inherently dangerous aspects of the half-breed male, but this was an increasingly inadequate, unstable solution. On the one hand, a harder, more pejorative "science" of racial anthropology, on the other, a growing feminist challenge to the ideal of a passive, childlike femininity, conspired to undermine it. Hearn toyed with such a masculine/feminine half-breed dichotomy in his stories of West Indian life, but ultimately got entangled in its contradictions. And so the graceful, childlike mulatto woman had to become a doomed type—as in the tale of "La Vérette" where a beautiful shop-girl, Pascaline, dies hideously of smallpox (surely a borrowing from Zola's *Nana*): "And they are all going thus, the beautiful women of color. In the opinion of the physicians, the whole generation is doomed."[247] The mixed-race woman in the West Indies (like all women?) was "changing," becoming "much less humble and submissive," and her "moral side is still half savage."[248]

Rodway's *In Guiana Wilds: A Study of Two Women* is the story of Alan Gordon, a young dry goods clerk from Glasgow, who, "exposed to many temptations" in Georgetown, is seduced into a secret marriage with a half-breed girl, Chloe. The child of a multiracial father (part Dutch, English, Indian, and Negro) and an Arawak mother, Chloe is portrayed as aggressive and sexually dominant—"her bosom throbbed, and the muscles of her bare arms stood forth like those of an athlete." In the inverted world of this tropical Eden ("They were in paradise"), she, like the temptress Eve, possesses exotic knowledge, and helps the innocent, feminine youth through the jungle ("Chloe went forward up the hill, her cutlass in her hand . . . [she] gave one cut and the obstruction fell; Alan chopped and chopped again at a bush rope, but it only bent").[249]

However, Chloe is an ultimately dangerous, destructive force. Once married, her half-breed nature swings from one identity to another, from her mother's "native" side—"a child of nature"—to that of her "shiftless" part-Negro father. As a wife, she is still dominant, but now a mere vampire, draining away Alan's money with her demands for finery and luxury, the way she drains away his sexual energy. He dreams of being devoured by a poisonous snake, while his wife's "horrid sardonic laugh" pierces his ears.[250] This is unendurable, and Alan flees into the bush, where he goes native among possible cannibals, undergoes scarification, and at last (although "out of his element") finds happiness with the alternative-feminine, a pure-blood Indian girl, Yariko, with a tattooed face and a "naked body [that] seemed to harmonize with her surroundings."[251] Her obscured face but sexy body make Yariko the perfect emblem of a male fantasy of undemanding female compliance, not a sexual partner, but an unintimidating sexual object. She is entirely passionless, submissive, carries great burdens, and does all the domestic work.[252]

The double image of the feminine here can be found exactly replicated in, for instance, the self-serving autobiographical representations of Hearn, who fled from his early connection with the illiterate mulatto "Mattie," a woman he said he had tried to lift up, but who sank back into "violence and viciousness," to her opposite, a Japanese woman with bashful, downcast eyes who would quietly and undemandingly look after his creature comforts.[253] The parallel contrast in James Rodway's fantasy—of dominating (half-breed) bitch and submissive (full-blood) slave ("were all women like these two . . . ?")[254]—is more, however, than a man's construction of female duality. Gender and sexuality serve other purposes as well here. Yariko's submissiveness (like Hearn's search for Oriental bashfulness) is, no doubt, the anxious male's answer to the late-nineteenth-century challenge of the masculine woman. Rodway, an unrelenting social Darwinist in his observations on Guianan natural history had claimed that "we can hardly consider the imperfect working females among insects as other than degenerate"; Hearn, who believed that education was destroying the simplicity and charm of the "child-like" West Indian coloreds, thought that women in general were being overeducated and told a friend that he did not want intellectual companionship in a wife. He refused to teach his Japanese wife English.[255] But Rodway's tale also suggests, via the counterimage of Chloe the unstable, unnatural half-breed, a wished-for solution to a central late-Victorian imperial dilemma—the growing demand, especially among Europeanized nonwhite colonial elites, for power-sharing and equality.

Rodway elsewhere despaired of the future of "native" Guiana—the flora and fauna being eradicated by mining, hunting, and urbanization, including the pure-blood Indians, who faced extermination. In their place was evolving a world populated by the cultural (and biological) half-breed: "The general effect of education is a desire to become clerks, office-boys and shopmen. Field work is beneath the notice of the rising generation of black and coloured . . . a lot of idlers who have no visible means of subsistence."[256] For Rodway the naturalist, the true Guiana native, the pure-blood Indian, was inseparable from his habitat, the jungle, and, as an exotically adapted species, could only flourish there in his proper realm:

> Those who have only seen Indians in town can hardly conceive how perfectly at home they are in the forest. In streets and among crowds they are out of their element, and appear dull and heavy. As they file along the

pavement, perhaps headed by one who wears a tall hat and a blue shirt, a stranger might almost fancy them near akin to the *half-idiots* seen here and there in most English towns. But see them in the forest or on the river, and the case is reversed. Here the white man is the fool.[257]

In Rodway's novel, half-breed Chloe, having become a thing of the town rather than the jungle, having tasted the good life, wants more, and Alan must retreat to an "authentic" race of noble savages. Clearly, this is an expression of a very general contemporary anxiety over the maintenance of European authority in rapidly changing colonial societies. The strategy it offers—denigration of the "corrupted" urban native and idealization of the "real" savage in his own special, and restricted, milieu—is also that of the popular press, with its comic images of the absurd nonwhite in Western dress, and of the well-attended imperial entertainments of late-Victorian London, such as the "Savage South Africa" exhibition in 1899.

Race, Gender, and Moral Panic —
Miss Jewell's Marriage Revisited

The unusually warm summer of 1899 witnessed an extravagant display of imperial entertainments at Earl's Court in London. The "Greater Britain" exhibition was a fin de siècle affirmation of empire, orchestrated in the afterglow of the Diamond Jubilee as a multiring circus–cum–geography, history, and anthropology lesson by promoters hoping to cash in on the popular appetite for jingoistic spectacle. It was a profitable success, combining as it did aspects of panorama, theater, music hall, and zoo in a celebratory way, which drew both popular and respectable middle-class audiences.

"Greater Britain" offered drama and an animal and human menagerie—like the illustrated press, which also fed a late-Victorian hunger for the exotic and for a self-confirming romance of empire. In fact, such an exhibition could be browsed by the curious and read in much the same way as a cheap adventure novel or an illustrated magazine of the "tit-bits" variety. For the average Londoner, the empire was in any event an imagined place, half-real, half-fantasy, a land of bizarre contrasts—of cannibals and cowboys, the tom-tom and the telegraph—established in the mind's eye by the adventure story, the illustrator's tableau, and the photographer's set piece. At Earl's Court, one could wander down "a street in Cairo," with camel and donkey rides for the children. There were a Wild West panorama and a Hong Kong opium den. But the central event was an elaborate entertainment called "Savage South Africa," mounted by a Mr. Fillis, who brought from Cape Town a large collection of animals, Boers, and blacks.

The Earl's Court exhibition, and the sensationalized interracial union of one of its black performers, "Prince" Lobengula (Peter Loben), and a

Ill. 19. Miss Jewell and Lobengula (*The Graphic,* 19 Aug. 1899). (British Library).

young white woman, Miss Jewell (ill. 19), has been excavated by Ben Shephard in a well-known essay on "Showbiz Imperialism."[1] Here it is proposed to reexamine the affair, focusing more closely on the way it demonstrates a racial framing of domestic obsessions and following its deployment in the London press in August of that year as an example of orchestrated moral panic with typically gothic overtones.

"To Join in Holy Matrimony"

Opening in May and running through the August Bank Holiday, Savage South Africa proved a popular draw at just the time when imperial relations in southern Africa were coming to a violent crisis. It offered the daily crowd of spectators—women and children were especially prominent—dramatic recreation of scenes of recent war and rebellion, like the attack in 1896 on the Gwelo stage coach (using, it was claimed, the original coach and driver). Most colorful, perhaps, was the "last stand" of Lobengula's warriors, led in savage war dress of feathers and paint by a tall, muscular son (Fillis claimed) of the Matabele king himself (ill. 20). These performances, three times daily, consistently filled the lower-priced seats of the theater where they were held.[2] Outside there were also displays of Boer marksmanship and zebra-lassoing, performing elephants and lions.

Savage South Africa was by no means the first such display of "primitives" in the metropolis of empire. Three years earlier, the Reverend

Joseph Salter had complained of the popular taste (which had grown up since at least the 1870's) for just such exotic circuslike attractions—for snake charmers, "devil-dancers," jugglers, conjurers, wrestlers, Arab horsemen, "Zulus, Maories, Japs, Chinese, even American Indians, and Dahomian Amazons . . . amply applauded and rewarded by the public."[3] What gave the 1899 exhibition its particularly attractive character, however, was the opportunity the crowd had of themselves entering the "Kaffir Kraal," an area set aside for the huts and crafts of Zulu, Matabele, Basuto, and Swazi tribesmen, a simulacrum of their domestic world. Here in this open reserve, black men scantily dressed in "native" fashion sang, danced, and sat around fires cooking their meals and eating "with savage simplicity without knife or fork,"[4] and here the white (often fe-

PRINCE LOBENGULA IN HIS NATIVE COSTUME

Ill. 20. "Loben in War Dress" (*The Graphic,*
19 Aug. 1899). (British Library).

male) spectator had the opportunity of herself entering the tableau vivant of primitivism, of participating in a kind of (safe, temporary, and exciting) dissolution of gender and racial boundaries.

The Kaffir Kraal was not appreciated as a locus of sexual and racial danger, however, until a threatened case of "miscegenation" was seized upon by Alfred Harmsworth's half-penny dailies the *Evening News* and the *Daily Mail* in August and sensationalized in tones of high moral outrage. The proposed marriage of Peter Loben and a Miss Florence ("Kitty") Jewell drew first an amused response, which in some papers took the form of crude racial humor—aimed largely at the presumptuous "nigger," but quickly descending to the dangerously unfeminine appetite and racial disloyalty of Kitty Jewell. The suddenness of this reversal of press and press-driven public opinion, catalyzed by a both humorized and gothicized report of a single interracial marriage, contrasts sharply with the nearly universal applause that had greeted the exhibition's opening in May and the enthusiasm that followed it right up to the Bank Holiday panic of August. These approving reviews owe something to a patriotic enthusiasm for empire and to a reading of the show that stressed its informative, improving, as well as entertaining aspect: "novel," "exciting" entertainment (the *Globe*); "delightful," "most interesting" (the *Morning Post*); "wonderful," "a microcosm of the colonial empire" (the *Morning Advertiser*); "realistic picture of savage life," "physically fine specimens of a race of savage warriors" (the *Standard*). Even a radical paper like *Reynold's*, strongly pro-Boer and anti-Rhodes, could recommend it as "something not to be missed by anyone who appreciates realistic spectacle."[5]

Peter Loben and Kitty Jewell announced their intention to marry on the 9th of August, and this was reported in at least some of the papers in a bemused but not overtly concerned fashion. The *Morning Advertiser*, for instance, treated the announcement as merely a bit of interesting gossip, noting what the pair were wearing and Miss Jewell's background as the 24-year-old daughter of a deceased Cornish mining engineer. The *Church Family Newspaper* published an interview with Loben that dwelt on his background (he had been educated by Wesleyan Methodists) but offered no unfriendly commentary on interracial union—except to note that Loben had been surprised by "several offers of marriage" from white women: "I must say this strikes me as rather strange, because in my country women do not offer themselves in marriage. They wait until they are asked."[6]

As the story rapidly widened in the popular press and in public discourse, there was a transforming process by which it passed from curiosity and humor to derision, and thus into "disgust" and "horror" (emotions central to the gothic sensibility), ultimately arriving at a moral outrage in which the marriage, indeed the whole exhibition itself, became emblematic of a much larger threat of social and biological degeneration. Ostensibly a racial scandal, the event quickly transcended this boundary. Ultimately, the marriage of Peter Loben and Kitty Jewell became, not only in the hands of the sensationalist *Daily Mail*, but in the calmer realm of the quality press, an opportunity for a homiletic and proscriptive excursion, via the racially unnatural and essentially gothic image of "miscegenation," into the areas of domestic gender and class relations. In this, it was driven as much by misogyny and social apprehension as by racial prejudice.

The affair produced three distinct, if closely intertwined, texts. First, there is that of Peter Loben as an uppity nigger who is himself a cultural half-breed and a sexual/social opportunist. Second, the text expands from the personal to the collective and engages the "problem" of those "Savage South Africa" blacks who had taken residence in the poorer neighborhood to the west and south of Earl's Court and of the lower-class white women who fraternized with them in the kraal, touched their bodies, and encouraged their attentions. Here the reading inevitably wanders from its racial locus and subsides into a well-established discourse about crime, lower-class sexuality, social control, and rough versus respectable urban culture. Finally, and I would argue most significantly, Kitty Jewell becomes the image of a willful, disobedient daughter, unnaturally empowered by financial independence and enabled thereby to gratify an unrestrained sexual appetite. She is both "new woman" and foolish girl.

"A Just Impediment"

The two mass-readership Harmsworth papers, the *Evening News* and the *Daily Mail*, following the lead, perhaps, of an indignant columnist in the South African–oriented London weekly, *The Critic*,[7] treated the "black scandal" of Loben's marriage announcement from the start as a dangerous issue of public and private morality. Much of the rest of the daily London press, however, at first employed in tone and anecdote a kind of sportive flippancy in their reportage that was both amused and distanced. This may represent the actual tone of the throng that gathered in hopes of witnessing the couple at church on the 10th and 11th (the clergyman refusing on either occasion to conduct a service). The *Pall Mall Gazette* wrote of "good-humoured banter from the crowd." Other papers no doubt worked up overheard "conversations" to conform to the kind of race and working-class joke formulas found in *Punch* and other

Ill. 21(a). "Loben and His Jewell" (*The Morning Herald*, 14 Aug. 1899).

humor magazines, but their treatment does not suggest that the curious common crowd in the street saw the affair as much other than an excuse for a little diversion and some light, if crude, raillery. The *Morning Herald* offered a Cockney "admirer of the bride" who sighed "Oh, lor! I wish I was a nigger!" The *Sun*, in an "Extra Special. Lo Ben and the Bride," had a butcher's man grumble to a baker's man, "I don't know what a white woman wants with a nigger for a husband," to be answered by a small boy, "P'raps she wants him to clean stoves."[8] Illustrations followed in some of the papers, which continue to locate the affair in the tradition of the racial joke, with Loben appearing as alternately a gentleman in light trousers, informal coat, bow tie and straw boater—suggesting a black-face minstrel dandy—and as feathered and painted warrior. One cartoon combined the two, picturing a thick-lipped savage in a grass skirt, with top hat and cane/spear (ill. 21).[9]

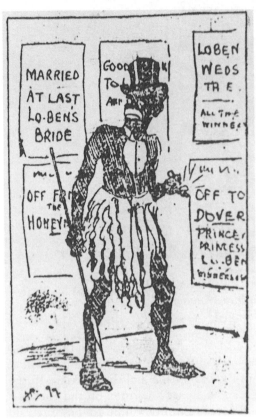

Ill. 21(b). "I Suppose I Am Married" (*The Star*, 12 Aug. 1899). (British Library).

As the story made its way upward into the establishment press, low humor was displaced by a more serious reading, one that followed the direction of the cheap dailies, which commonly served up divorce stories and other scandal as basic fare. The *Evening News* had chastised the public on the 12th of August for viewing the proposed marriage as "a theme for merriment." "[T]he mating of a white girl with a dusky savage" ought to "inspire a feeling of disgust among the vast majority of Englishmen and Englishwomen . . . to use it as a theme for jesting is not only in bad taste, but distinctly dangerous." Here the strategy was to appeal, in a way that was the stock-in-trade of such papers, to the class snobbery and status anxiety of the lower-middle-class reader, to clothe prurient sensationalism in the language of moral purity and patriotic duty: "Such acts of disgusting folly are well known to be infectious, and there are

Ill. 22. "Imperialism" (*The Morning Leader*, 16 Aug. 1899). (British Library).

plenty of silly women in the world."[10] Finally, even within the humorous representation itself, there was a shift toward a larger moral, toward a social and political reading of the exhibition and the marriage in the following week. The *Morning Leader*'s page 3 cartoon on the 16th is a political satire featuring Cecil Rhodes in military uniform holding a lid labeled "Imperialism" above a pot called "Kaffir Kraal," which gives off noxious fumes of "Brutality," "Drunkenness," "Rioting," "Cheap Vulgarity," and "Vice." John Bull is a sanitary inspector who "must condemn it" (ill. 22).[11]

The confusion of biological and social danger, and ambiguity over the nature of the problem—either a rampant black sexuality or a corrupted and inadequate domestic moral character—was paralleled by a similar confusion over the role of white women, as alternatively victims and villains, in the different narratives of the affair. "Savage South Africa" and the Loben-Jewell marriage forcefully relocated the characteristically British race-mixing phobia from the periphery of empire, the "natural" locus, as it were, of miscegenation and the half-breed, to the metropolitan heart of British society, at a time when the domestic issues of gender and class, of feminism and socialism, ran throughout an anxious debate over social and sexual anarchy, cultural malaise and biological degeneration. In this context, the affair demanded an analysis that, within a contemporary racial fear of "reverse colonization," nevertheless centered issues of feminine and class behavior in white, urban society.

As the discussion of the affair evolved, it was the white women, rather than the black men, who took center stage as the willful—that is, unnatural—agents of their own degradation: "The Kaffir exhibition at Earl's Court has, in fact, degenerated into an exhibition of White women visitors; and a very disgusting exhibition it is . . . a very pandemonium of sensuality."[12] Kitty Jewell's transgression, as a respectable, middle-class woman,[13] at first complicated, but ultimately served to close and secure a moral reading that both reinforced and depended upon an upper-class male hegemony.

In effect, there is a deeper message in the affair, which does not lie in the surface discourse about race at all, but in a contemporary male concern to resist the erosion of boundaries in the late-Victorian city, which had long restricted the social independence of, particularly, middle-class women. The whole brouhaha over the immorality of the Earl's Court exhibition may be read rather as Judith Walkowitz has read the panic over Jack the Ripper—as an event that entrenched gender divisions and confirmed the need for male supervision and protection. The calls in 1888 for the closure of common lodging houses and the harping on the dangers awaiting the unchaperoned woman have their parallel in the demands in 1899 for the closure of the "Savage South Africa" exhibition, or at least the Kaffir Kraal, to women.[14] On 29 August, management in fact bowed to public pressure, and the Kraal was closed to women, some 400 being turned away, it was claimed, the first day.

The "several offers of marriage" Loben had received from white women who did not "wait until they [were] asked," an item repeated in several of the press accounts of the affair, clearly served to ridicule female independence generally. As a *racial* story, however, it carried an additional message. It inverted an important myth that had served to justify rigid racial segregation and subordination of black men in the late-Victorian empire—the vulnerability of the white woman to rape.

Significantly, the first warnings to be raised in the press over the exhibition and the marriage expressed fears that somehow the brazenness of white women in London would erode the respect and awe with which blacks in South Africa properly regarded white women there: "Do the *unsexed* females who are lavishing their lascivious attentions on these men of a lower race ever stop to think how they may be creating for their sisters across the water untold humiliation and danger?"[15]

This quickly assumed a larger shape, threatening the whole of the fragile structure of an empire in which the white presence was a small minority. The *Daily Mail* worried that "such marriages destroy this feeling of respect and substitute for it the idea that Kaffir and white are equal."[16] The theme of "empire in danger," already much in the air owing to the rapidly unfolding South African crisis, was seized upon by other papers in the following week. "The tales that these black men will take back to their own land about the white people in the capital of the Empire—in that mysterious city which they have always connected with the power of the Great Queen and of a superior race—will be a precious result of a show supposed to help the Empire," the *Morning Leader* claimed.[17] A London weekly, *South Africa*, thought that it would be necessary to tighten the pass system for blacks back in Africa because of the danger that the "virus" of the "black plague at Earl's Court" would spread there with the returning Zulu warriors, unless a "moral quarantine can be devised."[18]

"Being now come to Years of Discretion"

The rhetorical use of the idea of quarantine—moral or otherwise—seems to me significant. In the context of Earl's Court, it applied as much to the white women as to the black men, and suggests a bridge of sorts between the apparently contradictory images of the vulnerable white woman abroad and the brazen woman at home. The chivalric attitude toward colonial womenfolk was grounded, not only in the presumed threat of the black male, but in the necessary weakness of women, who were to be "protected," in effect quarantined, as much from their own susceptibility as from violent assault.

We might note here a certain contradiction that weaves in and out of the European representation of the Negro male from the eighteenth to the end of the nineteenth centuries—that is, from the maturity of the system of slavery in America, through abolition, to the fin de siècle empire in Africa. On the one hand, there was the passive black, humbled and made obedient (that is, feminized) by slavery and imperial subordination, an image that parallels the common mid-nineteenth-century observation of many missionaries and explorers that the African male in his "native" environment had exchanged roles with his (masculine) womenfolk. Against this, however, was the powerful image of the rogue black, displaced—by escape or emancipation—from the quarantine of the slave system, or in Africa drawn out of his "own" world, his village, into the margins of the white society of the town. Moreover, as the nineteenth century progressed, African exploration and conflict generated

contrasting images, similar to those of the Columbian Caribbean between gentle Arawak and cannibal Carib, of the lazy, effeminate black
male on the one hand (the majority), and the fierce warrior, the Ashanti,
Zulu, or Masai, on the other (whose very fierceness helped to define the
unmanliness of the others). In the first case, the association of the
rogue—the escaped slave and displaced "native"—with rape-as-revenge
and, in the second, the exceptional stature and fierce character of the
Zulu warrior both reinforced long-standing traditions of black sexual potency and threat.

At Earl's Court, the long Western obsession with the famed size of the
black penis collaborated with the traditional European assumption of
female emotionalism and sexual excitability. The upper-class (at least
vis-à-vis her black servants) Englishwoman "in danger" in the colonies
and the lower-class women at Earl's Court were indeed "sisters across
the water" in that they were both thought to be susceptible—although
in different ways—to the fantasized potency of the black male member.
The former, like children, were danger of an unnatural sexual awakening
by rape or its equivalent and a consequent loss of self-control; the latter
were thought to be overtly ruled by sexual appetite. This difference between passive loss of self-control and active pursuit of gratification was
essentially one of class.

It is obvious that the furor over the exhibition and the marriage rested
on more than a panic about "miscegenation" and empire. It derived from
a particularly masculine reading of the affair, which suggested that both
Miss Jewell and the other women enjoying both independence and a light
sexual frisson in the Kaffir Kraal, were mastered by their natures—by a
hunger for the super-penis of racial myth. Here the women's uninhibited
responsiveness to the undoubtedly sexual nature of the exhibition was
itself constructed as female weakness, and served to advance ideas of
"protection" via a policed quarantine of immoral events and regulation
of public spaces that restricted for upper- and lower-class women alike
free access to areas of the city that were open territory for a male of any
class.

A hundred years earlier, the detached and preserved black penis had
been a commonplace of anatomical exhibition in London. Dr. Charles
White, a London physician who spent much effort examining the genitalia of living black men, claimed that he had confirmed the long-held
belief in the disproportionate length of their members, and that "prepa-
rations of them are preserved in most anatomical museums; and I had
one in mine."[19] Such anatomical curiosities, even in the all-male sanc-
tuary of the anatomical museum, where they actually suggest a juvenile

male obsession with relative size, disappeared in the more prudish nine-teenth century. But the myth, thus informed and confirmed by science, lived on powerfully in popular culture, entrenched perhaps by a gothic reading of "unnatural" racial difference. Hyam claims that a preoccupation with the black super-penis became obsessional once again after the 1860's, partly as a result of post-Reconstruction negrophobia in the American South.[20] Partly too, in the British context at least, as a result of violent conflict with warrior societies in Africa—with the Ashanti in the west and the Zulu in the east—which complicated the view that the African male *ordinarily* lacked stoicism, discipline, and masculinity.

The unresolved contradiction of the black male as both masculine-active and feminine-passive was, in fact, graphically represented at Earl's Court. On stage, the African "warriors" acted out a fierceness that served to confirm their position as noble adversaries, although ulti-mately, of course, defeated by white courage and resolution. But in the confining "Kraal," a very different identity was suggested by the essen-tially domestic surroundings of cooking and crafts.[21] Their sexuality here, unlike the active threat they posed in the eyes of the press outside the exhibition, in the shabby streets behind Earl's Court,[22] was seduc-tively passive. They were objects to be petted by "brazen"—that is, mas-culinized—white women.

"Savage South Africa" did not merely encourage "Brutality," "Drunk-enness," and "Rioting" among the urban working classes; significantly and specifically, it was held to precipitate a *feminine* loss of sexual con-trol. In the August heat, the sweaty Zulu warriors, smooth-skinned and scantily clothed, became themselves emblematic of that which their loincloths concealed. And the touching, slapping, and stroking of their "backs and chests" by curious and admiring women disturbed many who recognized in it an essentially sexual experience. In the eyes of the middle-class male observer, this was merely a confirmation of the tradi-tion—as old as that of the black penis—that, in the words of one late-eighteenth century critic, "the lower classes of [white] women" had a "strange partiality" for the black body.[23] In the colonies, the mulatto was usually the product of a white father and black mother, but in Britain the black population was overwhelmingly male, and consequently the child of miscegenation was generally seen to be the living sign of a white, usu-ally working-class, female transgression. At mid-century, a member of the City of London Mission deplored the fact that "many of our fallen ones prefer devoting themselves entirely to the dark races of men." For such an observer, distanced by class, education, and sensibility, the working class itself was becoming, in both a metaphorical and biological sense, Africanized:

It would be a surprise to many people to see how extensively these dark classes are tincturing the colour of the rising race of children in the lowest haunts of this locality: and many of the young fallen females have a visible infusion of Asiatic or African blood in their veins. They form a peculiar class, but mingle freely with the others.[24]

To such even charitably inclined observers, parts of London had become "an Asiatic jungle of courts and alleys," in which "a mixed population of half-castes [has begun] to spring up." The white women who lived there, Ruth Lindeborg has argued, had become cultural mulattas, and they were popularly known by names such as "Chinese Emma," "Lascar Sally," and "Canton Kitty."[25]

At some level, then, the affinity of the lower-class London women for the Zulu warriors at Earl's Court might suggest, not only female weakness for an eroticized exotic, but that the working class itself, and especially its women, might already have been "contaminated" by a racial virus. Certainly in the late-Victorian social discourse, the idea that the pauper class, the very poor "residuum" of London and other large cities, was a "race apart," a savage and bestial alien presence, was more than a metaphor. During the Ripper panic in 1888, at least one paper passed from the brutal (and perhaps racial) savagery of the unknown assailant, to paint the gothic image of a slum class regressing into the primitive half-breed:

> In fact, the Metropolitan Police are simply letting the first city of the world lapse into primeval savagery. . . . Marylebone was recently scourged by tribal warfare. . . . [The young ruffian of the slums] is becoming more and more akin to the monster—half-man, half-brute—who is now prowling round Whitechapel like the "were-wolf" of Gothic fable. But where is this process of hideous evolution to stop?[26]

"Brute Beasts that have no Understanding"

As the story of the immorality of the exhibition spread through the press, an ever-increasing number of hack reporters fanned out to find copy. At one point, Loben was harried by more than 50 reporters in the space of a single hour; every movement of Kitty Jewell and the African "prince" was followed by journalists in Hansom cabs and on bicycles; their servants were interviewed and probably bribed; and inevitably the fact that the couple were already living together in rooms added sensational material to the miscegenation-as-immorality story. A significant side effect was also to "expose" stories about other black males associated with the exhibition who lived in or frequented houses in the vicinity of Earl's Court. Here the racial panic merged into the general contemporary sensational treatment of crime and poverty in the capital, or rather the one amplified the other:

> For some time the monotonous record of drunken orgies, of wild escapes and escapades in the streets, went on, and all that was bad enough. But since then it has become notorious that English women have petted and pampered these specimens of a lower race in a manner which must sicken those who know the facts. The gloomy theories preached by those who believe in "decadence," are, in a general way, it is well to know, mere moonshine. But if ever a champion of that doctrine wants an object lesson in support of his creed he has only to point to "Savage South Africa."[27]

The same newspaper proceeded to unearth stories of blacks who had been found begging, had been charged with drunkenness, and had been cautioned by the police for "running after women and catching hold of them."[28] The text of such reports would appear to project upon the blacks who had escaped from the potential "quarantine" of Earl's Court the deep anxieties that respectable society felt about the presumed criminality and bestiality of the domestic pauper class.

The behavior of the blacks within and beyond the confines of Earl's Court could be regarded as natural and uncomplicated—their position at the bottom of a racial hierarchy made them already homologous to the lowest class of "savage" Londoner. The white women who admired the blacks pose, however, a rather more complex problem. As an upper-class woman (at least as she was portrayed by the press), Kitty Jewell had to be seen as an unnatural, "unsexed" female because she stepped outside her own class-defined role by actively pursuing a husband. The fact that her husband of choice was black only deepened this representation. But the working-class women had to be read otherwise. They were *expected* to be vulgar and brazen, and the most forward of them naturally attracted another class-constructed representation of the female—that of the lower-class prostitute: "Let the Vigilance and Purity Societies momentarily take their eyes off Leicester-square and Piccadilly; let them direct their attention to the immoral procedure now winked at within the precincts of the Greater Britain Exhibition."[29]

Here we may note that the frequent use of disease metaphor, the exhibition as a locus for "virus," "plague," and "pestilence," worked in more than one direction. Most obviously, it referred to a danger of racial infection, but it also resonated with the venereal illnesses of the prostitute, the airborne contagion of the slum, and, more broadly still, perhaps even with a deeply buried male distaste for the "pollution" of menstruating women. The lower-class women at Earl's Court were "free-and-easy," with no "sense of delicacy," and were themselves in fact infecting the black "natives" by leading them astray, while seriously degrading and morally "weakening" the empire.[30] As a result of the publicity focused on the area, one woman, Amy Hopkins of Finborough Road, was actually charged with operating a brothel frequented by the blacks, and her husband, an Earl's Court employee, with living on her earnings.[31]

This shift of blame from the blacks to women is instructive and indicates an important ulterior strategy behind the panic as a whole. Ostensibly the potential victims of black seduction, "silly and selfish" women become the architects of their own degradation.[32] The shift of guilt was even more pronounced in the press's treatment of Kitty Jewell and Peter Loben. A close reading of the coverage does not bear out Ben Shephard's claim that Loben's "association with Kitty Jewell transformed him into the blackest of villains."[33] Peter Loben *was* variously represented as contemptuous of the white women who threw themselves at him and as a presumptuous nigger servant-boy misrepresenting himself as a "prince," but he was not constructed as the central threat. Peter Loben was, essentially, an object—largely passive, and "on view" three times daily. Kitty was the mobile, seducing, secret, and unnatural actor.

The presence of Kitty Jewell as a rogue element was centrally significant in the play and resolution of the "black scandal" affair. While the interest in the working-class women can be associated with the noxious vapors of the cartoon, with the ignorance, vulgarity, and criminality of the slum, Miss Jewell's role begged for another reading, one *Vanity Fair* provided with a surprising directness.

> Why the lady wants to marry Lobengula is, perhaps, hardly intelligible. But while women hold meetings and congresses whose object it is to cry down the mere male as vicious and generally inferior, it may occur to that mere male at a time like this that the weaker sex itself may need a little attention in this direction. Man seldom makes a show of himself as this amorous lady has been making of herself. The modern woman—superior as she is—affects to adore the highest in man, not the lowest. Yet here is a specimen of her sex most eager to tie herself to a savage! We should like to regard her as an exception; but why do so many women take pleasure in touching and patting and even stroking these black persons? These blacks do not represent the highest, but the lowest, part of man. . . . she is a type; and her act is not self-regarding.[34]

It was Kitty Jewell's respectability, in conjunction with her level-headed, active pursuit of the sexual, that made the Loben-Jewell marriage problematic for contemporary male observers: "Her manner was entirely free from any nervousness . . . a frank open expression. . . . Miss Jewell is quite sane."[35] Sane, and determined, empowered as she presumably was by her inheritance from her father to take charge of her own social life, to override a deep-seated social taboo, and advertise her self-control and independence.

"Ordained for the Procreation of Children"

> Miss Jewell laughed derisively at the group of women and children who had awaited her arrival since nine o'clock.
> — *The Standard*, 12 August 1899

The observed, a woman of means; the observing, women of little means. Both caught in a moment of staring exchange, recorded in the word-pictures of journalists seeing and hearing, perhaps, what they wanted to see and hear. The *Daily Mail* found the mostly lower-class crowd "unfriendly." The day before, however, the *Pall Mall Gazette* had called the curious onlookers "good-humoured."[36] If the mood at St. Mathias's Church, Warwick Street, Kensington, did in fact change overnight, it is likely that the intensive press campaign of Thursday evening and Friday morning had played a role. Even a clearly sympathetic spokesman from the London Missionary Society was rattled by a journalist's prodding into opposing the marriage "as a man and an Englishman" while empathically supporting it "as a Christian."[37] It is also apparent that the crowd itself was swollen with many outsiders with an interest in a more sensational confrontation. By Friday morning, there were twenty newsmen and six artists hoping to record the scene for the illustrated weeklies. And there were self-appointed or paid troublemakers: one report noted that three certainly unfriendly men had positioned themselves to protest the wedding.[38]

The scene on a fine summer morning is significant. It places in the same frame both classes of women who bore the brunt of blame in representations of "Savage South Africa" as a scandal. In the press, the "brazenness" of upper-class women who plied the black warriors with favors and attention—"dames taking a savage for a drive in Hyde Park; and presents of bracelets and other trinkets were not uncommon"—was often purposefully juxtaposed with accounts of lower-class prostitutes supposedly offering favors of a more carnal nature—"a large portion" of the visitors at Earl's Court were "women of the lowest character."[39] But in the scene outside St. Mathias's Church there was an important difference. Here the focus was clearly on Miss Jewell's transgression, rather than on the supposed "savagery" and "primitivism" of the lowest class of female Londoner. The lower-class women had themselves become a kind of witnessing chorus of honest respectability. Significantly (a point made in more than one press report), they were women *and children*—

that is, they were represented as mothers, not prostitutes. The setting was also significant—a church, symbolic of bourgeois respectability, not a locus of common entertainment like Earl's Court or of rough and deviant society like the back streets and brothels linked to the blacks who had escaped from their kraal.

There were, in fact, two competing themes to the scandal. On the one hand, there was the representation of the exhibition as an opportunity for lower-class women to revel in disgraceful and licentious behavior, for the silly and the degraded to make a public mockery of moral order and social control. This implied a solution of, for the blacks, confinement and restriction, of a policed segregation. The kraal was to be closed to visitors and the entertainment kept a matter of a distanced, proscenium-style nonparticipatory theater. The intention here was not so much to reform the underclass as to keep a *public* display of immorality from infecting respectable, but weak and impressionable, women and their children. This theme found its focusing moment, not at Earl's Court, but outside St. Mathias's Church. Outraged authority, the clerical officials who ruled against allowing the marriage to proceed, prevented the movement of the affair into the citadel of middle-class morality. Kitty Jewell's drive around St. Mathias's, her exclusion from her own kind, and her juxtaposition with a crowd of common, but respectable, women, itself had a kind of theatricality that was highly symbolic.

In short, both Loben and the blacks at Earl's Court, and the lascivious lower-class women as well, receded into the background. Even the panic over miscegenation—the contamination of the race—that framed the whole event and provided the apparent motive for the interest the quality press took in the affair in the fortnight following Friday's scene at the church, does not "explain" the manipulation of the event at the deepest level of motivation and strategy. Mixed-race marriages were, after all, common enough among the working class of Liverpool and Limehouse. And although there may have been a heightened need to separate the "decent" working class from an immoral "residuum" in the post–Dock Strike 1890's, the press did not dwell on this beyond the useful but fleeting symbolism of the working-class mothers at the church. In fact, the primary object of attention was Kitty Jewell and her image as dangerous rogue, as both race and class traitor. Underlying and guiding this representational strategy was an even deeper and more demanding need among the middle-class, male-dominated press to restrain and vilify female independence. Kitty Jewell could become a traitor to her class and race *because* she was, first, a gender-anarchist. In order to be seen as a bogey-woman, she had to be seen as both an unnatural, willfully aberrant individual and a type. Kitty Jewell was constructed by the press as deviant—and not least in the humorous, as well as the indignant, literary treatment she received. But her personal transgression had to be made to expose a more general threat to social values and social order.

The Loben-Jewell marriage was gothicized, not only in the sensational dailies, but, more obliquely, in educated discourse as well. The more respectable press took up the general issue of "miscegenation" with an ostensibly more balanced and objective treatment. The *Spectator*, for instance, published a long article on mixed-race unions in other countries and admitted that such relationships had long been common among the lower classes in England, and that there was little indication that "a half-caste nation would necessarily be a base nation either in intelligence or character." Nevertheless, there was a mystery at the center of the issue. "Cultivated people" *felt* not only a disgust, the writer claimed, but a "horror" at the idea—a feeling that was "quite universal" among them and "in part shared by the present writer." It was an emotion grounded, he thought, in a "rooted distaste" ultimately traceable to "the common dislike of *mésalliance*," to the "pride of caste": "The lady who marries her groom is almost invariably degraded by her marriage, and if the groom is black the degradation is deeper."[40]

One must note two somewhat buried aspects of this overtly calm and objective analysis. First, inspired by the Loben-Jewell scandal, the text focuses the problem of an irrational but powerful aversion—the scorn and disgust that greet such unions—as essentially a response to white *female* misalliance. But equally important is the mysterious force of this response, inexplicable and gothic in its glissade from disgust into *horror*, a word that appears six times as a repeatedly jarring chord throughout the article. As in the long European discourse about cannibalism, the language of a physical revulsion, of a "disgust and horror," itself inspires, reiterates, and manipulates personal anxiety in a way that is characteristic of Victorian racial and sexual representation.

"Envy, Hatred, and Malice"

And so Kitty Jewell and her transgression became a text for a somewhat covert, but essentially gothic—that is, monstrous and aberrant—representation. This need had its first expression, perhaps, in her own mother's claim that her daughter was "insane." Mrs. Jewell, who apparently lived apart, and was perhaps already alienated, from her independent 24-year-old daughter, rushed back from Paris to try to stop the wedding, motivated, one may suppose, by the social horror with which such a union would be regarded among her own set. Mrs. Jewell's story, which received wide publicity before being dismissed by the press, was that

Kitty had fallen, injured her head, and never completely recovered. Unfortunately, her daughter was far too articulate, coherent, and firm in her resolution for such an "explanation" to convince. On another track, there were also crude hints in some of the papers that Kitty, who had recently returned from a stay in Johannesburg, had "acquired sufficient means [there] to retire into private with the African native."[41] This thinly veiled charge of prostitution did not play much better than that of insanity beyond the most sensational press, but both indicate a search for something "wrong" with Kitty Jewell, some deep but hidden defect in her character, not unlike that of Marryat's secretly mulatto heiress.

It is clear that the real text underlying this search for aberration is the unnaturalness, as felt by middle-class male observers, of an independent middle-class woman taking an active, indeed, dominant, role in arranging her sexual life. Both Marryat's Harriet Brandt and Kitty Jewell (at least as she was constructed in the press)[42] inherited sufficient means to live lives of their own choosing. In both cases, this unusual empowerment was accentuated by a lack of male influence. There was no father, brother, or husband to guide and restrain. In both cases, "race" was used as an obscuring or screening device—one that apparently moved the center of attention away from "the woman question," yet powerfully served to combine the public shame of miscegenation with female independence.

Mental illness and prostitution: these were perhaps unconvincing charges leveled at the daughter of a respectable Cornish mining engineer. The search continued, and the press finally found an element that served to tie everything together—that reached back into the earliest of the gothic as a racial tradition and discovered a secret shame, drawing together the discourses of racial pollution, sexual perversion, and the dangerous subversion of national character.

The "black scandal" of the exhibition and the marriage were played out in the press in competition with two other headline-grabbing items. The first was the deteriorating situation in southern Africa. Some of the more radical, pro-Boer papers made connections between the scandal at Earl's Court and the supposed immorality of Cecil Rhodes's clique of monied and corrupt diamond and gold speculators. When war came, radical journalists like J. A. Hobson and W. M. Thompson, the editor of *Reynold's Newspaper*,[43] were quick to see in the crisis a conspiracy of Jewish financiers. The other item that received attention throughout that August bank holiday week was the sensational retrial of Captain Alfred Dreyfus at Rennes, which began on 7 August 1899. Are there connections? The *Morning Leader*'s story of Kitty Jewell's pending marriage appeared on the 14th of August under the heading *"l'affaire* Lobengula."

On the preceding page, the same paper drew attention, in a separate report of "Lo Ben and his Lady," to rumors that Kitty Jewell was "a Mexican Jewess." Other papers picked this up, and turned hearsay into fact. Miss Jewell, the *Graphic* merely asserted, "is of Jewish extraction." *To-Day* told its readers that Miss Jewell was "a Mexican Jewess" and went on to link her marriage to the audacity of "women of the lowest character" at Earl's Court.[44]

Was Kitty Jewell Jewish? Perhaps there was nothing more to this than the suggestive resonance of "Jewell" and "Jewish," or the fact that many papers made little jokes about her being Loben's diamond, his "precious jewell" of a girl. It hardly matters. The strategy of the charge is obvious in its linkage of miscegenation with un-Englishness, and with an anti-Semitic tradition that Jews were already a "hybridized" (Negro and Semitic) race. The *Jewish Chronicle*, London's most respected Jewish newspaper, ignored the "black scandal" panic. But an element of defensiveness may be suggested by an editorial on 25 August that attacked an American anthropologist's claim that Jews were a mixed race.

In the Ripper panic eleven years earlier, horror had taken an anti-Semitic turn, drawing heavily upon the well-established gothic tradition of the secrecy, unnaturalness, and criminality of the immigrant Jew. Subsequently, the great popularity of Stoker's *Dracula* derived to some extent from the anti-Semitic tradition of alien bloodsuckers. Both "Jack" and Dracula preyed upon women who were at best ambiguous victims: the Ripper's prostitutes and the vampire's chosen find death in a sexual embrace and themselves are, or become, polluters. We have seen that the "black scandal" affair attempted to connect Kitty Jewell's willfulness to the lascivious deviance of the prostitute, and, at the same time, saw in her public encouragement of miscegenation a "plague" or "virus" that might contaminate the morality of her weaker middle-class sisters. Kitty, who, the papers suggested, had proposed to Loben, who had the money to establish a domestic sphere of her choosing, who laughed at her critics, transgressed the boundaries of gender, class, and race. Ultimately, she cannot be contained in a female, bourgeois, or English identity. A century of racial gothic led her male critics naturally and inevitably to discover in her aberration a secret biology, to locate the source of danger in an otherness that could "explain" her transgression of gender and class. They reconstructed Kitty as a Jew attempting to pollute a Christian church with an act of racial perversion. She became, not Scott's innocent maiden, the Jewess Rebecca, but the gothic image of the cunning, corrupting, defiling, *masculine* Jew.

Reference Matter

Notes

Introduction

1. Mannoni, *Prospero and Caliban* (written in 1948 and first published in Paris in 1950), 19.

2. Said, *Orientalism*, 3.

3. Hulme, *Colonial Encounters*; Greenblatt, *Marvelous Possessions*; Dening, *Mr. Bligh's Bad Language*.

4. See, e.g., Mosse, *Nationalism and Sexuality* and *Toward the Final Solution*. And see, too, Gilman, *Difference and Pathology*; *Disease and Representation*; *Freud, Race, and Gender*; *Jewish Self-Hatred*; *Jew's Body*; and *On Blackness Without Blacks*.

5. De Groot, "'Sex' and 'Race,'" 91.

6. One must note here the double importance of the gothic literary genre to the nineteenth-century discourse on race. In the first place, as Gerald Newman has argued, there was the direct contribution of the gothic in its larger sense (as an antiquarian as well as a literary and aesthetic movement) to the construction of racial myths of a Teutonic or Saxon past, providing "a broad bottom on which to build the sense of nationality and citizenship" (Newman, *Rise of English Nationalism*, 118). It is the second sense of "the gothic," however, that is the object of the present study—a literary fascination with secrecy and taboo, with hidden theat and pollution.

7. Gilman, *Difference and Pathology*, 27–28.

8. Margaret Hunt, "Racism," 346.

9. Stocking, *Race, Culture, and Evolution* and *Victorian Anthropology*; Herbert, *Culture and Anomie*; Kuklick, *Savage Within*.

10. Brantlinger, *Rule of Darkness*; Showalter, *Sexual Anarchy*; Walkowitz, *City of Dreadful Delight*.

11. Following David Punter's influential study, *Literature of Terror*, 1–6.

12. Ibid., 5–6.

13. Shephard, "Showbiz Imperialism."

14. As Homi K. Bhabha has observed, it is necessary to move beyond the mere

identification of positive and negative images to "the *process of subjectification* made possible (and plausible) through stereotypical discourse" ("Other Question," 149).

Chapter 1

1. Anonymous English ballad inspired by the contest between the British boxing champion Tom Cribb and the Negro challenger Thomas Molineaux in 1811. See Fryer, *Staying Power*, 447–48.

2. Baldick, *In Frankenstein's Shadow*, 5.

3. For the novel as allegory of the class struggle, see O'Flynn, "Production and Reproduction," 194–213; and, less convincingly, Moretti, *Signs Taken for Wonders*, ch. 3, "Dialectic of Fear." For the feminist interpretation, see Moers, "Female Gothic"; Gilbert and Gubar, *Madwoman in the Attic*, ch. 7, "Horror's Twin"; Poovey, "My Hideous Progeny"; and Spivak, "Three Women's Texts." Moers argues that the novel is a dream both of awakening sexuality and of the horror of maternity, while Gilbert and Gubar assert that Mary Shelley took the male cultural myth of *Paradise Lost* and rewrote it into a mirror of female experience. Poovey emphasizes the dilemma of the female artist expected to produce literature with a moral, while Spivak offers a deconstructionist perspective on the novel as "a text of nascent feminism," where the binary male-female opposition is undone in Frankenstein's womb-laboratory.

4. Mannoni, *Prospero and Caliban*, 19; also see Curtin, *Image of Africa*.

5. Hayden White, "The Noble Savage Theme as Fetish," in *Tropics of Discourse*, 192.

6. Ibid., 193.

7. See, e.g., Pollin, "Philosophical and Literary Sources"; O'Rourke, "'Nothing More Unnatural'"; David Marshall, *Surprising Effects of Sympathy*; Sterrenburg, "Mary Shelley's Monster"; Small, *Ariel Like a Harpy*; and Mellor, *Mary Shelley*.

8. Fryer, *Staying Power*, 212–13.

9. Godwin, *Political Justice*, 147–53.

10. Ibid., 151–53.

11. Gilman, "Black Bodies, White Bodies." Also see Honour, *Black Models*, 47–56, and Gould, "The Hottentot Venus," in *Flamingo's Smile*, 291–305.

12. Godwin, *Fables*, 165.

13. Fryer, *Staying Power*, 68. Estimates run from 10,000 to 20,000.

14. See Honour, *Black Models*, 30.

15. *Annual Register . . . for the Year 1811*, 110–11.

16. Peter Marshall, *William Godwin*, 76, 81.

17. Cited in ibid., 207.

18. Ibid., 234.

19. Honour, *Slaves*, 50–57 and 62–66.

20. Park, *Travels* and *Journal. Mary Shelley's Journal*, ed. Jones, 32, 71.

21. Bryan Edwards, *History*. Gerald McNiece, in *Shelley and the Revolutionary Idea*, first suggested (29) that there might be some connection between Edwards's work and *Frankenstein*. This was taken up briefly by Suvin Darko, *Metamorphoses*, where he discusses a "curious feedback system between fiction and social history" and locates the Monster in what he calls the "Caliban Complex of bourgeois imagination" (135–36, 135n).

22. *Mary Shelley's Journal*, ed. Jones, 34.

23. Davis, *Travels*, 92. It may also be worth mentioning that, although it may seem an obscure and distant "source," *The Arabian Nights' Entertainments* was childhood reading that the Shelleys continued to dip into when abroad. Black slaves feature in many of the stories, sometimes with a relevant twist, as in that in which "an ugly, tall, black slave" causes a young man to murder his wife (trans. Galland, 1: 178–80). *Mary Shelley's Journal*, ed. Jones, 47, notes that they read from this in 1815. Godwin recommended it for children (Mellor, *Mary Shelley*, 9). Mungo Park claimed that the African stories he had heard bore some resemblance to those of the Arabian Nights (*Travels*, 1: 31).

24. Mary Shelley first had the idea for the story in June 1816. Lewis, she later recalled, arrived in August, and she finished chapter 4 in December. The Creature makes his first appearance in the next chapter. *Frankenstein* was completed in May the following year. Mary Shelley to Percy Shelley, 5 Dec. 1816; Mary Shelley to John Cam Hobhouse, 10 Nov. 1824 (in *Letters*, ed. Bennett, 1: 22, 455, 456n).

25. Lewis, *Journal*, 125–27, 145, 149–50, 151–52.

26. Lewis, *The Castle Spectre* (first performed Drury Lane, 1798), 48–50.

27. Park, *Travels*, 1: 21, 239.

28. Bryan Edwards, *History*, 2: 58, 69.

29. Shelley, *Frankenstein*, 1831 edition (Penguin Books, 1985), 105, 261. All following references, except where indicated, are to this version. The 1831 edition was the one most commonly available in the nineteenth century and, although Mary Shelley made some significant alterations of the 1818 text, for our purposes these changes are not ordinarily of much significance.

30. Volney, *Ruins*, 331. One should also note in this context that Bryan Edwards attempted to associate the West Indian superstition of Obeah with ancient Egyptian sources (*History*, 2: 83).

31. Although, as we have seen, some writers drew attention to the yellowish skin and eyes of some Negroes.

32. Musselwhite, *Partings*, 60, argues that "the lustrous black hair and pearly white teeth suggest 'feminine' attributes, contrasted with the straight black lips and the prominent musculature, which suggest predominantly 'masculine' traits." Also see Veeder, *Mary Shelley*.

33. Shelley, *Frankenstein*, 166.

34. A point made by Davis (*Travels*, 95), among many others.

35. An inversion perhaps suggested to Mary Shelley by her father's discussion of the impact of climate on character: "In their extreme perhaps heat and cold may determine the character of nations, of the negroes for example on the one side, and the Laplanders on the other" (Godwin, *Political Justice*, 151). It may also be relevant to note that Edwards described the snow-covered mountains of South America in his history of the West Indies, and the lesser mountains of the islands that "have never yet, that I have heard, been fully explored" (1: 20). Davis in the American South alludes to the Alps when in sight of the Blue Ridge Mountains, and associates both with escape and melancholy (376).

36. Knoepflmacher, "'Face to Face,'" 319. Park, *Travels*, 1: 279–80.

37. Godwin, *Fables*, 165–68.

38. Bate, *Airs, Ballads, &c*, 17–18.

39. Park, *Travels*, 1: 16, 235. B. Edwards, *History*, 2: 59.

40. Leyden, *Historical and Philosophical Sketch*, 98, as quoted by Curtin, *Image of Africa*, 223.

41. Park, *Travels*, 1: 15–16. B. Edwards, *History*, 1: 31–36.

42. See Lorimer, *Colour*, who cites (147) Joseph Hooker (to John Tyndall, 15 Feb. 1867): "It depends on the definition of the term 'SAVAGE'. Johnson defined savage as 'a man untaught, uncivilized'; in general parlance the world now super-adds CRUELTY to the above. Now I hold the Negro in W. Africa and Jamaica is untaught, uncivilized, and CRUEL TOO."

43. B. Edwards, *History*, 1: 33–36, 2: 74.

44. Honour, *Slaves*, 93, and *Black Models*, 25–26.

45. *Parliamentary Register*, 44: 337.

46. B. Edwards, *History*, 2: 60–61.

47. Ibid., 82.

48. Shelley, *Frankenstein*, 124.

49. Mellor, *Mary Shelley*, 9. On cannibalism and the Colombian Caribbean, see Hulme, *Colonial Encounters*, and Greenblatt, *Marvelous Possessions*, and Chapter 2 below.

50. Bryan Edwards, *History*, 1: 29–30, where he attempts to refute Labat's claim that cannibalism had been rare.

51. Shelley, *Frankenstein*, 187.

52. Mellor, *Mary Shelley*, 135–36.

53. Godwin, *Political Justice*, 152.

54. Bryan Edwards, *History*, 2: 76.

55. Shelley, *Frankenstein*, 105.

56. Ibid., 83. For the 1818 description, see *Frankenstein* (University of California Press, 1968), 31.

57. Shakespeare gave Othello the "bloody thoughts" of "a capable and wide revenge," suggesting not only the fury of male jealousy but also the racialized characteristic of the African slave.

58. Shelley, *Frankenstein*, 210–11.

59. *Annual Register . . . for the Year 1816*, 77.

60. Something emphasized by the playbills advertising the popular stage adaptation of the novel in 1823, where the Monster is designated only by "———".

61. Shelley, *Frankenstein*, 165.

62. Bryan Edwards, *History*, 2: 78.

63. Shelley, *Frankenstein*, 165. The De Laceys read Volney's *Ruins*.

64. Ibid., 159, 262–64.

65. Bryan Edwards, *History*, 2: 20.

66. Ibid., 69–70, 80.

67. Lewis, *Journal*, 89–90.

68. Shelley, *Frankenstein*, 164–65, 171.

69. Ibid., 131, 190, 192, 262.

70. Bryan Edwards, *History*, 2: 25, 69–70.

71. Shelley, *Frankenstein*, 131, with reference to public opinion of Justine.

72. T. L. Peacock to P. B. Shelley, Aug. 1818. Italics in the original; quoted by Florescu, *In Search of Frankenstein*, 155.

73. In 1839, 1849, 1856, 1882, and 1886, not counting unauthorized and American printings of this edition. See the British Library Catalogue and Glut, *Frankenstein Catalogue*.

74. Nicoll, *History*, 1: 96, 2: 261, 346, 454; Leathers, *British Entertainers*, 55–57; Forry, "Dramatizations," and "Hideous Progenies."

75. Forry, *Hideous Progenies*, 22.

76. Also see Darko, *Metamorphoses*, 135n.

77. Nichols, "Silencing the Other," 2–3.

78. The American minstrel show was introduced in London in 1836, and had its heyday in the 1850's and 1860's. See Pickering, "White Skin, Black Masks," for a sophisticated analysis of the cultural meaning of "nigger minstrelsy" in Victorian England.

79. Quoted by Blunt, *Ark in the Park*, 38.

80. Poe, "Murders." Is there a further (perhaps unintended) significance in Poe's invocation of Rousseau in the last lines of this tale? For a recent essay on the anthropological treatment of apes, monkeys, and humans, and its relationship to the construction of race and gender in the nineteenth and twentieth centuries, see Haraway, *Primate Visions*.

81. Forry, *Hideous Progenies*, 4.

82. *Hansard*, n.s., 10, 16 Mar. 1824, col. 1103.

83. Handbill reproduced in Florescu, *In Search of Frankenstein*, 164.

84. Baldick, *In Frankenstein's Shadow*, 60.

85. See Forry, *Hideous Progenies*, 43–54; Maurice Hindle's introduction to *Frankenstein* (Penguin Books, 1985), 37; Lee Sterrenburg, "Mary Shelley's Monster," 166; and L. P. Curtis, *Apes and Angels*.

86. Eliot, *Middlemarch*, 177–78.

87. Gaskell, *Mary Barton*, 219–20. See Baldick, *In Frankenstein's Shadow*, 86–87. In an essay of 1871, Matthew Arnold similarly confused Frankenstein with his Monster in an allusion condemning Periclean democracy ("Curtius's History of Greece," 139).

88. Dickens, *Great Expectations*, 354.

89. Mellor (*Mary Shelley*, 89–114), I believe, somewhat exaggerates Shelley's intention in this direction, although Shelley did, in attempting to improve the morals of the tale for the edition of 1831, herself shift emphasis to this aspect. See O'Flynn, "Production and Reproduction," 201.

90. Mellor, *Mary Shelley*, 38–39, 128.

91. Ibid., 136.

92. Emily Brontë, *Wuthering Heights*, 77; Charlotte Brontë, *Jane Eyre*, 313.

93. Ainsworth, *Rookwood* 2: 269, 282; Haggard, *King Solomon's Mines*: "the wizened monkey-like figure . . . made up of a collection of deep yellow wrinkles . . . the whole countenance might have been taken for that of a sun-dried corpse" with eyes "like jewels in a charnel-house" (147); Godwin, *Caleb Williams*, 222.

94. See Chapter 4.

Chapter 2

1. W. Cooke Taylor, *Natural History*, 1: 124–25.

2. See Arens, *Man-Eating Myth*. For the Renaissance in particular, see Greenblatt, *Marvelous Possessions*.

3. Herbert, *Culture and Anomie*, 160–61.

4. Earle, *Narrative*, 13.

5. Dening, *Islands and Beaches*, 248–49.

6. This strongly suggests the similar inversion by which the burden of guilt for the slave trade was shifted onto the Africans themselves in the mid nineteenth century. See Brantlinger, "Victorians and Africans," 173.

7. See Mannoni, *Prospero and Caliban*. On the construction of the Caribbean cannibal in particular, see Hulme, *Colonial Encounters*. For cannibalism and identity, also see Kilgour, *From Communion to Cannibalism*.

8. Greenblatt, *Marvelous Possessions*, 6.

9. Kilgour, *From Communion to Cannibalism*, 149, 194.

10. Hulme, *Colonial Encounters*, 1–3, 20–21, 34, 46–47, 66, 85–86.

11. On the subject of the changing notion (in early modern Europe) of the Wild Man, see Hayden White, "The Forms of Wildness: Archaeology of an Idea," in *Tropics of Discourse*, 150–82.

12. Turner, *Boys Will Be Boys*, 32–35.

13. Ibid.

14. *Sweeney Todd, the Demon Barber of Fleet Street*.

15. See Brantlinger, *Rule of Darkness*, 234–35.

16. [Rymer?], *Varney*, 638.

17. St. Johnston, "Cannibalism," 395.

18. *North British Review* 19 (Feb. 1859): 48 [quoted in end papers, T. Williams, *Fiji*].

19. "From Greenland's Icy Mountains."

20. John Williams, *Narrative*, 7–8, 20. Williams was seen to be "the most successful" (*DNB*) missionary of the time. Killed and, it was widely presumed, "eaten" in 1839, he became an icon of the missionary enterprise, "the Martyr of Erromanga."

21. Richards, "Medical Notes," 614–25. Richards discounted the rumors of cannibalism as "doubtful . . . except in the absence of food."

22. St. Johnston, "Cannibalism," 395.

23. Sue, *Wandering Jew*, 85; Melville, *Moby-Dick*, 546; Rodway, "Day and Night," 609–12, and "Up a Creek," 592–602.

24. H. M. Stanley, *Great Forest*, 7–10; Wolseley, *Soldier's Life*, 2: 332–33. Meg Merrilies is the old gypsy woman in Scott's *Guy Mannering*, ch. 3: "She was full six feet high, wore a man's greatcoat . . . and . . . seemed rather masculine than feminine. Her dark elf-locks shot out like the snakes of the gorgon . . . while her eye had a wild roll that indicated something like real or affected insanity."

25. Herbert Ward, of H. M. Stanley's Emin Pasha expedition (*Five Years*, 127).

26. Ibid., 105, 117, 118, 122, 127, 132, 148.

27. Seemann, *Viti*, 183.

28. Thomas Williams, *Fiji*, 1: 211–12.

29. Mitchell's *Three Expeditions to the Interior of Eastern Australia*, as quoted (with the relevant passage in italics for emphasis) in Lang's *Cooksland*, 429n.

30. Quoted by Hogg, *Cannibalism*, 23–24.

31. Quoted in ibid., 25.

32. Wallace, *Narrative*, 498–99.

33. David and Charles Livingstone, *Narrative*, 67.

34. Knox, *Races of Men*, 470. Knox had been to Africa as a young man, serving at the Cape from 1817 to 1820 (Biddiss, "Politics of Anatomy," 246).

35. Livingstone, *Missionary Travels*, 129.

36. Livingstone, *Last Journals*, 2: 49, 149.

37. Goya did a series of sketches of robber-cannibals "preparing their victim" and "contemplating human remains" (1800–1808 [Musée des Beaux-Arts et d'Archéologie, Besançon]). Cannibalism is, of course, more graphically portrayed in Goya's well-known wartime gothic painting of Chronos devouring one of his children.

38. Arbousset and Daumas, *Narrative*, 52–57. Also see Bowker, Bleek, and Beddoe, "Cave Cannibals," 121–28, where the "gloomy sepulchre" is revisited and the Arbousset and Daumas narrative is given a pseudo-scientific gloss.

39. Reade, *Savage Africa*, 5–6.

40. Schweinfurth, *Heart of Africa*, 2: 18–19.

41. St. Johnston, *Camping Among the Cannibals*, 227.

42. Melville, *Moby-Dick*, 327.

43. See Simpson, *Cannibalism*.

44. Dickens, "Lost Arctic Voyagers."

45. A Travelling Correspondent, "African Cannibals," 544. Also see Peacock, "Executed Criminals," 281, and Frazer, *Golden Bough*, 2: 154–55.

46. Gordon-Grube, "Anthropophagy," 407, 408n. Also see Charnock, "Cannibalism in Europe," xxx, and Peacock, "Executed Criminals," 268–83.

47. Souden, *Short Breaks*, 114.

48. Cited by Wootton, *Chronicles of Pharmacy*, 2: 23–25.

49. Gordon-Grube, "Anthropophagy," 405–9.

50. Darnton, *Great Cat Massacre*, 15.

51. Winterbottom, *Account*, 166n; David and Charles Livingstone, *Narrative*, 67.

52. Darnton, *Great Cat Massacre*, 15.

53. Katherine M. Briggs, *Dictionary of British Folk-Tales*.

54. Ibid., A, part 2: 512.

55. Ibid., 541.

56. Ibid., 530–31.

57. Ibid., A, part 1: 553.

58. Ibid., 378–79, 414.

59. See Slights, "Incarnations of Comedy," 13–27, for the Christian iconography of the Agnus Dei and the comic substitution of baby for succulent lamb in the Wakefield Nativity Plays.

60. The savagery of blacks was frequently focused by their sadistic abuse of the young, as in Augustus Earle's account of a boy who, for neglecting to guard a field from hogs, was killed, roasted and eaten (*Narrative*, 14); or as in a missionary's report of 1804 that the Bushmen of southern Africa would kill their children "without remorse . . . they will strangle them, smother them, cast them away in the desert or bury them alive" (cited by Gould, *Flamingo's Smile*, 295).

61. J. Ross Browne, *Crusoe's Island*, 172.

62. On English caricatures of the French diet, see Duffy, *Englishman and the Foreigner*, 34–35.

63. Sterrenburg, "Psychoanalysis," 241–64.

64. Burke, *French Revolution*, 210.

65. Corbin, *Village of Cannibals*, 93.

66. Corbin cites this as a defining characteristic of the early nineteenth century, when, admittedly, there were legal and administrative actions taken to remove cruelty and slaughter from public view. But the sensibility had been "spreading" for some time, downwards into the general population.

67. Burke, "First Letter," 245–46.

68. Burke, as cited in Todd's expanded edition of Samuel Johnson, *Dictionary of the English Language*, vol. 1.

69. *Encyclopedia Britannica*, 1768, 1: 327.

70. Dampier, *Voyage Round the World*, 1: 485–86.

71. *Encyclopedia Britannica*, 2d ed., 1:480–81.

72. *Encyclopedia Britannica*, 3d ed., 2: "Anthropophagi." This passage was lifted from John Hawkesworth's very popular *Account*, 3: 448. Library borrowing statistics from Bristol for 1773–84 indicate that this was the most borrowed book in the collection (Margaret Hunt, "Racism," 336–37).

73. Cited by Boucher, *Cannibal Encounters*, 123.

74. Colley, *Britons*, 332.

75. The "Anthropophagi" article in the 3d ed. of the *Encyclopedia Britannica*, which appeared in weekly installments, was probably first published toward the end of 1788.

76. Singer, "Violence," 162–63.

77. Corbin, *Village of Cannibals*, 89.

78. See Outram, *Body*, 61–64, for a discussion of detachable body parts in French folk tradition.

79. Lynn Hunt, *Politics, Culture, and Class*, 108–9, and *Family Romance*, 59–61. The body of the queen, however, was not regarded as sacred, and its destruction was more overtly an act of vengeance against a "bloodsucker." Jacques-René Hébert suggested that she be chopped up like meat for paté (Hunt, "Many Bodies of Marie Antoinette," 122).

80. Outram, *Body and the French Revolution* (citing Ronald Paulson, *Representations of Revolution*), 64.

81. *Gentleman's Magazine*, 5 Sep. 1798.

82. Aufrere, *Cannibal's Progress*, 3, 6, 7, 27, 21, 29.

83. Himmelfarb, *Idea of Poverty*, 435–52.

84. [Smith], "Use of the Dead to the Living," 84–85.

85. Sue, *Wandering Jew*, 660–61.

86. [Rymer?], *Varney*, 231.

87. See, e.g., Yate, *Account of New Zealand*, 132.

88. Reade, *Savage Africa*, 20, 144–45.

89. H. Faulkner, *Elephant Haunts* (1869), 202–3, cited by Cairns, *Prelude to Imperialism*, 97.

90. See Stocking, *Victorian Anthropology*, 213–14.

91. Herbert, *Culture and Anomie*, ch. 4, 204–52.

92. Gallagher, "Body," 90–91.

93. Stocking, *Victorian Anthropology*, 234. Also see Kuklick, *Savage Within*, ch. 2.

94. Although Douglas Lorimer's study, *Colour, Class and the Victorians*, establishes (92ff.) the significance of domestic class prejudice in the emerging racial, especially African, stereotype of the mid nineteenth century, he does little with the traditional ethnic prejudices that often underlay class prejudice.

95. Johnson, *General History*, 132–33.

96. Judith Walkowitz notes the use of *labyrinthine* and *Cimmerian* in descriptions of the East End during the Ripper affair (*City of Dreadful Delight*, 191–94).

97. See Flynn, *Body*, ch. 7; Cornelius Walford, *Famines of the World* (1879), cited by Tannahill, *Flesh and Blood*.

98. Quoted by Fitzpatrick, *Ireland Before the Union*, 32–33.

99. Carlyle, *Reminiscences of My Irish Journey in 1849*, 70, 182–83.

100. Cited by L. P. Curtis, *Anglo-Saxons and Celts*, 140.

101. *Hansard*, 3d ser., 105: Commons (25 May 1849), cols. 978–79, (1 June 1849), cols. 1032–34.

102. An engraving a century later by J. Caulfield, "The Crimes of Mary Aubrey" (1798 [Guildhall Library]) shows her hacking away at her husband's limbs.

103. Whitehead, *Lives and Exploits*, 1: 26–32.

104. Gilman, *Jew's Body*, 112.

105. Charnock, "Cannibalism in Europe," xxvi–xxvii.

106. *The Times*, 13 Mar. 1850.

107. *The Times*, 6 Jan. 1869. For another example, among many, see *The Times*, 17 Nov. 1874.

108. Ruth Richardson, *Death, Dissection and the Destitute*, 222.

109. Carlyle, *Sartor Resartus*, 183.

110. Richardson, *Death, Dissection and the Destitute*, 222.

111. Ibid., 97. For a treatment of the gothic representation of the factory system in mid-Victorian literature, see Catherine Gallagher, *Industrial Reformation*, 44–46, 91, and 99–100.

112. Although the subject is African rather than Polynesian, Sir Charles Bell's striking drawing of a dissected Negro head (ca. 1797) offers such a reading: the commodification of a significant (in the era of the Revolution and the Terror) body part that also suggests the ironic reversals of beheaded savage and cannibal anatomist (see Bell, *Manuscript Drawings*, plate no. 4).

113. Yate, *Account of New Zealand*, 130–31; Richard Taylor, *Te Ika a Maui*, 154.

114. Johnson, *General History*, 132. As early as 1590, although he does not specifically mention cannibalism, Thomas Harriot drew a pointed parallel between savage Picts in Britain and the Indians of Virginia, "to show how that the inhabitants of the Great Britain have been in times past as savage as those of Virginia" (cited by Orgel, "Shakespeare and the Cannibals," 44).

115. Lord John Manners complained that Anti–Corn Law League speakers used terms like "vampires, Bloodsuckers, calling them [the landowners] a class of men living upon the bones and sinews of the labouring class" (Rhodes Boyson, *Ashworth Cotton Enterprise*, 207, cited by Searle, *Entrepreneurial Politics*, 34–35).

116. Sanday, *Divine Hunger*, 6.

117. Cited by Marlow, "English Cannibalism," 649.

118. Carlyle, *Past and Present*, 4.

119. "Man-Eating and Man-Sacrificing," 426.

120. *Encyclopedia Britannica*, 3d ed., 2, s.v. "Anthropophagia." Emphasis added.

121. W. Cooke Taylor, *Natural History*, 1: 49.

122. John Williams, *Narrative*, 566. Emphasis added.

123. Schweinfurth, *Heart of Africa*, 2: 224.

124. Yate, *Account of New Zealand*, 98n. He denies cannibalism of children, however, as "too horrible, even for them!"

125. *Clarissa*, as cited by Hilliard, "*Clarissa* and Ritual Cannibalism," 1084. Although in *Tom Jones*, Fielding serves up womankind as sexual food ("as no Glutton is ashamed to apply the Word Love to his Appetite, and to say he *Loves* such and such Dishes; so may the Lover of this Kind, with equal Propriety say, he *Hungers* after such and such Women" [VI, i]), it is a mutual banquet, and Mrs. Waters "feasts" on Tom at the "Table of Love" (IX, vi) (cited by Rawson, "Cannibalism and Fiction [II]," 233).

126. De Sade, *Juliette*, part 2. On cannibalism-as-sadistic-vengeance in literature generally, see Rawson, "Cannibalism and Fiction: Reflections," 667–711 and "Cannibalism and Fiction [II]," 227–313. On de Sade and Africanist discourse see C. L. Miller, *Blank Darkness*, ch. 5, 184–200.

127. Jordanova, *Sexual Visions*, cited by Elaine Showalter, *Sexual Anarchy*, 128–30.

128. Ruth Richardson, *Death, Dissection and the Destitute*, 132, 234.

129. Corbin, "Commercial Sexuality," 210–11.

130. Porter and Russell, "Social Biology," 148–49.

131. Reynolds, *Mysteries of London*, 1: 125, 130.

132. Quoted by Simpson, *Cannibalism*, 117.

133. See Alexander, *Mrs Fraser*.

134. Mariner, *Account*, 1: 116–17. Mariner was captured by and lived among Tongan natives for four years.

135. Earle, *Narrative*, 112–21.

136. Thomas Williams, *Fiji*, 1: 209–11, and *Journal*, 2: 399n.

137. Polack, *Manners and Customs*, 1: 287–88n. The quotation, however, was lifted from William Ellis's *Polynesian Researches*, 2: 224. Ellis himself had copied it from the missionary Bourne's relation of 1825. Such passage of suspect reportage seems to confirm one of William Arens's arguments, that the "knowledge" of cannibalism often involves a reworking over and over again of the same stories, gaining a spurious authenticity by this very density of repetition.

138. Arbousset and Daumas, *Narrative*, 57.

139. Douglas, *Purity and Danger*, 1.

140. See the discussion of a paper read by Winwood Reade in the *Anthropological Review* 3 (1865), clxiii–clxix, where Sir George Denys tells this anecdote, and is corrected by the bishop of Natal, who protests that it was originally about a New Zealand chief.

141. Reade, *Savage Africa*, 488. For Haggard's "sexual geography" of Africa, see Stott, "Dark Continent," and Bunn, "Embodying Africa."

142. Wordsworth, *The Prelude*, book 7, line 243.

143. Wordsworth, "1802," cited by Dykes, *Negro in English Romantic Thought*, 20, 70–71, 154.

144. Compare Reade's passage with the anthropomorphic account of a mortally wounded giraffe in W. C. Harris, *Wild Sports of Southern Africa*: "the tears trickling from his full brilliant eye . . . bowing his graceful head from the skies, his proud form was prostrate in the dust. Never shall I forget the tingling excitement of that moment" (quoted by Cairns, *Prelude to Imperialism*, 28).

145. Reade, *Savage Africa*, 400. Compare this passage with a strangely parallel one in Francis Parkman's account of his adventures on the Oregon Trail: "When I stood by his side, the antelope turned his expiring eye upward. It was like a beautiful woman's, dark and rich. 'Fortunate that I am in a hurry,' thought I; 'I might be troubled with remorse, if I had time for it'" (*Oregon Trail*, 126).

146. Reade, *Savage Africa*, 193.

147. Cited by Curtin, *Image of Africa*, 178.

148. Kipling also invokes a metaphoric female cannibalism in his poem "The Vampire" (1897):

> A fool there was and he made his prayer
> (Even as you and I!)
> To a rag and a bone and a hank of hair
> (We called her the woman who did not care),
> But the fool he called her his lady fair
> (Even as you and I!). . . .

149. See Hertz, "Medusa's Head: Male Hysteria Under Political Pressure," in *End of the Line*, 161–216.

150. Praz, *Romantic Agony*, 215–16. Lévi-Strauss (*La Pensée sauvage*, 141) sees the image of the *vagina dentata* as the reverse mythological form of the "near universal" conception of the male as devourer and the female as devoured (cited by Rawson, "Cannibalism and Fiction [II]," 227–28).

151. Cited by Hulme, *Colonial Encounters*, 327n.

152. Godwin, *Caleb Williams*, 222, 240.

153. Reynolds, *Mysteries of London*, 1: 125.

154. Parkman, *Oregon Trail*, 133.

155. Marryat, *Phantom Ship*, 356.

156. Reynolds, *Mysteries of London*, 1: 23, 255.

157. Flower, "Comparative Anatomy," 80.

158. Hawkesworth, *Account*, 3: 449.

159. Simpson, *Cannibalism*, 248.

160. This conforms to the common seventeenth-century English prejudice that Scotswomen were particularly unclean: "Their breath commonly stinks of Pottage, their linen of piss, their hands of Pigs turds, their body of sweat" (quoted by Duffy, *Englishman and the Foreigner*, 19).

161. Johnson, *General History*, 132–33.

162. Viaud, *Shipwreck*, 165–70.

163. Cited by Simpson, *Cannibalism*, 126–27.

164. See, e.g., W. Cooke Taylor on native Americans: "In all the accounts of the horrid tortures and mutilations inflicted by the Indians of North America on their unfortunate prisoners, we find the squaws the principal agents in the work of torture, instigating the men both by exhortation and example to increase the bitterness of death by the most bitter insults and agonizing inflictions" (*Natural History*, 1: 50).

165. John Curtis, *Shipwreck*, 107–9, 239.

166. Lang, *Cooksland*, 430.

167. Thomas Williams, *Journal*, 2: 310.

168. Thomas Williams, *Fiji*, 53–54.

169. Romilly, *Western Pacific*, 53, 61; Curtis, *Shipwreck*, 78n; John Watford (1846), cited by Hogg, *Cannibalism*, 31; Alexander Berry (1810), in Augustus Earle, *Narrative*, 47n.

170. Stepan, "Biological Degeneration," 104.

171. Rusden, *History of New Zealand*, 1: 5.

172. Thomson, *Story of New Zealand*, 1: 84.

173. Thomas Williams, *Fiji*, 53–54.

174. Bates, *Naturalist*, 2: 408.

175. As was commented upon at the time, Reade's account, although he had been to Africa himself, is a kind of pastiche of anecdotes and themes culled from previous writers (see the review "Savage Africa").

176. Reade, *Savage Africa*, 193, 367, 546.

177. There is a kind of circularity here. De Sade had himself taken lists of savage customs from travelers' books to corroborate his own fantasies of torture and sexual gratification (see Praz, "The Shadow of the Divine Marquis," in *Romantic Agony*, 100).

178. Gautier, "Une Nuit de Cleopatre," in *One of Cleopatra's Nights*, trans. Lafcadio Hearn, 55–56. Gautier himself suggests a Medusa and Cleopatra parallel in his first description of Cleopatra—of her head only, "one look of which caused the loss of half-a-world" (7). Also see Praz, *Romantic Agony*, 215.

179. Reade, *Savage Africa*, 366.

180. Livingstone, *Missionary Travels*, 49, and *Narrative*, 67.

181. Reade, *Savage Africa*, 549.

182. Flaubert, *Salammbô*, 140.

183. Reade, *Savage Africa*, 549–50.

184. Ibid.

185. Berthold Seemann, "Fiji and Its Inhabitants," in Galton, ed., *Vacation Tourists*, 251.

186. Reade, *Savage Africa*, 549–50.

187. Gilman, *Freud, Race, and Gender*, 38.

188. Reade, *Savage Africa*, 545.

189. Cited by Mort, *Dangerous Sexualities*, 49.

190. Gautier, *One of Cleopatra's Nights*, 55.

191. For a recent discussion of Freud's theory, as applied to Medusa images of revolutionary women in France, see Hertz, "Medusa's Head," in *End of the Line*, 165.

192. Reade, *Savage Africa*, 545–46. For a discussion of the contemporary European belief that female masturbation led to an enlarged clitoris and lesbianism, see Laqueur, "'Amor Veneris,'" 113–19.

193. Reade, *Savage Africa*, 524.

194. Cited by Dykes, *Negro in English Romantic Thought*, 10.

195. Reade, *Savage Africa*, 487–88. This vivid passage would appear to bear some resemblance to the graphic description of the monster Error in Spenser's *Faërie Queene*, suggesting perhaps the kind of borrowing that the 24-year-old Reade, recently down from Magdalen College, Oxford, followed in constructing his text (with thanks to John Fyler for drawing my attention to the similarity).

196. *The Times*, 24 Nov. 1871.

197. *The Times*, 15 Apr. and 26 Dec. 1831, cited by Durey, *Return of the Plague*, 182.

198. Dickens, *Great Expectations*, 36–38.

199. An Anatomy Act Inspector, quoted by Richardson, *Death, Dissection, and the Destitute*, 248.

200. The convict/cannibal tradition worked its way, for instance, into Tolstoy's last novel, *Resurrection*, where cannibalism among escaped prisoners, and the other "vices" associated with prison life, are the consequences of a cannibalistic system itself: "the inevitable result of the incredible delusion that one group of human beings has the right to punish another" (III, xix, 527).

201. Cited by Alexander, *Mrs Fraser*, appendix 2.

202. Curtis, *Shipwreck*, 82n.

203. Lang, *Cooksland*, 426–27.

204. Thomas Williams, *Fiji*, 1: 4.

205. These concerns were reflected in an anonymous verse of 1847 published in the *Launceston Examiner*:

> Shall Tasman's Isle so fam'd
> So lovely and so fair
> From other nations be estrang'd—
> The *name* of *Sodom* bear?

Cited by Hughes, *Fatal Shore*, 531.

206. See Hyam, *Empire and Sexuality*, 101–3; also Hughes, *Fatal Shore*, 267–71, 529–79.

207. Quoted by Hughes, *Fatal Shore*, 38.

208. Clarke, *His Natural Life*, 222.

209. Ibid., 451–53.

210. Hughes, *Fatal Shore*, 539.

211. Quoted in ibid., 264.

212. Mayhew, *London Labour*, vol. 4: *Those That Will Not Work*, 229. Emphasis added.

213. Simpson, *Cannibalism*, 121, 130–32, 139, 292.

214. W. Cooke Taylor, *Natural History*, 1: 129–30.

215. St. Johnston, "Cannibalism," 398.

216. Watt, *Rise of the Novel*, 68. Also see Rawson, "Cannibalism and Fiction [II]," 227–34 ("The Sexual Metaphor"): "There is a recurrent close connection in literary texts between that normally prohibited form of eating and the 'forbidden' or 'abnormal' forms of sexual activity."

217. Johnston, "Ethics of Cannibalism," 28.

218. Boswell, *Life of Johnson*, 246–47.

219. Dew, *I Caught Crippen*, 94–112.

220. See Simpson, *Cannibalism*.

221. Ibid., 128.

222. Ibid., 116–25; Viaud, *Shipwreck*, 165–70.

223. Viaud, *Shipwreck*, 168.

224. Ibid., 165–70.

225. Alexander, *Mrs Fraser*, 132–33.

226. Poe, *Narrative*, 84, 142, 205, 238. A few years later, in Poe's classic tale of gothic mystery "The Murders in the Rue Morgue," it is, significantly, a sailor returning from exotic Borneo who allows his murderous "Ourang-Outang" to escape into the streets of Paris.

227. [Guernsey], "Cruise," 461–63.

228. Dening, *Mr Bligh's Bad Language*, 35, 56.

229. "Old Stories Re-Told," 12–18.

230. Ibid., 15–16.

231. Quoted by James A. Browne, *North-West Passage*, 53.

232. For Dickens's interest in this affair generally, see Brannan, ed., *Under the Management*, introduction, 1–90.

233. "Lost Arctic Voyagers," 361–65, 392.

234. Ibid., 392.

235. Ibid., 362.

236. Hakluyt, *Principal Navigations*, 7: 227.

237. Browne, *North-West Passage*.

238. Peter C. Newman, *Company of Adventurers*, 1: 394.

239. *The Times*, 20 Oct. 1880.

240. Skewes, *Sir John Franklin*, 119.

241. Marlow, "The Fate of Sir John Franklin," 3–11, sees "a kind of national identity crisis" in the popular reluctance to believe that the Franklin expedition resorted to cannibalism.

242. "Lost Arctic Voyagers," 387.

243. Ibid.

244. Hulme, *Colonial Encounters* (15–19), discusses the histories of the two words, although as his thesis requires him to assert a premature displacement of "anthropophagi" for "cannibals," he is in some difficulty in explaining the relatively late coinage of the term *cannibalism*, and he underestimates the survival of the classical term, at least among the educated public, where, in any event, it had been located all along.

245. Marsden, *History of Sumatra*, 300–302. A similar (pre-Victorian) observation can be found in Earle's *Narrative*: an old chief, "King George," explains, "You flog and hang, but we shoot and eat" (121).

246. *Encyclopedia Britannica*, 8th ed. (1854), s.v. "Cannibal."

247. Ibid. cf. St. Johnston's account of the Fijians, "approaching the African type" with black skin, flat noses, protruding lips, and fuzzy hair (*Camping Among the Cannibals*, 211).

248. See, e.g., Herbert Spencer's view that cannibalism evolved by stages (via mutilation and tattoos) into the social institution of servitude, with the Fijians in a "transitional" stage where both exist (*Principles of Sociology*, 2 [1882]: 53–54, 60; 3 [1896]: 459–60).

249. *Encyclopedia Britannica*, 9th ed. (1876), s.v. "Cannibal."

250. Clarke, *For His Natural Life*, 222, 257.

251. C. Gilson, *In the Power of the Pygmies* (1919), as cited by Street, *Savage*, 76.

252. "Apologists for Cannibalism," 1199.

253. *The Times*, 20 July 1874.

254. Quoted by Ruth Richardson, *Death, Dissection and the Destitute*, 131.

255. Quoted by Durey, *Return of the Plague*, 177. Robert Knox was the surgeon implicated, but not charged, in the Burke and Hare murders.

256. Berlioz, *Mémoires*, quoted by Maulitz, *Morbid Appearances*, 83.

257. Desmond, *Politics of Evolution*, 9.

258. Ruth Richardson, *Death, Dissection and the Destitute*, 72.

259. When cholera broke out in Gateshead in 1832, it was said that the common people "firmly believe the doctors stupefy their patients with laudanum and then hurry them off to the grave while yet alive and that they have dissected living bodies; many well-informed people too, think some have been buried alive." There were similar fears expressed in Hull, York, Dewsbury, Droitwich, and Plymouth, and in Falkirk doctors were called "resurrectionist vagabonds" (cited by Durey, *Return of the Plague*, 168–70).

260. "Use of the Dead to the Living," 59–60.

261. Ibid., 61.

262. Desmond, *Politics of Evolution*, 189; French, *Antivivisection*, 306–7.

263. Drew, *I Caught Crippen*, 127.

264. Desmond, *Politics of Evolution*, 160, 189.

265. Marsden, *History of Sumatra*, 300–302; Schweinfurth, *Heart of Africa*, 1: 517, 2: 18.

266. Stocking, *Victorian Anthropology*, 280; Simpson, *Cannibalism*, 147–49.

267. "Stanley's Discoveries," 167, 171, cited by Fancher, "Francis Galton's African Ethnography."

268. Reade took this first tour of western Africa in 1862–63, but he did not have the means for another trip until Henry Walter Bates, the Amazon traveler and secretary of the Royal Geographical Society, introduced him to a wealthy patron, Andrew Swanzy. Swanzy paid for Reade's second African expedition in 1868–70 (Reade, *Martyrdom of Man*, preface).

269. Wolseley, *Story of a Soldier's Life*, 2: 342.

270. Reade, *Ashantee Campaign*, 117–19, 252–53.

271. Ruth Richardson, *Death, Dissection and the Destitute*, 143.

272. Cited by Durey, *Return of the Plague*, 175.

273. Corbin, *Village*, 149n, citing Jean-Claude Caron, "La Jeunesse des écoles de Paris, 1815–1848" (U. of Paris I, diss., 1989).

274. Albert Smith, *Medical Student*, 62.

275. *The Lancet*, as quoted by *The Times*, 20 Sept. 1867.

276. Albert Smith, *Medical Student*, 34. Much of this text was a reworking of earlier series in *Punch*: "The Physiology of the London Medical Student" [1 (1841)], "Curiosities of Medical Experience" [2 (1842)], and "The Medical Student" [3 (1842)].

277. From Edwin Chadwick's *Report on the Sanitary Condition of the Labouring Population of Great Britain* (London, 1842), 253–54 (cited by Childers, "Observation and Representation," 405).

278. Dickens, *Pickwick Papers*, 350.

279. Dickens, *Our Mutual Friend*, 124. Much could be written on the cannibalic associations of teeth (and on the comic pulling of teeth by dentists and the demonic filing of teeth by "primitives") in Victorian literature. See, e.g., Kunzle, "Art of Pulling Teeth."

280. Dickens, *Bleak House*, 500.

281. For a perceptive analysis of Dickens's use of a cannibal metaphor in this novel, see Gallagher, "Bio-Economics," 345–65. For the view that *Great Expectations* is permeated with "the taint of male-male carnivorous consumption" as a parody of economic competition, see Walsh, "Bodies of Capital," 73–97.

282. Dickens, *Bleak House*, 696.

283. Marlow, "English Cannibalism," 655, argues that after 1859 the themes of orality, predation, and the transformation of human flesh into economic gain come to dominate Dickens's fiction.

284. A. Millard, *An Account of the Circumstances Attending to the Imprisonment and Death of the Late William Millard* (London, 1825), 14, quoted by Richardson, *Death, Dissection and the Destitute*, 95.

285. *Index Librorum Prohibitorum* (1877), 415, cited by Ruth Richardson, *Death, Dissection and the Destitute*, 327n.

286. *Punch*, 11 Mar. 1865, cited by Simpson, *Cannibalism*, 143.

287. Cited by Kilgour, *From Communion to Cannibalism*, 194.

288. Peter Hulme's brief, and rather hesitant, discussion of the cannibal joke (*Colonial Encounters*, 81–83) is hindered by his, erroneous I believe, assumption that it did not flourish until the "imperial twilight" of the twentieth century. Moreover, his interest in seeing it only in terms of the civilized/primitive dichotomy of colonial discourse prevents him, here as elsewhere, from addressing the issue of a domestic context well beyond issues of ethnic or racial identity.

289. "Stories of the Black Men," 234–37.

290. Pickering, "White Skin, Black Masks," 90. Pickering challenges Douglas Lorimer's assertion that there was a mid-century shift in the image "of the Negro from an object of pity into a figure of fun" (Lorimer, "Bibles, Banjoes and Bones," 34) by reminding us that there had long been some comic element in Negro representation. True as this is—and, of course, the cannibal joke also had a long, pre-Victorian provenance—the shift in *dominant* representation seems to be much as Lorimer suggested: from the sympathy of "Uncle Tom" to the more purely comic and derisive racist clichés of the late-Victorian stage.

291. "Banjo and Bones," 739–40.

292. When the Anthropological Society discussed Richard Charnock's paper on cannibalism, the conversation moved inevitably from Prichard's observations on Fijian cannibals to a Dr. Chaplin's recollection of "a horrid practical joke that had been played on a medical student, whose comrades cut out a piece from a body in the dissecting-room, and had it fried and served up to him as a beef-steak, which he ate, and thought very good" (Charnock, "Cannibalism in Europe," xxx).

293. "The Surgeon's Warning," cited by Cole, *Things for the Surgeon*, preface.

294. Stocking, *Victorian Anthropology*, 252.

295. *The Times*, 19 Sept. 1866.

296. Freud, *Jokes*, 19–20, 104–5.

297. St. Johnston, *Camping Among the Cannibals*, 325–26.

298. See, e.g., the comical naturalist professor in Charles Gilson's boys' African adventure story *The Captives of the Caves*.

299. *The Times*, 19 Sept. 1866.

300. Thomas Williams, *Fiji*, 1: 212.

301. Ibid., 205. Christopher Herbert has recently argued (*Culture and Anomie*, 203) that Thomas Williams's account of Fijian cannibalism, as a customary, ritu-

alized practice rather than demonic madness, moves toward a modern ethnographic relativism—but it does not move very far. The irony Williams employs serves, it seems to me, to deepen rather than diminish the abnormality of the savage.

302. Romilly, *Western Pacific*, 58.

303. *The Times*, 4 Sept. 1869.

304. Seemann, *Viti*, 173–84.

305. Seemann, "Fiji and Its Inhabitants," 249–50. This "joke," like others, traveled, and may have originated in a witticism of Sydney Smith's a generation earlier: "He recommended Bishop Selwyn, on his departure from New Zealand, to receive the cannibal chiefs of that country with the following speech: 'I deeply regret, sirs, to have nothing on my table suited to your tastes, but you will find plenty of cold curate and roasted clergyman on the sideboard'" (cited in Thomson, *Story of New Zealand*, 2: 68–69).

306. T. M. Reid, *Odd People*, 174.

307. Rowe, *John Hunt*, 99.

308. John Williams, *Narrative*, 558n.

309. Ellis Hanson has recently written that the gaze of the male homosexual invokes the gaze of the vampire—he with whom one is forbidden to identify (Hanson, "Undead," 328–29).

310. Burton, *Lake Regions*, 2: 114.

311. Conrad, "Falk" Frazer, *Golden Bough*; Freud, *Drei Abhandlungen*. Frazer knew and befriended Australian anthropologists, and he made use of their researches in his own speculations. He also, as he was working on the first edition of *The Golden Bough* in the late 1880's, was a keen reader of Robert Louis Stevenson (Crawford, "Frazer and Scottish Romanticism," 30–32). Conrad wrote *Falk* during the period in which *The Golden Bough* was being widely discussed in the press (Hampson, "Frazer, Conrad," 172).

312. "Man-Eating and Man-Sacrificing," 424.

313. Reade, *Savage Africa*, vii. Reade's self-image as a *flâneur* directly invokes the Jamesian image of the detached, privileged *urban* spectator strolling across the metropolis, "slumming" among the working poor (see Walkowitz, *City of Dreadful Delight*, 16).

Chapter 3

1. Flaubert, *Salammbô*, 161–62.

2. Johnson, *General History*, 132–33; Singer, "Violence in the French Revolution," 162–63; Simpson, *Cannibalism*, 126–27; Thomson, *Story of New Zealand*, 1: 147.

3. Burton, "Day Amongst the Fans," 43–54, and *Vikram*; "Vampyres," *Household Words*, 3 Feb. 1855.

4. Cited by Street, *Savage in Literature*, 165 (emphasis added). Conan Doyle made use of the vampire myth in at least one of his Holmes tales, "Adventure of the Sussex Vampire."

5. Gilman, *Jew's Body*, 64. Also see Rosenberg, *From Shylock to Svengali*, 214.

6. Punter, *Literature of Terror*, 239–40: "They are all concerned in one way or another with the problem of degeneration."

7. Showalter's *Sexual Anarchy* offers the best synthesis of work on the "problem" of the New Woman.

8. Franco Moretti, as cited by Seed in "Narrative Method of *Dracula*," 65–65.

9. Besides Le Fanu's "Carmilla" (1872) and Stoker's *Dracula* (1897), the two vampire stories that frame the period, there were at least seventeen other such titles published between 1880 and 1900. See Dalby, comp., *Dracula's Brood*, introduction.

10. See, e.g., Burn, *Age of Equipoise*, ch. 5.

11. Poe's "Murders in the Rue Morgue" joins the two, and M. Dupin's rational reconstruction of the "crime" anticipates the methods of Conan Doyle's Holmes.

12. For some connections between at least Stevenson's gothic and the detective story, see Hirsch, "*Frankenstein*, Detective Fiction, and *Jekyll and Hyde*," 223–46. Conan Doyle's first Holmes book, *A Study in Scarlet*, was published in 1887.

13. See Bentley, "Monster in the Bedroom"; Bierman, "Dracula"; Byers, "Good Men and Monsters"; Craft, "'Kiss Me with Those Red Lips'"; Demetrakopoulos, "Feminism"; Griffin, "'Your Girls'"; Hatlen, "The Return of the Repressed/Oppressed"; Hennelly, "*Dracula*: The Gnostic Quest"; Howes, "Mediation of the Feminine"; Leatherdale, *Dracula*; Moretti, "Dialectic of Fear"; Pick, "'Terrors of the Night'"; Maurice Richardson, "Psychoanalysis of Ghost Stories"; Roth, *Bram Stoker* and "Suddenly Sexual Women"; Seed, "Narrative Method"; Senf, *Vampire*; Stade, "Dracula's Women"; J. A. Stevenson, "Vampire in the Mirror"; and Weissman, "Women as Vampires." Most recently, Halberstam has added her "Technologies of Monstrosity."

14. Dr. John William Polidori, Lord Byron's physician-companion at the house party at Geneva in 1816, published his own ghost story, *The Vampyre*, in 1819. David Punter maintains that the vampire in English culture "is a fundamentally anti-bourgeois figure" (*Literature of Terror*, 119). Franco Moretti has argued, however, that Dracula, with his piles of gold coins and engorged with the lifeblood of innocent victims, is an image of the bloated capitalist (*Signs Taken for Wonders*, 84), while Hatlen sees him as a representation of *both* aristocrat and dangerous proletariat—a view that, as Seed has observed, is difficult to sustain. Moretti's argument becomes more plausible if one sees Dracula as a particular kind of capitalist—the Jew, who is, like the aristocrat, an ancient and cosmopolitan type.

15. Following Ernest Jones's argument (in *On the Nightmare*) that the fear of vampires derives from incest conflict. See, e.g., Bentley, "Monster in the Bedroom": Bierman, "Dracula: Prolonged Childhood Illness and the Oral Trid"; Byers, "Good Men and Monsters"; and Richardson, "Psychoanalysis of Ghost Stories." Stevenson, "Vampire in the Mirror," argues against a Freudian interpretation.

16. See, e.g., Griffin, "'Your Girls That You All Love Are Mine'"; Roth, "Suddenly Sexual Women"; Stade, "Dracula's Women"; Senf, *Bram Stoker*; or Weissman, "Women as Vampires." Senf traces Stoker's ambiguous attitude to strong women to his mother's character, and to his supposed resort, in response to his wife's frigidity, to London prostitutes (63–64).

17. Craft, "'Kiss Me with Those Red Lips'," 169–71, 176; Howes, "Mediation of the Feminine."

18. Hatlen, "Return of the Repressed/Oppressed," 133. Also see Stevenson, "Vampire in the Mirror," who also argues (140) for an interracial sexual competition in *Dracula*.

19. Arata, "Occidental Tourist."

20. Stoker, "Censorship of Fiction," 480. Although there are recent biographies, Stoker did not leave very rich material for the biographer, and none are fully satisfying. The best is the most recent, that by Phyllis Roth. But also see Farson, *Man Who Wrote Dracula*, and Ludlam, *Biography of Dracula*. All rely to a great extent on what can be gleaned about Stoker himself from his own large and discursive biography of Irving.

21. Stoker, *Famous Imposters*. Stoker asserted he "aimed at dealing with his material as with the material for a novel, except that all the facts given are real and authentic." He made "no attempt to treat the subject ethically" (Preface, v).

22. Although Marjorie Howes ("Mediation of the Feminine") has drawn attention to an essay in which Stoker presents sexuality as not a matter of either-or, but a continuum from strong masculinity through sexual passivity to strongly sexual femininity, this, it seems to me, is not an admission that "inverted" or confused sexuality may be natural, but rather confirms opposing polarities by asserting that they meet only where there is a lack of sexual motivation. The majority of people may, he says, be "close to the borderline," but they do not transgress it.

23. Farson, *Man Who Wrote Dracula*, 233.

24. A point made by Hatlen, "Return of the Repressed/Oppressed," 132.

25. Foster, Foreword to Murray, *Fantastic Journey*, xi, xiv.

26. Foster, cited by Murray, *Fantastic Journey*, 32.

27. James Huneker in the *New York Times*, 1 Dec. 1906, cited by Murray, *Fantastic Journey*, 310.

28. Stoker, *Personal Reminiscences of Irving*, 1: 3.

29. Ibid., 2: 94.

30. For the concept of "homosexual panic," see Sedgwick, *Between Men*.

31. Stoker, *Personal Reminiscences of Henry Irving*, 2: 99.

32. Ibid., 1: 14.

33. Ibid., 2: 94.

34. Ibid., 2: 106–7.

35. Ibid., 97.

36. Stoker to Whitman, 1877. Quoted by Callow, *Walt Whitman*, 337.

37. Stoker, *Personal Reminiscences of Henry Irving*, 2: 97, 100–101, 106–7.

38. Quoted by Roth, *Bram Stoker*, 3.

39. Stoker, *Personal Reminiscences of Henry Irving*, 1: 31–33. Emphasis added.

40. Ibid., 44, 52, 54.

41. Ibid., 61.

42. Ibid., 364. There has been some speculation that Florence's frigidity compelled Stoker to turn to prostitutes, thereby incurring the syphilis that may have killed him—and instilling in him a hatred of women. This, if plausible, is only guesswork.

43. Roth, *Bram Stoker*, 136. Also see Irving, *Henry Irving*, 448.

44. Farson, *Man Who Wrote Dracula*, 62, 70.

45. *Dracula*, 281. See Sedgwick, *Between Men*, for a discussion of the need of the middle class to distance its own new range of homosocial bonds from the effeminacy of the aristocrat (p. 207). Curiously, the Wilde trial also appears to

have influenced that other classic of 1890's gothic, H. G. Wells's *The Island of Dr. Moreau*. See Showalter, "Apocalyptic Fables of H. G. Wells," 80.

46. Stoker, *Personal Reminiscences of Henry Irving*, 2: 22.

47. Ibid., 7–9.

48. Ibid., 20–21.

49. See, e.g., Stoker, *Glimpse of America*, 45–46; and in *Personal Reminiscences of Henry Irving*, 2: 100, he worries about the public vulgarity of American actors strutting through the streets: "It was most undignified."

50. Stoker on Ellen Terry's performance in *The Wandering Heir*: "She played a girl masquerading as a boy so delightfully because she was so complete a woman. She had to the full in her nature whatever quality it is that corresponds to what we call 'virility' in a man" (*Personal Reminiscences of Henry Irving*, 2: 202).

51. Stoker, *Personal Reminiscences of Henry Irving*, 1: 140.

52. Mosse, *Nationalism and Sexuality*, 138.

53. Immediately after *Dracula* was published, Stoker ordered a stage performance, really merely a reading, to stake out his copyright claim.

54. See, e.g., the suggestive comments of Marigny, *Le Vampire*, 2, 709–10.

55. Sedgwick, *Between Men*, ch. 5: "Toward the Gothic: Terrorism and Homosexual Panic," 91–92.

56. See Weeks, *Coming Out*.

57. See Sedgwick, *Between Men*, 94, 207.

58. Stoker, *Famous Imposters*, 280.

59. Lewis, *The Monk*; Maturin, *Melmoth*.

60. See Corber, "Representing the 'Unspeakable'."

61. Wilde, *Picture of Dorian Gray*, 132.

62. Stoker, *Dracula*, 62.

63. In *The Foul and the Fragrant*, Alain Corbin has traced Western attitudes toward strong body odors, especially those imagined to be sexual in origin, such as the "seminal humor that . . . produced 'that fetid odor which vigorous males exude'." Moreover, "the seminal odor of the continent priest" brings us back to the anti-Catholic roots of the gothic genre (35–37).

64. Stade, "Dracula's Women," 200. Lesley Hall cautions, however, that masturbation, either self-abuse or even mutual masturbation, was not *necessarily* associated with homosexuality, especially in the matey discourse of working-class subculture ("Forbidden by God," 374). True as this may be, it is clear that it often was, and that masturbation and homosexuality resonated in the Victorian mind—as similarly unfruitful excesses and as addictive vices.

65. Ellis Hanson has argued that the ruined chapel at Castle Dracula "is especially suggestive of the anal-erotic. 'At the bottom there was a dark, tunnel-like passage, through which came a deathly, sickly odour'" ("Undead," 337).

66. Note that Seward's lunatic asylum, where Renfield is held, is also in the lower part of the house, with the respectable rooms above (see Hennelly, "Dracula," 84). Such a location was, of course, a commonplace in gothic literature, from at least Horace Walpole's *Castle of Otranto*, with its "subterranean regions . . . that long labrinth of darkness" (25).

67. "Stoker's modern Prometheus is, as we shall see, both far less the tragically heroic overreacher, and in fact far less the focus of the tale, than his counterparts in romantic fiction and poetry and in contemporary film" (Roth, *Bram Stoker*, 97).

68. Roth, *Bram Stoker*, 111–12; Senf, *Vampire*, 63–64.

69. Howes, "Mediation of the Feminine," 104, 106.

70. Quoted by Farson, *Man Who Wrote Dracula*, 209.

71. "I doubt if Bram realised the homosexual implications of Whitman's concept of idyllic boy-love; I doubt if he recognized the lesbianism in *Carmilla*, the novel that influenced him so deeply; and I am sure he was unaware of the sexuality inherent in *Dracula*" (Farson, *Man Who Wrote Dracula*, 22).

72. Cited by Dyer, "Children of the Night," 47. Ulrichs was an early advocate of emancipation of homosexuals as a valid "third sex."

73. Stenbock, "True Story of a Vampire," 120–47. Emphasis added.

74. Stoker, *Personal Reminiscences of Henry Irving*, 1: 350–51, 359. Perhaps Stoker was also fascinated with Burton as an actor, as a man of many identities—who had famously made his way into Mecca disguised as a Muslim.

75. Burton, perhaps more than latently homosexual, had as we have seen published an adaptation/translation of *Vikram and the Vampire; or, Tales of Hindu Devilry* in 1870. Another edition appeared in 1893.

76. Stoker, *Personal Reminiscences of Henry Irving*, 1: 260.

77. See Craft, "'Kiss Me with Those Red Lips,'" 170–71.

78. Stoker, *Dracula*, 52.

79. Ibid.

80. Ibid., 53.

81. Ibid., 54.

82. Ibid., 67–68.

83. Leatherdale, *Dracula*, 156.

84. Craft, "'Kiss Me with Those Red Lips,'" 170–71.

85. Hanson, "Undead," 326.

86. Stade, "Dracula's Women," 209.

87. Craft, "'Kiss Me with Those Red Lips,'" 188.

88. Showalter (*Sexual Anarchy*) has drawn attention to this element in Stevenson's *Jekyll and Hyde*, and argues that French medical reports of a case of male hysteria may have influenced him (88).

89. Stoker, *Dracula*, 275.

90. Ibid., 209–10.

91. Ibid., 275.

92. For a description of *Frankenstein; or The Vampire's Victim*, see Forry, *Hideous Progenies*, 57–72.

93. See Stedman, "From Dame to Woman," and Laurence Senelick, "Evolution of the Male Impersonator."

94. In Greek mythology, Galatea is the Nereid loved by the cannibal Cyclops Polyphemus.

95. Forry, *Hideous Progenies*, 57.

96. As quoted by Forry, *Hideous Progenies*, 72. William Thomas Stead was the editor of the *Pall Mall Gazette* and anti-vice campaigner.

97. Craft, "'Kiss Me with Those Red Lips,'" 171.

98. Conan Doyle, "Adventure of the Sussex Vampire," 1041, 1043.

99. See Hatlen, "Return of the Repressed/Oppressed," 120.

100. Le Fanu, "Carmilla," 254.

101. Sue, *Wandering Jew*, 85.

102. Conan Doyle, "Adventure of the Sussex Vampire," 1036.

103. Sue, *Wandering Jew*, 105.

104. Hatlen, "Return of the Repressed/Oppressed," 129.

105. Knox, *Races of Men*, 197–98: "lips very full, mouth projecting, chin small, and the whole physiognomy, when swarthy, as it often is, has an African look."

106. See, e.g., Gilman, *Freud, Race, and Gender*, 20–21.

107. Van Onselen, *Studies*, vol. 1.

108. Hyam, *Empire and Sexuality*, 142–45. Also see, e.g., van Onselen, *Studies*, vol. 1: 109–11, 137, 138. See, for one instance among many, Lord, *Jewish Mission Field*, 20, where he asserts "the sad and incontrovertible fact" that "a very considerable portion" of the European Jewish community of Bombay were either the victims or the purveyors of vice.

109. Jackson, "Aryan and the Semite," 343.

110. Seemann, "On the Anthropology of Western Eskimo Land," ccci.

111. Livingstone, *Last Journals*, 2: 85. *The Merchant of Venice*, act 3, sc. 1: "I would my daughter . . . were hears'd at my foot and the ducats in her coffin!"

112. Cited by Arens, *Man-Eating Myth*, 64.

113. See Polack, *Manners and Customs*, 1: 287–88n, for a reference to 2 Kings 6:29 in conjunction with cannibalism in the South Pacific.

114. Thomson, *Story of New Zealand*, 1: 71, 78.

115. Nicholas, *Narrative*, 1: 62–63n, 285.

116. Richard Taylor, *Te Ika a Maui*, 8, 56.

117. Russell, *Polynesia*, 379.

118. Poe, *Narrative*, 236, 241.

119. Thomas Williams, *Fiji*, 1: 53–54, 117. This curiously parallels the connection the Protestant Jean de Lery made in the sixteenth century between the sonorous chanting of his Brazilian cannibals and the chanting of Catholic monks.

120. A letter of ca. 1841, quoted by Rowe, *John Hunt*, 123.

121. St. Johnston, *Camping Among the Cannibals*, 221.

122. "Cannibalism," 404.

123. Mariner, *Account*, 2: 265.

124. Spencer, *Principles of Sociology* 2 (1882), 66–68, and 3 (1896): 459–60.

125. Gilman, *Jew's Body*, 93.

126. Stoker, *Dracula*, 66.

127. Cheyette, *Constructions of "The Jew*," xi.

128. See Anderson, "Popular Survivals."

129. Cheyette, *Constructions of "The Jew*," 92.

130. There may be some significance in the fact that in France the word *vampire* appears to have been introduced by the marquis d'Argens's popular *Lettres juives* of 1737 (published in London as *The Jewish Spy* in 1740). Although the fictional Jewish author of the letters introduces the stories of eastern European vampirism in order to dismiss them as nonsense, the proximity here of the Jew and the vampire is suggestive. See Wilson, "History of the Word 'Vampire,'" 579, and d'Argens, *Jewish Spy*, letter 137, 122–24.

131. Zanger, "Sympathetic Vibration."

132. Halberstam's interesting essay "Technologies of Monstrosity" appeared after I wrote this section, but while she confirms the relationship between Jew and vampire through a reading of the text centered on the "productions of sexuality," her analysis is more concerned with elucidating Foucault's "great sur-

face network" than with grounding the work in a biographical and historical context.

133. Stoker, *Snake's Pass*, 26.

134. The list includes Sir Ernest and Miss Cassell, Barney Barnato, Alfred Beit, Mr. and Mrs. Felix Moschelles, Albert Sterner, and Alfred de Rothschild (Stoker, *Personal Reminiscences of Henry Irving*, 1: 315–26).

135. Ibid., 1: 84.

136. Brereton, *Life of Henry Irving*, 315.

137. Stoker, *Personal Reminiscences of Henry Irving*, 2: 9.

138. Ibid., 140. For Irving's portrayal of Shylock, also see Irving, *Henry Irving*, 339–58.

139. Caine, *My Story*, 349.

140. Stoker, *Famous Imposters*, 115.

141. When Irving played in a stage version of *Oliver Twist* in 1868, he took the role, not of Fagin, but of Bill Sykes (Landa, *Jew in Drama*, 167). In *The Lyons Mail*, he played a dual role.

142. Stoker, *Famous Imposters*, 116.

143. Stoker, "The Wandering Jew," in *Famous Imposters*, 105–20.

144. Caine, *My Story*, 97.

145. Ibid., 113.

146. Stoker, *Personal Reminscences of Henry Irving*, 2: 122–23.

147. See Rosenberg, *From Shylock to Svengali*, 197.

148. There were at least five more editions by 1873.

149. Stoker, "Wandering Jew," *Famous Imposters*, 114.

150. Landa, *Jew in Drama*, 125–26.

151. Lander, "Wandering Jew," 14. This adaptation had been first produced at the Britannia Theatre in 1873.

152. Hall Caine to Stoker, quoted by Ludlam, *Biography of Dracula*, 87.

153. Cited in ibid., 87–88.

154. Stoker, *Personal Reminiscences of Henry Irving*, 2: 117.

155. Caine, *Scapegoat*, 1: 17, 25.

156. Stoker, *Personal Reminiscences of Henry Irving*, 2: 54. Although Caine left for Russia with an "open mind, easily touched with sympathy," he in fact already suspected that "the Jews themselves" might "have helped to bring these evils upon them" (Hall Caine's letter to *The Times*, 12 Oct. 1891, on his projected trip).

157. These were articles that had previously appeared in *Pearson's Magazine*. The expression "white slavery"—not the forcing of girls into prostitution, its common meaning at the end of the century, but the bad pay and conditions of, usually industrial, labor generally—was a metaphor employed as a critique of a capitalist system that was thought often to be operated by "foreigners," especially Jews. It was a commonplace of radical rhetoric earlier in the century, and provided, for example, the title for a study of London seamstresses by the gothic novelist and radical G. W. M. Reynolds in 1850 (see Catherine Gallagher, *Industrial Reformation of English Fiction*, ch. 1).

158. Sherard, *White Slaves*, 112–28.

159. Booth, *Life and Labour*, 3: 170.

160. Arnold White, *Problems of a Great City*, 26.

161. Stoker, *Dracula*, 364.

162. Forman, *Some Queries*, from a pamphlet dated 1733, 11n.

163. As quoted by Baldick, *In Frankenstein's Shadow*, 128, 130.

164. Robb, *White-Collar Crime*, 97.

165. Maturin, *Melmoth*, 262–63.

166. Arnold White, *Destitute Alien*, 91, 92, 95–96, 189.

167. Arnold White, *Problems*, 143. It may also be significant, in such a juxtaposition of the gothic Jew and a gothic Chinese, that the Chinese were thought to be, like the Jew, addicted to gambling—and to sodomy, while China was commonly thought to be the source of cholera.

168. Arnold White, "Invasion of Pauper Foreigners," 417, 418, 422. Emphasis added.

169. Much precedent for mob violence directed against the "Other" can of course be found in early gothic: the parricide who is pulled to pieces by the enraged crowd in *Melmoth* (256) and the evil prioress who is hounded down in *The Monk* (356). And in *The Wandering Jew*, we find Dagobert's tale of French peasants, "pitchforks, stones, mattocks" in hand, who rush upon Prussian soldiers separated from their units: "It was a true wolf-hunt!" (33).

170. Marigny, *Le Vampire*, 1: 394–95, 2: 590–91.

171. Sue, *Wandering Jew*, 69. Compare with Groom Napier's observation in 1870 that the vampire bats of South America were like priests who suck the juices of the state (*Book of Nature*, 264).

172. Stoker, *Dracula*, 56.

173. Ibid., 415.

174. Stade, "Dracula's Women," 204, has written of "the paradox of the primitive" in the vampire legend.

175. Leatherdale, *Dracula*, 176.

176. *Dracula*, 280.

177. Arata, "Occidental Tourist," 623, 630.

178. *Dracula*, 31.

179. Schloss, "Jew as a Workman," 104.

180. Pearson, *National Minorities*, 98.

181. See Evans, *Death in Hamburg*.

182. Drage, "Alien Immigration," 41.

183. Arnold White, *Modern Jew*, xvi, 3–4.

184. Wilkins, *Alien Invasion*, 39, 95.

185. In his apologia for the Jewish workman, David Schloss felt a need to associate the Jew, against popular opinion, with Mendoza the pugilist, and to deny that the Jewish physique was naturally one of "narrow chests and limp limbs" ("Jew as Workman," 47).

186. Arnold White, *Modern Jew*, 279.

187. *Lloyd's Weekly Newspaper*, 7 Oct. 1888.

188. Dew, *I Caught Crippen*, 125.

189. Gilman, *Jew's Body*, 113–19. Also see Walkowitz, "Jack the Ripper," 542–74, and *City of Dreadful Delight*, ch. 7.

190. X. L. [Julien Osgood Field], *Aut diabolus aut nihil*, 145–226.

191. Ibid., 153–54, 156, 177–78, 225.

192. Stoker, "Censorship of Fiction," 485–86.

193. Stoker, *Snake's Pass*, 59.

194. Sue, *Wandering Jew*, 1.

195. Three of Bram Stoker's brothers in fact studied medicine.

196. J. B. Bailey, *Diary of a Resurrectionist* (1896), cited by Richardson, *Death, Dissection and the Destitute*, 62.

197. Arata, "Occidental Tourist," 640.

198. Halasz, *Captain Dreyfus*, 121.

199. Ellmann, *Oscar Wilde*, 449n.

Chapter 4

1. See Twitchell, *Living Dead*, ix.

2. In *Les Fleurs du Mal* of 1857, Baudelaire vividly anticipates the vampire as a gothic female threat; see "Les Métamorphoses du vampire" (one of the pieces removed by the censor). Also see Praz, *Romantic Agony*, 218–20.

3. Patrick Brantlinger has argued that Captain Marryat's adventure novels are themselves a kind of early-Victorian percursor of later "imperial gothic," focusing as they often do on the carnage of warfare—the violent dissection of bodies— and savages who can only be half-civilized (*Rule of Darkness*, 63–64).

4. Florence Marryat, *Blood of the Vampire*, 3–4. I am indebted to Dr. Alex Warwick for drawing my attention to this work.

5. Ibid., 26.

6. Ibid., 37–38.

7. "One tenet of the professional psychiatry developing in the nineteenth century was the conviction that insanity could be fearsomely latent, biding its time, and visible only to the expert diagnostic gaze of the alienist," Roy Porter has observed (*Mind-Forg'd Manacles*, 35). The resonance of such views of the "latent" dangers of a "buried" mental instability with those of the hidden dangers of "bad blood" are obvious.

8. Florence Marryat, *Blood of the Vampire*, 120.

9. Ibid., 121–22.

10. Ibid.

11. Ibid., 139.

12. Ibid., 152.

13. Ibid., 298. Emphasis in the original.

14. Ibid., 267.

15. Ibid., 345.

16. Lorimer, "Bibles, Banjoes and Bones," 38; also Arbery, "Victims of Likeness," 60.

17. Anicet Bourgeois and Dumanoir, *Black Doctor*.

18. See, e.g., the review in the London literary magazine *The Athenaeum* of John Biggs's novel *The History of Jim Crow* in 1840. It deplores the theme of interracial union as "one of the signs of the times," and regrets that in such popular representations, the black man "is no longer a nigger, but a gentleman of colour, a favourite low comedian, the hero of a novel, and a jet ornament to society" (no. 640 [1 Feb. 1840], 94–95).

19. Although Reid, like other writers of the genre, preferred Red Indian/white crosses to mulattoes. Especially doubtful in his fiction were Negro/Spanish mixed bloods, like the innately cruel "Yellow Jake" of *Oçeola*. Reid was Robert Louis Stevenson's favorite boyhood author (Steele, *Captain Mayne Reid*, 9).

20. The Feringhees of Bengal were a long-established community of Portuguese and Indian mixture.

21. Sue, *Wandering Jew*, 123, 369.

22. Maturin, *Melmoth*, 337.

23. Zanger, "'Tragic Octoroon,'" 67. Also see Roach, "Slave Spectacles," 167–87.

24. Enkvist, "*Octoroon*," 166–70, argues that the change in sentiment, contrasting with the enormous public approval of *Uncle Tom's Cabin* a decade earlier, was a result of English sympathy for the Southern cause in the American Civil War.

25. Hulme, *Colonial Encounters*, 46–47.

26. Hyam, *Empire and Sexuality*, 5.

27. See Adams, "Woman Red," 7–27.

28. Shelley, *Frankenstein*, 210–11.

29. *Report of Proceedings*, ix.

30. Chancellor Harper of South Carolina, on race mixing in the 1830's, quoted by Genovese, *Roll, Jordan, Roll*, 420.

31. Whitman, "Half-Breed," 258, 272, 291.

32. Martineau, *Society in America*, 2: 320, 328–29.

33. Arbousset and Daumas, *Narrative* (also published in London in 1852), 9.

34. See, e.g., Henriques, *Children of Caliban*, ix. Ronald Hyam has reminded us that as late as the 1920's, military men were three or four times as likely to contract a sexually transmitted disease in India and Ceylon as in English port and barracks towns, which themselves offered no lack of sexual opportunity. The highest rate he records is that in Bengal, where between 1889 and 1892, 522/1,000 British soldiers were treated for venereal disease (Hyam, *Empire and Sexuality*, 89, 126).

35. Hyam, *Empire and Sexuality*, 201. Except, significantly, as we shall see, in the West Indies and Canada.

36. Ibid., 98.

37. Both were accidental peers—that is, distant cousins who unexpectedly inherited titles; neither ever came to England to confirm their inheritance, and in both cases the succession was contested in England by rival claimants. See Cokayne, *Complete Peerage*.

38. Hyam, *Empire and Sexuality*, 201–15.

39. The *Oxford English Dictionary* offers as its earliest citation of *half-breed* a 1775 source, and for *half-caste* one of 1789.

40. Bowring, *Visit to the Philippine Islands*, 109.

41. Undoubtedly, there was some evidence of lower fertility in some cross-race unions, but this can be explained, for instance, by the venereal and other infections that white men communicated to native women, as well as by social factors, such as abortion or destruction of infants, likely to be stigmatized by both white and black communities.

42. For instance, in 1884 J. Hawthorne described the "strange" custom of mere cobblers and tinkers occupying workshops in the lower floors of palaces, "and similar miscegenations," in ancient Rome (from *Nathaniel Hawthorne and Wife*, 2: 178; quoted in the *Oxford English Dictionary*).

43. Paul Broca finally inherited the dissected genitalia of "the Hottentot Venus," as well as her skeleton—both of which he donated, along with his own brain, to the Musée de l'Homme in Paris (Gould, *Flamingo's Smile*, 291–92).

44. Broca, *On the Phenomena of Hybridity*, 6, 29, 39–40.

45. See Porter and Russell, "Social Biology of Werewolves," 151, 146, and Marryat, *Phantom Ship*, 339–57.

46. Baring-Gould, *Book of Were-Wolves*, xii. The project apparently dried up.

47. Ibid., 6–7. Emphasis added.

48. Ibid., 250–51.

49. Ibid., 6–7.

50. Ibid., 132.

51. Ibid., 133.

52. Ibid., 138.

53. Ibid., 142–43.

54. See Julia Briggs, *Night Visitors*, 20–21.

55. *The Times*, 11 Nov. 1865.

56. See, e.g., Stocking, *Victorian Anthropology*.

57. Knox, *Races of Men*, 497. Also see Biddiss, "Politics of Anatomy."

58. W. Cooke Taylor, *Natural History*, 1: 30.

59. Emerson, Journal 36 (1845), published in Emerson and Emerson, eds., *Journals*, 7: 115–16.

60. See Stepan, "Biological Degeneration."

61. See Nicoloff, *Emerson*, 129.

62. Quoted by Himmelfarb, *Darwin*, 415.

63. As late as 1844, Mrs Flannagan noted in her travel book about Antigua cases of albino Negroes: "One, in particular, of the appropriate name of 'Wonder' . . . astonished all who beheld him. He was said to be as repelling in temper as he was in person" (*Antigua*, 2: 148).

64. [Parsons], "An Account," 483–85. This was copied from *Philosophical Transactions*, vol. 55.

65. Lewis, *Journal*, 74.

66. See Hulme, *Colonial Encounters*, 227, for the eighteenth-century cult of the romance of Inkle the Englishman and Yarico the Indian girl who saves him but whom he sells into slavery.

67. Lewis, *Journal*, 66–67.

68. Ibid., 70–71.

69. Ibid., 281.

70. Ibid., 94–95.

71. Ibid.

72. Arbousset and Daumas, *Narrative*, 10.

73. Lewis, *Journal*, 278.

74. "Maceo and His Race," 892–93 (italics added).

75. Greenblatt, *Marvellous Possessions*, 140–41.

76. De Lery, *History*, 128, 132.

77. See Brain, *Decorated Body*, 58–59.

78. Darwin, *Journal*, 388, 404–5.

79. Polack, *Manners and Customs*, 2: 44n.

80. Ibid., 2: 43–44.

81. *A Narrative*, 70–71.

82. Polack, *Manners and Customs*, 2: 46.

83. Hearn, "West Indian Society," 340.

84. Earle, *Narrative*, 49–50.

85. By 1830 there were at least 74 Aboriginal women living with sealers in Bass Strait. That year the government sent George Augustus Robinson "to rescue the Aboriginal women. He regarded all Europeans in the Strait as fugitives from the law and all Aboriginal women associated with them as their slaves" (Ryan, *Aboriginal Tasmanians*, 71).

86. Hughes, *Fatal Shore*, 332–33.

87. Unsigned memo on Bass Strait sealing to Lieutenant Governor Arthur, 29 May 1826, cited by Hughes. Ironically, though, it was Lord Sydney himself who, in the original plan of settlement in 1786, envisioned the capturing of native women from the South Pacific islands for the purpose of what he regarded as a necessary and healthful concubinage that would preserve the settlement from "gross irregularities [sodomy] and disorders" (ibid., 245).

88. Quoted by Hughes, *Fatal Shore*, 573.

89. Meredith, *Notes and Sketches*, cited by Hughes, *Fatal Shore*, 342.

90. Savage, *Some Account*, 91–92.

91. Ibid., 90.

92. Cruise, *Journal*, 288–90.

93. Although he admits that they deny this and that, in general, the New Zealanders were "very fond" of their children. But then, he also is ready to accept stories of the cannibalization of children (ibid., 110–12, 288–90).

94. A quarter of a century later, it was still claimed that the low survival rate in New Zealand reflected, not the European diseases introduced by the sailors, but a strategy of infanticide ([Chapman?], "Polynesians," 461).

95. Flannagan, *Antigua*, Vol. 2: 93.

96. Shortland, *Southern Districts*.

97. Ibid., 67, 77–78, 114–15.

98. Thomson, *Story of New Zealand*.

99. Ibid., 1: 74.

100. Ibid., 2: 289.

101. Ibid., 305–7.

102. Compare Thomson's picture with, e.g., the cover illustration of H. A. Stark's defense of the Indian half-caste, *Hostages to India*.

103. Quoted by Ryan, *Aboriginal Tasmanians*, 236.

104. Hyam, *Empire and Sexuality*, 115–16.

105. Ibid., 200.

106. Ballhatchet, *Race, Sex and Class*, 98.

107. Huggins, *Sketches*, 83–84. Huggins was an indigo planter in Tirbut.

108. Sir John Shore, quoted in *The Indo-Briton*, 132, 139, 141.

109. Sir Ashley Eden, Address at St. Xavier's College, Dec. 1878, quoted by Thomas Edwards, "Eurasians," 38.

110. See, e.g., Digby, "Eurasians of Ceylon," 173–74.

111. For recent scholarship on the Jews of India—the Cochin Jews of the Malabar Coast, the Bene Israel of western India, and the Baghdadi (or Iraqi) Jews of Bombay and Calcutta—see Roland, *Jews in British India* and Isenberg, *India's Bene Israel*.

112. There were probably well under 20,000 Jews in India by the end of the nineteenth century. The census of 1891 counted just over 17,000. Cited by Lord, *Jewish Mission Field*, 1–2.

113. Roland, *Jews in British India*, 14, 17, 22.

114. Bruce, *Letters*, 47–49.

115. Although it is the degeneracy of the Asian-Jewish mixture that is insisted upon here, the image of the Jew was infinitely serviceable and emerges as "evidence" on both sides of the "race-mixing" debate. In the 1870's, for instance, Surgeon-General W. J. Moore, in his eccentric defense of the Indo-British (but not the Indo-Portuguese) community, cited the ancient Jewish race (along with Gypsies) as evidence for both the social and biological disadvantages of exclusivity: "By keeping to themselves they [the Jews] have been hated and despised, and as a distinct nation are dying out" ("Eurasian Future," 487).

116. Huggins, *Sketches in India*, 85–91. Although, citing Prichard, he believed generally in the biological advantages of racial amalgamation in India, Moore thought that the Portuguese-Indian cross had failed because of insufficient "renewal" of the European blood ("Eurasian Future," 503).

117. "Feringhees of Chittagong," 82, 86.

118. "Percival's *Account*," 139.

119. "Feringhees of Chittagong," 88.

120. Cited by Davies, "Miscegenation Theme," 328. Thackeray's father had taken a native mistress in India and had a daughter there, for whom he provided in his will.

121. Thomas Edwards, "Eurasians," 40–41.

122. See *The Indo-Briton*, 145–46.

123. Lee, ed., *Guide*, 4. The idea of a return to the soil, "colonization" of less-populated parts of India, along the lines of a familiar nineteenth-century utopianism, was not new in the Eurasian community. See Fenwick, *Essay*.

124. Thurston, "Eurasians," 69–114; also see the critical review in the *Anglo-Indian Journal* (Bombay), 1, 13 (Oct. 1898): 3.

125. Significantly, perhaps, the professional tattooers whom Thurston interviewed were females, and of a Gypsylike tribe notorious, he claims, for robbing and begging. The first woman he questioned "arrived in a state of maudlin intoxication" (Thurston, "Note on Tattooing," 115–18).

126. Ibid., 78–79.

127. *The Lancet* (1 Apr. 1899), 929–30. With an unintended significance, these observations on the half-caste are immediately followed by a report on the progress of the plague in India. The Bombay death rate for the past year stood at only 5/1,000 for the European population, but at 96/1,000 for the Eurasian, while low-caste Hindus suffered an estimated 250/1,000 (930).

128. *Anglo-Indian Journal*, 1, 1 (Oct. 1897): 1 (emphasis added). The *Journal* was a pro-Eurasian organ, and its editor admonished such behavior as likely to lay the half-caste community "open to the charges of cowardice, untruthfulness and disloyalty."

129. Kincaid, *British Social Life in India*, 220.

130. Ibid.

131. Charles Forgett, superintendent of police in Bombay, Colonel Hearsey of Calcutta, and General Henry Charles Van Cortlandt in the Punjab were types of Indo-Briton as hero who "spoke their [the Indian] language like themselves, and knew them better than themselves" (Holmes, of Hearsey, *History*, 87–88).

132. Quoted by Anthony, *Britain's Betrayal*, 86. Canning also warned, however, that left to themselves, the Eurasians might form a "floating population" that would exhibit "the worst qualities of both races" and become perhaps in the long run "a class dangerous to the state" (quoted by Thomas Edwards, "Eurasians," 48).

133. In Ballhatchet, *Race, Sex and Class*, 100.

134. Moore, "Eurasian Future," 502–3. Spokesmen for the Eurasian community continued to express this wishful view well into the twentieth century.

135. Hope, *Story*, 38.

136. Stark, *Call of the Blood*, 2–5. See also *Hostages to India*, 137, and Anthony, *Britain's Betrayal*, 5.

137. Fitchett, *Tales*, 52–53 (emphasis added).

138. *Parliamentary Papers*, sess. 1832, "Report of the Select Committee (House of Commons) on the Affairs of the East India Company," Appendix (Minute of Sir J. Malcolm, 10 Oct. 1829), 532.

139. Bruce, *Eurasian*, 91.

140. Paxton, "Mobilizing Chivalry," 5–30.

141. Quoted in ibid., 8.

142. See, e.g., Knapman, *White Women*.

143. Thurston, "Eurasians," 77.

144. "Aleph Bey" was a common pseudonym. The author is identified, however, as "an European long resident in India."

145. Bruce began his literary career in the early 1890's with biographical studies drawn from American history (a *Life of General Ogelthorpe* [1890] and a *Life of General Houston, 1793–1863* [1891]). In the Edwardian period, he followed a visit of some months to India with a travel memoir (*Letters from Malabar and on the Way* [1909]), and subsequently turned to writing highly sensational novels, mostly about the Raj (*The Native Wife; or, Indian Love and Anarchism: A Novel* [1909]; *The Residency: An Indian Novel* [1914]; *The Song of Surrender: An Indian Novel* [1915]; *The Temple Girl: An Indian Story* [1919]; *Bride of Shive* [1920]).

146. Bruce, *Eurasian*, 90.

147. Ibid., 206.

148. Ibid., 217.

149. Ibid., 234, 243–45. In Kipling's well-known tale of miscegenation, "Without Benefit of Clergy" (1890), the "impossibility" of such race-mixing is confirmed in the death of both native mother and half-caste child, and the washing away of their mud-brick house by an angry deluge.

150. Ibid., 320.

151. In fact, G. O. Trevelyan's "history of horrors," *Cawnpore*, was published the same year (1865) that the Jamaican rebellion broke out. The best treatment of the Jamaican rebellion and its aftermath in England is still Semmel, *Governor Eyre Controversy*.

152. See Holt, *Problem of Freedom*, 298.

153. *The Times*, 13 and 17 Nov. 1865.

154. Ibid., 13 Nov. 1865.

155. Ibid., 18 and 20 Nov. 1865.

156. Ibid., 17 Nov. 1865.

157. Quoted by Semmell, *Governor Eyre Controversy*, 89, 102–3.

158. Finlason, *History of the Jamaica Case*, vi.

159. *The Times*, 23 Nov. 1865.

160. Ibid., 20 Nov. 1865. Emphasis added.

161. Sensational stories of the killing of women and children, and particularly that of the Cawnpore massacre, provided a rich source of racial gothic. See Mukherjee, "'Satan Let Loose,'" 92–116.

162. *The Times*, 16 Nov. 1865.

163. Ibid., 20 Nov. 1865.

164. Carlyle, no friend of the Negro in Jamaica, called Gordon an "incendiary mulatto" and a "half-brutish type" (quoted by Semmel, *Governor Eyre Controversy*, 106, 107).

165. Eyre's dispatch of 20 October, published in *The Times*, 20 Nov. 1865.

166. Ibid., 16 Dec. 1865.

167. Quoted by Genovese, *Roll, Jordan, Roll*, 418.

168. Fowler, *Northern Attitudes*, 233ff.

169. Williamson, *New People*, 3–6, 86–87.

170. "Miscegenation," 116–21; Arbery, "Victims of Likeness," 53.

171. Semmell, *Governor Eyre Controversy*, 85.

172. Napier, "Notes on Mulattoes"; Sir William Lawrence, *Lectures on Physiology, Zoology, and the Natural History of Man* (London: Smith, 1822), 200–204, cited by Stepan, "Biological Degeneration," 107.

173. Even the French anthropologist Quatrefages, who, unlike Broca, took a strongly positive view of the physical and mental characteristics of mixed-race people, contrasted these merits with contradictory vices: the half-breed is "almost everywhere indolent, passionate, and addicted to gaming, *always ready to foment civil discord* [emphasis added]" (Quatrefages, "Formation of the Mixed Human Races," 24).

174. Napier, "Notes on Mulattoes," lvii–lx. Napier, *Book of Nature*, 417. Also see C. L. Miller, *Blank Darkness*, for Baudelaire's sense of the feminine beauty of male Creole writers and their "women's souls" (95).

175. If Groom saw half-breeds as metaphoric (or actual) homosexuals, Edward Carpenter later (in *The Intermediate Sex*) turned this about, and portrayed homosexuals as "half-breeds" of the Inner Self (cited in S. Somerville, "Scientific Racism," 259).

176. Whitman, "Half-Breed," 272; Parkman, *The Oregon Trail* (1849), quoted by Scheick, *Half-Blood*, 18.

177. Riel's paternal grandmother was half Chipewyan.

178. Wolseley, 21 Aug. 1870, in George, ed., *Letters*, 5. For the story of both of the Riel rebellions, see George F. G. Stanley's standard history, *Birth of Western Canada*, and his *Louis Riel*.

179. Wolseley had seen service in the second Burma war, the Crimea, the Indian Mutiny, and China, but it was the Red River expedition that brought him

to the public's, and the government's, attention. He was rewarded with a knighthood and made an assistant adjutant general in the War Office.

180. John E. Foster, "Origins of the Mixed Bloods," 71.

181. Van Kirk, "'Custom of the Country,'" 56–64.

182. A. P. Reid, "Mixed or 'Halfbreed' Races," 46.

183. Parkman, *California and Oregon Trail*, 93.

184. Wolseley, *Story of a Soldier's Life*, 2: 206. Curiously, one can find a similar opposition in the French novelist "Gustav Aimard" [I. E. Olivier Gloux], whose Anglo-Indian half-breed, "Cherokee Bill" is the heroic protagonist, while the French-Indian half-breeds, or "Bois-Brûlés," are little better than malignant Crow renegades (*Red River Half-Breed*, 38 and passim).

185. Ballhatchet, *Race, Sex and Class*, 99; Jeal, *Livingstone*, 153–54. Also see Rowley, "Slavery," who retells the familiar story of the rebel slaver Mariano, "a barbarous despot . . . [who] indulged in the unrestrained use of his passions and temper, and gave way to the wickedest caprices that his reckless vanity, gross nature, unchecked authority and green age suggested" (200–201).

186. Whitman, "Half-Breed," 272.

187. Newman, *Company of Adventurers*, 2: 157n.

188. Keating, *Narrative*, 79–80.

189. *Hansard*, Commons, 3d ser., vol. 201, cols. 1089–90, 20 May 1870.

190. Aimard, *Red River Half-Breed*, 8–11.

191. Newman, *Company of Adventurers*, 2: 175.

192. Ross, *Red River Settlement*, 168.

193. Ibid., 79–80.

194. Ibid., 242.

195. Van Kirk, "'What if Mama is an Indian?'"

196. Ross, *Fur Hunters*, 1: 298.

197. Ibid., 289–91.

198. Hearn, *Two Years*, 329, 332, 332n.

199. Ibid., 329.

200. See, e.g., the American James Ross Browne's story "A Dangerous Journey," where a half-blood woman is both seductress and murderess, a "devil incarnate" (*Crusoe's Island*, 240).

201. On the ambivalence of Ross, also see Scheick, *Half-Blood*, 3–4.

202. *Red River*, 169.

203. Newman, *Company of Adventurers*, 3: 42–52. The news of Scott's execution was published in the Toronto *Globe* and the Montreal *Herald* on 26 Mar. 1870; there followed a vigorous press campaign for "vengeance and retribution" (G. F. G. Stanley, *Louis Riel*, 136).

204. *The Times*, 25 Jan. 1870.

205. Ibid., 27 Jan. 1870.

206. Wolseley, *Story of a Soldier's Life*, 2: 172–73.

207. Ibid., 169.

208. G. F. G. Stanley, *Louis Riel*, 116–17.

209. *Hansard*, Commons, 3d ser., vol. 201, cols. 1093–94, 20 May 1870.

210. Arnstein, *Protestant Versus Catholic*, 127–41.

211. *The Times*, 17 Nov. 1885.

212. Reported in ibid., 18 May 1885.

213. A. P. Reid, "Mixed or 'Halfbreed' Races," 47.

214. *The Times*, 18 May and 17 Nov. 1885.

215. Quoted in Brown, *Strangers in Blood*, 179.

216. Quoted in ibid., 188–89.

217. Livingstone, *Missionary Travels*, 442.

218. Belich, *New Zealand Wars*, 316.

219. Cowan, *Kimble Bent*, vii–ix.

220. Poe, *Narrative*, 85 and passim.

221. Cowan, *Kimble Bent*, vii–ix, 7–8.

222. Crowder, *Senegal*, 10.

223. Wolseley, 17 Oct. 1873, in George, ed., *Letters*, 12.

224. Wolseley, 4 Nov. 1873, in ibid., 14. For his low opinion of the Jamaican regiment, see Wolseley, *Story of a Soldier's Life*, 2: 258.

225. Wolseley, *Story of a Soldier's Life*, 2: 291.

226. Ibid., 357.

227. Reade, *Savage Africa*, 58, 142, 271, 274.

228. Burton, *Wanderings*, 1: 271.

229. Brantlinger, *Rule of Darkness*, 54, 227–49.

230. See, e.g., Arata, "Occidental Tourist," and McBratney, "Lovers Beyond the Pale," and "Imperial Subjects." Although not interested in the gothic per se, Green's *Dreams of Adventure* and Street's *Savage in Literature* are valuable precursors to much of this work.

231. Showalter, *Sexual Anarchy*; Jordanova, *Sexual Visions*; Harris, *Murders and Madness*; and Walkowitz, *City of Dreadful Delight*.

232. See, e.g., Street, *Savage in Literature*, 101–4, and McBratney, "Lovers Beyond the Pale," passim.

233. Macdonald, "Discourse."

234. Kipling, "Beyond the Pale," 147.

235. Stevenson's elemental evil, Mr. Hyde, for instance, may indeed suggest contemporary psychological theories of multiple personalities, or, more allusively, homosexual "rough trade" and male "self-begetting," as Elaine Showalter has argued (*Sexual Anarchy*, 76, and ch. 6 passim) or a contemporary panic over lower-class street crime in London, but beneath all of this there is the reading suggested by David Punter and Patrick Brantlinger—of Hyde, whose apelike appearance demands a racial recognition, as a kind of "going native" or the degenerative effect of "race mixing" or at least a buried trace of past evolution, the "primitive" in the European himself (Punter, *Literature of Terror*, 239–40; Brantlinger and Boyle, "Education of Edward Hyde," 265–82; Brantlinger, *Rule of Darkness*, 232–33).

236. Punter, *Literature of Terror*, 252–53.

237. Showalter, "Apocalyptic Fables," 70.

238. Wells, "Pollock and the Porroh Man."

239. Mackay, *Violent Friend*, 282.

240. Quoted by Sanchez, *Life of Mrs. Robert Louis Stevenson*, 149.

241. RLS had visited a leper colony on the island of Molokai and wrote letters to Fanny in Samoa about his experiences there (Mackay, *Violent Friend*, 281–82).

242. Fanny Van de Grift Stevenson, "Half-White," 282–88.

243. Linden, "Half-Caste," 19–26.

244. His first wife Kate Reedon's genealogy is unclear in the sources I have seen—*Who Was Who* for 1926, where she is simply described as a "Creole," and obituaries in the Georgetown press.

245. Murray, *Fantastic Journey*, 40–41.

246. Hearn, "Study," 167–72.

247. *Two Years in the West Indies*, 219.

248. Ibid., 331–32.

249. Rodway, *In Guiana Wilds*, 18–19, 30–33.

250. Ibid., 77.

251. Ibid., 135.

252. Ibid., 141.

253. Murray, *Fantastic Journey*, 42, 44.

254. *In Guiana Wilds*, 141.

255. Rodway, *In the Guiana Forest*, 324; Murray, *Fantastic Journey*, 44, 143; Hearn, "West Indian Society," 339. Hearn was clearly intimidated by strong-willed women, one reason, presumably, why his marriage to the assertive Mattie collapsed so quickly. In 1884 he wrote that "you are afraid even to think of sex with" the "magnificent type of womanhood" one associated with the "Northern Races" (cited by Murray, 43–44).

256. Rodway, *Guiana: British, Dutch and French*, 158–59, cited by Rodney, *History*, 201.

257. Rodway, "Up a Creek," 600 (emphasis added).

Epilogue

1. Shephard, "Showbiz Imperialism," 94–112. On the general topic of public exhibitions, see Brain, *Going to the Fair*; on exhibition and empire, see Greenhalgh, *Ephemeral Vistas*, 52–81.

2. *Morning Post*, 8 Aug. 1899.

3. Salter, *East in the West*, 143–49. Robert Brain has drawn attention to the parading of African blacks in "showcases of empire" at international exhibitions: West Africans were on view in Paris in 1887 and 1889, and Dahomey villagers played a part at the Chicago Columbian Exposition of 1893 (*Going to the Fair*, 138–39, 144, 172–86).

4. *Church Family Newspaper*, 11 Aug. 1899.

5. *Globe*, 6 May 1899; *Morning Post*, 8 Aug. 1899; *Morning Advertiser*, 11 Aug. 1899; *Standard*, 7 Aug. 1899; *Reynold's Newspaper*, 6 Aug. 1899.

6. *Morning Advertiser*, 11 Aug. 1899; *Church Family Newspaper*, 11 Aug. 1899.

7. An angry review of "Savage South Africa" and Loben's marriage plans, titled "The Earl's Court Scandal," was published in the *Critic*, in an issue dated 5 Aug., although in fact this appeared on 9 Aug., the delay being caused by the Bank Holiday. The *Evening News* attacked the marriage the next day, and the *Daily Mail*'s first attack appeared on 11 Aug., to be followed the day after by a more sustained assault, similarly titled "The Black Scandal."

8. *Pall Mall Gazette*, 11 Aug. 1899; *Morning Herald*, 11 Aug. 1899; *Sun*, 10 Aug. 1899.

9. *Morning Herald*, 14 Aug. 1899; *Star*, 12 Aug. 1899.

10. *Evening News*, 12 Aug. 1899.

11. *Morning Leader*, 16 Aug. 1899.

12. *Critic*, 5 [i.e. 9] Aug. 1899.

13. What the real Kitty Jewell may have been is, and was then, obscure. She was constructed in the press, however, as independent and propertied.

14. Walkowitz, *City of Dreadful Delight*, 566; "The Black Scandal," *Daily Mail*, 17 Aug. 1899.

15. *Critic*, 5 [9] Aug. 1899. Emphasis added.

16. *Daily Mail*, 11 Aug. 1899.

17. *Morning Leader*, 14 Aug. 1899.

18. *South Africa*, 26 Aug. 1899.

19. Charles White, *An Account of The Regular Gradation in Man* (1799), 58–59, quoted by Gossett, *Race*, 48.

20. Hyam, *Empire and Sexuality*, 204–5.

21. In fact, the "native" setting in which they were confined would in southern Africa have been a particularly female arena; Zulu and Swazi males would have found it demeaning to cook meals and hang around the huts.

22. Although the vicinity of Earl's Court was generally one of fashionable prosperity, it was bordered to the west and southwest by much shabbier streets and pockets of extreme poverty, areas colored by Charles Booth's survey in blacks and blues, which contrast sharply with the bright reds and yellows of most of the area (Booth, *Life and Labour*, map, southwest London).

23. James Tobin, *Cursory Remarks on the Reverend Mr. Ramsay's Essay on the Treatment and Conversion of African Slaves in the Sugar Colonies* (1785), 118n, as quoted by Hecht, *Continental and Colonial Servants in Eighteenth-Century England*, 47.

24. *London City Mission Magazine* 22 (Aug. 1857), 217, quoted by Lorimer, *Colour, Class and the Victorians*, 41.

25. Lindeborg, "The 'Asiatic' and the Boundaries of Victorian Englishness," 382, 388, citing Joseph Salter (London City Missionary), *The Asiatic in England: Sketches of Sixteen Years' Work Among Orientals* (1873), 29, and *East in the West*, 24.

26. *Daily Chronicle*, 10 Sept. 1888.

27. *Morning Leader*, 14 Aug. 1899.

28. Ibid., 16 Aug. 1899.

29. *Critic*, 5 [9] Aug. 1899.

30. *Daily Mail*, 18 and 19 Aug. 1899.

31. *South Africa*, 19 Aug. 1899.

32. *Vanity Fair*, 17 Aug. 1899, 111.

33. Shephard, "Showbiz Imperialism," 108.

34. *Vanity Fair*, 17 Aug. 1899.

35. "Lobengula's Marriage: Interview with the Bride," *Daily Graphic*, 12 Aug. 1899.

36. *Daily Mail*, 12 Aug. 1899; *Pall Mall Gazette*, 11 Aug. 1899.

37. *Morning Leader*, 14 Aug. 1899.

38. *Daily Graphic*, 12 Aug. 1899.

39. Both quotations are from *To-Day*, 17 Aug. 1899, which devoted a full page to the affair.

40. "Miscegenation," *Spectator*, 19 Aug. 1899, 245–46.

41. *Sun,* 11 Aug. 1899.

42. In August most of the papers assumed that Kitty Jewell was a woman of some property (with "rows of houses" in London). But, as Ben Shephard has shown, Loben had difficulty meeting arrears of rent only a year later (Shephard, "Showbiz Imperialism," 104). Whether this indicates that Jewell in fact had little means of her own, or that the couple had gone through her money, or whether they fell out, and she was no longer willing to support him, is unclear.

43. See Hirshfield, *"Reynold's Newspaper* and the Modern Jew."

44. *Graphic,* 19 Aug. 1899, 262; *To-Day,* 17 Aug. 1899, 81.

Bibliography

Books and Articles

Adams, James Eli. "Woman Red in Tooth and Claw: Nature and the Feminine in Tennyson and Darwin." *Victorian Studies* 33, 1 (Autumn 1989): 7–27.

Aimard, Gustav [I. E. Olivier Gloux]. *The Red River Half-Breed: A Tale of the Wild North-West*. Trans. by H. L. Williams, of *Les Bois-Brûlés*, ed. Percy B. St. John. London: J. & R. Maxwell, n.d. (1876?).

Ainsworth, William Harrison. *Roockwood.* 1824. London: Bentley, 1834.

Alexander, Michael. *Mrs Fraser on the Fatal Shore*. London: Michael Joseph, 1971.

Anderson, G. K. "Popular Survivals of the Wandering Jew in England." In *The Wandering Jew*, ed. G. Hasan-Rokem and A. Dundes, 76–104. Bloomington: Indiana University Press, 1986.

Anicet Bourgeois, Auguste, and Philippe Françoise Pinel Dumanoir. *The Black Doctor: A Drama in Five Acts*. London: Lacy's Acting Edition, 1855.

Anthony, Frank. *Britain's Betrayal in India: The Story of the Anglo-Indian Community*. Bombay: Allied, 1969.

"The Apologists for Cannibalism." *Spectator*, 13 Sept. 1884, 1199.

Arata, Stephen D. "The Occidental Tourist: Dracula and the Anxiety of Reverse Colonization." *Victorian Studies* 33, 4 (Summer 1990): 621–46.

Arbery, Glenn Canon. "Victims of Likeness: Quadroons and Octoroons in Southern Fiction." *Southern Review* 25 (Winter 1989): 52–71.

Arbousset, T., and F. Daumas. *Narrative of an Exploratory Tour to the North-East of the Colony of the Cape of Good Hope*. 1842. Trans. John Croumbie Brown. Cape Town: A. S. Robertson, 1846.

Arens, William. *The Man-Eating Myth: Anthropology and Anthropophagy*. Oxford: Oxford University Press, 1979.

Arnold, Matthew. "Curtius's History of Greece [1871]." In *Essays, Letters and Reviews*, ed. Fraser Neiman. Cambridge, Mass.: Harvard University Press, 1960.

Arnstein, Walter L. *Protestant Versus Catholic in Mid-Victorian England: Mr. Newdegate and the Nuns.* Columbia: University of Missouri Press, 1982.

"A Travelling Correspondent." "African Cannibals." *Saturday Review* 81 (30 May 1896): 544.

Aufrer[e], Anthony. *The Cannibal's Progress; or the Dreadful Horrors of French Invasion, as displayed by the Republican Officers and Soldiers, in their perfidy, rapacity, ferociousness and brutality, exercised towards the inhabitants of Germany.* London, 1798.

Baldick, Chris. *In Frankenstein's Shadow: Myth, Monstrosity, and Nineteenth-Century Writing.* Oxford: Clarendon Press, 1987.

Ballhatchet, Kenneth. *Race, Sex and Class Under the Raj: Imperial Attitudes and Policies and Their Critics, 1793–1905.* London: Weidenfeld & Nicolson, 1980.

"Banjo and Bones." *Saturday Review,* 7 June 1884.

Baring-Gould, Sabine. *The Book of Were-Wolves: Being an Account of a Terrible Superstition.* London: Smith, Elder, 1865.

Bate, Henry [Sir Henry Bate Dudley]. *Airs, Ballads, &c in "The Blackamoor Wash'd White."* London: Cox & Bigg, 1776.

Bates, Henry Walter. *The Naturalist on the River Amazons.* London: John Murray, 1863.

Belich, James. *The New Zealand Wars and the Victorian Interpretation of Racial Conflict.* Auckland: Auckland University Press, 1986.

Bell, Sir Charles. *Manuscript Drawings of the Arteries.* Ca. 1797. Meriden, Conn.: Meriden Gravure Co., for Editions Medicina Rara, n.d. (1979?).

Bentley, C. F. "The Monster in the Bedroom: Sexual Symbolism in Bram Stoker's *Dracula.*" In *"Dracula,"* ed. M. L. Carter (1988), 25–34. Reprinted from *Literature and Psychology,* 22, 1 (1972).

Bey, Aleph. *That Eurasian.* Chicago: F. Tennyson Neely, 1895.

Bhabha, Homi K. "The Other Question: Difference, Discrimination and the Discourse of Colonialism." In *Literature, Politics and Theory. Papers from the Essex Conference 1976–84,* ed. F. Barker, P. Hulme, M. Iverson, and D. Loxley, 148–72. London: Methuen, 1986.

Biddiss, M. D. "The Politics of Anatomy: Dr Robert Knox and Victorian Racism." *Proceedings of the Royal Society of Medicine* 69 (Apr. 1976): 245–50.

Bierman, Joseph S. "Dracula: Prolonged Childhood Illness and the Oral Triad." In *"Dracula,"* ed. M. L. Carter (1988), 51–55. Reprinted from *American Imago* 29 (1972).

———. "The Genesis and Dating of *Dracula* from Bram Stoker's Working Notes." *Notes and Queries* 222 (1977): 39–41.

Blunt, Wilfrid. *The Ark in the Park: The Zoo in the Nineteenth Century.* London: Hamish Hamilton, 1976.

Booth, Charles. *Life and Labour of the People in London.* First Series: *Poverty.* Vols. 1–4. London: Macmillan, 1902.

Boswell, James. *Life of Johnson.* 1791. Oxford: Oxford University Press, 1970.

Boucher, Philip. *Cannibal Encounters: Europeans and Island Caribs, 1492–1763.* Baltimore: Johns Hopkins University Press, 1992.

Bowker, James Henry, Dr. Bleek, and Dr. John Beddoe. "The Cave Cannibals of South Africa." *Anthropological Reivew* 7, 25 (Apr. 1869): 121–28.

Bowring, John. *A Visit to the Philippine Islands.* London: Smith, Elder, 1859.

Brain, Robert. *The Decorated Body.* London: Hutchinson, 1979.

———. *Going to the Fair: Readings in the Culture of Nineteenth-Century Exhibitions.* Cambridge: Whipple Museum of the History of Science, 1993.

Brannan, Robert Louis, ed. *Under the Management of Mr. Charles Dickens: His Production of "The Frozen Deep."* Ithaca, N.Y.: Cornell University Press, 1966.

Brantlinger, Patrick. *Rule of Darkness: British Literature and Imperialism, 1830–1914.* Ithaca, N.Y.: Cornell University Press, 1988.

———. "Victorians and Africans: The Genealogy of the Myth of the Dark Continent." *Critical Inquiry* 12 (Autumn 1985): 166–203.

Brantlinger, Patrick, and Richard Boyle. "The Education of Edward Hyde: Stevenson's 'Gothic Gnome' and the Mass Readership of Late-Victorian England." In *Dr Jekyll and Mr Hyde After One Hundred Years,* ed. W. Veeder and G. Hirsch, 265–82. Chicago: University of Chicago Press, 1988.

Bratton, J. S., ed. *Music Hall Performance and Style.* Milton Keynes, Eng.: Open University Press, 1986.

Brereton, Austin. *The Life of Henry Irving.* 1908. New York: Benjamin Blom, 1969.

Brewer, John. *The Common People and Politics, 1750–1790s.* London: Chadwyck-Healey, 1986.

Briggs, Julia. *Night Visitors: The Rise and Fall of the English Ghost Story.* London: Faber, 1977.

Briggs, Katherine M. *A Dictionary of British Folk-Tales in the English Language.* London: Routledge & Kegan Paul, 1970–71.

Broca, Paul. *On the Phenomena of Hybridity in the Genus Homo.* Ed. C. Carter Blake. London: Longman, 1864.

Brontë, Charlotte. *Jane Eyre.* 1847. London: Penguin Books, 1985.

Brontë, Emily. *Wuthering Heights.* 1847. London: Penguin Books, 1965.

Brown, Jennifer S. H. *Strangers in Blood: Fur Trade Company Families in Indian Country.* Vancouver: University of British Columbia Press, 1980.

Browne, J. Ross. *Crusoe's Island: A Ramble in the Footsteps of Alexander Selkirk with Sketches of Adventures in California and Washoe.* New York: Harper, 1864.

Browne, James A. *The North-West Passage and the Fate of Sir John Franklin.* Woolwich, Eng.: W. P. Jackson, 1860.

Bruce, Henry. *The Eurasian.* London: John Long, 1913.

———. *Letters from Malabar and on the Way.* London: Routledge, 1909.

Bunn, David. "Embodying Africa: Women and Romance in Colonial Fiction." *English in Africa* 15 (1988): 1–28.

Burke, Edmund. *The French Revolution.* London, 1790.

———. "First Letter on a Regicide Peace." 1796. In *The Writings and Speeches of Edmund Burke,* vol. 9, ed. R. B. McDowell. Oxford: Clarendon Press, 1991.

Burn, W. L. *The Age of Equipoise.* London: Unwin, 1968.

Burton, Richard F. "A Day Amongst the Fans." *Anthropological Review* 1, 1 (May 1863): 43–54.

———. *The Lake Regions of Central Africa.* London: Longman, Green, Longman & Roberts, 1860.

———. *Vikram and the Vampire; or, Tales of Hindu Devilry.* 1870. London, 1893.

————. *Wanderings in West Africa, from Liverpool to Fernando Po.* London: Tinsley Brothers, 1863.

Byers, Thomas B. "Good Men and Monsters: The Defenses of *Dracula.*" In *"Dracula,"* ed. M. L. Carter (1988), 149–57.

Caine, Hall. *My Story.* London: Heinemann, 1908.

————. *The Scapegoat: A Romance.* London: Heinemann, 1891.

Cairns, H. Alan C. *Prelude to Imperialism: British Reactions to Central African Society, 1840–1890.* London: Routledge & Kegan Paul, 1965.

Callow, Philip. *Walt Whitman: From Noon to Starry Night.* London: Allison & Busby, 1992.

Carlyle, Thomas. *Past and Present.* 1843. New York: Scribner's, 1897.

————. *Reminiscences of My Irish Journey in 1849.* London: Sampson Low, 1882.

————. *Sartor Resartus: The Life and Opinions of Herr Teufelsdrokh.* 1833–34. New York: Scribner's, 1899.

Carpenter, Edward. *The Intermediate Sex.* London: Swan Sonnenschein, 1908.

Carter, Margaret L., ed. *"Dracula": The Vampire and the Critics.* Ann Arbor, Mich.: UMI Research Press, 1988.

Chamberlain, J. Edward, and Sander L. Gilman, eds. *Degeneration: The Dark Side of Progress.* New York: Columbia University Press, 1985.

[Chapman, H. S.?] "The Polynesians: and New Zealand," *Edinburgh Review* 91 (Apr. 1850): 443–71.

Charnock, Richard Steven. "Cannibalism in Europe." *Anthropological Review* 4, 12 (Jan. 1866): xxii–xxxi.

Cheyette, Bryan. *Constructions of "The Jew" in English Literature and Society: Racial Representations, 1875–1945.* Cambridge: Cambridge University Press, 1993.

Childers, Joseph W. "Observation and Representation: Mr. Chadwick Writes the Poor." *Victorian Studies* 37, 3 (Spring 1994): 405–32.

Clarke, Marcus. *His Natural Life.* 1870. London: Penguin Books, 1970.

Cole, Hubert. *Things for the Surgeon: A History of the Resurrection Men.* London: Heinemann, 1964.

Colley, Linda. *Britons: Forging the Nation, 1707–1837.* London: Pimlico, 1992.

Conan Doyle, Arthur. "The Adventure of the Sussex Vampire." *The Case Book of Sherlock Holmes,* in *The Penguin Complete Sherlock Holmes.* London: Penguin Books, 1981.

Conrad, Joseph. "Falk: A Reminiscence." In *Typhoon and Other Stories.* London, 1903.

Corber, Robert J. "Representing the 'Unspeakable': William Godwin and the Politics of Homophobia." *Journal of the History of Sexuality* 1, 1 (1990): 85–101.

Corbin, Alain. "Commercial Sexuality in Nineteenth-Century France: A System of Images and Regulations." In *The Making of the Modern Body,* ed. C. Gallagher and T. Laqueur (1987), 209–19.

————. *The Foul and the Fragrant: Odor and the French Social Imagination.* Cambridge, Mass.: Harvard University Press, 1986.

————. *The Village of Cannibals: Rage and Murder in France, 1870.* Trans. Arthur Golhammer. Cambridge, Mass.: Harvard University Press, 1992.

Cowan, James. *The Adventures of Kimble Bent: A Story of Wild Life in the New Zealand Bush.* London: Whitcombe & Tombs, 1911.

Craft, Christopher. "'Kiss Me with Those Red Lips': Gender and Inversion in Bram Stoker's *Dracula*." In *"Dracula,"* ed. Carter (1988), 167–94. Reprinted from *Representations* 8 (1984).

———. *Another Kind of Love: Male Homosexual Desire in English Discourse, 1850–1920.* Berkeley: University of California Press, 1994.

Crowder, Michael. *Senegal: A Study of French Assimilation Policy.* Rev. ed. London: Methuen, 1967.

Cruise, Richard A. *Journal of a Ten Months' Residence in New Zealand.* London: Longman, 1823.

Curtin, Philip D. *The Image of Africa: British Ideas and Action, 1780–1850.* London: Macmillan, 1965.

Curtis, John. *Shipwreck of the Stirling Castle.* London: George Virtue, 1838.

Curtis, L. P., Jr. *Apes and Angels: The Irishman in Victorian Caricature.* Newton Abbot, Eng.: David & Charles, 1971.

———. *Anglo-Saxons and Celts: A Study of Anti-Irish Prejudice in Victorian England.* Bridgeport, Conn.: Conference on British Studies, 1968.

Dalby, Richard, comp. *Dracula's Brood.* London: Crucible, 1987.

Dampier, William. *Voyage Round the World.* 1688. London: James & John Knapton, 1729.

d'Argens, Jean Baptiste de Boyer, Marquis. *The Jewish Spy.* London: D. Browne, 1740.

Darko, Suvin. *Metamorphoses of Science Fiction.* New Haven, Conn.: Yale University Press, 1979.

Darnton, Robert. *The Great Cat Massacre and Other Episodes in French Cultural History.* New York: Vintage Books, 1985.

Darwin, Charles. *Journal of . . . the Beagle.* 1839. London: J. M. Dent [Everyman], 1906.

Davies, P. G. "The Miscegenation Theme in the Works of Thackeray." *Modern Language Notes* 76 (Apr. 1961): 326–31.

Davis, John. *Travels of Four Years and a Half in the United States of America; During 1798, 1799, 1800, 1801, and 1802.* London: Edwards, 1803.

De Groot, Joanna. "'Sex' and 'Race': The Construction of Language and Image in the Nineteenth Century." In *Sexuality and Subordination,* ed. S. Mendus and J. Rendall, (1989), 82–128.

De Lery, Jean. *History of a Voyage to the Land of Brazil, Otherwise Called America.* Trans. Janet Whatley. Berkeley: University of California Press, 1990.

Demetrakopoulos, Stephanie. "Feminism, Sex Role Exchanges, and Other Subliminal Fantasies in Bram Stoker's *Dracula*." *Frontiers* 2 (Fall 1977): 104–13.

Dening, Greg. *Mr Bligh's Bad Language: Passion, Power and Theatre on the Bounty.* Cambridge: Cambridge University Press, 1992.

———. *Islands and Beaches: Discourse on a Silent Land: Marquesas, 1774–1880.* Honolulu: University Press of Hawaii, 1980.

Desmond, Adrian. *The Politics of Evolution: Morphology, Medicine, and Reform in Radical London.* Chicago: University of Chicago Press, 1989.

Dew, Walter. *I Caught Crippen: Memoirs of Ex-Chief Inspector Walter Dew, C.I.D. of Scotland Yard.* London: Blackie & Son, 1938.

Dickens, Charles. *Bleak House.* 1853. London: Penguin Books, 1971.

———. *Great Expectations.* 1861. London: Penguin Books, 1965.

———. "The Lost Arctic Voyagers." *Household Words*, 2 and 9 December 1854.

———. *Our Mutual Friend*. 1864–65. London: Penguin Books, 1971.

———. *The Pickwick Papers*. 1836–37. New York: Dodd, Mead, 1944.

Digby, William. "The Eurasians of Ceylon." *Calcutta Review* 63, 125 (1876): 173–206.

Douglas, Mary. *Purity and Danger: An Analysis of the Concepts of Pollution and Taboo*. London: Routledge, 1966.

Drage, Geoffrey. "Alien Immigration." *Fortnightly Review*, n.s., 57 (1 Jan. 1895): 37–46.

Duffy, Michael. *The Englishman and the Foreigner*. The English Satirical Print, 1600–1832. Cambridge: Chadwyck-Healey, 1986.

Durey, Michael. *The Return of the Plague: British Society and the Cholera, 1831–2*. Dublin: Gill & Macmillan, 1979.

Dyer, Richard. "Children of the Night: Vampirism as Homosexuality, Homosexuality as Vampirism." In *Sweet Dreams*, ed. Radstone (1988), 47–72.

Dykes, Eva Beatrice. *The Negro in English Romantic Thought; or, A Study of Sympathy for the Oppressed*. Washington, D.C.: Associated Publishers, 1942.

Earle, Augustus. *A Narrative of a Nine Months' Residence in New Zealand, in 1827*. London: Longman, 1832.

Edwards, Bryan. *The History, Civil and Commercial, of the British Colonies in the West Indies*. Dublin: Luke White, 1793.

Edwards, Thomas. "Eurasians and Poor Europeans in India." *Calcutta Review* 72, 143 (1881): 38–56.

Eliot, George. *Middlemarch*. 1872. London: Penguin Books, 1965.

Ellis, William. *Polynesian Researches, During a Residence of Nearly Six Years in the South Sea Islands*. London: Fisher, Son, & Jackson, 1829.

Ellmann, Richard. *Oscar Wilde*. London: Penguin Books, 1988.

Emerson, Ralph Waldo. *Journals of Ralph Waldo Emerson*. Ed. Ralph Edward Emerson and Forbes Emerson. Boston: Houghton Mifflin, 1912.

Enkvist, Nils Erik. "The *Octoroon* and English Opinions of Slavery." *American Quarterly* 8 (Summer 1956): 166–70.

Evans, Richard J. *Death in Hamburg*. Oxford: Oxford University Press, 1987.

Fancher, R. E. "Francis Galton's African Ethnography and Its Role in the Development of his Psychology." *British Journal of the History of Science* 16 (Mar. 1983): 67–79.

Farson, Daniel. *The Man Who Wrote Dracula: A Biography of Bram Stoker*. London: Michael Joseph, 1975.

Feher, Ferenc. *The French Revolution and the Birth of Modernity*. Berkeley: University of California Press, 1990.

Fehler, M., ed. *Fragments for a History of the Human Body*. Cambridge, Mass.: Urzone, 1989.

Fenwick, C. A. *Essay on the Colonization of Hindoosthan by East Indians*. Calcutta: Baptist Mission Press, 1828.

"The Feringhees of Chittagong." *Calcutta Review* 53, 105 (1871): 57–89.

Finlason, W. F. *The History of the Jamaica Case*. 2d ed. London: Chapman & Hall, 1869.

Fitchett, W. H. *Tales of the Indian Mutiny*. London: Smith, Elder, 1901.

Fitzpatrick, William J. *Ireland Before the Union*. 2d ed. Dublin: W. B. Kelly, 1867.

Flannagan, Mrs. *Antigua and the Antiguans*. London: Saunders & Otley, 1844.

Flaubert, Gustave. *Salammbô*. 1862. Trans. A. J. Krailsheimer. London: Penguin Books, 1977.

Florescu, Radu. *In Search of Frankenstein*. London: New English Library, 1975.

Flower, W. H. "Comparative Anatomy of Man." *Nature* 22 (20 & 27 May, 3 June 1880): 59–61, 78–80, 97–100.

Flynn, Carol Houlihan. *The Body in Swift and Defoe*. New York: Cambridge University Press, 1990.

Forman, Charles. *Some Queries and Observations upon the Revolution in 1688*. London: Olive Payne, 1741.

Forry, Steven Earl. "Dramatizations of *Frankenstein*, 1821–1986: A Comprehensive List." *English Language Notes* 25 (1987): 63–79.

———. *Hideous Progenies: Dramatizations of "Frankenstein" from the Nineteenth Century to the Present*. Philadelphia: University of Pennsylvania Press, 1990.

———. "The Hideous Progenies of Richard Brinsley Peake: *Frankenstein* on the Stage, 1823 to 1826." *Theatre Research International* 11, 1 (1986): 13–31.

Foster, John E. "The Origins of the Mixed Bloods in the Canadian West." In *Essays on Western History*, ed. L. H. Thomas (1976), 69–80.

Foster, R. F. Foreword to *A Fantastic Journey*, by Paul Murray (1993).

Fowler, David H. *Northern Attitudes Towards Interracial Marriages: Legislation and Public Opinion in the Middle Atlantic and the States of the Old Northwest, 1780–1930*. New York: Garland, 1987.

Frazer, J. G. *The Golden Bough: A Study in Comparative Religion*. London: Macmillan, 1890.

French, Richard D. *Antivivisection and Medical Science in Victorian Society*. Princeton, N.J.: Princeton University Press, 1975.

Freud, Sigmund. *Drei Abhandlungen zur Sexualtheorie*. Vienna, 1905.

———. *Jokes and Their Relation to the Unconscious*. Trans. James Strachey. New York: Norton, 1989.

Fryer, Peter. *Staying Power: The History of Black People in Britain*. London: Pluto Press, 1984.

Fuss, Diana, ed. *Inside/Out: Lesbian Theories, Gay Theories*. London: Routledge, 1991.

Gallagher, Catherine. "The Bio-Economics of *Our Mutual Friend*." In *Fragments for a History of the Human Body*, ed. M. Fehler, vol. 3 (1989), 345–64.

———. "The Body Versus the Social Body in the Works of Thomas Malthus and Henry Mayhew." In *The Making of the Modern Body*, ed. C. Gallagher and T. Laqueur (1987), 83–106.

———. *The Industrial Reformation of English Fiction. Social Discourse and Narrative from 1832–1867*. Chicago: University of Chicago Press, 1985.

Galland, M., trans. *The Arabian Nights' Entertainments; or, The Thousand and One Nights*. Liverpool: Nuttall, Fisher, & Dixon, 1814.

[Galton, Francis]. "Stanley's Discoveries and the Future of Africa." *Edinburgh Review* 147, 301 (Jan. 1878): 166–91.

Galton, Francis, ed. *Vacation Tourists and Notes of Travel in 1861*. London: Macmillan, 1862.

Gaskell, Elizabeth. *Mary Barton*. 1848. London: Penguin Books, 1970.

Gautier, Théophile. *One of Cleopatra's Nights and Other Fantastic Romances.* Trans. Lafcadio Hearn. New York: Worthington, 1886.

Genovese, Eugene D. *Roll, Jordan, Roll: The World the Slaves Made.* London: André Deutsch, 1975.

George, Arthur, ed. *The Letters of Lord and Lady Wolseley, 1870–1911.* London: Heinemann, 1922.

Gilbert, Sandra, and Susan Gubar. *The Madwoman in the Attic: The Woman Writer in the Nineteenth-Century Literary Imagination.* New Haven, Conn.: Yale University Press, 1979.

Gilman, Sander L. "Black Bodies, White Bodies: Toward an Iconography of Female Sexuality in Late Nineteenth-Century Art, Medicine, and Literature." *Critical Inquiry* 12 (Autumn 1985): 204–42.

———. *Difference and Pathology: Stereotypes of Sexuality, Race, and Madness.* Ithaca, N.Y.: Cornell University Press, 1985.

———. *Disease and Representation: Images of Illness from Madness to Aids.* Ithaca, N.Y.: Cornell University Press, 1988.

———. *Freud, Race, and Gender.* Princeton, N.J.: Princeton University Press, 1993.

———. *Jewish Self-Hatred.* Baltimore: Johns Hopkins University Press, 1986.

———. *The Jew's Body.* London: Routledge, 1991.

———. *On Blackness Without Blacks: Essays on the Image of the Black in Germany.* Boston: Hall, 1982.

Gilson, Charles. *The Captives of the Caves.* London: Cassell, 1919.

Glut, Donald F. *The Frankenstein Catalogue.* Jefferson, N.C.: McFarland, 1984.

Godwin, William. *Caleb Williams.* 1794. London: Penguin Books, 1988.

———. *An Enquiry Concerning Political Justice.* 1793. London: Penguin Books, 1985.

———. *Fables, Ancient and Modern, Adapted for the Use of Children.* London: Thomas Hodgkins, 1805.

Gordon-Grube, Karen. "Anthropophagy in Post-Renaissance Europe: The Tradition of Medicinal Cannibalism." *American Anthropologist* 90 (June 1988): 405–9.

Gossett, Thomas F. *Race: The History of an Idea in America.* Dallas: S.M.U. Press, 1963.

Gough, Barry M., ed. *In Search of the Visible Past.* Waterloo, Ont.: Wilfrid Laurier University Press, 1975.

Gould, Stephen Jay. *The Flamingo's Smile: Reflections in Natural History.* New York: Norton, 1985.

Green, Martin. *Dreams of Adventure, Deeds of Empire.* London: Routledge & Kegan Paul, 1980.

Greenblatt, Stephen. *Marvelous Possessions: The Wonder of the New World.* Chicago: University of Chicago Press, 1991.

Greenhalgh, Paul. *Ephemeral Vistas: The "Expositions Universelles", Great Exhibitions and World's Fairs, 1851–1939.* Manchester: Manchester University Press, 1988.

Griffin, Gail B. "'Your Girls That You All Love Are Mine': *Dracula* and the Victorian Male Sexual Imagination." In *"Dracula,"* ed. M. L. Carter (1988), 137–

48. Reprinted from *International Journal of Women's Studies* 3, 5 (1980).

[Guernsey, A. H.] "A Cruise After and Among the Cannibals." *Harper's* 7, 40 (Sept. 1853): 461–75.

Haggard, H. Rider. *King Solomon's Mines*. London: Cassell, 1885.

Hakluyt, Richard. *The Principal Navigations. . . . 1589*. London: J. M. Dent, 1927–28.

Halasz, Nicholas. *Captain Dreyfus*. New York: Simon & Schuster, 1955.

Halberstam, Judith. "Technologies of Monstrosity: Bram Stoker's *Dracula*." *Victorian Studies* 36, 3 (Spring 1993): 333–52.

Hall, Lesley A. "Forbidden by God, Despised by Men: Masturbation, Medical Warnings, Moral Panic, and Manhood in Great Britain, 1850–1950." *Journal of the History of Sexuality* 2, 3 (1992): 365–87.

Hanson, Ellis. "Undead." In *Inside/Out*, ed. D. Fuss (1991), 324–40.

Haraway, Donna. *Primate Visions: Gender, Race, and Nature in the World of Modern Science*. London: Routledge, 1990.

Harris, Ruth. *Murders and Madness: Medicine, Law, and Society in the "fin de siècle."* Oxford: Clarendon Press, 1989.

Harris, William Cornwallis. *The Wild Sports of Southern Africa*. 4th ed. London, 1844.

Hasan-Rokem, Galet, and Alan Dundes, eds. *The Wandering Jew*. Bloomington: Indiana University Press, 1986.

Hatlen, Burton. "The Return of the Repressed/Oppressed in Bram Stoker's *Dracula*." In *"Dracula,"* ed. M. L. Carter (1988), 117–35. Reprinted from *Minnesota Review*, n.s., 15 (1980).

Hawkesworth, John. *An Account of the Voyages Undertaken by the Order of his Present Majesty for Making Discoveries in the Southern Hemisphere*. London: W. Strahan and T. Cadell, 1773.

Hearn, Lafcadio. "A Study of the Half-Breed Races in the West Indies." *Cosmopolitan* 9, 2 (June 1890): 167–72.

——. *Two Years in the West Indies*. New York: Harper & Brothers, 1890.

——. "West Indian Society of Many Colorings." *Cosmopolitan* 9, 3 (July 1890): 337–41.

Hecht, J. Jean. *Continental and Colonial Servants in Eighteenth-Century England*. Northampton, Mass.: Smith College, 1954.

Hennelly, Mark M., Jr. "*Dracula*: The Gnostic Quest and Victorian Wasteland." In *"Dracula,"* ed. M. L. Carter (1988), 79–92. Reprinted from *English Literature in Transition* 20 (1977).

Henriques, Fernando. *Children of Caliban: Miscegenation*. London: Secker & Warburg, 1974.

Herbert, Christopher. *Culture and Anomie: Ethnographic Imagination in the Nineteenth Century*. Chicago: University of Chicago Press, 1991.

Hertz, Neil. *The End of the Line: Essays on Psychoanalysis and the Sublime*. New York: Columbia University Press, 1985.

Himmelfarb, Gertrude. *Darwin and the Darwinian Revolution*. New York: Norton, 1968.

——. *The Idea of Poverty: England in the Early Industrial Age*. London: Faber & Faber, 1985.

Hirsch, Gordon. "*Frankenstein*, Detective Fiction, and *Jekyll and Hyde*." In *Dr Jekyll and Mr Hyde After One Hundred Years*, ed. W. Veeder and G. Hirsch (1988): 223–46.

Hirshfield, Claire. "*Reynolds's Newspaper* and the Modern Jew." *Victorian Periodicals Review* 14, 1 (Spring 1981): 3–11.

Hogg, Gary. *Cannibalism and Human Sacrifice*. London: Hale, 1958.

Holmes, T. R. E. *A History of the Indian Mutiny*. London: W. H. Allen, 1883.

Holt, Thomas C. *The Problem of Freedom: Race, Labour and Politics in Jamaica and Britain, 1832–1938*. Baltimore: Johns Hopkins University Press, 1992.

Honour, Hugh. *Black Models and White Myths*. Vol. 4, part 2, of *The Image of the Black in Western Art*. Cambridge, Mass.: Harvard University Press, 1989.

———. *Slaves and Liberators*. Vol. 4, part 1, of *The Image of the Black in Western Art*. Cambridge, Mass.: Harvard University Press, 1989.

Hope, Ascott R. *The Story of the Indian Mutiny*. London: Warne, 1896.

Howes, Marjorie. "The Mediation of the Feminine: Bisexuality, Homosexual Desire, and Self-Expression in Bram Stoker's *Dracula*." *Texas Studies in Literature and Language* 30 (Spring 1988): 104–19.

Huggins, William. *Sketches in India*. London: Letts, 1824.

Hughes, Robert. *The Fatal Shore: A History of the Transportation of Convicts to Australia, 1787–1868*. London: Pan, 1988.

Hulme, Peter. *Colonial Encounters: Europe and the Native Caribbean, 1492–1797*. London: Methuen, 1986.

Hunt, Lynn. *The Family Romance of the French Revolution*. Berkeley: University of California Press, 1992.

———. "The Many Bodies of Marie Antoinette: Political Pornography and the Problem of the Feminine in the French Revolution." In *Eroticism and the Body Politic*, ed. Lynn Hunt, 108–30. Baltimore: Johns Hopkins University Press, 1991.

———. *Politics, Culture, and Class in the French Revolution*. Berkeley: University of California Press, 1984.

Hunt, Margaret. "Racism, Imperialism, and the Traveler's Gaze in Eighteenth-Century England." *Journal of British Studies* 32, 4 (Oct. 1993): 333–57.

Hyam, Ronald. *Empire and Sexuality: The British Experience*. Manchester: Manchester University Press, 1990.

The Indo-Briton. Bombay: American Mission Press, 1849.

Irving, Lawrence. *Henry Irving: The Actor and His World*. London: Faber & Faber, 1951.

Isenberg, Shirley Berry. *India's Bene Israel: A Comprehensive Inquiry and Sourcebook*. Berkeley, Calif.: Judah L. Magnes Museum, 1988.

Jackson, J. W. "The Aryan and the Semite." *Anthropological Review* 7, 27 (Oct. 1869): 333–65.

Jeal, Tim. *Livingstone*. London: Pimlico, 1993.

Johnson, Capt. Charles [pseud.]. *A General History of the Lives and Adventures of the Most Famous Highwaymen, Murderers, Street-Robbers, Etc., to Which is Added, a General Account of the Voyages and Plunders of the Most Notorious Pyrates*. London: J. Janeway, 1734.

Johnston, H. H. "The Ethics of Cannibalism." *Fortnightly Review*, n.s., 45 (1 Jan. 1889): 18–28.

Jordanova, Ludmilla. *Sexual Visions: Images of Gender in Science and Medicine Between the Eighteenth and Twentieth Centuries.* Madison: University of Wisconsin Press, 1989.

Keating, William H. *Narrative of an Expedition to the Source of the St. Peter River.* London: G. P. Whittaker, 1825.

Kilgour, Maggie. *From Communion to Cannibalism: An Anatomy of Metaphors of Incorporation.* Princeton, N.J.: Princeton University Press, 1990.

Kincaid, Dennis. *British Social Life in India, 1608–1937.* London: Routledge, 1938.

Kipling, Rudyard. "Beyond the Pale." In *Plain Talk from the Hills,* 147–53. London: Thacker, 1888.

Knapman, Claudia. *White Women in Fiji, 1835–1930: The Ruin of Empire?* London: Allen & Unwin, 1986.

Knoepflmacher, U. C. "'Face to Face': Of Man-Apes, Monsters, and Readers." In *The Endurance of Frankenstein,* ed. G. Levine and U. C. Knoepflmacher (1979), 317–24.

Knox, Robert. *The Races of Men: A Philosophical Enquiry into the Influence of Race over the Destinies of Nations.* 2d ed. London: Renshaw, 1862.

Kuklick, Henrika. *The Savage Within: The Social History of British Anthropology, 1885–1945.* Cambridge: Cambridge University Press, 1991.

Kunzle, David. "The Art of Pulling Teeth in the Seventeenth and Nineteenth Centuries: From Public Martyrdom to Private Nightmare and Political Struggle?" In *Fragments for a History of the Human Body,* ed. M. Fehler, vol. 3 (1989), 28–89.

Landa, M. J. *The Jew in Drama.* London: P. S. King & Son, 1926.

Lander, George. *The Wandering Jew.* Adapted from Eugene Sue. London: Dicks' Standard Plays, no. 397, n.d. (1873?).

Lang, John Dunmore. *Cooksland in North-Eastern Australia: The Future Cotton-Field of Great Britain.* London: Longman, Brown, Green, & Longmans, 1847.

Laqueur, Thomas. "'Amor Veneris, vel Dulcedo Appeletur.'" In *Fragments for a History of the Human Body,* ed. M. Fehler, vol. 3 (1989), 91–131.

Leatherdale, Clive. *Dracula. The Novel and the Legend: A Study of Bram Stoker's Gothic Masterpiece.* Wellingborough, Eng.: Aquarian Press, 1985.

Leathers, Victor. *British Entertainers in France.* Toronto: University of Toronto Press, 1954.

Lee, Standish, ed. *Guide to the Eurasian and Anglo-Indian Villages Proposed to be Established in the Provinces of Mysore.* Madras: Eurasian and Anglo-Indian Association of Mysore [Banglalore], 1882.

Le Fanu, Joseph Sheridan. "Carmilla." In *In a Glass Darkly.* 1872. Bath: Alan Sutton, 1990.

Levine, G., and U. C. Knoepflmacher, eds. *The Endurance of Frankenstein: Essays on Mary Shelley's Novel.* Berkeley: University of California Press, 1979.

Lévi-Strauss, Claude. *La Pensée sauvage.* Paris: Plon, 1962.

Lewis, Matthew Gregory. *The Castle Spectre: A Dramatic Romance, in Five Acts.* London: John Cumberland, 1798.

————. *Journal of a West India Proprietor, 1815–17.* 1834. London: George Routledge & Sons, 1929.

————. *The Monk.* 1796. Oxford: Oxford University Press, 1973.

Leyden, John. *Historical and Philosophical Sketch of the Discoveries and Settlements of the Europeans in Northern and Western Africa at the Close of the Eighteenth Century.* Edinburgh: J. Moir, 1799.

Lindeborg, Ruth A. "The 'Asiatic' and the Boundaries of Victorian Englishness." *Victorian Studies* 37, 3 (Spring 1994): 381–404.

Linden, Annie. "The Half-Caste." *Pall Mall Magazine* 16, 65 (Sept. 1898): 19–26.

Livingstone, David. *Missionary Travels and Researches in South Africa.* London: Murray, 1857.

————. *The Last Journals of David Livingstone, in Central Africa, from 1865 to his Death.* Ed. Horace Waller. London: John Murray, 1874.

Livingstone, David, and Charles Livingstone. *Narrative of an Expedition to the Zambesi and Its Tributaries.* London: John Murray, 1865.

Lord, J. Henry. *The Jewish Mission Field in the Bombay Diocese.* Bombay: Education Society, 1894.

Lorimer, Douglas A. "Bibles, Banjoes and Bones: Images of the Negro in the Popular Culture of Victorian England." In *In Search of the Visible Past,* ed. B. M. Gough (1975), 31–50.

————. *Colour, Class and the Victorians: English Attitudes to the Negro in the Mid-Nineteenth Century.* Leicester: Leicester University Press, 1978.

Ludlam, Harry. *A Biography of Dracula: The Life Story of Bram Stoker.* Slough: W. Foulsham, 1962.

McBratney, John. "Imperial Subjects, Imperial Space in Kipling's *Jungle Book.*" *Victorian Studies* 35, 3 (Spring 1992): 277–93.

————. "Lovers Beyond the Pale: Images of Indian Women in Kipling's Tales of Miscegenation." *Works and Days* 8, 1 (Spring 1990): 17–36.

Macdonald, Robert H. "Discourse and Ideology in Kipling's "Beyond the Pale.'" *Studies in Short Fiction* 23 (Fall 1986): 413–18.

"Maceo and His Race." *The Spectator,* 19 Dec. 1896, 892–93.

Mackay, Margaret Mackprang. *The Violent Friend: The Story of Mrs. Robert Louis Stevenson, 1840–1914.* New York: Doubleday, 1968.

MacKenzie, John M., ed. *Imperialism and Popular Culture.* Manchester: Manchester University Press, 1986.

McNiece, Gerald. *Shelley and the Revolutionary Idea.* Cambridge, Mass.: Harvard University Press, 1969.

"Man-Eating and Man-Sacrificing." *All the Year Round,* n.s., 36, 868 (18 July 1885).

Mannoni, O. *Prospero and Caliban: The Psychology of Colonization.* Trans. P. Powesland. London: Methuen, 1956.

Marigny, Jean. *Le Vampire dans la littérature anglo-saxonne.* Paris: Didier Erudition, 1985.

Mariner, William. *An Account of the Natives of the Tonga Islands.* London: Murray, 1817.

Marlow, James E. "English Cannibalism: Dickens After 1859." *Studies in English Literature* 23 (1983): 647–66.

————. "The Fate of Sir John Franklin: Three Phases of Response in Victorian Periodicals." *Victorian Periodicals Review* 15, 1 (Spring 1982): 3–11.

Marryat, Florence. *The Blood of the Vampire*. London: Hutchinson, 1897.

Marryat, Frederick. *The Phantom Ship*. 1839. London: Bentley, 1853.

Marsden, William. *The History of Sumatra, Containing an Account of the Government, Laws, Customs, and Manners of the Native Inhabitants*. London: Payne & Son, 1783.

Marshall, David. *The Surprising Effects of Sympathy: Marivaux, Diderot, Rousseau, and Mary Shelley*. Chicago: University of Chicago Press, 1988.

Marshall, Peter H. *William Godwin*. New Haven, Conn.: Yale University Press, 1984.

Martineau, Harriet. *Society in America*. London: Saunders & Otley, 1837.

Maturin, Charles. *Melmoth the Wanderer*. 1820. Oxford: Oxford University Press, 1989.

Maulitz, Russell C. *Morbid Appearances: The Anatomy of Pathology in the Early Nineteenth Century*. Cambridge: Cambridge University Press, 1987.

Mayhew, Henry. *London Labour and the London Poor*, vol. 4: *Those That Will Not Work*. London: Griffin, Bohn, 1862.

Mellor, Anne K. *Mary Shelley: Her Life, Her Fiction, Her Monsters*. London: Routledge, 1989.

Melville, Herman. *Moby-Dick; or, The Whale*. 1851. London: Penguin Books, 1992.

Mendus, Susan, and Joan Rendall, eds. *Sexuality and Subordination: Interdisciplinary Studies of Gender in the Nineteenth Century*. London: Routledge, 1989.

Michelsen, Oscar. *Cannibals Won for Christ: A Story of Missionary Perils and Triumphs in Tonga, New Hebrides*. London: Morgan & Scott, 1893.

Miller, Christopher L. *Blank Darkness: Africanist Discourse in French*. Chicago: University of Chicago Press, 1985.

"Miscegenation." *Anthropological Review* 2, 5 (May 1964): 116–21.

Moers, Ellen. "Female Gothic." In *The Endurance of Frankenstein*, ed. G. Levine and U. C. Knoepflmacher (1979), 77–87. Reprinted from *Literary Women* (1974).

Moore, W. J. "The Eurasian Future." *Indian Annals of Medical Science* (Calcutta) 16 (Jan. 1874): 486–503.

Moretti, Franco. *Signs Taken for Wonders: Essays in the Sociology of Literary Forms*. London: Verso, 1983.

Mort, Frank. *Dangerous Sexualities: Medico-Moral Politics in England Since 1830*. London: Routledge, 1987.

Mosse, George L. *Nationalism and Sexuality: Middle-Class Morality and Sexual Norms in Modern Europe*. Madison: University of Wisconsin Press, 1985.

Mukherjee, Rudrangshu. "'Satan Let Loose upon Earth': The Kanpur Massacres in India in the Revolt of 1857." *Past and Present* 128 (Aug. 1990): 92–116.

Murray, Paul. *A Fantastic Journey: The Life and Literature of Lafcadio Hearn*. Sandgate, Eng.: Japan Library, 1993.

Musselwhite, David E. *Partings Welded Together: Politics and Desire in the Nineteenth-Century Novel*. London: Methuen, 1987.

Napier, Charles Ottley Groom. *The Book of Nature and the Book of Man*. London: John Camden Hotten, 1870.

───── [Napier Groom]. "Notes on Mulattoes and Negroes." *Anthropological Review* 6 (Apr. 1968): lvii–lx.

Newman, Gerald. *The Rise of English Nationalism: A Cultural History, 1740–1830*. London: Weidenfeld & Nicolson, 1987.

Newman, Peter C. *Company of Adventurers*, vol. 1: *The Story of the Hudson's Bay Company*. London: Penguin Books, 1985.

─────. *Company of Adventurers*, vol. 2: *Caesars of the Wilderness*. New York: Viking, 1987.

─────. *Company of Adventurers*, vol. 3: *Merchant Princes*. New York: Viking, 1991.

Nicholas, John Liddiard. *Narrative of a Voyage to New Zealand*. London: James Black & Son, 1817.

Nichols, Ashton. "Silencing the Other: The Discourse of Domination in Nineteenth-Century Exploration Narratives." *Nineteenth Century Studies* 3 (1989): 1–22.

Nicoll, Allardyce. *A History of Early Nineteenth Century Drama, 1800–1850*. Cambridge: Cambridge University Press, 1930.

Nicoloff, Philip L. *Emerson on Race and History*. New York: Columbia University Press, 1961.

O'Flynn, Paul. "Production and Reproduction: The Case of *Frankenstein*." *Literature and History* 9, 2 (1983): 194–213.

"Old Stories Re-Told: Driven to Cannibalism." *All the Year Round*, n.s., 8, 181 (18 May 1872).

Orgel, Steven. "Shakespeare and the Cannibals." In *Cannibals, Witches, and Divorce: Estranging the Renaissance*, ed. Marjorie Garber. Baltimore: Johns Hopkins University Press, 1987.

O'Rourke, James. " 'Nothing More Unnatural': Mary Shelley's Revision of Rousseau." *ELH* 56 (1989): 543–69.

Outram, Dorinda. *The Body and the French Revolution: Sex, Class and Political Culture*. New Haven, Conn.: Yale University Press, 1989.

Park, Mungo. *The Journal of a Mission to the Interior of Africa, in the Year 1805*. London: John Murray, 1815.

─────. *Travels in the Interior Districts of Africa: Performed under the Direction and Patronage of the African Association in the Years 1795, 1796, and 1797*. London: W. Bulmer, 1799.

Parkman, Francis, Jr. *The California and Oregon Trail*. New York: Putnam, 1849.

[Parsons, James]. "An Account of the White Negro, shewn before the Royal Society." *British Magazine* 7 (Sept. 1766): 483–85.

Paxton, Nancy L. "Mobilizing Chivalry: Rape in British Novels About the Indian Uprising of 1857." *Victorian Studies* 36, 1 (Fall 1992): 5–30.

Peacock, Mabel. "Executed Criminals and Folk-Medicine." *Folk-Lore* 7, 3 (1896): 268–83.

Pearson, Raymond. *National Minorities in Eastern Europe, 1848–1945*. London: Macmillan, 1983.

"Percival's *Account of the Islands of Ceylon*." *Edinburgh Review* 2 (Apr. 1803): 136–47.

Peterson, Jacqueline, and Jennifer S. H. Brown, eds. *The New People: Being and Becoming Métis in North America*. Winnipeg: University of Manitoba Press, 1985.

Pick, Daniel. "'Terrors of the Night': Dracula and 'Degeneration' in the Late Nineteenth Century." *Critical Quarterly* 30 (Winter 1988): 71–88.

Pickering, Michael. "White Skin, Black Masks: 'Nigger' Minstrelsy in Victorian England." In *Music Hall Performance and Style*, ed. J. S. Bratton (1986), 70–91.

Poe, Edgar Allan. "The Murders in the Rue Morgue." In *The Complete Poems and Stories of Edgar Allan Poe, with Selections from his Critical Writings*. Ed. Edward H. O'Neill. Introduction by Arthur Hobson Quinn. Vol. 1. New York: Knopf, 1958.

———. *The Narrative of Arthur Gordon Pym of Nantucket*. 1838. Introduction by Harold Beaver. London: Penguin Books, 1975.

Polack, J. S. *Manners and Customs of the New Zealanders*. London: James Madder, 1840.

Pollin, Burton R. "Philosophical and Literary Sources of *Frankenstein*." *Comparative Literature* 17, 2 (1965): 97–108.

Poovey, Mary. "My Hideous Progeny: Mary Shelley and the Feminization of Romanticism." *PMLA* 95, 3 (1980): 332–47.

Porter, Roy. *Mind-Forg'd Manacles: A History of Madness in England from the Restoration to the Regency*. London: Penguin Books, 1990.

Porter, W. M. S., and Claire Russell. "The Social Biology of Werewolves." In *Animals in Folklore*, ed. Porter and Russell, 143–82. London: Bremer, 1978.

Praz, Mario. *The Romantic Agony*. 1933. Trans. Angus Davidson. 2d ed. Oxford University Press, 1970.

Punter, David. *The Literature of Terror: A History of Gothic Fictions from 1765 to the Present Day*. London: Longman, 1980.

Quatrefages, M. de. "The Formation of the Mixed Human Races." *Anthropological Review* 7, 24 (Jan. 1869): 22–40.

Radstone, Susannah, ed. *Sweet Dreams: Sexuality, Gender and Popular Fiction*. London: Lawrence & Wishart, 1988.

Rawson, C. J. "Cannibalism and Fiction: Reflections on Narrative Form and 'Extreme' Situations." *Genre* 10, 4 (1977): 667–711.

———. "Cannibalism and Fiction [II]." *Genre* 11, 2 (1978): 227–313.

Reade, W. Winwood. *The Martyrdom of Man*. London: Trubner, 1872.

———. *Savage Africa: Being the Narrative of a Tour in Equatorial, South-Western, and North-Western Africa*. London: Smith, Elder, 1863.

———. *The Story of the Ashantee Campaign*. London: Smith, Elder, 1874.

Reid, A. P. "The Mixed or 'Halfbreed' Races of North-Western Canada." *Journal of the Anthropological Institute* 4 (1875): 45–52.

Reid, Thomas Mayne. *Oçeola*. 3 vols. London: Hurst & Blackett, 1859.

———. *Odd People: Being a Popular Description of Singular Races of Men*. London: Routledge, 1860.

———. *The Quadroon; or, Adventures in the Far West*. London: J. & C. Brown, (1856).

———. *The White Squaw, and The Yellow Chief: A Romance of the Rocky Mountains*. London: Charles H. Clarke, 1870–71.

———. *The Wild Huntress*. 3 vols. London: Richard Bentley, 1861.

Report of Proceedings Connected with the East Indians' Petition to Parliament. Calcutta: Baptist Mission Press, 1831.

Reynolds, George W. M. *The Mysteries of London.* London: George Vickers, 1846.

———. *Wagner, the Wehr-Wolf.* Originally serialized in *Reynolds Miscellany,* 1846–47. Ed. E. F. Bleiler. New York: Dover, 1975.

Richards, Vincent. "Medical Notes on the Convict Settlement, Port Blair." *Indian Annals of Medical Science* (Calcutta) 16 (Jan. 1874): 614–25.

Richardson, Maurice. "The Psychoanalysis of Ghost Stories." *Twentieth Century* 166 (Dec. 1959): 419–31.

Richardson, Ruth. *Death, Dissection and the Destitute.* London: Penguin Books, 1989.

Roach, Joseph R. "Slave Spectacles and Tragic Octoroons: A Cultural Genealogy of Antebellum Performance." *Theatre Survey* 33 (Nov. 1992): 167–87.

Robb, George. *White-Collar Crime in Modern England: Financial Fraud and Business Morality, 1845–1929.* Cambridge: Cambridge University Press, 1992.

Rodney, Walter. *A History of the Guyanese Working People, 1881–1905.* London: Heinemann, 1981.

Rodway, James. "Day and Night in the Guiana Forest." *Longman's Magazine* 20 (Oct. 1892): 603–12.

———. *Guiana: British, Dutch and French.* London: T. Fisher Unwin, 1912.

———. *In Guiana Wilds: A Study of Two Women.* London: T. Fisher Unwin, 1898.

———. *In the Guiana Forest: Studies of Nature in Relation to the Struggle for Life.* 1894. London: T. Fisher Unwin, 1911.

———. "Up a Creek in Demerara." *Cornhill Magazine* 19 (Dec. 1892): 592–602.

Roland, Joan G. *Jews in British India: Identity in a Colonial Era.* Hanover, N.H.: New England Press for Brandeis University Press, 1989.

Romilly, Hugh Hastings. *The Western Pacific and New Guinea: Notes on the Natives, Christian and Cannibal.* London: John Murray, 1886.

Rosenberg, Edgar. *From Shylock to Svengali: Jewish Stereotypes in English Fiction.* London: Peter Owen, 1961.

Ross, Alexander. *The Fur Hunters of the Far West: A Narrative of Adventures in the Oregon and Rocky Mountains.* London: Smith, Elder, 1855.

———. *The Red River Settlement: Its Roots, Progress, and Present State.* London: Smith, Elder, 1856.

Roth, Phyllis A. *Bram Stoker.* Boston: Twayne, 1982.

———. "Suddenly Sexual Women in Bram Stoker's *Dracula.*" In *"Dracula,"* ed. M. L. Carter (1988), 57–67. Reprinted from *Literature and Psychology* 27 (1977).

Rowe, George Stringer. *The Life of John Hunt, Missionary to the Cannibals.* London: Hamilton, 1860.

Rowley, H. "Slavery Among the Portuguese in Eastern Africa." *Mission Life,* 1 Mar. 1868, 197–206.

Rusden, G. W. *History of New Zealand.* London: Chapman & Hall, 1883.

Russell, Michael. *Polynesia; or, An Historical Account of the Principal Islands in the South Sea.* Edinburgh: Oliver & Boyd, 1842.

Ryan, Lyndall. *The Aboriginal Tasmanians.* Brisbane: University of Queensland Press, 1981.

[Rymer, James M.?] *Varney, the Vampyre; or, the Feast of Blood: A Romance.* London: E. Lloyd, n.d. (1847).

Sade, Comte Donatien-Alphonse-François, marquis de. *Juliette.* 1797. Trans. Austryn Wainhouse. New York: Grove Press, 1968.

Said, Edward W. *Orientalism.* New York: Vintage Books, 1979.

St. Johnston, Alfred. *Camping Among the Cannibals.* London: Macmillan, 1883.

———. "Cannibalism." *Gentlemen's Magazine* 257 (Oct. 1884): 395–416.

Salter, J[oseph]. *The East in the West; or, Work Among the Asiatics and Africans in London.* London: S. W. Partridge, [1896].

Sanchez, Nellie Van de Grift. *The Life of Mrs. Robert Louis Stevenson.* London: Chatto & Windus, 1920.

Savage, John. *Some Account of New Zealand.* London: John Murray, 1807.

"Savage Africa." *Anthropological Review* 2, 5 (May 1864): 123–26.

Scheick, William J. *The Half-Blood: A Cultural Symbol in Nineteenth-Century American Fiction.* Lexington: University Press of Kentucky, 1979.

Schloss, David F. "The Jew as a Workman." *Nineteenth Century* 29 (Jan. 1891): 96–109.

Schweinfurth, Georg. *The Heart of Africa: Three Years' Travels and Adventures in the Unexplored Regions of Central Africa from 1868 to 1871.* Trans. Ellen E. Frewer. London: Sampson Low, 1873.

Sedgwick, Eve Kosofsky. *Between Men: English Literature and Male Homosocial Desire.* New York: Columbia University Press, 1985.

Seed, David. "The Narrative Method of *Dracula*." *Nineteenth-Century Fiction* 40, 1 (1985): 61–75.

Seemann, Berthold. "Fiji and Its Inhabitants." In *Vacation Tourists,* ed. F. Galton (1862), 249–92.

———. "On the Anthropology of Western Eskimo Land, and on the Desirability of Further Arctic Research." *Anthropological Review* 3, 10 (1865): ccxciv–cccviii.

———. *Viti: An Account of a Government Mission to the Vitian or Fijian Islands in the Years 1860–61.* London: Macmillan, 1862.

Semmel, Bernard. *The Governor Eyre Controversy.* London: Macgibbon & Kee, 1962.

Senelick, Laurence. "The Evolution of the Male Impersonator on the Nineteenth-Century Popular Stage." *Essays in Theatre* 1, 1 (1982): 31–44.

Senf, Carol A. *The Vampire in Nineteenth-Century English Literature.* Bowling Green, Ohio: Bowling Green State University Popular Press, 1988.

Shelley, Mary Wollstonecraft. *Frankenstein.* 1818 ed. Berkeley: University of California Press, 1968.

———. *Frankenstein; or, The Modern Prometheus.* 1831 ed. Introduction by Maurice Hindle. London: Penguin Books, 1985.

———. *The Letters of Mary Wollstonecraft Shelley.* Ed. Betty T. Bennett. Baltimore: Johns Hopkins University Press, 1980.

———. *Mary Shelley's Journal.* Ed. Frederick L. Jones. Norman: University of Oklahoma Press, 1947.

Shephard, Ben. "Showbiz Imperialism: The Case of Peter Lobengula." In *Imperialism and Popular Culture,* ed. J. M. MacKenzie (1986), 94–112.

Sherard, Robert H. *The White Slaves of England.* London: Bowden, 1897.

Shortland, Edward. *The Southern Districts of New Zealand: A Journal with Passing Notices of the Customs of the Aborigines*. London: Longman, Brown, Green, & Longmans, 1851.

Showalter, Elaine. "The Apocalyptic Fables of H. G. Wells." In *Fin de Siècle / Fin du Globe: Fears and Fantasies of the Late Nineteenth Century*, ed. John Stokes, 69–84. London: Macmillan, 1992.

———. *Sexual Anarchy: Gender and Culture at the Fin de Siècle*. New York: Viking, 1990.

Simpson, A. W. Brian. *Cannibalism and the Common Law: The Story of the Tragic Last Voyage of the "Mignonette" and the Strange Legal Proceedings to Which It Gave Rise*. Chicago: University of Chicago Press, 1984.

Singer, Brian. "Violence in the French Revolution: Forms of Ingestion / Forms of Expulsion." In *The French Revolution and the Birth of Modernity*, ed. F. Feher (1990), 150–73.

Skewes, J. Henry. *Sir John Franklin: The True Story of the Discovery of His Fate*. London: Bemrose & Sons, 1889.

Slights, William W. E. "The Incarnations of Comedy." *University of Toronto Quarterly* 51 (Fall 1981): 13–27.

Small, Christopher. *Ariel Like a Harpy: Shelley, Mary and "Frankenstein."* London: Gollancz, 1972.

Smith, Albert. *The Medical Student*. London: Routledge, 1861.

[Smith, Thomas Southwood]. "The Use of the Dead to the Living." *Westminster Review* 2 (July 1824): 59–97.

Somerville, Siobhan. "Scientific Racism and the Emergence of the Homosexual Body." *Journal of the History of Sexuality* 5, 2 (Oct. 1994): 243–66.

Souden, David. *Short Breaks in Historic Country Towns*. London: George Philip, 1991.

Spencer, Herbert. *The Principles of Sociology*. London: Williams & Norgate, 1876–96.

Spivak, Gayatri Chakravorty. "Three Women's Texts and a Critique of Imperialism," *Critical Inquiry* 12 (Autumn 1985): 243–61.

Stade, George. "Dracula's Women." *Partisan Review* 53, 2 (1986): 200–215.

Stanley, George F. G. *The Birth of Western Canada: A History of the Riel Rebellions*. London: Longmans, 1936.

———. *Louis Riel*. Toronto: Ryerson Press, 1963.

Stanley, H. M. *The Great Forest of Central Africa: Its Cannibals and Pigmies*. London: William Clowes & Sons, 1890.

Stark, Herbert Alick. *The Call of the Blood, or Anglo-Indians and the Sepoy Mutiny*. Rangoon: British Burma Press, 1932.

———. *Hostages to India*. Calcutta: Star Printing Works, 1936.

Stedman, Jane W. "From Dame to Woman: W. S. Gilbert and Theatrical Transvestism." In *Suffer and Be Still*, ed. Martha Vicinus, 20–37. Bloomington: Indiana University Press, 1972.

Steele, Joan. *Captain Mayne Reid*. Boston: Twayne, 1978.

Stenbock, Eric, Count. "The True Story of a Vampire." In *Studies of Death: Romantic Tales*, 120–47. London: David Nutt, 1894.

Stepan, Nancy. "Biological Degeneration: Races and Proper Places." In *Degenera-*

tion: The Dark Side of Progress, ed. J. E. Chamberlain and S. L. Gilman (1985), 97–120.

———. *The Idea of Race in Science: Great Britain, 1800–1960*. London: Macmillan, 1982.

Sterrenburg, Lee. "Mary Shelley's Monster: Politics and Psyche in *Frankenstein*," In *The Endurance of Frankenstein*, ed. G. Levine and U. C. Knoepflmacher (1979), 143–71.

———. "Psychoanalysis and the Iconography of Revolution." *Victorian Studies* 19 (Dec. 1975): 241–64.

Stevenson, Fanny Van de Grift. "The Half-White." *Scribner's Magazine* 9 (3 Mar. 1891): 282–88.

Stevenson, J. A. "A Vampire in the Mirror: The Sexuality of Dracula." *PMLA* 103 (Mar. 1988): 139–49.

Stocking, George W., Jr. *Race, Culture, and Evolution: Essays in the History of Anthropology*. 1968. Chicago: University of Chicago Press, 1982.

———. *Victorian Anthropology*. New York: Free Press, 1987.

Stoker, Bram. *A Glimpse of America: A Lecture Given at the London Institution, 28th December 1885*. London: Sampson Low, 1886.

———. "The Censorship of Fiction." *Nineteenth Century* 64 (Sept. 1908): 479–88.

———. *Dracula*. 1897. London: Penguin Books, 1979.

———. *Famous Imposters*. London: Sidgwick & Jackson, 1910.

———. *Personal Reminiscences of Henry Irving*. London: Heinemann, 1906.

———. *The Snake's Pass*. 1890. Dingle, Ireland: Brandon, 1990.

"Stories of the Black Men." *All the Year Round* 6, 136 (30 Nov. 1861).

Stott, Rebecca. "The Dark Continent: Africa as Female Body in Haggard's Adventure Fiction." *Feminist Review* 32 (Summer 1989): 69–89.

Street, Brian. *The Savage in Literature: Representations of "Primitive" Society in English Fiction, 1858–1920*. London: Routledge, 1975.

Sue, Eugène. *The Wandering Jew*. Paris, 1844–45. London, 1846. Dublin: Dedalus, 1990.

Sussman, Charlotte. "Women and the Politics of Sugar, 1792," *Representations* 48 (Fall 1994): 48–69.

Sweeney Todd, The Demon Barber of Fleet Street. London: Charles Fox, n.d. [ca. 1880].

Tannahill, Reay. *Flesh and Blood: A History of the Cannibal Complex*. London: Hamish Hamilton, 1975.

Taylor, Richard. *Te Ika a Maui; or, New Zealand and Its Inhabitants*. London: Wertheim & Macintosh, 1855.

Taylor, W. Cooke. *The Natural History of Society in the Barbarous and Civilized State: An Essay Towards Discovering the Origin and Course of Human Improvement*. 1840. 2 vols. New York: D. Appleton, 1841.

Thomas, Lewis, H., ed. *Essays on Western History*. Edmonton: University of Alberta Press, 1976.

Thomson, Arthur S. *The Story of New Zealand: Past and Present—Savage and Civilised*. London: John Murray, 1859.

Thurston, Edgar. "Eurasians of Madras City and Malabar." [Madras Government Museum] *Bulletin* 2, 2 (1898): 69–114.

————. "Note on Tattooing." [Madras Government Museum] *Bulletin* 2, 2 (1898): 115–18.

Tolstoy, L. N. *Resurrection.* 1899. Trans. Rosemary Edmonds. London: Penguin Books, 1966.

Trevelyan, George Otto. *Cawnpore.* London: Macmillan, 1865.

Turner, E. S. *Boys Will Be Boys.* 1948. London: Michael Joseph, 1975.

Twitchell, James B. *The Living Dead: A Study of the Vampire in Romantic Literature.* Durham, N.C.: Duke University Press, 1981.

"Vampyres." *Household Words* 11, 254 (3 Feb. 1855).

Van Kirk, Sylvia. "'The Custom of the Country': An Examination of Fur Trade Marriage Practices." In *Essays on Western History,* ed. L. H. Thomas (1976), 47–68.

————. "'What if Mama is an Indian?': The Cultural Ambivalence of the Alexander Ross Family." In *The New People: Being and Becoming Métis in North America,* ed. J. Peterson and J. S. Brown (1985), 207–17.

Van Onselen, Charles. *Studies in the Social and Economic History of the Witwatersrand, 1886–1914.* New York: Longman, 1982.

Veeder, William. *Mary Shelley & "Frankenstein": The Fate of Androgyny.* Chicago: University of Chicago Press, 1986.

Veeder, William, and G. Hirsch, eds. *Dr Jekyll and Mr Hyde After One Hundred Years.* Chicago: University of Chicago Press, 1988.

Viaud, Pierre. *The Shipwreck and Adventures of Monsieur Pierre Viaud, A Native of Bordeaux, and Captain of a Ship.* Trans. Mrs. Griffith. London: T. Davies, 1771.

Vicinus, Martha, ed. *Suffer and Be Still: Women in the Victorian Age.* Bloomington: Indiana University Press, 1972.

Volney, Constantin François Chasseboeuf, comte de. *Ruins; or, A Survey of the Revolutions of Empires.* London: J. Johnson, 1795.

Walkowitz, Judith R. *City of Dreadful Delight: Narratives of Sexual Danger in Late-Victorian London.* Chicago: University of Chicago Press, 1992.

————. "Jack the Ripper and the Myth of Male Violence." *Feminist Studies* 8 (Fall 1982): 542–74.

Wallace, Alfred Russell. *A Narrative of Travels on the Amazon and Rio Negro.* London: Reeve, 1853.

Walpole, Horace. *The Castle of Otranto: A Gothic Story.* 1764. Oxford University Press, 1964.

Walsh, Susan. "Bodies of Capital: *Great Expectations* and the Climacteric Economy." *Victorian Studies* 37, 1 (Autumn 1993): 73–98.

Ward, Herbert. *Five Years with the Congo Cannibals.* London: Chatto & Windus, 1890.

Watt, Ian. *The Rise of the Novel: Studies in Defoe, Richardson and Fielding.* 1957. London: Hogarth Press, 1987.

Weeks, Jeffrey. *Coming Out: Homosexual Politics in Britain from the Nineteenth Century to the Present.* London: Quartet Books, 1990.

Weissman, Judith. "Women as Vampires: *Dracula* as a Victorian Novel." In *"Dracula,"* ed. M. L. Carter (1988), 69–77. Reprinted from *Midwest Quarterly* 18 (1977).

Wells, H. G. *The Island of Dr. Moreau.* 1896. New York: Berkley, 1964.

————. "Pollock and the Porroh Man." In *The Plattner Story and Others*, 142–64. London: Methuen, 1897.

White, Arnold. "Alien Immigration: A Rejoinder." *Fortnightly Review*, n.s., 57 (1 Mar. 1895): 501–7.

————. *The Destitute Alien in Great Britain.* London: Swan Sonnenschein, 1892.

————. "The Invasion of Pauper Foreigners." *Nineteenth Century* 23 (Mar. 1888): 414–22.

————. *The Modern Jew.* London: Heinemann, 1899.

————. *The Problems of a Great City.* London: Remington, 1886.

White, Hayden. *Tropics of Discourse: Essays in Cultural Criticism.* Baltimore: Johns Hopkins University Press, 1978.

Whitehead, C. *Lives and Exploits of English Highwaymen, Pirates and Robbers.* London: Bull & Churton, 1833.

Whitman, Walt. "The Half-Breed: A Tale of the Western Frontier." In *The Early Poems and the Fiction*, ed. Thomas L. Brasher, 257–91. New York: New York University, 1963. Originally published under the title "Arrow-Tip" in *The Aristidean*, Mar. 1845.

Wilde, Oscar. *The Picture of Dorian Gray.* 1890. Oxford University Press, 1981.

Wilkins, W. H. *The Alien Invasion.* London: Methuen, 1892.

Williams, John. *A Narrative of Missionary Enterprises in the South Sea Islands.* London: J. Snow, 1837.

Williams, Thomas. *Fiji and the Fijians.* Ed. George Stringer Rowe. 2d ed. London: A. Heylin, 1860.

————. *The Journal of Thomas Williams, Missionary in Fiji, 1840–1853.* Ed. G. C. Henderson. Sydney: Angus & Robertson, 1931.

Williamson, Joel. *New People: Miscegenation and Mulattoes in the United States.* New York: Free Press, 1980.

Wilson, Katharina M. "The History of the Word 'Vampire'." *Journal of the History of Ideas* 46, 4 (1985): 577–83.

Winterbottom, Thomas. *An Account of the Native Africans in the Neighbourhood of Sierra Leone.* London: C. Winterbottom, 1803.

Wolseley, Garnet Joseph, 1st viscount. *The Story of a Soldier's Life.* London: Constable, 1903.

Wootton, A. C. *Chronicles of Pharmacy.* London: Macmillan, 1910.

Wordworth, William. *The Prelude.* 1805 text. Ed. J. C. Maxwell. London: Penguin Books, 1971.

X. L. [Julien Osgood Field]. *Aut diabolus aut nihil and Other Tales.* London: Methuen, 1894.

Yate, William. *An Account of New Zealand; and of the Formation and Progress of the Church Missionary Society's Mission in the Northern Island.* 2d ed. London: R. B. Seeley & W. Burnside, 1835.

Zanger, Jules. "A Sympathetic Vibration: Dracula and the Jews." *English Literature in Transition, 1880–1920* 34, 1 (1991): 33–44.

————. "The 'Tragic Octoroon' in Pre-Civil War Fiction." *American Quarterly* 18, 1 (1966): 63–70.

Periodicals

Note: Unless otherwise indicated, the place of publication was London.

All the Year Round
The Anglo-Indian Journal (Bombay)
The Annual Register
The Athenaeum
The Church Family Newspaper
The Critic
The Daily Chronicle
The Daily Graphic
The Daily Mail
The Evening News
The Gentleman's Magazine
The Globe
The Graphic
Household Words
The Jewish Chronicle
The Lancet
Lloyd's Weekly Newspaper
The Morning Advertiser
The Morning Herald
The Morning Leader
The Morning Post
The Pall Mall Gazette
Punch
Reynold's Newspaper
The Saturday Review
South Africa
The Spectator
The Standard
The Star
The Sun
The Times
To-day
Vanity Fair

Standard Reference Works

Cokayne, G. E. *Complete Peerage of England, Scotland, Ireland, Great Britain and the United Kingdom*, ed. Vicary Gibbs. London: St. Catherine Press, 1910–1959.
The Dictionary of National Biography.
Encyclopedia Britanica, 1st ed. (Edinburgh, 1768); 2d ed. (Edinburgh, 1778); 3d ed. (Edinburgh, 1788–97); 8th ed. (Edinburgh, 1853–54); 9th ed. (Edinburgh, 1875–76).

Hansard's Parliamentary Debates.
Johnson, Samuel. *A Dictionary of the English Language.* Todd's expanded edition. London, 1827.
The Oxford English Dictionary.
Parliamentary Papers.
The Parliamentary Register.

Index

In this index an "f" after a number indicates a separate reference on the next page, and an "ff" indicates separate references on the next two pages. A continuous discussion over two or more pages is indicated by a span of page numbers, e.g., "57–59." *Passim* is used for a cluster of references in close but not consecutive sequence.

Library of Congress Cataloging-in-Publication Data

Malchow, Howard L.
  Gothic images of race in nineteenth-century Britain /
H. L Malchow.
    p. cm.
  Includes bibliographical references and index.
  ISBN 0-8047-2664-7 (alk. paper)
    1. English fiction—19th century—History and
  criticism. 2. Horror tales, English—History and
  criticism. 3. Race in literature. 4. Popular culture—
  Great Britain—History—19th century. 5. Gothic
  revival (Literature)—Great Britain. 6. Cannibalism in
  literature. 7. Vampires in literature. 8. Racism in
  literature. I. Title.
  PR868.T3M25   1996
  823'.809355—dc20   95-25870
                                                          CIP

  ⊚ This book is printed on acid-free, recycled paper.

  Original printing 1996
  Last figure below indicates year of this printing:

  05 04 03 02 01 00 99 98 97 96